WRITING WITH A PURPOSE

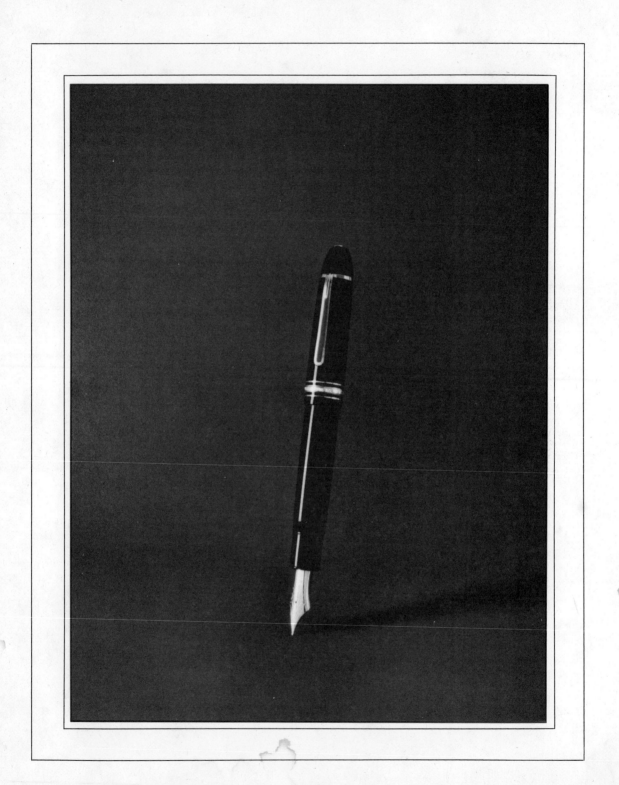

WRITING WITH A PURPOSE

SEVENTH EDITION

JAMES M. McCRIMMON

CONTRIBUTING AUTHORS

SUSAN MILLER
THE UNIVERSITY OF WISCONSIN – MILWAUKEE

WEBB SALMON
FLORIDA STATE UNIVERSITY

HOUGHTON MIFFLIN COMPANY
BOSTON

DALLAS   GENEVA, ILLINOIS   HOPEWELL, NEW JERSEY
PALO ALTO   LONDON

Printed in the U.S.A.

Library of Congress Catalog Card Number: 79-88599

ISBN: 0-395-28253-5

CREDITS

ILLUSTRATIONS

STUDENT ESSAYS

CONTENTS

PREFACE

The seventh edition of *Writing with a Purpose* retains the theme of purpose, the emphasis on prewriting and revision, and the general organization of earlier editions. The book assumes that composition is a process and that students can best learn that process not by fragmentary experiences with particular types of essays but by studying the process itself and by using it in any kind of expository writing, including persuasion. What is essential to the process is a set of interrelated decisions about what the writer wants to say about a subject in a given situation and how that best can be said for the kind of reader being addressed. The synthesis of these decisions is the writer's purpose, and that purpose provides a standard by which alternative choices at any stage of the writing can be judged. The book further assumes that a considerable number of students, though not all, can learn to write purposefully in this sense within the limits of a freshman composition program.

The major changes in this edition have been suggested by constructive feedback from teachers who have used the book in the past. The most important of these changes are summarized below.

Especially in Part 1, an increased effort has been made to involve students in the discovery of basic concepts through an inductive procedure. In part, this has been done by extensive use of problems for discussion: usually a set of questions that require students to make individual analyses of student writings, to discuss their judgments, and to seek a class consensus on the merits or weaknesses of the work. But the text itself has frequently been revised to lead students into a concept rather than to give them the concept ready-made. The most obvious examples of this procedure are the cumulative approach to an understanding of *purpose* in Chapter 1 and the treatment of thesis and outline in Chapter 3. An inductive procedure is admittedly time consuming and cannot be consistently used in all the concerns of a composition course. But in those areas—chiefly those dealing with invention—in which induction can be efficiently used, the time spent is often justified by the results achieved.

In Chapter 2 the sections on observation and inference making have been expanded, both to emphasize the centrality of observation in writing and to provide a clearer account of the process by which observations are converted to judgments. This process is basic to interpretation, criticism, and argument, and the emphasis on inference making is intended to provide students with a nontechnical explanation of the kind of thinking they will use in much of their writing.

A new Chapter 3, "Stating and Outlining a Thesis," has been added to show students how to determine a thesis and develop it through an outline. In previous editions, *Writing with a Purpose,* like other textbooks, was more helpful in identifying the characteristics of a good thesis than in helping students to formulate a satisfactory thesis from the material available to them. The procedure for deriving a thesis is probably the most difficult lesson to teach to a composition class, chiefly because each thesis is a unique discovery and can be discussed only in relation to the information from which it emerges. Chapter 3 makes at least a start toward a general method of abstracting a thesis from given material. The inductive approach emphasizes that the thesis is derived from the data, not the data from the thesis. Then the outline is presented as a structure for selecting and organizing the pertinent data to establish the content of the paper. The chapter contrasts the relative advantages of topic and sentence outlines so that the student can decide which form is better for a particular purpose.

A new section on definition in Chapter 4 emphasizes an extended definition that combines the patterns of development previously discussed—illustration, comparison, classification, and process—and so serves to show that these patterns are not limited to types of essays but are primarily means of developing expository writing.

The chapter on style has been divided into two parts: *tone* and *style*. These parts are of course inseparable, but it has seemed wiser—or at least more convenient—to deal with considerations of the writer's attitudes toward the subject and the reader before dealing with linguistic choices. One change in this chapter may need explanation. In discussing the range of styles, I have reluctantly substituted the term *moderate* for *informal*. The reason for this change is that *informal* sometimes evokes a negative reaction leading to the assumption that only a formal style is appropriate in an English class. Since such an unjustifiable assumption undermines any sensitive approach to stylistic choices, I have attempted to by-pass it by inviting the more favorable connotations of *moderate*.

The major changes in the chapter on the research paper are required to make the treatment of bibliography and documentation conform to the recommendations of the *MLA Handbook*. In addition, a new model research paper on a nonliterary subject is provided as a practical review of the research paper assignment and, incidentally, of the composing process itself.

The new chapter on business letters, while not ignoring the conventional forms, puts most of its emphasis on content and style. The writer's main concerns are not the conventional forms, which can be easily learned or copied, but decisions on what to say and how to say it in a situation that the writer recognizes as real and important. The business letter is another application of the theme of purpose to a practical writing assignment.

At the request of some instructors, the glossary of previous editions has been reorganized and expanded into two sections: a glossary of technical terms and a list of troublesome usages. As in previous editions, the judgments about usage are the result of a survey of the scholarship in the field.

In the preparation of this edition I have had more help than a brief acknowledgment can describe. My greatest indebtedness is to Professors Miller and Salmon, who, as contributing authors, have provided many of the professional and student samples used for illustration and analysis and have participated in shaping the revision.

For general criticism of the sixth edition, made before actual work on the seventh edition began, I am indebted to David Bartholomae of the University of Pittsburgh; Joseph Comprone of the University of Louisville; Richard L. Larson of Herbert Lehman College, City University of New York; James C. Raymond of The University of Alabama; and Robert S. Rudolph of the University of Toledo.

For detailed criticism of an early draft of this edition, I owe thanks to Jean Brenkman of the University of Wisconsin; Forrest D. Burt of Texas A&M University; Kenneth W. Davis of the University of Kentucky; Robert R. Green of the Community College of Allegheny County; Patrick G. Hogan, Jr. of the University of Houston; and Joseph F. Trimmer of Ball State University.

To Kenneth W. Davis and Patrick G. Hogan, Jr. I owe additional and special thanks for their thorough and helpful criticism of what I then thought was the final version of the manuscript.

To the Dictionary and Reference Division of Houghton Mifflin Company I express gratitude for sending me a considerable body of material on usage from the files of *The American Heritage Dictionary*. The usage notes in that dictionary provided a basic, though not exclusive, selection of items for the "Checklist of Troublesome Usages." The job of preparing such a list would have been much more onerous without this assistance.

Finally, I again acknowledge the help of my wife, who not only revised the chapter on the library and typed extensive parts of the manuscript but also exerted a pervasive influence in several chapters of the book.

JAMES M. McCRIMMON
TALLAHASSEE, FLORIDA

WRITING WITH A PURPOSE

PART
1

PREWRITING

1

PURPOSE:
AN
OVERVIEW

Writing is, first of all, a way of thinking, and the quality of your writing will depend to a large extent on the quality of the thinking you do about your subject both before and during the writing. Throughout Part 1 of this book we emphasize the kind of thinking you should be doing as you try to bring out your thoughts and feelings on a subject in order to discover what you want to say about it.

THE THREE STAGES
OF THE WRITING PROCESS

We will begin by dividing the whole writing process into three stages: *prewriting, writing,* and *rewriting.* In the *prewriting* stage you try to get clear in your mind what your specific approach to the subject should be, what kinds of materials you need, how these materials should be organized and presented for the particular kind of reader you have in mind; in short, you plan the organization and content of your projected paper. In the *writing* stage you work out your plan in detail through the first draft. In *rewriting* you examine what you have done and consider where and how the first draft can be improved.

The three stages are not always so separate as the previous paragraph may suggest. Sometimes, of course, they are separate. Especially in working on long research papers, you may gather extensive notes and prepare and revise several outlines before you begin the first draft, and then—perhaps days later—you may do a thorough revision of that draft. But sometimes, especially in writing short papers, you may plan and revise as you write. And often you will modify your original plan during the writing stage, as the actual writing clarifies your ideas.

The following excerpts from an interview with a professional writer, William Allen, describe one writer's procedure. Other writers may use a somewhat different sequence, but Allen's comments are typical enough to provide a practical example of the process discussed throughout this chapter. Read them and answer the questions that follow them.

INTERVIEWER: Can you describe what you usually do when you write?
ALLEN: First I need to want to write—and this happens in a number of ways. For instance, I feel an urge to create. Or to publish. Or to make money. Or maybe an editor will call and motivate me. Then I get an idea. Either I come up with it or an editor does. I think about this idea for a while, then I start gathering information. I do research. Then I start selecting things that relate from almost everything around me—for instance, I'll hear a good line that I can fit in. I take notes. Finally I reach the point where I've done all the thinking I want, so I begin putting something on paper.

Once I begin, the material I've gathered starts to take shape. During the first draft, I'm aiming to make my purpose clear, and to keep the reader involved in . . . what I want to do, the direction I'm taking. . . . Then I do another draft, which I write slowly in an effort to improve my ideas and perfect the language. I put the piece aside for a while and then come back to it to look at the structure; sometimes it has to be reshaped. If I got off on a tangent, I may have had to write it before I knew that it didn't fulfill my purpose. I never worry about throwing away material or even starting completely over.

INTERVIEWER: Do you become your own critic?

ALLEN: Yes, but I try to find someone to talk to about the piece, and luckily I'm receptive to criticism. I try to incorporate other people's ideas if I think they're good. A lot of writers can't accept criticism, but I've found that if you can please one careful reader, you can probably count on pleasing others. But I have to be my own critic, too. I don't really know everything I think about something until I put it on paper. I have to see the words. Then I can reshape them. I can see them as if somebody else wrote them. Sometimes I *pretend* I'm somebody else to facilitate this. By the way, often I find what I write is a trigger toward something bigger that I didn't realize I knew. Writing is a way of reaching into yourself. . . .

QUESTIONS FOR DISCUSSION

1.   The two paragraphs following the question "Can you describe what you usually do when you write?" report the prewriting, writing, and rewriting stages of Allen's writing procedure. What does Allen do in each stage?

2.   To which stages does he give most attention in these paragraphs?

3.   Compare Allen's procedure with the one you yourself use when you are writing. Do you seem to spend more time or less time than Allen does on prewriting? On rewriting?

4.   Allen says, "I don't really know everything I think about something until I put it on paper." Do you think that this statement probably holds true for other writers, too—that is, that writing helps the writer learn something new about the subject? Do you learn about your subject when you write? If so, can you give an example?

5.   What have you learned about the process of writing from this interview?

Insofar as Allen's procedure can be called typical of the way professional writers approach their work, this interview suggests that a great deal of writing is rewriting. Because of their experience, professional writers can trust themselves to see from the first draft what still needs to be done. Inexperienced writers have more trouble detecting major flaws in a first draft. They tend to be bound by what they have written and therefore cannot easily see where the draft has drifted away from the subject or what should be cut or added or changed. For this reason we are going to emphasize the importance of prewriting as a necessary initial stage in the writing process. As far as possible we will urge you to plan your work fully enough to avoid the need for extensive rewriting of the sort Allen describes.

YOUR VIEW
OF THE WRITING SITUATION

Writing does not take place in a vacuum. Always a writer (*W*) is trying to communicate his or her ideas about some subject (*S*) to some reader (*R*) in some situation, as shown in the following diagram:

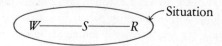

If you look at this set of relations from the point of view of the writer, you recognize that the flow of communication is from the writer through the treatment of the subject to the reader. But what you as a writer have to say is influenced both by the situation in which you are writing and by your view of the reader. For example, if you are writing an answer to an examination question, both what you say and how you say it are influenced by (1) the wording of the question, (2) the amount of time and space available for your answer, (3) your awareness of the grader's interests, and (4) your understanding of the relation of the question to the work in the course. These four considerations dictate the form of your answer. You are not free to respond as you wish; you are limited by the situation in which you are writing.

YOUR VIEW
OF YOUR READER

You know from experience that what you say and how you say it depend in part on whom you are talking to and in what situation the conversation is being held. A student complaining about a grade on a paper will talk very differently to a roommate and to an instructor. These differences apply equally in writing. A writer must think of the reader before beginning to write, and that concern affects the choice of subject, the organization of the work, the kinds of illustrations to be used, and the style of the work. Your view of your reader is therefore an important thing to consider during prewriting.

The need to understand your readers is greatest when you are trying to persuade them to do or believe something, and we will have to pay considerable attention to this need when we come to the chapter on persuasion. But for the moment we will concentrate on finding an answer to just two questions: "Where is the reader now?" and "What is it going to take to move the reader from there to where I want him or her to be?" The first question attempts to discover what the reader's knowledge, beliefs, and attitudes about the subject are likely to be. The second invites careful consideration of what kinds of information or appeals are likely to be most influential with that reader.

The easiest way to illustrate this kind of analysis is to use a set of directions. Consider the following telephone conversation, in which a woman from out of town is given directions on how to drive to a friend's house:

"Where are you now?"

"At the Holiday Inn on Main Street."

"All right, drive east on Main about two miles to Magnolia. As you approach Magnolia you'll see on the left a big school with a sign reading 'Central High School. Home of the Cougars.' About half a mile later you'll come to Magnolia. Turn right on Magnolia and go about a mile to the Parkway Shopping Center at the intersection of Magnolia and U.S. 27. Continue across 27 and go through two lights. After the second light continue for two short blocks to Pine Street. Turn left on Pine and count the driveways on the left side of the street. The fifth driveway is mine. Is that clear?"

"Yes, I think so: east on Main to Magnolia, then right on Magnolia across 27 to Pine, then left on Pine to the fifth driveway on the left."

To give these directions the speaker first identified the visitor's starting point and then guided her through each stage of the journey. Everything that was said was chosen for its usefulness to the driver. The references to the high school, the shopping center, and the lights were necessary landmarks given to inform the driver that she would be approaching a turning point. In other words, the selection of information was controlled by what the speaker thought the visitor would need to know. A similar control is at work in all communication situations. Just as the man giving directions had to place himself imaginatively in the driver's seat and see the route as the driver would see it, so you as writer must try to see your writing as your reader will see it.

For inexperienced writers this is often a difficult requirement. It is certainly more difficult in writing than in speech. A speaker can make adjustments to the feedback of a puzzled look or a "What-do-you-mean?" But in writing there is no such direct feedback. Your best safeguards are these: first, to try to get your reader's needs clearly in mind; second, to cultivate the habit of asking yourself in prewriting, writing, and rewriting, "Will this be clear to a reader?" If you are in doubt, consult someone—a roommate, a classmate, or your instructor. The one thing *not* to do is to assume that there must be something wrong with a reader who has trouble with your writing.

EXERCISES **A.** The advertisements on these two pages are addressed to different kinds of readers. Probably anything that can be done at one resort can be done at the other, but each advertisement emphasizes certain activities and ignores or plays down others. On the evidence of this selectivity, write a brief description of the sort of people that each advertisement is addressing.

Come to the tropical island with only one hotel.

Our island is called Marco. Very tropical. Very secluded. Very beautiful.

An island where you can make a three and a half mile trail of footprints on a sugar white beach.

Where the crack of a golf ball, the twang of a racquet, the call of a sandpiper, the ripple of laughter, all act to punctuate the serenity.

And when the sun goes down, life on our island rises to the occasion.

Our nights are filled with tinkling pianos, clinking glasses, sizzling crepes, strumming guitars, excited applause and warm feelings for one of life's most delightful island vacations.

It's all here. At the Marco Beach Hotel. On Florida's southwest coast.

For brochures or reservations, see your travel agent. Or call toll free: 800-237-7509. (In Florida: 813-394-2511.) Marco Beach Hotel & Villas, Dept. NY, Marco Island, Fla. 33937.

Ad prepared by Hume/Smith/Mickelberry

Peter Island offers nothing.

This is why people keep coming back. Certainly you can sail, snorkel and ride. But you can also think, in peace and solitude. Of course you can fish, canoe, play tennis and scuba dive. But you can also do nothing at all and enjoy it as never before.

Peter Island Yacht Club is in the British Virgin Islands. It is remote, beautiful, expensive and exclusive. Very good travel agents know about it. Peter Island.

Not for every Tom, Dick or Harry.

Peter Island
Peter Island Yacht Club, British Virgin Islands

Call Loews Reservations, Inc. throughout the United States for immediate confirmed reservations.

Courtesy of Peter Island Yacht Club

B. Suppose you have been asked to write for your school paper an advertisement for a resort that is seeking to attract college students. You may select any material from the advertisements you used in exercise A, and add anything you think appropriate for the readers you are addressing. But make the advertisement a serious one that the resort might be willing to publish and pay for.

YOUR VIEW
OF YOUR SUBJECT

The subjects of some of your papers will be decided for you by the wording of your assignments. For example, if you are asked in an essay examination to contrast two characters in a play the class has read, you know quite specifically what your subject is, even though you may not yet know what you are going to say about it. But when you have a free choice of subjects, do not shuttle indecisively between alternatives. Pick a subject that lies close to your interests and experience and start to think about it. You may begin by jotting down at random some leads that might seem worth following, but do not be in a hurry to commit yourself to any of them. Certainly do not begin to write on them. At this stage you are not trying to find out what you are going to say about the subject; you are merely reconnoitering the subject to see what your options are.

GENERAL AND "REAL" SUBJECTS

In choosing a subject it is useful to keep in mind the difference between a general subject and what we will call a "real" subject. A general subject is not a specific topic to write about; it is an area within which to look for a topic that you can develop thoroughly within the length of your paper. For example, ecology is a general subject. Dictionaries define it as the relation between organisms and their environment. That relation includes dozens, perhaps hundreds, of other general subjects, such as erosion, contamination of the water supply, overpopulation, the destruction of species by excessive hunting or by pesticides, and the effects of all of these on plant and animal life. Each of these subjects is too broad for a student essay of three or four typewritten pages.

Students who commit themselves too quickly to a general subject are likely to run into two difficulties. First, if they try to deal with a large subject in a few pages, they can treat it only in a sketchy summary that gives a reader no detailed understanding. The result is a paper that has no grounding in the writer's experience and therefore does not reflect what the writer sees in the subject or thinks about it. Such a paper has little value to either the reader or the writer. Second, the subject will be so all-inclusive that it will give the writer no help in deciding what to emphasize and what to leave out. The result will be a paper that has no focus, no central point on which the reader can concentrate.

The obvious solution to these problems is to *restrict* the general subject to something that can be treated in some detail within the space available—that is, to reduce the scope of the subject in order to treat it in more depth. But although restriction is a necessary first step, it does not of itself guarantee a successful paper. Even if a writer restricts a general subject like pollution to, say, the problem of nuclear waste, there is still the question of what is to be said about nuclear waste. Only when that question has been answered does the writer have a real subject.

The choice of the real subject, then, establishes the focus of the paper. "Dating" is a general subject. Restricting it to "Dating in College" helps but still does not commit a writer to any particular focus. But when a student decides that she is going to show that dating in college is much more informal and relaxed than it used to be, not only does she have a subject she can deal with in a short paper, but she knows what kind of information that paper needs and, as the following student essay shows, she can easily get it from her own experience:

Is Dating Outdated?

It used to be that the rules were pretty well cut and dried. A guy would call a girl, ask her out, get all dressed up, and take her to a movie. Afterwards they would go to the local hangout for a hamburger and a shake. They would part with a sweet, simple, and quick handshake. And in every case the guy took the initiative; the girl merely reacted. It was out of the question for a girl to call a boy.

Dating has changed quite a bit since then. Guys don't formally ask girls out as much as they used to. If a guy happens to meet a girl on the street, he may ask her out, but more often than not they date in groups and nobody makes an effort to dress up. The ever-popular jeans have taken over the fashion scene.

One day last semester, I was walking home from school when one of the guys in my class started walking with me. Before we parted to go to our separate dorms, he asked me if I wanted to go to "dime a draft" at the Cabin. It sounded like fun, so I said yes. Twelve of us went as a group with an even number of girls and guys.

Dutch dating has become quite common, especially among college students. Girls realize that guys are in just as much of a financial bind as they are. The first few dates are usually guys' treats. But when a girl dates a guy steadily over a period of time, she becomes pretty open-minded and open-pocketed when it comes to the question of who's going to buy the next pitcher of beer.

I've been dating a guy for almost two semesters now. He goes to a different college, so I don't see him much. But when it happens that we manage to make it home on the same weekend, I usually make sure that I pay an equal share of the expenses when we go out. If we go to a bar, I pay for my own drinks and try to pay for some of his, although I usually have to catch him off guard on both accounts.

Another example of the way dating has changed is kissing on the first date. In Mother's day that just wasn't done. The guy had to wait until the second or third date, so he wouldn't get any wrong ideas. But kissing on the first date is no longer a big event. Kids just do it. There's nothing wrong with a simple sign of affection to show thanks for a good time. It's just as natural as a handshake and a "Thank you for a pleasant evening," and it means about the same thing.

Dating is not on its way out. It's just changing, and most of the changes add up to a more relaxed way of girls and guys getting to know each other.

Often a well-chosen title will summarize the real subject of a paper. Such a title as "College: Four More Years of High School" clearly suggests to both writer and reader what the paper is going to say about college and even the tone in which it is going to say it. Similarly, such titles as "The Registration Nightmare" and "College Is a Breeze" suggest very different real subjects drawn from the same general subject, "My Impressions of College."

QUESTIONS FOR DISCUSSION

As preparation for a class discussion, read this essay and answer the questions following it.

On Your Own

Before I came to this campus I knew things would be rough. I had heard from friends ahead of me in high school how big the U was and that a new freshman was sure to feel lost and lonely for a time. I had also been told that the work would be much harder than I was used to and that students got less help from the teachers. All this advice got summed up in the phrase, "At the U you're on your own." Now after three weeks here I know what the older fellows meant.

During Freshman Week I didn't know whether I was coming or going. I never had so many different activities crowded into one week. The first thing I did when I arrived on campus was to go to the dormitory and get my room. There I met my roommate, whom I had written a couple of times to during the summer. He introduced me to some of the other fellows in the dorm, and we compared notes about what we had done in high school and what we wanted to do here. It was a nice beginning for college, for I got to know several students who have been my good friends ever since.

During the next three or four days we had something scheduled every minute. We took physical examinations and scholastic tests and I had to take an extra math test because I did not have enough math in high school. After the tests we went to see our advisers, who told us what subjects we should take and helped us plan our programs. I didn't have too much trouble because one of the older boys in the dorm had briefed me on the courses I'd have to take, although the adviser almost refused to OK my program because I had forgotten to bring the slip showing I had taken my physical.

Registration wasn't as bad as I had been told. I was lucky to get an early registration time, so I was able to get all of the classes my adviser had approved, except that I had to switch hours for my PE section. Those who came later were less lucky. By then classes were pretty well filled up and some students practically had to tear up their programs and start over again.

My real troubles began when classes started. Where my most difficulty was was the assignments. I thought I understood the work as it was being taken up in class, but it was a different story when I tried to do the assignments. Worst of all, every one of my instructors seemed to have the idea that his class was the only one I was taking. I had more homework for each course than I had for all my courses together in high school. Fortunately several of us in the dorm studied together and were able to help each other out.

1. From the evidence of the title and first paragraph, what do you, as a reader, expect this paper to be about—that is, what do you expect its real subject to be?

2. Does the second paragraph bear out your expectations? Why or why not?

3. What is the third paragraph about? The first two sentences suggest that it will deal with unpleasant experiences. But does the rest of the paragraph follow up that lead? Do the things that are happening to the student here help to explain that students in college are on their own, and that being on one's own can be "rough"?

4. Did the student have a difficult or a relatively easy time during registration? Was he on his own during this time?

5. The student did have trouble with his first assignments. But was he alone with his difficulties, or did he get help from others?

6. Do your answers to the questions above make you feel that the student consistently developed the idea expressed in the title and opening paragraph, or do you feel that he drifted away from the subject he began with? If you think that he drifted, where did the drifting begin?

7. Would this have been a more consistent paper if its title were "Not as Bad as They Said It Would Be"? If so, has the student merely chosen the wrong title, or does the paper have a more serious fault than that?

8. How would you rate this paper: superior? average? poor? Explain your rating.

9. From studying this paper, what conclusion do you draw about writing?

Since the real subject depends partly on the personal interests of the individual writer, for any general subject there will be as many real subjects as there are writers. And any paper written on a real subject will reflect the writer's personal views. We can illustrate the truth of this statement by the accompanying drawings made by children. The general subject of each drawing is a thumbprint, but each child sees different possibilities in it, and so each drawing (real subject) is unique. It reflects the interests of the child as much as it conveys the impression of the thumbprint.

It is this personal element that gives writing individuality. Probably no amount of thinking will give you a subject that has never been used before. Yet a paper that expresses *your* observations, *your* ideas, *your* values, even on a subject that everyone is familiar with, will be worth writing and reading. It will be worth writing because it will give you the experience and satisfaction of working out in detail how *you* feel about the subject. This is one of the educational values of writing. Writing forces us to examine our general impressions and clarify them. Often our ideas on a topic are vague and undeveloped. Writing requires us to develop them more fully and specifically, so that in the process of writing, including prewriting, we learn to see and understand the subject more clearly than we did before.

Furthermore, a paper that reflects something of the personality of its author is likely to be more interesting to a reader than one that does not. There are, of course, occasions in which an assignment requires the writer to suppress his or her

Drawing by Fred Gettings, reprinted with permission of the Hamlyn Group, London, from *You Are An Artist: A Practical Approach to Art,* by Fred Gettings. Copyright 1965, The Hamlyn Group.

own personal attitudes toward a subject, but in many of the essays written in a composition class, the reader expects to see the subject through the writer's eyes. After all, a writer's view of the subject should be a personal view, not everybody's view or the view of no one in particular. An essay on role-playing written by a freshman girl should be different from a paper on the same topic by a psychologist. If the girl tries to write like a psychologist or contents herself with repeating the kinds of things that psychologists say, what will be the appeal of such a paper to a freshman audience? If the girl is going to write on role-playing, she would be wise to deal with it on a personal level, as the author of the following paper does:

The Roles I Play

I have thought seriously about role-playing since our discussion in class last week, and while I fought the idea for a while, feeling that it cut down my image of myself, I finally had to admit it's true. I do play roles. I guess we all do. And now that I've admitted it, I think I understand myself a little better, and maybe other people too.

One important role I have played for the last eighteen years is that of being a daughter. My parents have been great to me. But there are times when I just can't tell them what is on my mind. At those times my parents seem to have a sixth sense and to know something is worrying me. And I know they feel left out and maybe frustrated to be told, "Oh, Mom, everything's fine," or "Dad! Whatever gave you that idea?" But there are things I just can't tell them. It is easier to play the role of a carefree girl than to upset them with all my doubts and misgivings.

I have been in college for just six weeks, but already I have found that I play a different role for each of my professors. They all have a particular kind of response that they expect from their students, and it is impossible for me not to respond the way they want. It's not that I am apple-polishing. It's just that each of them creates a different situation and I adjust to it. It seems the natural thing to do. For instance, I usually do not like to draw attention to myself by asking questions or volunteering answers in class, but my sociology instructor is disappointed when students do not respond. He has a thing about dialogue. So I ask questions, even when I know the answers, to show him I am responsive. In the physics lab I am the cool, methodical scientist who never makes a mistake, though I sometimes have to doctor the results of an experiment to make it come out the way it is supposed to. I sometimes think I am doing most of my work for my professors, not for myself, and I don't always like it, but it seems right at the time.

More important to me is the role I play with the man I love. This relationship means everything to me. To him I am a person he can tell his problems to, a shoulder to lean on, and most important the woman he loves. The role I am playing with him is the one that is nearest to my real self. I am not afraid to let him know what is on my mind. He listens and does not laugh or make me feel embarrassed, and he understands. I value his opinion, for he often makes me see my problems more clearly than I did before. Yet even he has an image of me, and I try to live up to it. I could not bear it if he was disappointed in me.

There are many other roles I play. My best girlfriend and I have been very close for the last five years. Yet there are personal things on which she and I do not communicate. We talk about our boyfriends and about where we went and what we did. But it's all on an impersonal level. I would be embarrassed—and so would she—if I tried to tell her what Ted and I mean to each other. Sometimes I catch myself playing roles with people I have never seen before—a policeman, an old lady, a boy who tried to pick me up. I even play different roles in different clothes. When I had a job in a store before Christmas last year I tried to be as cheerful and helpful and interested in other people as I like others to be with me. Some nights when I got home from work I felt like taking off my face and frowning for a week.

I see now that I play almost as many roles as there are people I meet. Usually, without even knowing it, I try to be what they think I am, or what I want them to think I am. I have learned already that role-playing works two ways, and that sometimes I play a particular role for the sake of others, because I want to please them, and sometimes for my own sake, because I want to make an impression. I don't like myself any better for my new knowledge, but I do understand myself better. And everybody else too, I suspect.

YOUR VIEW
OF YOUR PURPOSE

Now that we have considered the writer's view of the situation, reader, and subject, let us put these particular concerns together into one comprehensive view of what we will call *purpose*. As it is used in this book, the word *purpose* is a technical term. It does not mean what it usually means in such a question as, "Is the purpose of this article to inform, persuade, or amuse?" because these terms are so general that they offer little help to a writer planning a paper. By *purpose* we mean *the basic commitments writers make when determining* (1) *what they want to do, and* (2) *how they want to do it.* The first commitment determines the *what,* or content, of the work; the second determines the *how,* or style. We cannot really say that these are separate decisions, because often content and style are so interrelated that they must be considered together, but in this definition of *purpose* it will be convenient to treat them separately.

Suppose a student decides that she is going to write her next paper about television. This, you will recognize, is a general subject. When she asks herself what she is going to do with television, she can easily identify a number of restricted topics: sex and violence on television, educational television, TV commercials, westerns, soap operas, the influence of television on children, and so on and on.

Suppose she chooses westerns. Now she has a restricted subject, but still she has not decided what to do with that subject. Thinking about the various possibilities, she decides she is going to make fun of TV westerns. Now she has a real subject, a *what,* but is still faced with the question of *how.* The answer to that question must take into account her audience (her classmates), the situation (a 500-v.ord paper to be read in class), the kinds of illustrations she needs, and, most important, the kind of language she will use.

Here is what she wrote. Read her paper as preparation for the discussion that follows it.

Why We Need More Westerns on Television

The other night I saw a wonderful western on television. It had just about everything you'd want—fast horses, handsome men, beautiful women, mean outlaws, sneaky Indians, waving grass, rolling plains, covered wagons, smoking pistols, hard liquor, torrid love, bitter tears, bloody death—just about everything you could ask for, all packed together into one little hour, and early enough for the kids to see it, too. This program was really something and I think we need lots more just like it, because programs like that teach lots of things that everybody ought to know—things that help us in our everyday life, and at other times, too. I'll tell you what I mean.

Take making friends, for instance. Most people are pretty slow at this, but they don't have to be. This program showed that a person can make friends quickly if he really tries. There was a trail scout in this story and a Russian countess, and at the beginning, they didn't even know each other, but before the first commercial, which came about four minutes after they met, they were already lying in the grass and kissing, just as if they'd known each other for years. I think we should all take a lesson from this—it's sort of a symbol. A Russian and an American making love on the prairie under the sky. It has a lot of meaning to it.

Another thing about westerns is that they show the difference between good and bad people. After you watch a few westerns, it's pretty easy to tell which is which. A good man never shoots a person in the back—he waits until the person turns around to face him, which is the decent thing to do. On the other hand, bad men will shoot a man anywhere and will even shoot a woman or a dog sometimes. Speaking of women, there are good ones and bad ones, just like men. The good ones are usually married, while the bad ones usually aren't. The bad women usually wear real low-cut dresses or

short ones, and the good women usually have on aprons; they might wear
pretty tight dresses (the young good ones, that is; the old good women wear
loose dresses), but they're hardly ever cut low. All these things are very
helpful to people watching the program, because they know right away
whose side to be on. And just like knowing how to make friends quickly, it's
very helpful in life to know whose side to be on.

One of the best things westerns teach is our country's history. I'll bet
people with television sets know lots more about history than people without television sets, because westerns on television are just crammed with
history. They tell how we had to fight the pagan Indians every step of the
way to get them to give us this land so that we could really make something
out of it. (We let them go on living here, after we won the land fair and
square, and we even gave them special areas called "reservations" to live on.
They're real nice places—sort of like wild game preserves to keep animals
from becoming what they call "extinct.")

When you start thinking about all the advantages of watching westerns,
it's pretty plain to see that we ought to have more of them. There has been a
lot of progress made toward getting more westerns on television, and you
can see a good western almost any time except Sunday. Unfortunately, on
Sunday afternoons there are things like symphony orchestras, documentary
films, and panel discussions—real dull, long-hair stuff that most Americans
wouldn't be interested in. The only good thing about Sunday is that before
you know it, it's Monday again, and the beginning of a whole new week of
interesting, educational, realistic, historical westerns. But friends, we've got
to do something about Sunday afternoons.

QUESTIONS
FOR
DISCUSSION

1. We cannot ask the author what her purpose was. All we can do is perceive the
purpose from the paper itself. Does the paper suggest that from the beginning the
writer knew what she was going to do and how she was going to do it? Does she
seem to be in command of her writing, so that everything in the paper seems to fit
together into a consistent treatment of her subject?

2. Consider the structure of the paper. Of the five paragraphs, what is the
function of the first one, the next three, and the last one? Is the content of each
paragraph consistent with the apparent purpose of the paper? Explain your answer.

3. When does the reader first discover that this paper is going to be a spoof of
TV westerns?

4. Are there enough illustrations to make clear to a reader each of the main
points the writer is trying to make? How effective are these illustrations?

5. Consider the language. Some people object to such informal expressions as

"kids," "lots of," "sort of," and "real low-cut" in a paper for an English class. Do you object to them in this paper? Why or why not?

6. Is the statement in the final paragraph that most Americans are not interested in symphony orchestras, documentary films, and panel discussions a digression, or does it seem appropriate in this essay? Explain your answer.

7. What is the writer's attitude toward her readers? Does she seem to be taking her readers into partnership by counting on them to see that she is really making fun of TV westerns? If so, was this author-reader partnership something that was planned from the beginning?

8. We can distinguish between the author and the narrator of a story by saying that the author is the real person who did the writing and the narrator is a character invented by the author to tell the story. If the speaker in this essay is the *author,* then the student who wrote the essay is truly enthusiastic about TV westerns for the reasons given. If the speaker is a *narrator,* then the author can give her any personality that is appropriate to the purpose of the paper. Do you think the speaker is the author or a narrator? Is the personality of the speaker appropriate to the purpose of the paper? Was the personality of this speaker decided on before the writing began?

At every point in the composition process, a writer is making choices between alternatives—between one view of the subject and another, between different kinds of materials and different ways of organizing it, between different styles of presentation. If the choices are consistent they will support each other, and the writing will move forward smoothly and logically, as it did in the paper about TV westerns. But if the choices are inconsistent they will work against each other and will result in awkward, confused, or contradictory writing.

To be consistent a writer needs some control that will be a guide toward good choices and away from bad ones. Your best control will come from a sure awareness of your purpose. If you know what you want to do in a paper and how you want to do it, this sense of purpose will lead you toward the right choices and will help you detect and correct any wrong choices you may make. In effect, a sense of purpose acts as a guideline along the path marked out in prewriting.

The dominant idea of this book is that the effectiveness of your writing will depend on the clearness with which you see your purpose. As fully as possible you should discover your purpose in prewriting, since a wrong turn at the beginning of the composition can cause you to continue in the wrong direction during the rest of the writing stage, as the writer of the paper "On Your Own" wandered away from the direction of his title and opening paragraph. You will not, of course, be able to plan everything in detail before you begin to write. But a firm sense of purpose offers the best assurance that the basic plan of your work will be right, and it tends to reduce the amount of rewriting you will have to do after the first draft.

REVIEW
EXERCISES

A. As a review of what you have learned about purposeful writing, read the paper that follows and discuss the questions after it. The paper was written by a student whose father is an officer on a narcotics squad. The instructor had said he wanted papers showing careful prewriting that took into account both the writers' view of their subject and their view of their readers. The audience was identified as the class itself, and it was understood that the best papers would be read by the authors to the class. The student who wrote this paper assumed that some members of the class might be hostile to narcotics officers. His major prewriting decision was how to say what he wanted to say to such an audience.

Three Points of View

Put yourself in the position of this man.

The YMCA where your son takes swimming lessons is located in a section of the city that has been plagued with drug traffic problems in recent months. So on this Saturday afternoon you rush away from the golf course as soon as your match is over to be at the Y to pick him up. You are waiting in your car, reading a newspaper, when a man dressed in a business suit approaches you, flashes something that is inside his wallet, says he is a police officer, and tells you to step outside of your car. You are shocked and scared and you refuse. He pulls a gun and orders you out. This time you do get out of the car. He searches you and then puts away his gun. He says he has had a report that leads him to suspect you may be selling heroin, and he asks you for identification. You object indignantly, but you reach for your wallet. Unable to find it, you remember that in your haste you left it in the safety deposit box at the clubhouse, and you become more upset. The man asks you to get into his car to go to the police station and establish your identity. You demand a better look at his police credentials and protest his actions with threats of legal action, but you go with him. At the station your identity is quickly proved by a couple of telephone calls, and you are released with an apology and a lecture about driving without a license.

You have experienced the scene with the innocent citizen. Now look at it from the policeman's point of view.

You are a plainclothes officer assigned to a high-crime area. A former prostitute who now operates a boardinghouse and who has given the police valuable tips in the past telephones the station that a man in a late-model blue car with a black top is parked in front of the Y across the street from her house. She names the man and says that he has a reputation for pushing hard drugs and for always carrying a pistol. The call is relayed to you by radio and you proceed to the Y. There you see a man in a blue Impala with a black acrylic top. You park and approach him. When you identify yourself and ask the man to step out of the car, he acts nervous and refuses. One of his hands is underneath a newspaper, and you know that he is supposed to be armed. You draw your revolver and order him to get out. This time he does. You search his clothing and find no weapon, so you holster your gun. The man protests loudly. When you ask him for identification, he cannot produce any, not even a driver's license. You ask him to accompany you to the station.

Who was right in this situation? Granted, the man was nervous and frightened. He had good reason to be. However, had he responded to the officer's request and been able to identify himself, the whole encounter would have taken only a few minutes.

But by what right does a policeman pull a gun on an innocent citizen? Was there a violation of the Fourth Amendment to the Constitution?

The right of the people to be secure in their persons, houses, papers, and effects, against unreasonable searches and seizures, shall not be violated, and no warrants shall issue, but upon probable cause. . . .

The terms "unreasonable" and "probable cause" are the basis for the legality of "stop-and-frisk" actions. Probable cause to stop and search exists if there are facts and circumstances that satisfy "a man of ordinary caution" that a crime has been or is about to be committed and that a danger to personal or public safety exists. In the incident just described, the officer had reason to suspect that a crime was being committed, for he was in a high-crime district, his informant had been reliable in the past, and he was ordered to investigate. He had reason to believe that the man was armed and that the newspaper covered up a possible place of concealment. So when he drew his revolver he thought that an immediate danger to himself existed. The suspect had no identification. This, along with his actions, left reasonable doubt of his innocence in the officer's mind. So he asked the man to accompany him to the police station where further investigation could be conducted. All of these actions seemed reasonable according to the officer's view of "a man of ordinary caution."

It is extremely important that a police officer be "a man of ordinary caution." One who is not can destroy much of the public trust that is necessary for efficient law enforcement. A decision an officer makes in a split second may harm a person permanently or may be a cause for an extended and expensive lawsuit. There is no place on the force for a policeman who

abuses his authority or does not understand its limits. Such a man should be
screened out as soon as possible.

It is also important that citizens know how their rights can be protected
against abuse of the probable-cause ruling. We have seen that an officer must
have probable cause to believe that an individual is or is about to be involved
in a crime. Once he is satisfied of this, he may approach the suspect, identify
himself, and ask reasonable questions related to his suspicions. He may search
the suspect only if he has reason to believe he may be armed. Even then, he
may search only the suspect's clothing and the area of immediate reach. If the
officer finds anything other than a weapon, such as contraband or narcotics,
these may not be used as evidence against the suspect. This is as far as an
officer can go without placing the person under arrest, and he must have
additional probable cause to believe that an arrest is warranted.

Should you ever be subjected to a "stop-and-frisk" situation, the first
thing to do is to assure the officer that you are unarmed. Until he knows that
you are a potential source of danger to him, and he may be as much afraid of
you as you are of him. Once he knows you are not armed, you can express
your indignation firmly. The officer may not like your lecture, but as long as
your protest is kept within legal bounds, he will put up with it.

If you believe that an officer had no probable cause or that he overstepped
his authority and acted unlawfully, there are several actions you can take.
You may write a letter to his superior and offer to meet with him and the
policeman in order to make your accusation. You may consult an attorney
and sue the officer civilly. If some physical violence took place, you may
charge the officer with assault or any other crime you and your attorney feel
he committed. You should not hesitate to take appropriate action against a
law-enforcement man who has mistreated you, for his kind must not be
entrusted with police authority. But until you are mistreated, the best policy
is to recognize that he has a duty to perform and to cooperate with him.

1.   Do you think this is an appropriate essay for a freshman audience? Why or
why not?

2.   Does the author seem to have his audience clearly in mind? Give reasons to
support your answer.

3.   What are the "three points of view" mentioned in the title? The first two are
obvious, but what is the third?

4.   What are the main parts of this essay? How are these related to the title?

5.   Do you think that the structure of the essay is the result of a definite plan
made during prewriting? What is the evidence for your opinion?

6.   Do you think that the plan is an effective one? Why or why not?

7. Does the information in the paper seem to you both complete enough and clear enough for a freshman audience?

8. What do you think were the principal sources of the student's information— conversations with his father, reading, or both?

9. Considering the instructor's directions for the assignment, how would you rate this paper: excellent? good? average? unsatisfactory?

B. As a result of the total discussion of the questions in exercise A, write a short paper in which you express your personal evaluation of "Three Points of View." Be as specific as you can in supporting your evaluation by references to the paper.

2

GETTING
AND
USING
INFORMATION

You saw in Chapter 1 that once William Allen had an idea for an article, his next step was to gather information with which to develop the idea: "I think about this idea for a while, then I start gathering information. I do research. Then I start selecting things that relate from almost everything around me." The quotation summarizes briefly what a writer does when trying to find out what to say on a subject. This chapter will show the common sources of information available to you and the means of using that information in your writing.

SOURCES OF INFORMATION

The research Allen mentions may require you to read up on the subject, the way a lawyer searches through legal decisions to find a precedent for a case, or the way a student goes to the library to find material for a research paper. It may include talking with people, as the interviewer talked with Allen. But it may also be a search into one's memory, what Allen calls "reaching into yourself." We will consider four major ways of obtaining material for writing: selecting information from previous experience, observing the subject, asking questions about the subject, and drawing conclusions from the information these sources give you.

SELECTING INFORMATION
FROM EXPERIENCE

You will often be your own best source of information. You do not come to a writing problem with a blank mind. Since infancy you have accumulated a tremendous amount of information about people and places, historical events, your country and neighborhood, sports, politics, hobbies, and many other subjects. And you have opinions on these subjects—some that you got from conversations with parents, friends, and teachers; some that you acquired through reading; and some that you formed yourself. Often your problem in writing is not so much to gather new information as to select what you need from your memory.

The selection will be guided by your sense of purpose. If you know what idea you want to develop, that understanding will lead you to look for certain kinds of materials and to reject others. In effect, your purpose gives you a principle of selection that both suggests and controls your choices of material.

Suppose a writer wants to develop the opinion that people never blame themselves for what happens, but always blame somebody or something else. To do that he needs illustrations of people blaming others. Where does he get them? The most obvious source is his memory. As he scans his memory, he selects three bits of information:

1. a quotation from Jack Kerouac's novel *On the Road,* in which the main character says, "It's not my fault! Nothing in this lousy world is my fault, don't you see that? I don't want it to be and it can't be and it won't be."
2. letters to Abigail Van Buren, who writes a syndicated column giving advice to people who have social and domestic problems
3. an incident in a popular cartoon strip in which Dennis (the Menace) disowns any responsibility for the muddy footprints he has tracked onto the carpet

The writer could probably think of more examples, but these are enough for the moment. He works them into his paper this way:

> "It's not my fault! it's not my fault! Nothing in this lousy world is my fault, don't you see that? I don't want it to be and it can't be and it won't be." This outcry comes from Kerouac's Sal Paradise, but it expresses the deep conviction of multitudes of irresponsibles in the age of self-pity. It is a curious paradox that, while the self is the center of all things, the self is never to blame for anything.
>
> The fault is always the fault of someone or of something else. This is implicit in all the letters which are addressed to Abigail Van Buren. "Dear Abby: This is my problem. . . . My husband. . . ." "Dear Abby: Here is my problem. . . . My wife. . . ." Or it may be my son, my daughter, my mother-in-law, my neighbors. It is never Me.
>
> Blame it on God, the girls, or the government, on heredity, or on the environment, on the parents, on the siblings, on the cold war, on the pressures toward conformity, on being unloved and unwanted. But don't blame it on me, the very center around which the whole universe revolves. This me is like the innocent and apparently unmenacing Dennis, who stands before an accusing mother, in the middle of the parlor, with his body twisted about as he looks back on the carpet at some curious mud tracks which lead right up to his heels. Says Dennis, in bewilderment, "I don't know what that stuff is . . . it just keeps following me around." (Robert Elliot Fitch, *Odyssey of the Self-Centered Self*)

1. Reread the passage, but this time leave out the three illustrations. How does the unillustrated passage affect you?

2. What does your answer to question 1 tell you about the value of appropriate illustration in developing an idea or opinion?

3. Which of the following bits of information might be appropriate in the paper you have just read, and which would not? Explain your answer.

a. the quotation, "There's nothing either good or bad but thinking makes it so."

b. the following dialogue:

> DENNIS: "Oh, is my teacher mad at you!"
> HIS MOTHER: "Why?"
> DENNIS: "For the way you've brought me up."

c. a student who excuses her poor spelling with the remark, "I know. All my family are poor spellers."

d. a golfer who penalizes himself by one stroke because his caddy accidentally kicked his ball slightly while looking for it in the rough.

QUESTIONS
FOR
DISCUSSION

EXERCISE   Consider the opinion, "Often it is not what we did (or said) that we most regret, but what we did not do (or say)." Jot down possible illustrations of this idea from your own experience. Then choose two of these illustrations and write a two-paragraph paper that uses one illustration in each paragraph.

OBSERVING THE SUBJECT

An important source of information is the knowledge we get from close observation of a subject. Most of us, most of the time, notice only a little of what we see, hear, touch, taste, and smell. This is natural, because usually we are selective in what we notice. When we are looking for a golf ball that we drove into the rough, we do not distract ourselves by examining the bark on the trees. But when our interest is aroused or we feel a real need to observe, we can train ourselves to see what we have often ignored, and to recall it when necessary. Writers who understand how important specific details are in helping readers to understand general statements cannot be content with a general impression of a subject. They must have observed the subject in concrete detail, as Mark Twain has observed watermelons before composing the following paragraph:

> . . . I know how a prize watermelon looks when it is sunning its fat rotundity among pumpkin vines . . . ; I know how to tell when it is ripe without "plugging" it; I know how inviting it looks when it is cooling itself in a tub of water under the bed, waiting; I know how it looks when it lies on the table in the sheltered great floor space between house and kitchen, and the children gathered for the sacrifice and their mouths watering; I know the crackling sound it makes when the carving knife enters its end . . . ; I can see its halves fall apart and display the rich red meat and the black seeds. . . . I know how a boy looks behind a yard-long slice of that melon, and I know how he feels; for I have been there. I know the taste of the watermelon which has been honestly come by, and I know the taste of the watermelon which has been acquired by art. Both taste good, but the experienced know which tastes best. *(The Autobiography of Mark Twain)*

A famous critic once described good writing as "writing with one's eye on the object." He did not mean that good writers were literally looking at an object as they wrote about it, but that writing should be done only after careful observation, and that writers should have their observations clearly in mind while writing. They should see them in their mind's eyes, as Twain did.

It is useful to distinguish between two kinds of observing: looking *at* and looking *for*. When we are leafing through a magazine, looking at the pictures, we are usually not looking *for* anything. We see each picture separately and are not trying to find any relationship among them. But when we pick up the magazine to see whether it contains a picture or a cartoon by a favorite artist, our attention is concentrated on certain details of subject or style that signal the work of that artist. Our looking is conditioned by a previous judgment that some details are more significant than others. In this frame of mind we look purposely for certain features and tend to ignore or hurry over anything not pertinent, much as we do when we look up someone's number in the telephone book.

Although looking *at* is usually a first step in looking *for,* it is less important in purposeful observation. Looking *for* goes beyond seeing things to seeing a relationship between things. When we are looking for a particular piece of a jigsaw puzzle, our attention is concentrated on the color and shape the piece must have if it is going to fit into the pattern. Looking *for* demands greater selectivity than looking *at.*

The following passage illustrates both the difference between looking *at* and looking *for* and the importance of observation in studying a subject. The author (a graduate student of Louis Agassiz, a great American naturalist of the last century) is describing Agassiz's method of teaching. At his first lesson the student was given a jar containing a fish preserved in alcohol and was told to take out the fish and study it, and to moisten it with alcohol whenever it began to dry out. After giving these instructions, Agassiz left the laboratory.

> In ten minutes I had seen all that could be seen in that fish, and started in search of the professor, who had however left the museum; and when I returned, after lingering over some of the odd animals stored in the upper apartment, my specimen was dry all over. I dashed the fluid over the fish as if to resuscitate the beast from a fainting-fit, and looked with anxiety for a return of the normal, sloppy appearance. This little excitement over, nothing was to be done but return to a steadfast gaze at my mute companion. Half an hour passed,—an hour,—another hour; the fish began to look loathsome. I turned it over and around; looked it in the face—ghastly; from behind, beneath, above, sideways, at a three-quarters' view,—just as ghastly. I was in despair; at an early hour I concluded that lunch was necessary; so, with infinite relief, the fish was carefully replaced in the jar, and for an hour I was free.
>
> On my return, I learned that Professor Agassiz had been at the museum, but had gone, and would not return for several hours. My fellow-students were too busy to be disturbed by continued conversation. Slowly I drew forth that hideous fish, and with a feeling of desperation again looked at it. I might not use a magnifying-glass; instruments of all kinds were interdicted. My two hands, my two eyes, and the fish: it seemed a most limited field. I pushed my finger down its throat to feel how sharp the teeth were. I began to count the scales in the different rows, until I was convinced that that was

nonsense. At last a happy thought struck me—I would draw the fish; and now with surprise I began to discover new features in the creature. Just then the professor returned.

"That is right," said he; "a pencil is one of the best of eyes. I am glad to notice, too, that you keep your specimen wet, and your bottle corked."

With these encouraging words, he added:

"Well, what is it like?"

He listened attentively to my brief rehearsal of the structure of parts whose names were still unknown to me: the fringed gill-arches and movable operculum; the pores of the head, fleshy lips and lidless eyes; the lateral line, the spinous fins, and forked tail; the compressed and arched body. When I had finished, he waited as if expecting more, and then, with an air of disappointment:

"You have not looked very carefully; why," he continued, more earnestly, "you haven't even seen one of the most conspicuous features of the animal, which is as plainly before your eyes as the fish itself; look again, look again!" and he left me to my misery.

I was piqued; I was mortified. Still more of that wretched fish! But now I set myself to my task with a will, and discovered one new thing after another, until I saw how just the professor's criticism had been. The afternoon passed quickly; and when, towards its close, the professor inquired:

"Do you see it yet?"

"No," I replied, "I am certain I do not, but I see how little I saw before."

"That is next best," said he, earnestly, "but I won't hear you now; put away your fish and go home; perhaps you will be ready with a better answer in the morning. I will examine you before you look at the fish."

This was disconcerting. Not only must I think of my fish all night, studying, without the object before me, what this unknown but most visible feature might be; but also, without reviewing my discoveries, I must give an exact account of them the next day. I had a bad memory; so I walked home by Charles River in a distracted state, with my two perplexities.

The cordial greeting from the professor the next morning was reassuring; here was a man who seemed to be quite as anxious as I that I should see for myself what he saw.

"Do you perhaps mean," I asked, "that the fish has symmetrical sides with paired organs?"

His thoroughly pleased "Of course, of course!" repaid the wakeful hours of the previous night. After he had discoursed most happily and enthusiastically—as he always did—upon the importance of this point, I ventured to ask what I should do next.

"Oh, look at your fish!" he said, and left me again to my own devices. In a little more than an hour he returned, and heard my new catalogue.

"That is good, that is good!" he repeated; "but that is not all; go on"; and so for three long days he placed that fish before my eyes, forbidding me to look at anything else, or to use any artificial aid. "Look, look, look," was his repeated injunction.

This was the best entomological lesson I ever had—a lesson whose influence has extended to the details of every subsequent study; a legacy the professor has left to me, as he has left it to many others, of inestimable value, which we could not buy, with which we cannot part. (Samuel Scudder, "In the Laboratory with Agassiz," *Every Saturday,* April 4, 1874)

QUESTIONS FOR DISCUSSION

1.   What was Agassiz's method of teaching?

2.   Did the student think it was a good method for training young scientists? Do you? Why or why not?

3.   When he first began his study of the fish, was the student looking *at* or looking *for* something?

4.   Why did Agassiz say, "a pencil is one of the best of eyes"? In what sense would drawing the fish help the student to see it in more detail?

5.   Why was Agassiz so pleased when the student discovered that the fish had symmetrical sides with paired organs?

6.   In this excerpt what was the difference between looking *at* and looking *for*?

EXERCISE

Study the picture on page 32 called *Edith, Christmas A.M.* with the intention of writing a description of the scene. First, list what seem to you the significant details. Then group these details in whatever order you decide. Finally, write the description.

ASKING QUESTIONS
ABOUT THE SUBJECT

One way of gaining information about a subject is to ask yourself questions about it. What is it? How does it resemble or differ from something else? What is it used for? The following passage shows an application of this method:

Imagine that sitting opposite you is a person who knows nothing whatever about our modern civilization—a transplanted Cro-Magnon man, in effect. You are to assume that this man does know the English language. If you can go along with this impossible paradox, you will realize that no object will mean much to your primitive listener unless you tell him *all* about it. Now, suppose you try to describe to him a common, undecorated, plain-shaped *water glass*. Here is one of our most common articles of use. How would you go about describing it to someone who hadn't the faintest idea what it was unless you told him?

Get a plain water glass and put it in front of you. Ask questions of the glass.

What is it for? What is its function? How does it perform that function? Why is it round-shaped instead of square-shaped? Exactly what "shape" is it?

EDITH, CHRISTMAS A.M.

Emmet Gowin, 1972

Is this the best shape for its function? Why is it made of glass? Could it be made of some other material? Why is glass a better material than, say, copper?

The trick is to ask *why* of every relevant part of the article. When you ask *why* of something persistently enough, you get quickly to essentials. You have to be direct and specific. You can't drag in details that have nothing to do with the object—because as soon as you ask "why" of those irrelevant details, they are eliminated.

Now sit down and write a description of the water glass in a hundred words or less. You will find yourself writing short sentences. You will discover that every word has to be exact. You won't be able to weasel with vague terms or bluff with generalities, because each word you use—especially nouns and adjectives in this exercise—stands for a fact. The facts are not alterable, and you need to find the precise words to match them. For example, you cannot say, vaguely, that the water glass is "round." It *is* round, in a way, but so is a ball or a wheel or an egg round after a fashion.

But if you say that the glass is *cylindrical,* then you are getting closer. If it is a slightly tapered cylinder, then your limiting adjectives to the noun *cylinder* have to be exact. In what direction does it taper? And so on. (Roger H. Garrison, *A Creative Approach to Writing)*

The advantages of this kind of questioning are threefold. First, asking yourself questions requires you to observe the subject in specific detail. Second, the questions direct your thinking by telling you what to think about. Third, your attempts to answer the questions force you to report your findings accurately, fully, and clearly.

Another kind of questioning helpful in gathering information about an event is the traditional advice given to cub reporters to ask *who, what, where, when, why,* and *how.* This advice serves as a formula that a young reporter can follow in covering a story. An experienced reporter may vary the formula on particular assignments. For example, in covering the hijacking of an airplane, the reporter may emphasize or "feature" the personality of the hijacker *(who)* or his motivation *(why)* or the means he used *(how).* The formula need not be followed slavishly, but it is good general advice for someone who is looking for the significant facts in an event.

Choose any event that has happened recently on campus. Take each of the six   EXERCISE
questions that the cub reporter is advised to ask, and, for each, jot down all the information you can obtain. Then examine your material to see which, if any, of the data should be emphasized for the readers you are addressing. Finally, write your report of the event.

MAKING INFERENCES
FROM THE FACTS

Once you have gathered specific bits of information, you will want to find a relationship among the bits. Professor Agassiz used to tell his students, "Facts themselves are stupid things until brought into connection with some general law." What he meant was that facts alone are of little importance to a scientist until he or she can relate them to some conclusion.

It is customary to call the relationship between an observation and a conclusion an *inference.* An inference is a thought pattern that refers an observation to previous experience and then draws a conclusion. A student who looks at his watch while he is having breakfast and says, "Seven-forty; I'll be late for my eight o'clock!" is thinking a relationship between the hands of his watch and getting to class on time. He knows from experience how long it takes to go to class; therefore, he is able to make the inference that he will be late.

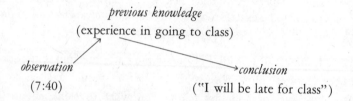

previous knowledge
(experience in going to class)

observation   →*conclusion*
(7:40)   ("I will be late for class")

This illustration identifies the three steps in the process of making an inference:

1. the observation from which the inference starts (in this case the time on the watch)

2. the previous knowledge or belief to which the observation is related (the time required to get to class)

3. the conclusion or end point of the inference ("I will be late for class")

When the student in the illustration completes the process, we say he *infers* the conclusion from the observation. *Infers* is simply a short way of saying "goes through the mental process from observation to previous knowledge to conclusion." In this short form the beginning and end stages of the process are emphasized, and the second stage (previous experience) is taken for granted or assumed and is usually called an *assumption.*

EXERCISE   Because this book will make frequent use of the words *inference* and *infer,* especially in dealing with interpretation and argument, we urge you to become familiar with these two terms. In the following statements identify the three stages of each inference:

1. This is a green apple; it will be sour.

2. See that black cloud; it's going to rain.

3. The faucet keeps dripping; it needs a new washer.

4. My car is not in the parking lot. It has been stolen.

5. I answered only three of the five questions on the test. I probably failed.

6. Her symptoms point to appendicitis.

7. It is the third accident at that intersection this month. The city should install a traffic light.

8. Although there's plenty of gas in the car, it won't start. Maybe I need to replace the spark plugs.

9. She has not done any of the assignments. She is sure to fail.

10. Red sky at morning, sailors take warning,
    Red sky at night, sailors' delight.

INTERPRETING INFORMATION

Interpretation is the act of giving meaning to observations by inferring a judgment or conclusion from them. A simple example will illustrate. Robinson Crusoe, on his desert island, one day discovered the print of a naked foot on the sand. He had believed he was alone, but seeing the footprint caused him to infer that there was somebody else on the island. He reacted to that conclusion by drawing another conclusion from it: the person who had left that footprint represented a possible threat to his security. Until Crusoe could find out whether the newcomer was friend or foe, he would have to be careful.

Crusoe's thinking went through three stages: he *observed* something (the marks in the sand), he *interpreted* it (a human footprint), and he *inferred a conclusion* (it could mean trouble). This observation–interpretation–conclusion sequence is the chain of reasoning used by a doctor in diagnosing a patient's symptoms, by a scientist in conducting an experiment, and by you when the bulb of your study lamp does not light. In simple situations, such as Crusoe's, the mind may leap from observation to conclusion instantaneously. In more complex situations it may take time to go from observation to interpretation and on to conclusion. But the process is the standard way of responding to information.

You can use this three-step method in many of your college courses for observing and interpreting information. In step 1 you concentrate on individual details, looking *at* them as though to describe each detail separately. In step 2 you try to see in what ways individual details are related to each other, how they fit together. You are looking *for* a pattern. In step 3 you combine all the information into a comprehensive view of the subject.

The following illustration will show the method in operation. Suppose someone brought you a paper bag containing all the pieces of a jigsaw puzzle, dumped the contents on your desk, and said, "I will give you ten dollars if you can put this puzzle together in less than an hour." And suppose you accepted the challenge.

Since you do not know what the puzzle will look like when it is finished, you must begin with individual pieces. You start by examining them, observing both their color and their shape. At this stage you are not organizing the material; you are simply taking an introductory look at it.

Soon you begin to sort the pieces into groups: all those that have the same color probably go together; all those that have one straight edge probably form part of the border. At this stage you are combining bits into small clusters or patterns; you are studying the interrelation of the parts.

As you develop these patterns by fitting pieces together, you begin to see small patterns combining into larger ones. You can begin to make guesses about the final picture, and these guesses help you to make further combinations until finally the picture is complete.

EXERCISE   To give you practice in using the three-step method of interpretation, we will first provide a demonstration, using the picture on page 37. Then we will ask you to use the same method to interpret the picture on page 40. Finally we will ask you to write a paper based on both pictures. These pictures were made by William Hogarth, an eighteenth-century artist whose work was often concerned with social criticism.

Observations   **A.**   As we look at the picture on page 37, we see the following details:

1.   In the foreground we see a child falling from the lap of a woman who is taking something from a can (snuff?). Her clothes are tattered, her leg is scratched or bruised, her breasts are bare (has she been nursing the child?), and there is a vacant grin on her face.

2.   Beneath her and to the right is a man who seems to be either dead or

GIN LANE (B-4, 613), William Hogarth

National Gallery of Art, Washington, Rosenwald Collection

unconscious. Except for a coat, he is almost naked. In his left hand he holds a bottle in a basket that contains a paper on which the most conspicuous word is *Gin.* In his right hand he holds a glass, at which a dog seems to be gazing.

3.   Below and to the left of the woman a vessel of some kind (a pitcher?) is suspended over a door and shows the words *Gin Royal.* In this reproduction we cannot read the inscription over the door, but if the picture were enlarged we would see:

> Drunk for a penny.
> Dead drunk for twopence.
> Clean straw for nothing.

4.   Above the gin royal pitcher, an old man and a dog are gnawing at a bone; next to them a woman is either asleep or staring vacantly upward.

5.   Above this group are three people at the door of a pawnshop. One of them (the pawnbroker?) is well dressed and is examining a saw, which the man on his left is evidently trying to pawn. Next to them a woman in tattered clothes is offering her cooking utensils.

6.   To the right of this trio is a little mob scene in which the following details can be identified:

   a. Someone is being wheeled in a barrow while a woman is pouring a drink from a glass into the person's mouth.

   b. At the extreme right, a woman is giving her child a drink from the same kind of glass.

   c. Beyond her, two women are drinking from similar glasses.

   d. To the left of them a group of men seem to be fighting: one of them has a bandaged head and is brandishing a stool; another is striking with a crutch; some others are carrying sticks.

7.   To the right of this group is a distillery displaying the same kind of pitcher we noticed before and containing stored barrels of something (gin?).

8.   Beyond the distillery is a building with a wall so broken that it reveals a man hanging (a suicide?).

9.   The next building has a coffin displayed on a pole (an undertaker's establishment?). This building seems to be in good shape.

10.   The next building is falling down.

11.   In mid-center an almost naked corpse is being lifted into a coffin, beside which a man carrying a cross is standing (a priest or monk?). Beside the coffin is a child.

12. To the right a man carrying a pointed staff on which a child is impaled seems to be hurrying toward the fighting group.

13. In the distance, at the end of the street, is a mass of buildings, one falling over and another being supported by posts.

1. With some exceptions, the general impression of the scene is one of poverty, ruin, violence, and death.

2. One dominant symbol pervades the scene—the drinking of gin—and there seems to be a clear causal relation between the drinking of gin and the condition of the people and the buildings.

3. The exceptions to the general rule are the gin shop, the distillery, the pawn-broker and his shop, and the undertaker's building. These exceptions suggest a contrast between those who profit from the sale of gin and those who suffer from drinking it.

The "real" subject, as we used that term in Chapter 1, is the evils of drinking gin, and the artist's purpose is to communicate these evils by presenting the details already identified. If we wanted to give the picture an appropriate title, it would be one that featured the word *gin.* Hogarth called the picture *Gin Lane.*

B. Now use the same method to interpret the picture on page 40. If your instructor prefers, the exercise may be done by class discussion. But since we are principally interested in method here, do not jump hastily from a few observations to a conclusion. As much as possible, complete the observations before making major interpretations, and hold off any conclusion until the end. What title would you give this picture?

C. Finally, when both pictures have been interpreted, sum up the contrast between the two by completing the sentence, "In these two pictures Hogarth is contrasting. . . ." Use the completed sentence to begin your paper. Organize your notes and use them to develop that sentence into a paper.

Now that you have had experience in using the three-step method of interpretation, let us see how it is used in a piece of professional writing. But first you must understand that the method is a *prewriting* method. The observing and interpreting you did on the Hogarth pictures were done *before* you began to write. If you wrote a paper developing the sentence that you were asked to complete in part C of the exercise, you began with that sentence, which was the conclusion you had reached after studying both pictures. You could not have completed that sentence without

BEER STREET (B-4, 612), William Hogarth

National Gallery of Art, Washington, Rosenwald Collection

the detailed information provided by the prewriting sequence of observation, interpretation, and conclusion. But in writing the paper, you began with your conclusion and used your observations and interpretations to support and make clear that conclusion.

The following passage from a book published in 1963 begins with the author's conclusion—that "Negroes in this country . . . are taught really to despise themselves from the moment their eyes open on the world." Then it goes on to show how from observation and interpretation the author arrived at that conclusion. First read the passage carefully, then study the numbered statements that follow it.

. . . Negroes in this country—and Negroes do not, strictly or legally speaking, exist in any other—are taught really to despise themselves from the moment their eyes open on the world. This world is white and they are black. White people hold the power, which means that they are superior to blacks (intrinsically, that is: God decreed it so), and the world has innumerable ways of making this difference known and felt and feared. Long before the Negro child perceives this difference, and even longer before he understands it, he has begun to react to it, he has begun to be controlled by it. Every effort made by the child's elders to prepare him for a fate from which they cannot protect him causes him secretly, in terror, to begin to await, without knowing that he is doing so, his mysterious and inexorable punishment. He must be "good" not only in order to please his parents and not only to avoid being punished by them; behind their authority stands another, nameless and impersonal, infinitely harder to please, and bottomlessly cruel. And this filters into the child's consciousness through his parents' tone of voice as he is being exhorted, punished, or loved; in the sudden, uncontrollable note of fear heard in his mother's or his father's voice when he has strayed beyond some particular boundary. He does not know what the boundary is, and he can get no explanation of it, which is frightening enough, but the fear he hears in the voices of his elders is more frightening still. The fear that I heard in my father's voice, for example, when he realized that I really believed I could do anything a white boy could do, and had every intention of proving it, was not at all like the fear I heard when one of us was ill or had fallen down the stairs or strayed too far from the house. It was another fear, a fear that the child, in challenging the white world's assumptions, was putting himself in the path of destruction. A child cannot, thank Heaven, know how vast and how merciless is the nature of power, with what unbelievable cruelty people treat each other. He reacts to the fear in his parents' voices because his parents hold up the world for him and he has no protection without them. I defended myself, as I imagined, against the fear my father made me feel by remembering that he was very old-fashioned. Also, I prided myself on the fact that I already knew how to outwit him. To defend oneself against a fear is simply to insure that one will, one day, be conquered by it; fears must be faced. As for one's wits, it is just not true that one can live by them—not, that is, if one wishes really to live. That summer, in any case, all the fears with which I had grown up, and which were now a part of me and controlled my vision of the world, rose up like a wall between the world and me.... (James Baldwin, *The Fire Next Time)*

If we analyze the order of the experiences and the inferences made from them, not as they appear in the writing, but as they occurred to the boy while he was growing up, we can trace the following sequence, which was, in a sense, the sequence of Baldwin's prewriting:

1.   First the boy was disciplined to be "good." He saw no significance in this except the normal pattern of parental control, which would be similar in any family.

2.   He began to distinguish two kinds of reprimands: those that were limited to his relations with his parents, and those that extended beyond his parents to some power beyond the family, a power of which even his parents were afraid. This was an inference from his experience.

3.   He began to realize that people are divided into two groups—blacks and whites, and that his parents accepted whites as the dominant group and feared to offend them. This was a more comprehensive inference and a major step in his interpretation of what was happening to him.

4.   At first he rejected this grouping, then rebelled against it, but finally accepted it, and with that acceptance came the same fear that his parents had shown.

5.   Later he realized that the whole pattern of his upbringing was designed to make him feel inferior to whites and to impress on him the need of "keeping his place." This is a conclusion from all that has gone before.

6.   This pattern was built up by a series of cause-and-effect inferences: "The whites won't like this—you will be punished."

7.   The pattern was extended. It was not just that young Baldwin was inferior and must conform; the pattern was generalized to all blacks. This is the final conclusion.

When he came to write this passage in the book, Baldwin reversed this order. He began with the generalization, which was the last stage of his growing aware- ness that blacks were being brought up to think of themselves as inferior to whites. He stated this generalization in his first sentence and explained it in a general way in the next two. Then he went on to show the experience that had led him to his conclusion. The experiences themselves became the material by which the generalization was developed to show its full implications.

This illustration summarizes the process of getting and using materials for writing. The process starts with observations from experience. These observations are fitted into small patterns by inferences. The small patterns, in turn, are generalized into one large pattern that provides the main idea, focus, or real subject of the paper to be written. The main idea is then developed by the information (observations and inferences) from which it was derived.

3

STATING
AND
OUTLINING
A
THESIS

In Chapter 2 you learned how to gather, select, and interpret information in order to arrive at a conclusion. That conclusion, stated as the main idea that you are going to develop, we will now call the *thesis*. When you completed the sentence about the two Hogarth pictures, you were stating the thesis of your paper. When James Baldwin wrote the generalization that "Negroes in this country . . . are taught really to despise themselves from the moment their eyes open on the world," he was stating the thesis of one part of his book. These examples should show that a *thesis* is *an introductory statement that summarizes the content of an essay by stating the conclusion or main idea to be developed*. Such a statement serves two useful functions: it notifies the reader what the work is going to be about, and it reminds the writer what he or she is committed to do.

If you remember what a topic sentence is, you could say that a thesis is to an essay what a topic sentence is to a paragraph. The following sentences could serve either as topic sentences of paragraphs or as theses (note the plural form) of essays of several paragraphs:

> Honesty is not always the best policy.
>
> The antipollution devices in new cars are causing trouble.
>
> Inflation falls most heavily on people living on a pension.

These statements do not indicate *how* the material is to be presented, so they cannot properly be called statements of purpose. But they do tell *what* the general content of the writing is going to be; and therefore they state the real subject the writer is concerned with. Even without the rest of the paragraph or paper, you know what kinds of information these theses require.

Since the thesis states the main idea an essay will develop, it is used only in essays that *do* develop an idea. Many quite purposeful papers do not, but simply describe something or provide the reader with information. A report of an event may have a purpose—to make the reader see what happened. A directive about how to do something may have a purpose—to show the reader how to do it. But such papers usually do not develop a dominant idea. If your paper is not going to develop an idea, there is no point in making it look as though it were. If you wish only to explain how the Wankel engine works, any attempt to begin with such a thesis as "The Wankel engine is the most interesting automotive development in fifty years" distorts your purpose. Since all you want to do is to show how the engine works, a thesis saying that it is the most interesting automotive development in fifty years would actually lead you away from your real subject, or else it would raise expectations in a reader that you do not intend to fulfill.

Since a thesis is an introductory statement, it usually comes at or near the beginning of an essay. Sometimes a writer will lead into the thesis with an introductory paragraph or two, but the best practice for you to follow at present is to put the thesis of your essay as close to the beginning as possible. Remember, though, that although a thesis comes at the beginning of an essay, it usually comes late in the prewriting process. The thesis is the conclusion that the author intends to develop. Prewriting has led to that conclusion and has suggested at least some of the material needed to develop it. A writer who starts with a thesis for which he or she has no material has simply pushed the difficulties of prewriting into the writing stage. The author then has two sets of difficulties to handle at once: those of getting clearly in mind what to do and how to do it, and those of developing the purpose through the paragraphs and sentences of the paper. An experienced writer might be able to handle both sets of problems at once, but your safest procedure is to let the thesis grow out of the prewriting and to know how you are going to develop it before you begin to write.

If you do not make the discovery of your thesis a part of your prewriting, you are likely to encounter the difficulty that is bothering Snoopy in the accompanying cartoon. Can you tell Snoopy what his problem is and what he must do to solve it?

EXERCISE

DERIVING A THESIS
FROM YOUR MATERIAL

Most of the troubles students run into in writing a thesis come from one of two sources: from inadequate prewriting or from difficulty in composing a satisfactory statement of the main idea of the paper. We will discuss the first difficulty here and the second in the next section, "Good and Bad Theses."

A student who has not adequately prewritten a paper may have no conclusion to present. To draw a thesis out of thin air is futile. Even if the student is able to compose a sentence that looks like a thesis, that sentence is of no use without material to support it. There is no point in a student's writing "The antipollution devices in new cars are causing trouble" if he or she does not know what the antipollution devices are or what kinds of trouble they cause.

If you have conscientiously done the prewriting for an essay and still have trouble deriving a thesis, the logical thing to do is to go back to your notes and see what kinds of conclusions they suggest. For example, suppose you had done the prewriting on the second Hogarth picture but could draw no conclusion from your observations. What should you do? You could ask yourself, "What is the connection between all this beer-drinking and the condition of the people doing the drinking?" That question could suggest several possible conclusions.

Beer is a healthful drink.

Drinking beer makes you fat.

When beer is available, nobody works.

Beer drinkers are happy people.

Any one of these statements could serve as a thesis for a paper *if you have the material (the observations) to support it.* The thing to do, therefore, is to ask what conclusions can be drawn from your material and then pick the conclusion you can best support.

Or—to take a harder example—suppose that, as part of an orientation program, your class has been reading and discussing a summary of a questionnaire submitted to 200,000 freshmen, about equally divided between men and women. In one part of the questionnaire the freshmen had been asked to rate which of eighteen objectives they considered "very important." They could rate as many objectives in this category as they pleased. The accompanying table shows the results.

In this tabular form the information is not organized to suggest any thesis. You must find a thesis by deciding what significant conclusion you can draw from the data. Your first step is to organize the information by grouping like things together. Let us suppose that you begin by checking the table to see what

Ratings of Objectives as Very Important

No.	Objective	% of men	% of women
1	Achieving in a performing art	11	16
2	Becoming an authority in one's field	76	72
3	Obtaining recognition from colleagues	52	45
4	Influencing the political structure	19	12
5	Influencing social values	29	33
6	Raising a family	59	59
7	Having administrative responsibility	38	31
8	Being very well-off financially	66	51
9	Helping others who are in difficulty	57	73
10	Making a theoretical contribution to science	17	11
11	Writing original works	12	16
12	Creating an artistic work	12	19
13	Being successful in one's own business	56	39
14	Helping to clean up the environment	31	28
15	Developing a philosophy of life	56	62
16	Participating in community action	27	32
17	Promoting racial understanding	32	40
18	Keeping up with political affairs	45	35

Source: Adapted from Alexander Astin et al., *The American Freshman: National Norms for Fall 1977* (Washington: American Council on Education; Los Angeles: University of California at Los Angeles, 1977), pp. 29, 45. Used by permission.

objectives were rated higher by one sex than by the other. This check gives you the following groups:

Higher ratings by men

Becoming an authority in one's field
Obtaining recognition from colleagues
Influencing the political structure
Having administrative responsibility
Being very well-off financially
Making a theoretical contribution to science
Being successful in one's own business
Helping to clean up the environment
Keeping up with political affairs

Higher ratings by women

Achieving in a performing art
Influencing social values
Helping others who are in difficulty
Writing original works
Creating an artistic work
Developing a philosophy of life
Participating in community action
Promoting racial understanding

Equal ratings by both

Raising a family

As you study these groups, you begin to think that you see a pattern: that men tend to rate more highly those objectives that are important in practical affairs, such as successful careers and participation in political and environmental activities, whereas women tend to rate more highly objectives that relate to artistic and social activities. Since this conclusion seems consistent with what is generally believed about male and female interests, you accept it and write the tentative thesis:

> This study shows that, in rating objectives, men tend to emphasize those related to successful participation in practical affairs, and women tend to emphasize social and artistic values.

This looks like a good thesis; but as you check it against the table, you begin to see some weaknesses in it. First, some of the "higher" ratings do not seem to be significantly higher. For example, male and female ratings differ by only 3% in objective 14 and by 4% in objectives 2, 5, and 11. Second, some of the differences between male and female ratings become less significant when both sexes give an objective a low rating. For example, although women rated "achieving in a performing art" 5% higher than men did, only 16% of the women and 11% of the men thought that that objective was very important. A considerable majority in both sexes (84% of the women and 89% of the men) thought it was *not* very important. A similar situation exists for objectives 4, 10, 11, and 12. Finally, the tentative thesis distorts the result of the study by emphasizing the differences in the ratings of men and women and ignoring the similarities.

At this point you decide to see what the results would be if you contrasted those objectives that were rated very important by more than 50% of the men and of the women with those that were not so rated. Your new grouping becomes

1. Objectives rated very important by more than 50%
   a. of the men: 2, 3, 6, 8, 9, 13, 15
   b. of the women: 2,   6, 8, 9,   15
2. Objectives *not* rated very important by more than 50%
   a. of the men: 1,   4, 5, 7, 10, 11, 12,   14, 16, 17, 18
   b. of the women: 1, 3, 4, 5, 7, 10, 11, 12, 13, 14, 16, 17, 18
3. Objectives on which men and women disagree: 3 and 13

This kind of grouping greatly alters your interpretation of the data. Now the significant conclusion seems to be not that one sex rates an item higher or lower than the other, but that, except for items 3 and 13, a majority of both sexes agree on which objectives are very important and which are not. The thesis you now want to write is

> In this study sex is not a major factor in deciding the importance of objectives.

This thesis is more consistent with all of the figures than was the first one, but it tends to overstate the similarities and to ignore the differences. There are differences that deserve attention—a difference of 15% on objective 8 (being well-off financially), a difference of 16% on objective 9 (helping others), a difference of 17% on objective 13 (success in business), a difference of 10% on objective 18 (political affairs). These differences can be noted by revising the second thesis to read

> This study reveals that, though there were some differences in male and female ratings of objectives, sex was not a major factor in deciding which objectives freshmen considered very important.

This revision allows you to include the differences while still retaining your overall conclusion. There are, of course, other ways to state this conclusion without distorting the results of the study. If what interests you most is the particular objectives that do seem to be sex-determined, you can write the thesis

> This study shows that, although sex was not a major factor in deciding what objectives freshmen considered very important, the ratings of some objectives do suggest differences in male and female values.

In this form your thesis will allow you to discuss the differences without ignoring or understating the similarities between male and female ratings.

What must be emphasized here is that the thesis is derived from the material, not the material from the thesis. Of course, a writer can state a thesis and then search for information to support it. But usually that can be done only when the information can easily be recalled from memory, in which case the information actually occurred first and suggested the thesis. For example, a student who writes "High school was more fun than college" can easily recall from memory enough examples to support that thesis. But we are not concerned with such easy theses here. The question we are considering now is how to derive a thesis from information that does not clearly suggest a conclusion.

The answer to this question is the one just illustrated in the plan for a paper on freshman objectives. The procedure is as follows: (1) list the information, (2) group like things together, (3) try to reach a conclusion from the groupings. If, despite your best efforts, no conclusion emerges from your study, that may be because your information does not lead to the sort of paper that requires a thesis. It may lead to a description or to a set of directions or a how-to-do-it paper. None of these needs to focus on one main idea. Therefore none of them may require a thesis.

For example, when you wrote in Chapter 2 about *Edith, Christmas A.M.,* you were asked only to describe the room. You may or may not have begun with a conclusion—say, "This room is a mess." But the assignment did not require a thesis. You could have described the room without making any judgment of it.

Suppose now that we change that assignment and ask you to *interpret* the picture. Since interpretation ends in a conclusion, it suggests a thesis. Study the picture again and write down some conclusions. Each conclusion will serve as a possible thesis for a paper.

DISCUSSION PROBLEM Study the following information from a magazine and draw a conclusion that could serve as the thesis of a paper using all of the data. First organize the material into two groups, as was done with the freshman ratings of objectives. Then for each group write a sentence that summarizes the material in that group. Finally combine these two summarizing statements into one conclusion that will serve as the thesis of a two-paragraph paper. If your instructor wishes, some of the theses may be discussed in class.

1.   Girls and boys today are about three inches taller and ten pounds heavier than were youngsters of the same age in 1920.

2.   Investigators have noted that the average American sixteen-year-old has had five years more schooling than his or her counterpart in 1920.

3.   Because of progress in medicine, childhood diseases that stunt and maim have been largely prevented.

4.   The average student today scores approximately one standard deviation above the score of an average student of a generation ago.

5.   A level of performance that places a student in the middle of a graduating class today would probably have placed that student in the top 15 per cent thirty years ago.

6.   Improvements in nutrition and medicine have caused adolescents to mature physiologically much earlier than in the past.

7.   A recent U.S. Census Bureau study reveals that the number of young adults with high school diplomas has doubled since 1940.

8.   In the United States the average age for the onset of puberty has dropped for girls from 14 in 1920 to 12.4 today; for boys it has dropped from 15 to 13.5.

9.   In scholastic achievement teenagers today are approximately one grade ahead of where their parents were at the same age.

GOOD AND BAD THESES

Apart from the problem of deriving a thesis from the material, students sometimes have difficulty with the actual wording of a thesis. The pages that follow will focus on this problem by showing the requirements of a good thesis and the faults that can make a thesis a poor one.

A good thesis is *restricted, unified,* and *precise.* To be *restricted* it must limit the scope of the paper to what can be discussed in detail in the space available. A thesis such as "The United States has serious energy problems" might be suitable for a long magazine article, but it could not be treated in adequate detail in a three-page essay. The thesis is too big for any paper a student is likely to write, since the length of the usual student assignment would allow room for only a general summary of so broad an idea. It would be wise to restrict the thesis to something that can be treated with some thoroughness, perhaps one of the following:

The oil shortage is greatly increasing the cost of products derived from petroleum.

Because of the energy problem, homeowners and building contractors are paying more attention to insulation.

People are seriously thinking about solar energy as a supplementary source of heat for their homes.

Students are often tempted into an unrestricted thesis because it makes few demands on them. It allows them to write "about" a general subject without going through the discipline of finding a real subject. But the function of a thesis is to control the writing so that both writer and reader know what the essay is going to do. Any thesis that fails to make such a commitment is of little value to either the writer or the reader. Neither writer nor reader, for example, gets a clear focus from the thesis "Manufacturers often deceive their customers." That thesis could lead off in all sorts of directions and might result in no more than a list of miscellaneous deceptions. But if the thesis were restricted to "Some automobile manufacturers and dealers have withheld information about structural defects that a customer has a right to know," the real subject of the essay would be much clearer to both the writer and the reader. Restriction of the thesis is so essential to effective communication that it is worth all the effort it requires.

A good thesis is *unified* as well as restricted. It must express only one idea. The following thesis contains not one idea, but three: "The use of drugs has increased significantly in the last fifteen years. Hard drugs are admittedly dangerous, but there is considerable disagreement about marijuana." This thesis commits a writer to deal with three topics: (1) the increase in the use of drugs, (2) the dangerous effects of hard drugs, and (3) the disagreement about marijuana. Each of these topics could easily be made the thesis of a separate essay. To try to deal with all three in a short paper would invite the kind of superficial treatment that is common with unrestricted theses, and would almost surely result in a paper consisting of three unrelated parts and lacking focus.

Even such a thesis as "Compared with other languages, English has a relatively simple grammar, but its spelling is confusing" could lead to separate treatments of grammar and spelling. If these two topics are to be related in some way, that relationship has to be implied in the thesis, perhaps by such a statement as "In learning English, foreigners usually have less trouble with grammar than with spelling." In this form the thesis commits the writer to contrasting the ease of learning grammar with the difficulty of learning spelling and thus tends to prevent separate development of the two topics. If the writer's chief interest is spelling, it would be still safer to ignore grammar and confine the thesis to spelling: "Foreigners have a hard time with English spelling."

As the previous examples show, lack of unity is most likely to occur in a thesis that contains two or more coordinate parts, each of which could be developed separately. For example, the thesis "The amateur ideal of the Olympic Games is being threatened; professionalism is on the increase" might trap an unwary writer into treating each part separately and producing a paper that develops two ideas, not one. This possible fault can be avoided by embedding one part in the other, thus: "Increasing professionalism is creating a serious threat to the amateur ideal of the Olympic Games."

In the following contrasted theses the possible lack of unity at the left is minimized by the revision at the right:

Not unified	Unified
Many of the silent letters in English words were once pronounced. The pronunciation changed, but the old spelling was standardized.	Many of the silent letters in English words are a result of standardizing the spelling while the pronunciation was still changing.
The nuclear bomb has immense destructive power, and there is no adequate defense against it.	There is no adequate defense against the immense destructive power of the nuclear bomb.
Baseball players have achieved a new independence, and there is nothing the owners can do about it.	There is nothing the owners can do about the new independence of baseball players.

Finally, a thesis should be *precise*. It should be so stated that it can have only one interpretation. For example, the thesis "My home town is one of the most interesting in the state" does not indicate the content of the essay, since *interesting* is vague and can mean many things. Readers will want to know in what way the town is interesting. If they have to read the whole essay to find out, the thesis does not help them. Moreover, because of its vagueness, it does not help the writer to see what should be done to develop the paper.

Words such as *interesting, colorful, exciting, inspiring, unusual* are too vague for a thesis. So are metaphors. The thesis "Where instructors are concerned, all that glitters is not gold" may seem clever, but what does it mean? That the best scholars are not always the best teachers? That instructors who put on a good show in the classroom do not always help students to master the subject? Or something else? The precise meaning of a thesis should be immediately clear. Metaphors may be effective in the text of an essay, but they can be troublesome in a thesis.

Some of the following statements would make acceptable theses; some, because they lack restriction, unity, or precision, would not. Reject those that are unacceptable and explain why you do so.

DISCUSSION PROBLEM

1. The increasing cost of a college education is reducing enrollment in private institutions.

2. During my senior year in high school I had some very interesting trips.

3. The invasion of Fort Lauderdale by hundreds of college students during the spring vacation results in pollution of that city's beaches.

4. An educated electorate is necessary in a democracy.

5. Good housing is hard to find. The rents are too high and the locations are undesirable.

6. Student writing would be improved if more attention were paid to prewriting. *need definition*

7. The forthcoming conference with the USSR may reduce tension in the trouble spots of the world, but we had better not count our chickens before they are hatched.

8. The evils of professionalism in college athletics should be considered.

9. The United Nations Organization has major weaknesses and cannot prevent a war between major powers.

10. The major cause of today's violence is the influence of television and the fact that the courts are too lenient.

Ideas

OUTLINING A THESIS

An *outline* is a formal plan of organization that breaks the topic or thesis into main units (marked by Roman numerals) and subdivides these main units into subunits (marked by capital letters). The subunits may be further subdivided and their subdivisions marked by Arabic numerals. The Arabic-numeral subdivisions may be further broken into smaller units marked by small letters.

The headings of an outline may be words or phrases that merely identify the topic to be discussed; or they may be complete sentences. Whether a topic or a sentence outline should be used depends on the kind of paper to be written. In general, *topic outlines* are suitable for papers that do not have a thesis or that enumerate or classify the kinds of materials to be presented. *Sentence outlines* are preferable when the outline is intended to prove a conclusion stated in a thesis. The following contrast illustrates the form and use of both kinds of outlines:

Topic outline   My Reasons for Coming to College

  I. To improve my economic status
  II. To develop social poise
  III. To make myself a cultured person
  IV. To enjoy college activities

Comment: Assuming that the writer has the information to develop each of these headings, this outline might be a sufficient plan for a paper entitled "My Reasons for Coming to College."

Sentence outline   Thesis: The financial benefits of a college education are not as convincing a reason for going to college as they used to be.

  I. A college degree is no longer a guarantee of employment.
  II. The wage differential between college graduates and nongraduates is shrinking.
  III. The increasing cost of a college education now demands a greater investment than was required in the past.

Comment: In this kind of argument a sentence outline is more effective than a topic outline would be in supporting the conclusion stated in the thesis. A topic outline would only identify the headings (employment, wages, costs) under which the argument was to be presented. The sentences actually begin to develop the argument by stating the three judgments that led the writer to the conclusion in the thesis.

CONSTRUCTING AN OUTLINE

The amount of subdivision required depends on the length and complexity of the outline. Sometimes all that is necessary is to plan the main divisions. For example, if on page 51 you had chosen the thesis:

> Although sex was not a major factor in deciding what objectives freshmen considered very important, the ratings of some objectives do suggest differences in male and female values.

you would know that this thesis implied two main divisions of your paper:

I.   General agreement between men and women that certain objectives were very important

II. Ratings of particular objectives that seem to suggest different sex values

At this stage, with the aid of your notes, you might begin writing your first draft. But if you thought a more detailed plan would be helpful, you might outline the structure of your paper thus:

> Thesis: The Astin study shows that, though sex was not a major factor in deciding what objectives freshmen considered very important, the ratings of some objectives do suggest differences in male and female values.
>
> I. In decisions about what objectives were "very important," sex was not a major factor.
>   A. More than 50% of the men and more than 50% of the women rated the following objectives as very important:
>   1. Becoming an authority in one's field (M, 76%; W, 72%),
>   2. Raising a family (M, 59%; W, 59%),
>   3. Being well-off financially (M, 66%; W, 51%),
>   4. Helping others in difficulty (M, 57%; W, 73%),
>   5. Developing a philosophy of life (M, 56%; W, 62%).
>   B. In only two objectives did the majority of men and of women disagree.
>   1. Most men did, but most women did not, consider obtaining recognition from one's colleagues very important (M, 52%; W, 45%).
>   2. Most men did, but most women did not, consider being successful in one's own business very important (M, 56%; W, 39%).
> II. A contrast of the figures on each objective suggests that in four objectives sex may have been a significant factor in student responses.
>   A. In 14 of the 18 objectives the differences between male and female ratings range from only 0% to 8%.
>   B. In four objectives the differences are conspicuous.
>   1. On being well-off financially, there is a difference of 15% (M, 66%; W, 51%).
>   2. On helping others, the difference is 16% (W, 73%; M, 57%).
>   3. On success in business, the difference is 17% (M, 56%; W, 39%).
>   4. On political affairs, the difference is 10% (M, 45%; W, 35%).
>   C. This contrast of minor and major differences suggests that the greater the difference, the more it reflects interests that are likely to be stronger in one sex than in the other.

In this outline we have provided more detail than would normally be given, because we wanted you to examine the relationships between the outline units and the evidence from which they are to be developed. If you were constructing this outline, you would probably leave out the statements preceded by Arabic numerals. That information would be used to develop the capital-letter entries into paragraphs in your paper, but it need not appear in the outline.

TESTING AN OUTLINE

If an outline is needed, it is always wise to test it carefully before beginning to write from it, partly because the structure of a paper is easier to see in an outline than in an essay, and partly because structural revision of a first draft may require starting all over again. For these reasons it is sound practice to test an outline by asking the following questions:

1. Is the thesis satisfactory?
2. Is the relation among the parts clear and consistent?
3. Does the order of the parts provide a logical progression?
4. Is the outline complete?

Is the thesis satisfactory? Since the thesis controls the whole outline, a faulty statement invites trouble all along the way. A rigorous checking of the thesis is therefore the first and most important step in testing an outline. Neither the first nor the second of the theses about the ratings of objectives suggested on page 50 survived a careful check against the data. Any paper written from either of them would likely distort the results of the questionnaire.

Is the relationship among the parts clear and consistent? In a good outline one should be able to see how each main unit brings out an important aspect of the thesis and how each subdivision helps to develop its main heading. If there is any doubt about the relation of any entry to the rest of the outline, that entry is either poorly stated or a potential trouble spot. Whatever the reason, the difficulty should be removed before the writing is begun.

The arrows in the following outline show a clear and consistent relationship among the parts:

I. The four-year college is geared to a few specialized interests.
    A. It is geared to liberal arts education.
    B. It is geared to a limited number of professions such as law, medicine, and engineering.
    C. It is geared to the training of teachers.

Notice also that inconsistency in the form of the entries or parts would have made their relationship less clear:

I. The four-year college is geared to a few specialized interests.
  A. It is geared to liberal arts education.
  B. Professions such as law, medicine, and engineering are served by the four-year system.
  C. The training of teachers is one of its main activities.

Because A, B, and C are no longer parallel in form, their parallel relationship to the main heading is obscured. Consistency among entries in an outline is not just a matter of style; it emphasizes their relation to each other and to the topic or thesis they develop.

Does the order of the parts provide a logical progression?   If any parts of an outline are out of order, the disorder will be magnified in the essay. As you know, the federal government has three main divisions of authority: the Executive, the Legislative, and the Judicial. Each of the following outlines confuses that structure:

I. The Executive
  A. The President
  B. The Supreme Court
II. The Legislative
  A. The House of Representatives
  B. The Senate

I. The Legislative
II. The Senate
III. The President
IV. The Judicial

At the left, listing the Supreme Court as a division of the Executive distorts the organization of the government into two main branches, not three. Further, it places the Supreme Court under the Executive, although that court has no executive power. At the right, the failure to recognize the Senate as a division of the legislature results in what looks like four main branches of government; it also implies that the Senate has no legislative authority.

Is the outline complete?   Asking whether an outline is complete is really asking not one question, but two. First, are all major units of the subject represented? Second, is each major unit subdivided far enough to guide the development of the essay? The first question is especially important in outlines for papers that will classify something or explain how something is done, since failure to include all the classes or stages may cause the writer to omit essential material. The second question—how extensive must the outline be to serve as an adequate plan for the paper?—is relative. The answer depends on the paper and the writer. For short papers, the outline may not need to go beyond the main headings, and even for a fairly long paper a short outline may be enough for a writer who has all the necessary information clearly in mind; the main headings may give all the help needed. The test is whether the outline will clearly determine the structure of the paper so that the writer is freed from any worries about structure during the actual writing.

The following outline was made by an instructor from an unsatisfactory student paper, and was intended to show the student that the paper was so badly organized that it did not have any focus. The student evidently had not seen this weakness, and the instructor hoped that the outline would help him to see it. Study the outline and answer the questions concerning it.

Thesis: College sports have an important place in the university as a whole.
I. College football is like professional football in many ways.
   A. The sport is less dangerous.
   B. Recruiters use many of the same tactics.
II. College sports are great money raisers.
   A. Alumni often give money when a team is successful.
   B. Intramural teams do not require scholarships.
III. Some students and teachers think there is too much emphasis on college sports.
   A. They say players get special treatment from teachers.
IV. Players often find their academic work suffering because of the time spent in practicing, but sports improve everyone's social life.
   A. Some teams have special tutors.
   B. Players don't like to study.
   C. A basketball date is a traditional Saturday activity here.

1. Is the thesis satisfactory? Does it clearly indicate to both the reader and the writer what the paper is going to do? Is the wording of the thesis precise, or is "an important place" too vague a term in this thesis?

2. Re-examine each of the four main statements—those marked by Roman numerals—before looking again at the subordinate statements marked by capital letters. Ask of each main statement, "Is the relationship of this statement to the thesis clear?" For example, does the similarity of college football to professional football support or help develop the thesis? See if there is general agreement in the class that each main statement is or is not clearly related to the thesis.

3. Next, consider the relationship between each subordinate statement and the main statement above it. For example, do A, B, and C under IV all help to explain or prove the fourth main statement? Do the A and B statements under I and II develop their main statement?

4. Does A under III provide adequate development of its main statement, or are

additional subordinate statements necessary? If you think more are necessary, can you suggest some?

5.   What is the real subject of the outline? If you have difficulty identifying a real subject, whose fault is that?

6.   As a result of this analysis, do you think the whole outline is satisfactory or unsatisfactory?

7.   Do you think that the instructor's outline helps to show the weakness of the paper's organization?

8.   If the student had had such an outline available before revising the first draft, would it have helped him to revise the paper?

9.   Would it have been helpful to this student to make an outline before beginning to write?

10.   What have you learned from this discussion that might help you in planning a paper of your own?

4

COMMON
PATTERNS
OF
DEVELOPMENT

In the last chapter you studied the development of a thesis by means of an outline. Any paper can be outlined, and the longer the paper the more useful an outline is. But for some kinds of short papers an alternative or supplementary way of developing a thesis may be more convenient. It is with this kind of paper that we will be concerned in Chapter 4.

Most theses suggest their own kind of development. But five patterns of development are so common that they deserve attention here. These are *illustra-*

tion, *comparison, classification, process,* and *definition.* Argument, another common pattern, is treated in Chapter 9. As you will see later, choosing to develop a paper in one of these five patterns does not mean excluding the others, since a writer will often include one pattern with another. For example, all five of the patterns we are considering in this chapter make some use of illustration; classification depends on comparison; and definition may include classification, comparison, illustration, and process. If you can handle the common patterns of development individually, you will also be able to combine them to suit your needs.

ILLUSTRATION

The simplest way to explain something is to give an example of it; so the commonest and most useful pattern of organization consists of a thesis explained or illustrated by examples.

Thesis stated and clarified

Birds reared in isolation from their kind do not generally know what species they belong to: that is to say, not only their social reactions but also their sexual desires are directed towards those beings with whom they have spent certain impressionable phases of their early youth. Consequently, birds raised singly by hand tend to regard human beings, and human beings only, as potential partners in all reproductive activities.

Example 1

A female barnyard goose which I now possess was the only survivor of a brood of six, of which the remainder all succumbed to avian tuberculosis. Consequently she grew up in the company of chickens and, in spite of the fact that we bought for her, in good time, a beautiful gander, she fell head over heels in love with our handsome Rhode Island cock, inundated him with proposals, jealously prevented him from making love to his hens, and remained absolutely insensible to the attentions of the gander.

Example 2

The hero of a similar tragi-comedy was a lovely white peacock of the Schönbrunn Zoo in Vienna. He too was the last survivor of an early-hatched brood which perished in a period of cold weather, and to save him, the keeper put him in the warmest room to be found in the whole Zoo, which at that time was in the reptile house with the giant tortoises. For the rest of his life this unfortunate bird saw only in those huge reptiles the object of his desire and remained unresponsive to the charms of the prettiest peahens. . . .

Example 3

Another tame adult male jackdaw fell in love with me and treated me exactly as a female of his kind. By the hour, this bird tried to make me creep into the nesting cavity of his choice, a few inches in width. He became most importunate in that he continually wanted to feed me with what he considered the choicest delicacies. Remarkably enough, he recognized the human mouth as the orifice of ingestion and he was overjoyed if I opened my lips to him, uttering at the same time an adequate begging note. This must be considered as an act of self-sacrifice on my part, since even I cannot pretend to like the taste of finely minced worms, generously mixed with jackdaw saliva. You will understand that I found it difficult to cooperate with the bird in this manner every few minutes! But if I did not, I had to guard my ears against him; otherwise, before I knew what was happening, the passage of one of these organs would be filled right up to the drum with warm worm pulp, for jackdaws, when feeding their female or their young, push the food mass, with the aid of their tongue, deep down into the partner's pharynx. However, this bird only made use of my ears when I refused him my mouth, on which the first attempt was always made. (Konrad Z. Lorenz, *King Solomon's Ring)*

In the opening paragraph the author first states his thesis and clarifies it by a few additional sentences, so that the reader knows, as well as he or she can be told in a short paragraph, the main idea to be developed. Then he illustrates that idea by three examples drawn from his experience. These examples drive the point home for a reader. Without them, most readers would be less sure what the author meant by his introductory paragraph. The examples also provide most of the interest of the paper.

One professor uses the letters *T, R,* and *I* to label the parts of the illustrative pattern.* The *T* marks the thesis (or in a single paragraph the topic sentence); the *R* stands for restriction, the additional comment that explains the thesis; and the *I* indicates the illustrations or examples. Thus in the selection you have just read, the underlined sentence would be labeled *T,* the rest of the first paragraph would be marked *R,* and the three examples together would be marked *I.* If the author had added a concluding paragraph restating the thesis, that paragraph would also have to be marked *T.* In that case, the structure of the selection would be TRIT.

The use of this structure can be quickly seen in the following paragraph, in which the underlined opening sentence is *T.* The next two sentences explain or clarify the first and so are marked *R.* The next two sentences are examples of the claim made in the topic sentence and are marked *I.* The restatement of the topic sentence in the last sentence calls for a second *T.*

> By a strange perversity in the cosmic plan, the biologically good die T
> young. Species are not destroyed for their shortcomings but for their R
> achievements. The tribes that slumber in the graveyards of the past were not
> the most simple and undistinguished of their day, but the most complicated

---

* A. L. Becker, "A Tagmemic Approach to Paragraph Analysis," in *The Sentence and the Paragraph* (Champaign, Ill.: National Council of Teachers of English, 1966), p. 34.

I and conspicuous. The magnificent sharks of the Devonian period passed with the passing of the period, but certain contemporaneous genera of primitive shellfish are still on earth. Similarly, the lizards of the Mesozoic era have long outlived the dinosaurs who were immeasurably their biologic betters. Illus-

T trations such as these could be endlessly increased. The price of distinction is death. (John Hodgden Bradley, "Is Man an Absurdity?")

DISCUSSION PROBLEM The following paragraph is based on *The Once and Future King,* a story about King Arthur and the knights of the Round Table. It deals with the education of young Arthur, who for a brief time was turned into first an ant, then a goose, by his teacher, Merlin the magician. The paragraph has a TRIT structure. Can your class agree in labeling its parts?

> Arthur's adventures as an ant and a goose were contrasted lessons in government, designed by Merlin to prepare him for kingship. Each illustrated a society in operation, and Arthur was expected to learn a lesson from the contrast. As an ant, he saw the tyranny of a dictatorship which reduced individuals to automatons. The ants had no freedom. Their lives were governed by "Done" and "Not done," and what was done or not was decided by their leader. By contrast, as a goose, Arthur saw how individuals lived in a free society. The geese chose their leaders freely for their skill in navigation and followed them willingly but were not subject to them. They accepted the mutual responsibility of taking turns as guards to warn of the approach of danger, but the thought of war with their own kind was shocking to them. In the contrasted lessons of the ants and the geese, Merlin showed Arthur society at its worst and its best.

EXERCISE To demonstrate your ability to use the TRI pattern of development, write a short paper using that pattern. You may add a concluding *T* if you prefer. Use the appropriate symbols to mark the parts of your paper.

COMPARISON

Another way to explain something is to show how it is like or unlike something else—that is, to develop it by a comparison or a contrast. (A *contrast* is simply a comparison that emphasizes differences rather than similarities.)

THE DIVIDED PATTERN OF COMPARISON
(A + B)

When your thesis implies a comparison or a contrast, you have two ways of organizing your material. The more common way is called the *divided pattern,* which compares or contrasts two things (let's call them A and B), either in separate paragraphs or in the two halves of one paragraph. In this pattern all that is to be said about A is said before anything is said about B. The structure can be abbreviated to "A + B." Here is an example:

> As Edward T. Hall points out in *The Silent Language,* attitudes toward time are conditioned by cultural habits: what is a long time in the United States may be a short time in other cultures.
>
> For Americans "a long time" may be anything from forty years to forty minutes, depending on the circumstances. To an American businessman a proposal that could not be completed within forty years might be "too far into the future" to be considered. The Internal Revenue Service defines a "long term" capital gain as a gain from an investment that lasted six months or more. A motorist involved in an accident would be in trouble with the police if he waited twenty-four hours to report an accident. An hour would be too long a time to be late for a business appointment or a date. Americans are so time-conscious that promptness is not only a virtue; it is a binding obligation.
>
> But other cultures have no such limited concept of "a long time." Hall cites many examples of this judgment. During World War II a Truk Islander arrived breathless at military government headquarters to report that a murderer was running loose in his village. Under questioning he revealed that the murder had occurred seventeen years earlier and that the murderer had remained unmolested in the village all this time. In a Latin American city an American envoy calling, by appointment, to present his credentials to an official was kept waiting in an outer office for more than an hour. In a Pueblo village a ritual dance scheduled to be presented on Christmas Eve did not begin till one o'clock in the morning, although tourists had assembled to see the dance by nine o'clock in the evening. For such people our respect for promptness is not only unreasonable; it is positively irrational; and they wonder why we make such a fuss about it. To a South Asian a long time may be a thousand years, or even forever.

Thesis identifies A and B and states the contrast.
A: The American concept of "a long time" treated fully in the first paragraph of the contrast.

B: The contrasted concept of "a long time" treated fully after everything that has to be said about A has been said. The contrast is divided, with one half in the first paragraph and the other half in the second paragraph.

Notice that the introductory paragraph containing the thesis does three things: it identifies the contrasted topics, it states what the contrast is meant to show, and it therefore links the two paragraphs that follow into one unified contrast.

Notice also that the examples in the two main paragraphs match each other, since those in A are in clear opposition to those in B. There need not be a one-to-one pairing between the A and B examples. (There are actually more examples in the second paragraph than in the third.) But all the examples of A, taken together, are in direct contrast with those in B, taken together. The directness of the contrast tends to bind the paragraphs together as matching halves of one whole. This relationship is not accidental; it is the necessary working out of the control imposed by the writer's purpose.

The two main parts of an A + B comparison must develop a cumulative comparison or contrast. A simple description of two unlike houses, for instance, is not necessarily a contrast. It becomes one only when it points up dissimilarities implied in a thesis. The chief exception to this statement is the situation in which one side of the contrast is so well known to readers that it need not be stated. Thus a sportswriter contrasting English rugby with American football for an American audience might assume that readers will be familiar with football but not with those details of rugby that show how different the two games are. In such a contrast, A is already in the mind of the audience, and the writer needs only to explain the significant details of B and let the reader make the contrast. This, of course, is another illustration of a point made earlier, that how writers do what they want to do will be influenced by what they know about their readers.

THE ALTERNATING PATTERN
OF COMPARISON (A/B + A/B)

In the second way of organizing material for a comparison or contrast, details of A and B are not grouped separately but are presented in matched pairs, sometimes in the same sentence, sometimes in separate sentences. This arrangement results in a point-by-point comparison rather than the group-by-group comparison of the divided pattern. The following shows the structure of the *alternating pattern,* as this second type of organization is called:

Thesis   The process of gaining or losing weight can be explained by comparing
A/B   your body to your car. Both run on fuel, food for your body and gasoline for
A/B   your car. Both convert that fuel, first into heat, then energy, some of which
A/B   is used to do work, and some emitted as waste. And just as your car uses
more energy when the engine is racing than when it is idling, so does your
body use more energy when you are working hard than when you are
resting.

A/B   For the purpose of this comparison, however, there is one significant
difference between them. Your car cannot store fuel by turning it into
something else; all gasoline not used remains as gasoline. But your body
stores excess fuel as fat. When the gas tank is empty, the car won't run; but
your body can burn fat to provide more energy.

Therefore, if you want to gain weight, you must do either of two things: eat more calories (units of heat, therefore energy), or use less through inactivity. If you want to lose weight, you do the reverse: decrease your input of calories or increase the amount of energy you spend. There is no other way. Gaining or losing weight is always a relation between intake and output of potential energy.

Conclusion from the preceding paragraphs

Here the comparison alternates between A and B throughout the first two paragraphs. The third paragraph, a conclusion drawn from the first two, continues to echo the alternation between the two elements of the thesis.

The same pattern is used in the following paragraph, in which the underlined thesis is developed by a series of contrasting details of the computer (A) and the brain (B):

Presently it is a popular occupation among the computer fraternity to compare their mechanism to the human brain. The conclusions are not disheartening—marvelous as the machines are, the brain seems still a good deal more marvelous. Like the mills of the gods, it grinds slow compared to the machines, but it grinds exceeding fine—it is original, imaginative, resourceful, free in will and choice. The machine operates at a speed approaching that of light, 186,000 mi. per sec., whereas the brain operates at the speed at which impulses move along nerve fiber, perhaps a million times slower—but the machine operates linearly, that is, it sends an impulse of "thought" along one path, so that if that path proves to be a dead end the "thought" must back up to the last fork in the road and try again, and if the "thought" is derailed the whole process must be begun again; the brain operates in some mysterious multipath fashion whereby a thought apparently splits and moves along several different paths simultaneously so that no matter what happens to any one of its branches there are others groping along. And whereas even a transistorized computer has a fairly modest number of components, the brain, it seems, has literally billions of neurons, or memory-and-operation cells. To rival an average human brain a computer built by present techniques would have to be about as big as an ocean liner, or a skyscraper. And even then it would lack the capacity for originality and free will. To initiate free choice in a machine the operator would have to insert into its program random numbers, which would make the machine "free" but uncoordinated—an idiot. (Gerald S. Hawkins, *Stonehenge Decoded*)

Thesis

A/B (speed)

A/B (path)

A/B (components)

B/A (size)

A/B (free will)

This passage could have been written as a two-paragraph divided structure, with everything about the computer (A) in the first paragraph and everything about the brain (B) in the second. The structures of the two patterns are contrasted in the outlines in the box on page 70.

Neither the divided nor the alternating pattern can be said to be generally "better" than the other, though one may be preferred for a particular purpose.

The divided pattern is more common, perhaps because it is an easier pattern to write in. But unless the writer has a clear, controlling thesis to serve as a guide, this pattern may lead to a loosely related description of two subjects. The alternating pattern requires more control by the writer, but it is often easier and more interesting for the reader, since the point-by-point development reinforces the comparison with every pair of matched details, and often the balanced sentence structure emphasizes the comparison or contrast. Whenever the writer's purpose requires close attention to compared details, as in an analogy, the alternating pattern is usually to be preferred.

Alternating pattern		Divided pattern	
A/B 1	Speed	A	Computer
	Computer	1	Speed
	Brain	2	Path of thought
A/B 2	Path of thought	3	Number of components
	Computer	4	Relative size
	Brain	5	Free will
A/B 3	Number of components	B	Brain
	Computer	1	Speed
	Brain	2	Path of thought
A/B 4	Relative size	3	Number of components
	Brain	4	Relative size
	Computer	5	Free will
A/B 5	Free will		
	Computer		
	Brain		

EXERCISES

A. The accompanying cartoon represents the same couple at different times of their lives. In preparation for writing a contrast of the two parts of the cartoon, first study the pictures separately as you did with the Hogarth prints (pages 37–40) and for each picture jot down what seem to you the significant details. Then infer a thesis from your observations of both pictures. Finally, using the divided pattern, write a two-paragraph paper developing the contrast implied in your thesis.

B. Choose any two subjects that you can contrast. First, in parallel columns, list significant details of the contrast so that each detail in the first column contrasts with the detail opposite it in the second column. Then, using the alternating pattern, develop the contrast from the two columns.

Cartoon by Neil Adams. Courtesy of Harper's Magazine.

CLASSIFICATION

Classification is the process of organizing information into groups or classes. When you were organizing the student responses to the freshman ratings of objectives (pages 48–51), you were classifying these responses as *very important* and *not very important* and further grouping them into subclasses: *male* and *female* responses. Here we want to look at the process in more detail and at a more difficult level.

Perhaps the best way to begin is to plunge into a problem of classification and see what we learn from that experience. Suppose you have been given this list of twenty-four words and have been told that for each word the first meaning in parentheses was an old one and the second is a modern one. You are asked to classify the words according to the type of meaning change they show and to report your findings.

1. *arrive* (come to shore—come to any place)
2. *boor* (a farmer—an ill-mannered person)
3. *butcher* (a seller of goat meat—a seller of meat)
4. *cad* (younger son of an aristocratic family—an ungentlemanly fellow)
5. *count* (a companion—a nobleman)
6. *crafty* (skillful—cunning)
7. *cupboard* (a shelf for holding cups—a cabinet for holding dishes and utensils)
8. *dismantle* (take off a cloak—take apart anything)
9. *eaves* (edges—the edges of a roof)
10. *frock* (a monk's robe—a dress)
11. *hound* (a dog of any kind—one of several breeds of hunting dogs)
12. *liquor* (a liquid—an alcoholic beverage)
13. *marshal* (a companion in a stable—a high-ranking officer)
14. *nice* (ignorant—attractive)
15. *prude* (a modest person—a self-righteous person)
16. *rose* (a flower—a particular kind of flower)
17. *shrewd* (evil—having keen insight)
18. *silly* (blessed—lacking good sense)
19. *starve* (to die—to die of hunger)
20. *steward* (a keeper of a pigsty—an administrator)
21. *target* (a light shield—anything one aims at)
22. *villain* (a farm laborer—a scoundrel)
23. *voyage* (a journey—a sea journey)
24. *wench* (a girl—a woman of low morals)

The assignment defines the purpose of your study and suggests your principle of selection: you are looking for words that show the same kind of change in meaning. So you begin with *arrive*. What kind of change does it show? Since it has gone from "coming to shore" to "coming to any place," you decide that it has taken on a broader or more general meaning. So you check to see if other words in the list fit that pattern.

Boor does not; it seems to have moved toward a less favorable meaning. But *butcher* fits because the modern meaning is broader: it includes all kinds of meat, not just goat meat. *Cupboard* also has taken on a broader meaning; so has *dismantle*. You are satisfied that you have identified one class of meaning-change; and as you go down the list, you discover other members of that class. We need not identify them, since you can find them for yourself.

When you are satisfied that you have found all the words that show broader meanings, you go back to *boor* and see if other words in the list show a change toward less favorable meanings. You find *cad* and others, and so you complete your second class.

But when you have found all the words that fit into either of these classes, you still have to classify about half the words in your list. You now see that *count* and *marshal* have acquired more favorable meanings, and you look for other words that show the same kind of change. When you find them, you still have six words to account for. *Eaves* suggests a change toward narrower meaning, just the opposite of *arrive*. So do *hound* and *liquor,* and you are well on your way to the fourth class of meaning-change.

Since all twenty-four words now fit into your four classes, your classification of the material is complete. Another list, however, might contain words that have changed in some other way or have not changed at all. Such a list would require you to add more classes to take care of all the items.

Your final report will be easy to write. Your findings can be presented in a single paragraph that starts with the topic sentence: "These words have changed in one of four directions: toward broader meanings, toward narrower meanings, toward more favorable meanings, and toward less favorable meanings." This topic sentence would be developed by four sentences, each of which would explain and illustrate one of the four classes of change. If the list had been much longer, say two hundred words, you might have needed a separate paragraph for each type of change. Then, what was given above as a topic sentence would become the thesis of a paper. But that would not require any change in the procedure or organization.

We can generalize the procedure you followed in your study of twenty-four words into a five-step description of the classification process. This is not a hasty generalization from a single sample, because the assignment was designed to be typical, and so illustrated the process.

1.   *The classifier approaches a body of unorganized material with the intention of organizing it for some purpose.* Different purposes will result in different classifications. For example, people may be classified according to sex, age, income, IQ, marital status, blood types, and so on. The classifier's purpose determines the principle of selection to be used in deciding which items are to be placed in which class. Direction of change in meaning was the principle of selection in your word study.

2.   *The same principle of selection must be maintained for all main classes.* However, a different principle may be used in going from main classes to subclasses. For example, after people have been classified by sex, the sex groups may be subdivided into age groups. Age then becomes the principle of selection in the subgroups.

3.   *Items are grouped within a class as they are seen to be alike in some characteristic that is essential to the principle of selection.* Thus in your word study, all words showing change toward narrower meaning went in one group, all showing change toward wider meaning went in another.

4.   *Each class is given an identifying label.* The labels you used were descriptive phrases—"toward broader meanings," "toward narrower meanings," "toward more favorable meanings," "toward less favorable meanings." These were good enough for our study, though a linguist would use technical terms and call your classes respectively "extension," "restriction," "amelioration," "pejoration."

5.   *If a class is divided into subclasses, it must have at least two.* Whether a class should be divided into subclasses depends on the material being classified. Your four types of changes in meaning did not require subdivision, but some classes do. If there are not at least two subclasses, no subdivision is necessary.

The following extract from a long article illustrates the use of classification as a pattern of organization. The writer's detailed knowledge of the historical development of New York City provided him with data that he grouped into classes that correspond to four historical periods ranging from the city's beginning to the present. He decided to label each of the four classes or phases by calling it a particular kind of "face"—thus, New York as successively a port, a manufacturing city, a concentration of large corporations, and a cultural center. Each of these faces is described in two paragraphs that use the data from which the classification was made.

"Fourteen people love me, 22 people like me, 6 people tolerate me, and I only have 3 enemies. Not bad for a little kid, huh?"

By Scott. *Saturday Review,* April 17, 1976.

The Four Faces of New York

New York is a palimpsest.* Successive layers, never wholly erasing the earlier ones, have provided different outlines for the profiles of New York. And each of these profiles has given a different character to New York, providing at successive historical periods a distinctive face whose traces, etched deeply, remain visible.

New York was, first, a port city. The magnificent natural harbor—large, well-sheltered, deep enough for the largest ships, shallow enough for convenient anchorage—made New York the center for commerce as it became the primary transportation center for the exchange of raw materials from the West for the finished products of Europe and the eastern seaboard. Point-counterpoint followed with economic logic. Frequent ship sailings, the rail-canal system to the West, the concentration of freight forwarders, insurance specialists, banks to facilitate credit, wholesalers to distribute imports—all these spurred the development of the port.

The port gave New York its 19th-century character, topographical and social. Downtown was the intense concentration of insurance, finance and wholesale sections. Along the rim of the port lay the dives and saloons and open brothels—along Water Street and Green Street—which gave the city its brawling character. Hordes of immigrants poured through the port, and many stayed here, providing not only a floating labor supply but the distinctive "foreign" sections which created an ecological mosaic of the city.

The second face of New York, emerging strongly at the turn of the century, was a manufacturing profile. New York today has 40,000 manufacturing establishments, with the largest factory work force (nearly a million industrial workers) and the largest manufacturing payroll (close to $3 billion a year) of any American city. The garment industry is the dominant one, but printing and publishing are also huge, providing one-fifth of all the printing and publishing in the U.S.

But this manufacturing is of a special character. It has not been transport savings or labor costs that have attracted industry, but "external economies," the availability of a pool of specialized facilities and skills that could be shared by firms without their having to carry these items as part of permanent overhead costs. Typically, this has meant that industries located in New York tend to be composed of small, fast-moving, risk-taking and highly competitive firms engaged in a rough-and-tumble race. . . . These industries are characterized by uncertainty, by the capacity to make quick-change production shifts, the search for an item or product that will be a sudden "hit." Each of these industries depends upon a whole range of auxiliary services. Each manufacturer being, so to speak, a retailer, has behind him a range of wholesalers who supply his needs. Because decisions have to be

---

* "A written document . . . that has been written upon several times, often with remnants of earlier, imperfectly erased writing still visible . . ." (*The American Heritage Dictionary*).

made swiftly there is scarcely an intra-firm hierarchy, little bureaucratization, and usually only a single establishment. The number of one-plant firms in New York, averaging about 25 employees each, is enormous. In 47 industries composed almost entirely of single-plant firms, 30 per cent of the total employment is concentrated in New York. . . .

The "third face" of New York—the New York of the 1950s—is the New York of the corporate headquarters, a face displayed by the unbroken lines of the new glass houses on Park Avenue to the towering high-rental apartment houses along the upper East Side. All this is quite remarkable. In the late 1940s, the talk in the business world was largely about the impossibility of New York as a business center and the need for decentralization. (General Foods moved out to Westchester; Time Inc., which owned the site of the Hotel Marguery, sold it and took an option on land in Rye.) Jean-Paul Sartre, a visitor here in 1950, commented sourly on the grid-shadowed streets of Midtown New York and predicted that no new skyscrapers would be built in the city.

Yet how wrong all that talk was. Since 1947, nearly 150 new large office buildings have been built in Manhattan. In all, 58 million square feet of office space—or nearly two-thirds as much as existed before 1947—has been added to Manhattan in the last 20 years. Today, more than 135 of the 500 largest industrial corporations in America have their headquarters in New York. And with this concentration of managerial personnel, the ancillary services of the white collar world—law firms, accounting houses, management consultants, advertising agencies (some 70 per cent of the national advertising agencies have their central offices here)—have expanded. . . .

Each of these "faces" has been symbolic of the multifaceted nature of New York. Each, in its own way, has made or "remade" sections of the city. There is emerging now—its lineaments have always been present—a new, fourth face, a New York of the mid-'60s and '70s, with a set of new needs and a dominant style: the "cultural city."

New York has always been the publishing, music, art and drama center of the country. The United Nations has made it an international capital. It is a vast intellectual center, with more than 40 institutions of higher learning and one-fifth of all students in the United States doing postgraduate work concentrated here. Its score of museums give it the largest treasure trove of paintings in the world. Its several hundred art galleries and more than 2,000 art shows a year give it a centrality and excitement in the world of art. There are as many shows off-Broadway as there are on Broadway. And in the course of any week during the season one can find the greatest variety of opera, ballet, symphony concerts, experimental music and solo performance.

But several obvious elements conjoin to place a new emphasis on culture and learning as a new "face" of the coming decade. There is, first, the enormous expansion of higher education, undergraduate and graduate, which has given a new weight to the colleges and universities of the city. A new generation of younger businessmen and executives has brought a "culture-hungry" class to the fore, a class that has sought its own status symbols as well as desire for new taste, in the vast purchases of art and furnishings. The children of the immigrants, particularly the Jewish generation, with its own middle-class status, have vastly expanded the market for culture. It is in the creation of Lincoln Square as a new focal point of the city's performing arts, the expansion of Columbia University along Morningside Heights and the spread of New York University to engulf Washington Square, that we see the symbols of this new "fourth face" of the city. (Daniel Bell, "The Forces Shaping the City: The Four Faces of New York," *New York,* November 15, 1964)

EXERCISES   **A.**   To get practice in classifying, consider each of the following sports, arrange them in groups according to some similarity you see in them (your principle of selection), and for each group write a label that suggests that similarity:

baseball, basketball, boxing, football, golf, gymnastics, hockey, soccer, swimming, tennis, track, wrestling

When you have done this, reorganize the sports according to some other kind of similarity and so make a second classification for a different purpose.

B.   Choose *one* of the following topics and write a paper that classifies the topic under three or four headings and describes each heading in a paragraph:

1.   a classification of major areas in your home town

2.   a classification of teaching procedures you have observed in high school or college

3.   any classification topic of your own choosing

PROCESS

A *process* is a sequence of operations or actions by which something is done or made. The development of the human embryo from conception to birth is one process; the procedure by which the citizens of the United States elect a President is another.

To describe a process you must first know it thoroughly. Second, you must divide it into its steps or stages. Third, each step must be explained in enough detail so that a reader can "see" it and if necessary perform it. Following are the three types of processes most commonly described in essays:

1. The "how-to-do-it" process, which gives directions for doing something. A recipe is such a process; so are the directions given to the visitor on page 7.

2. The "how-it-works" or "how-it-is-done" process, which shows an operation in its successive stages.

3. The "why-it-happened" or causal process, which seeks to explain how an effect was produced.

The article that follows is an example of type 1, a how-to-do-it process. Its purpose is to show readers how to use a map. Judging that many people do not know how to interpret a map, the writer first explains how to do so and then shows four ways to "orient" a map—that is, to line it up with the territory so that points in the territory can be identified on the map. The article may be outlined thus:

    I. How to read a map
   II. How to orient a map
       A. By using a compass
       B. By using a watch
       C. By lining it up with a road
       D. By connecting known points
  III. How to find where you are on a map

Where Are You?

Ability to use a map intelligently is essential to the hunter, enjoyable to the camper, necessary to the fisherman, and valuable to the traveler.

But it has been found that an astonishing number of persons are unable to read a map beyond gleaning from it the barest essentials for following a main highway from one city to another.

Probably the most important thing to know about a map is that within certain qualifications, it is a representation on paper, on a reduced scale, of the surface of the ground in the region depicted.

In order to comprehend a map one must understand first, that each distance on it is scaled to the corresponding distance on the actual terrain; second, that relative directions of objects from each other on the map correspond to their directions from each other on the ground; and, third, that the relative height of mountains, the steepness of slopes, the direction of streams, and the shapes of features are often shown by contour lines and other symbols.

Many fine maps show water features, including seas, lakes, rivers, canals, and swamps; relief features, including mountains, hills, and valleys; as well as towns, cities, roads, railroads, and boundaries. . . .

For the camper who is going into the mountains, probably the most valuable information obtained from a map is that supplied by contour lines. These contour lines show the shapes of the hills, mountains, and valleys, as well as their altitudes. . . .

When the map is "oriented," these contours are of great help to the camper for locating an unfamiliar canyon or creek. For the fisherman such knowledge eliminates much unnecessary travel, while for the hiker it provides a quick means of locating available mountain trails.

A map is oriented when all lines on it are parallel with those they represent on the ground. And as a map is of little value until this is done, a few simple directions for orienting it follow:

One way is to spread the map out flat and lay a compass on it in such a manner that the N-S line of the dial coincides with a longitude line or the printed arrow which indicates true north. Revolve the map with the compass on it until the compass needle and the longitude line are parallel. Then move them both again the required number of degrees, as indicated on the map, to correct for magnetic variation. This variation represents the difference in degrees at your location between true north and "magnetic north" (to which your compass needle points). Some maps have arrows printed in the margins which point to magnetic north. If yours does, simply align this arrow with your compass needle. When this orientation has been done, all directions on the map are the same as the directions they represent on the ground.

However, if a compass is not handy, a map may be oriented roughly if one has a watch. Holding the watch in front of the body and level in the hand, revolve it until the hour hand points directly under the sun. Halfway between the hour hand and twelve o'clock will be due south.

Another simple way to orient a map is to line up a highway shown on the map with the road itself—that is, parallel the printed road with the actual road. Again, when this is done, all lines on the map are aligned with those on the ground.

There is yet another way to orient your map, provided the spot occupied at the moment is recognizable on the map as is also some distant object—say a mountain peak. Lay a pencil or other similar straightedge on the map so that it connects these two known points. Then turn the map until it is possible to sight along the pencil to the distant object—and your map is oriented.

To find one's place on the map when the place occupied is unknown, the first thing to do is to orient the map. Again, select a distant object that is recognizable both on the map and on the terrain. Lay a straightedge on the map and sight toward the distant object. Draw a line on the map by the straightedge. Repeat this procedure sighting on another recognizable point and where the two lines intersect is roughly where you are.

Remember that the study of a good map by a vacationer *before* he leaves on a trip will often enable him to choose a campsite that is particularly valuable for whatever activity he wishes to pursue—be it fishing, hunting, hiking, or . . . just sitting! (Daniel Clark, "Where Are You?" *Field and Stream)*

The following excerpt from an article is an example of the second type, the how-it-is-done process. It explains the procedure by which the female mosquito gets the animal blood she needs to produce eggs.

You are now taking a last turn around your yard before going in to dinner. Insect eyes are more sensitive to contrast and motion than to form or color. In your shirt of faded blue denim, you are a moving target no insect could miss. A mosquito zeroes in for a landing. The warmth, moisture and odor of your skin assure her that she has arrived, and the convection currents set up in the cool air by the heat of your body prompt her to cut the motor and let down the landing gear.

On six long legs, she puts down so lightly that you feel nothing. Sensors on her feet detect the carbon dioxide that your skin exhales. Down comes the long proboscis; up go the long back legs, as though to balance it. The little soft lobes at the tip of the proboscis are spread to test the surface. It will do. A sudden contraction of the legs with the weight of the body behind it bends the proboscis backward in an arc while the six sharp blades it has ensheathed are thrust into your skin. Two of the blades are tipped with barbs. These work alternately, shove and hold, shove and hold, pulling the insect's face down and carrying their fellows deeper into your skin.

Once the skin is penetrated, all the blades bend forward and probe as far as they can reach in all directions. (A scientist learned all this by watching through a miscroscope while a mosquito bit the transparent membrane between the toes of a frog.) With luck, the blades strike a capillary. If they don't, saliva pumped into the wound through a channel in one of the blades stimulates the flow of blood into a pool. And still you feel nothing. Your continued ignorance of attack is probably due, not to any anesthetic effect (although a few mosquitoes do have an anesthetic saliva) but rather to the minute size of the mouthparts, which have simply passed between nerve endings without touching any.

The taste of blood turns on two pumps in the insect's throat. The broadest blade of the mouthparts is rolled lengthwise to form a tube. Through it, blood passes upward into the mouth. In a blood meal, volume is what counts—the more blood, the more eggs—and even while the pumping is going on, excess water is passing out at the insect's other end.

In three to five minutes, her body is so swollen that your blood shows pinkly through the taut skin. The stretching of the stomach wall stimulates nerves that turn on a pair of glands in the thorax; the glands, in turn, release a hormone that sets the ovaries to work. Finally, when she has filled herself so full that she can't force in a single additional corpuscle, Madam Mosquito withdraws her mouthparts with a tug and drifts away.

All this time you may have felt nothing, but soon you will begin to itch and later a welt will appear. (From Alice Gray, "Daughters of Dracula," in *Sports Afield)*

A *causal process,* the type 3 process, attempts to explain the sequence by which some effect was produced. A writer seeking to explain what motivates a character in a novel or why parents and children disagree on certain issues or who is responsible for a political scandal usually shows the process by which the cause produced the effect.

Here is an example of causal process used to explain why large cities are in serious trouble:*

"I can tell you one thing," said Henry Ford the First in the early 1920's. "The cities are finished."

After last week's meeting of the mayors here in Washington, it begins to seem that Henry Ford may have been right. Perhaps our cities really are finished, as places where any sensible person would wish to live, and thus as viable social institutions. Great social institutions do die, after all—the British Empire is dead, for example; and the family farm, the foundation stone of the old American way, is busy dying. To judge from the way the mayors talked, the cities are dying too. . . .

The rot of the cities really started back in the decades when Henry Ford made his prediction. Then a small minority of city dwellers—those rich enough to own a car—discovered that it was pleasanter to live out among the trees and the fields and to drive in to work. Nearby farm villages began to be transformed into bedroom towns—in the close-in suburbs, you can see the big houses of that era still, often transformed into funeral parlors or dreary rooming houses. Thus began, in a very small way, the erosion of the tax base that is causing such anguish to the mayors who gathered in Washington last week.

When the rich move out and the poor stay behind, the tax base is fatally weakened. More and more poor people need more and more welfare or other financial support, and there are fewer and fewer rich people to support those poor people with their tax money. The result is inevitable. All the mayors said about the same thing. Let New York's Mayor John Lindsay speak for them all:

"In New York we have a deficit of $300 million and face a deficit next year of $1 billion. Frankly, even with help in Washington, I'm not sure we can pull out of the urban crisis in time."(Stewart Alsop, "The Cities Are Finished," *Newsweek*)

The writer explains the plight of big cities by showing the process by which the cause produced the effect. That causal process can be summarized as a pattern of related events:

1. The automobile made it possible for people who could afford to do so to move to the suburbs while continuing to hold their jobs in the city.

2. When they moved out, the cities lost the tax money of those who paid most of the taxes, but the cost of maintaining city services did not diminish.

3. The loss of taxes made it impossible to pay for these services.

4. The cumulative result is that the cities are facing a financial crisis that they cannot solve.

Choose any process you know well and explain it clearly in sufficient detail so that **EXERCISE** a reader who is not familiar with the process will be able to understand it.

These four organizational patterns you have been studying—illustration, comparison, classification, and process—will be useful to you in much of your writing both in and out of the composition class. Any one of them can be used to organize a whole paper or a particular paragraph. Moreover, they can be combined so that two or more of them may be used in the same piece of writing, as the next section, "Definition," will show.

DEFINITION

The function of definition is to provide a necessary explanation of a word or concept. The explanation may be simply the substitution of a familiar word for the one being defined, as when we substitute *cancer* for *carcinoma*. It may be the addition of a phrase, as when we define *rhetoric* as "the art of spoken or written communication." It may be a single sentence: "For tax purposes, a *short-term gain* is the increase of the selling price over the buying price when a stock is held for six months or less; a *long-term gain* is the increase when the stock is held for more than six months." Or the definition may consist of one or more paragraphs, or even a whole essay, as a writer explains a subject in depth.

The length and complexity of a definition depend on the writer's purpose. That is, they depend on what the writer wants to say about the subject and how he wants to say it for the kind of reader being addressed. No definition of *thrombosis* would be necessary for a physician, but one might be advisable for a general reader. In some situations all that would be necessary would be to insert "a blood clot in an artery or vein" in parentheses after the word *thrombosis;* in others the writer might feel it necessary to explain the process by which thrombosis develops and the effects it produces. How much definition is required is relative to the situation in which the definition is being made.

Definitions may be classified as three types: short, stipulative, or extended. A *short* definition, like the definitions of *carcinoma, rhetoric,* and *short-term gain* above, explains a word by a brief identification of its meaning. This is the kind of definition that dictionaries provide.

Stipulative definitions identify the particular meaning that a writer is using. Since words may have several meanings, it is sometimes important to specify which meaning is being used in a particular passage. For example, in the South the word *liberal* often has unfavorable connotations when applied to a politician. So a candidate for political office, on being called a liberal, is likely to reply, "I am not a liberal," or maybe, "Yes, I am a liberal, but only in the true sense of that word. I believe in the freedom of individuals to think, speak, and act according to their consciences. That is what the word *liberal* originally meant—freedom—and what it still means in reputable dictionaries." Here the candidate is making a stipulative definition by emphasizing one meaning to the exclusion of others. Provided that stipulative definitions are used to clarify an issue, not to obscure it, they are legitimate and useful means of defining. When the Supreme Court rules on how "due process of law" is to be interpreted, it is making a stipulative definition. It is saying in effect, "This is what 'due process' must mean in a court of law." The definition of *purpose* on page 16 is another example of stipulative definition.

Extended definitions may include both short and stipulative definitions, but they go far beyond both. They are essentially essays that seek to explain the writer's view of the subject, something that cannot be done effectively in a short definition. An extended definition may begin with a dictionary definition, but it goes on to add to, modify, and illustrate that definition. In so doing, it may use any of the patterns of development discussed earlier in this chapter: it may compare or contrast one meaning with another; it may classify the subject by showing to what class it belongs and what its subclasses are; it may provide illustrative examples; it may treat the subject as a process. It may even combine two or more of these patterns, as the following extended definition shows:

What is a limerick? Dictionaries define it as a form of light verse that differs from other light verse by its characteristic rhythmic pattern consisting of three long and two short lines rhyming *a-a-b-b-a*. This definition is satisfactory, as far as it goes:

God's plan made a hopeful beginning	*a*
But man spoiled his chances by sinning.	*a*
We trust that the story	*b*
Will end in God's glory—	*b*
But at present the other side's winning.	*a*

Dictionary definition by classification

Example

But a limerick may also be a short, short story, with characters involved in some action. It tells what happened to a young lady called Bright / who travelled much faster than light, or to an epicure dining at Crew / who found a large mouse in his stew; though sometimes the conclusion is left to the reader's imagination by saying "(Almost any last line will do here.)." Some of the stories are, to say the least, risqué; some are unprintably pornographic.

Comparison with examples

Although the rhymes of a limerick usually follow an *a-a-b-b-a* pattern, the writer may take considerable leeway in deciding what rhymes with what, such as spelling "inch" as "in-ich" to make it rhyme with "spinach" or using outlandish abbreviations, like the young Mr. who took out his girl and kr. with such ardor that her lips soon started to blr. Or the writer may challenge the reader with such monstrosities as this:

Classification by subtypes

Example   Said the chemist: "I'll take some dimethyloximidomesoralamide
                       And I'll add just a dash of dimethylamidoazobensaldehyde;
                          But if these won't mix,
                          I'll just have to fix
                       Up a big dose of trisodiumpholoroglucintricarboxycide."

Occasionally he may ignore rhyme completely as did W. S. Gilbert (of the Gilbert and Sullivan partnership) in

Example   There was an old man of St. Bees
                       Who was stung in the arm by a wasp.
                          When asked, "Does it hurt?"
                          He replied, "No, it doesn't,
                       But I thought all the while 'twas a hornet."

So, what is a limerick? Is it simply a five-lined stanza in which the writer will do anything for a laugh? Perhaps the best definition was given by an addict:

Concluding example   The limerick packs laughs anatomical
                       Into space that is quite economical.
                          But the good ones I've seen
                          So seldom are clean
                       And the clean ones so seldom are comical.*

At least four observations may be made from this essay. First, it is dominated by the writer's purpose, which was not only to explain what a limerick is but also to entertain the reader by pointing out characteristics that are not mentioned in a dictionary definition. Second, despite the variety of observations the writer is making, they have a common core—the verse pattern: its uses and abuses. Third, this extended definition proceeds mainly by classification and example. Fourth, the effect of the essay is not a neat, dictionary-like definition, but a more comprehensive view of the subject than such a definition can provide. The writer's comments are all pertinent to a fuller understanding of limericks and are therefore extensions of the dictionary definition.

Now let us look at a quite different way of developing an extended definition. The purpose of the next essay is to explain what something is by explaining how it is done. The subject is a game called "Definitions," and the best way to explain a game is to show how it is played. Therefore, the explanation must treat the subject as a process.

---

* The source of the limericks quoted in this essay is Anthony B. Lake's *A Pleasury of Witticisms and Word Play* (New York: Bramhall House, 1975).

The game of Definitions is a contest in which the players compete with each other by trying to write the most plausible definition of a word nobody knows. The only equipment required is paper, pencils, and a dictionary. At the beginning, one of the group is appointed lexicographer, an office that combines keeper of the dictionary and master of ceremonies. Since there is some advantage in being lexicographer, it is desirable to rotate that office after each word has been defined.

The lexicographer begins the game by choosing from the dictionary the word to be defined. It cannot be a word beginning with a capital letter. The lexicographer pronounces and spells it. Anyone who knows the word says so, and another word is then chosen. Each player writes a definition and passes it to the lexicographer, who then reads all definitions aloud, slowly and clearly, including the dictionary definition, which he or she has copied on a piece of paper so that it is not distinguishable from the others. For ease of reference, each definition is given a number.

The players respond by giving the number of the definition they think is correct. If a definition written by a player is chosen by another player, the writer of that definition gets one point each time it is chosen. For example, if, for the word *whiffletree*, two players choose the definition "a deciduous tree common in western Australia, the bark of which, when reduced to a powder and dissolved in water, makes an intoxicating drink," the player who wrote that definition gets two points, even though it is not the dictionary definition. Obviously the trick is to write a definition so plausible that it will be accepted by other players as the correct one.

Any player who chooses the dictionary definition gets a point. If no player chooses the dictionary definition, the lexicographer gets two points, so that, in any round, the lexicographer's score will be either two or zero. The game ends when any player gets ten points, or whatever number the group agrees on.

One complication of the game not covered by these rules is the influence that others have on a player's choice of definitions. If two players prove to be clever at writing plausible definitions, the others will say to themselves, "Number 2 sounds right to me, but I suspect that it was written by Bill or Jean, so I'll choose Number 4," only to find later that Number 2 is the dictionary definition and Number 4 was written by Jean. The ability of one player to fool the others helps the lexicographer, since it reduces the chance that the dictionary definition will be chosen. Obviously the lexicographer will avoid choosing scientific terms if one of the players is majoring in that science. In short, as in poker, sizing up the other players is part of the game.

Some may object that this is not a definition but a process. The answer is that it is both. It is a process used to provide a necessary explanation of the game of Definitions; therefore it defines that game. It is actually the only way the game can be defined extensively. The core of the definition is the opening sentence, which resembles a dictionary definition. The rest of the paper extends that definition by showing how the contest is conducted.

PRACTICAL ADVICE ON
WRITING AN EXTENDED DEFINITION

1.   Choose a subject on which you have something to say—something more than you could say in a short definition, and preferably a subject that will allow you to draw on your own experience and previous thinking. For example, if you know people who would not deliberately tell a lie but are often dishonest with themselves, that knowledge may suggest an extension of the usual meaning of honesty and provide examples to illustrate your definition. Do not settle on a subject until you have done some preliminary prewriting of it in your mind. It may be helpful to jot down some of the points or examples that occur to you as you think about the subject.

2.   Focus on the core of your definition. Ask yourself: "What is it essentially? What characteristics do I want to emphasize?" The answer to these questions will be the main idea of your essay, and the purpose of the essay will be to expand that idea.

3.   In deciding what your subject *is,* you may have to consider what it is *not:* freedom is not license, love is not infatuation, courage is not recklessness. The word *define* comes from a Latin phrase that means "set the boundaries," and boundary lines keep things out as well as in. The boundaries set by the definition of *limerick* exclude all prose, all serious poetry, and all witty verses with more or fewer than five lines. If you insist that all limericks must have an *a-a-b-b-a* rhyme scheme, that boundary will exclude W. S. Gilbert's nonrhyming verse about the old man of St. Bees. The point is that you decide the boundaries; and that decision determines what is pertinent and not pertinent to your purpose.

4.   Once you have decided what your real subject is and is not, develop it by any of the means discussed in this chapter. You may begin with a dictionary definition, as the limerick essay did, or with a summary statement, as the essay on Definitions did. But these are only introductions to your essay. It is what you say after the introduction that defines the subject as you see it. As you have seen from the examples given, there is no one way in which an extended definition must be developed. Any way is a good way if it helps you to do what you want to do.

5.   Above all, keep your readers in mind. Your explanation is meant for them and

must be clear to them. Any statement that is too technical or vague will interfere with communication. The best protection against vagueness is to illustrate your general statements by specific examples. You can hardly ever go wrong by supplementing a general explanation by a clear and appropriate example.

A. Choose any word that is not in your dictionary and write a short definition of it. The word may be campus slang, or it may be a term used in some specialized activity and not common enough to be included in a dictionary.

B. Following the five pieces of advice given above, choose any term you wish and write an extended definition of it.

PART
2

WRITING

AND

REWRITING

5

PARAGRAPHS:
UNITS
OF
DEVELOPMENT

As we go from Chapter 4 to Chapter 5, we move from the prewriting to the writing stage of the composition process, from planning a paper to actually writing it. We could have begun this stage with the writer's choice of words and then advanced to sentences and paragraphs. But since most of your writing assignments in college require you to write whole essays, or at least a paragraph, we have chosen to move from larger units to smaller ones, and so will begin with paragraphs. In this chapter we will be discussing two kinds of paragraphs: *topical* paragraphs—those that actually develop some topic or subject; and *special* paragraphs—those that introduce or conclude a paper or that provide a transition between major parts.

Paragraphing is a means of presenting ideas and information in units of related sentences. In *expository* writing—writing that tries to explain something—a paragraph consists of a set of sentences, all of which deal with a common topic. In effect, the writer breaks the whole task of writing a paper into paragraph units, each of which deals with one part of the composition. When the writer has said all that needs to be said in a particular unit, the paragraph is finished, and the writer moves on to the next one.

This division of the paper into paragraphs performs two useful functions. From the writer's point of view, it helps control the organization of the paper by providing a way to group like things together and to separate different groupings by separate paragraphs. From the reader's point of view, it breaks a long piece of prose into smaller units and so makes the job of reading easier. For both writer and reader, therefore, effective paragraphing makes for easier communication.

DEVELOPING TOPICAL PARAGRAPHS: FOUR REQUIREMENTS

To be effective, a topical paragraph must meet four requirements. First, it must discuss one topic only; that is, it must have unity of subject matter. Second, it must say all that a reader needs to know about the topic; that is, it must be complete enough to do what it is intended to do. Third, the sentences within the paragraph must follow some reasonable order that a reader can recognize and follow. Fourth, the sentences within a paragraph must have coherence; that is, they must be so tied together that a reader can read the paragraph as a unit, not as a collection of separate sentences. In the first major division of this chapter, we will try to show you how to make your paragraphs *unified, complete, orderly,* and *coherent.*

UNITY

Unity in a paragraph requires consistent development of the idea that the paragraph is intended to explain. The paragraph as a whole should focus on that idea. If it is to achieve such a focus, each succeeding sentence must show a clear connection to the topic idea, such as is shown in the following paragraph:

(1) The fall of Rome was not a sudden event, but a slow process of disintegration which came from many causes, some so gradual that they were scarcely noticeable at the time. (2) Because of high taxes and harsh laws forbidding workmen to change their trades, the population of the city slowly melted away to find work at great country houses and estates. (3) This decline in population and taxes so reduced the imperial treasury that it became harder to man and pay the legions, and the resulting military weakness offered an inducement to provincial generals who found a march on the capital too great a temptation to resist. (4) Thus, slowly the machinery of government ceased to function. (5) And when the barbarians came there was no organized power to resist.

The first sentence states the slow process of disintegration that the paragraph is intended to develop. Each succeeding sentence contributes to the explanation of that process, so that all the sentences together focus on the disintegration that led to the fall of Rome. It is this close relationship among individual sentences that gives the paragraph its unity.

Any sentence that has no clear relation to the intent of the paragraph will blur the focus and obscure the point the writer is trying to make. Consider, for example, the following paragraph:

(1) Excavations in the past ten years have really formed the complete city of Pompeii. (2) As it stands now, most of Pompeii has been uncovered. (3) The ancient city of Pompeii covered one hundred and sixty-three acres, and at this time there are about one hundred and fifty yards to go. (4) Scientists believe that Vesuvius is about to erupt again, and that would cover the city. (5) Archaeologists have not had to contend with Vesuvius at all in the past ten years, and progress has been faster. (6) Pompeii itself is now a museum, and people can walk on guided tours through all that the archaeologists have uncovered. (7) The techniques used in the past ten years have been more scientific and were more towards the preservation of this unknown city.

The first three sentences all deal with *the extent of the excavation of Pompeii.* Presumably, then, the paragraph is going to focus on that topic. A reader will have some difficulty with these sentences, because the first sentence suggests that the excavation is complete, whereas the second sentence says that *most* of the city has been uncovered. The third sentence gives the area of the original city but not the area of the uncovered part; instead, it gives only its length. But at least the sentences do deal with the extent of excavation.

Then in sentences 4 and 5 the focus shifts to Vesuvius, and neither sentence is clearly related to the extent of excavation. Sentence 6 shifts the focus again to Pompeii as a museum. This does have some relation to the uncovered part of the city, though readers will have to discover the connection by themselves. The last sentence shifts again, this time to a contrast between old and modern techniques of archaeological investigation. All this is hard going for readers, who expect to be able to see the main idea and to follow its development through the paragraph. As they proceed they become less sure what the main idea is, or even whether there is one, and they begin to suspect that the lack of unity in the paragraph is a result of the lack of unity in the writer's perception of the subject.

A contrast between this paragraph and the one on the fall of the Roman Empire shows the difference between an integrated paragraph, in which each sentence contributes to the idea the writer intends to develop, and a paragraph that is merely a collection of inadequately related sentences that do not focus on any one idea. The student who wrote the Pompeii paragraph moved from one sentence to another without proceeding in any consistent direction. If she had stuck to the intention of showing the extent of excavation, she might have begun with such a sentence as "During the last ten years so much of Pompeii has been uncovered that visitors can now take conducted tours through the ancient city." Such a beginning would have focused attention on the extent of excavation and would probably have suggested details about both the excavation and the tours that the paragraph obviously lacks. These details would have made the paragraph more informative than it now is.

Unless writers have a clear idea of what they want to do in a paragraph, they can drift away from their opening sentences and end in a digression or, even worse, a contradiction. For example, the following paragraph ends up saying just the opposite of what its readers have been led to expect:

(1) In college writing the main emphasis is on content. (2) It is what you have to say that counts, and you are expected to think out the content of a paper before you begin to write. (3) Mechanical correctness—grammar, punctuation, spelling, and the like—is still important, but you are supposed to have learned about those things in high school. (4) Such faults as period faults, comma splices, dangling modifiers, and faulty pronoun references can fail a paper. (5) So be sure you can recognize these errors and correct them. (6) I have found that it pays to go over my first drafts carefully to catch such mistakes, and I often wish we had spent more time on proofreading in high school. (7) Believe me, it is discouraging to plan carefully what you want to do in a paper and then have it returned with the comment, "The content of this essay is pretty good, but the grammar and spelling are atrocious."

The first two sentences clearly imply to a reader that the focus of the paragraph will be on content. The third sentence will be consistent with that focus if the writer immediately returns to content. But the introduction of "mechanical correctness" makes him forget his purpose and leads him astray. The result is that the second half of the paragraph digresses to a focus on correctness, which is the opposite of what the opening sentences require. The paragraph therefore becomes a conspicuous example of lack of unity.

Test the following paragraph for unity by asking of each sentence, "Does this sentence clearly refer to the topic of the itinerant preacher announced in the first sentence?" If you find any shift in focus within the paragraph, where does that shift occur? If you think the paragraph needs revision, can you suggest how it might be revised?

DISCUSSION PROBLEM

(1) The itinerant street preacher was a common sight in small Southern towns a generation ago. (2) He would come into town on Saturday afternoons in the summertime, after he had finished his week's work in his regular job, sometimes accompanied by a guitar player and one or two singers. (3) Once he had set up his microphone and loud speakers and had checked them by saying "Testing, testing, testing," he might begin the service with "Brothers and sisters, we have come here this blessed afternoon to bring the saving message of our Lord Jesus Christ to poor, lost, dying sinners! Amen!" (4) His audience would be located at various places in the block—some clustered around him, some scowling from the pool hall windows, some loafing on the taxi stand porch, and almost certainly a number sitting on the bank steps. (5) Almost certainly, I say, because the bank was a favorite gathering place in those days. (6) Farmers came there to get their loans against crops that had not yet made. (7) Mill workers only a generation removed from the farm came to make small payments against money borrowed during the last strike or the last illness in the family. (8) And these people stayed to relax and talk with friends on the bank steps through Southern Saturday afternoons.

The best way to keep your paragraphs unified is to be sure of what you intend them to do. One way to make your intention clear to yourself and your readers is to begin with a topic sentence. As you know from your high school work in composition, a *topic sentence* is a statement that summarizes the idea to be developed in a paragraph. It is often a single sentence, though sometimes a writer will take two sentences to state the topic. Not all topical paragraphs have topic sentences, and not all topic sentences appear at the beginning of their paragraph. But for relatively inexperienced writers it is good basic training to begin with a topic sentence in any paragraph that is intended to develop an idea or a judgment. The following paragraph, in which the topic sentence is underlined, illustrates the procedure:

> <u>In urban and developed economies such as ours, the four years that separate age 17 from age 21 are the true generation gap.</u> No period in a man's life—except perhaps the jump from fulltime work at age 64 and eleven months to complete retirement at 65—involves greater social or psychological changes. Seventeen-year-olds are traditionally (and for good reasons) rebellious, in search of a new identity, addicted to causes, and intoxicated with ideas. But young adults from 21 to 35—and especially young adult women—tend to be the most conventional group in the population, and one of the most concerned with concrete and immediate problems. This is the time of life when the first baby arrives, when one has to get the mortgage on one's first house and start paying interest on it. This is the age in which concern with job, advancement, career, income, furniture, and doctor's bills moves into the fore. (Peter F. Drucker, "The Surprising Seventies," *Harper's*)

The purpose of this paragraph is to contrast adolescents and young adults to show that the shift from one stage of life to the other is a far-reaching change. (Remember the cartoon on page 71?) Everything that follows the topic sentence helps to develop that contrast. Therefore, the paragraph consistently develops the judgment stated in the opening sentence.

Beginning with a topic sentence will not of itself guarantee unity in a paragraph, since a writer can veer away from a topic sentence after writing it. But if you deliberately begin with a topic sentence, you have made a decision about what you intend the paragraph to do. That decision will probably suggest what kind of information will be needed to develop the topic sentence. And if you should drift into inconsistencies, at least you have a standard by which to judge the paragraph during revision.

COMPLETENESS

Completeness, the second major requirement of an effective paragraph, is relative. How much explanation an idea requires depends on how much the reader needs. This is a decision you must make out of your knowledge of the subject and of the reader. It is an error to give too much information or not to give enough, though in freshman writing lack of adequate detail is more common than too much detail.

Consider the following example:

> Under the 1968 Gun Control Act, any resident of a state can purchase a gun anywhere in his state provided he meets the established requirements.

However, the law provides no foolproof way for gun dealers to check the background of the purchaser.

If that is all the writer is going to say about the Gun Control Act, this paragraph will be incomplete for most readers, since the two sentences do no more than state the topic. The only reader this paragraph will satisfy is one who already knows what "the established requirements" are and why the law provides "no foolproof way" to check a purchaser's identity. And such a reader would not need the paragraph in the first place. For one who does need it, the writer must provide a fuller explanation, perhaps something like this:

> Under the 1968 Gun Control Act, any resident of a state can purchase a gun anywhere in his state provided he meets specified minimum age requirements (twenty-one for hand guns and eighteen for long guns) and is not under indictment or has not been convicted of a crime punishable by more than a year's imprisonment. Nor can he be a fugitive from justice, a narcotics addict or unlawful user of drugs, an adjudged or committed mental incompetent, or anyone else otherwise disqualified from gun ownership by state or local laws. However, the federal law provides no foolproof way for gun dealers to check the background of a would-be purchaser or, for that matter, even to determine whether the person they are selling to is just who he says he is. A driver's license is usually considered sufficient identification to establish a person's name, address, and age. And so any proscribed person can easily get a gun, as well as ammunition for it, by presenting false credentials or by simply lying. (Carl Bakal, "The Failure of Federal Gun Control," *Saturday Review*)

The detailed information added in the expansion is necessary to make the meaning of the incomplete paragraph clear. Of course, writers can begin with a short paragraph if all they intend to do is to state the idea they are going to develop and then explain it in a subsequent paragraph. In that case, the second paragraph completes the first.

The following example further illustrates incompleteness and the way correct it:

> Pregnant women sometimes attempt to mold the character of an unborn child by studying poetry, art, or mathematics. What we know of prenatal development makes such attempts seem utterly impossible. How could such extremely complex influences pass from the mother to the child?

If the writer stops here, all he has given readers is an unsupported judgment that these attempts will have no influence on the child. But that is not enough. Readers still need to know why the attempts will not work. The rest of the paragraph explains why not.

> There is no connection between their nervous systems. Even the blood vessels of mother and child do not join directly. They lie side by side and the chemicals are interchanged through the walls by a process that we call osmosis. An emotional shock to the mother will affect her child, because it changes the activity of her glands and so the chemistry of her blood. Any chemical change in the mother's blood will affect the child—for better or worse. But we cannot see how a liking for mathematics or poetic genius can be dissolved in blood and produce a similar liking or genius in the child. (William H. Roberts, *Psychology You Can Use)*

The added sentences complete the paragraph by showing why "what we know of prenatal development makes such attempts seem utterly impossible." The information they provide is necessary for a complete explanation of the topic sentence.

The lesson to be learned from these contrasted examples is that you must spell out the implications of your topic sentences. Unless you give your readers the information they need, you make it difficult for them to understand you. Incomplete paragraphing is a common fault in freshman writing; yet it is an easy one to correct, once a student realizes the importance of developing generalizations with supporting details.

EXERCISE The following paragraph is incomplete as it now stands. Complete it by inserting after the second sentence a sustained illustration from any activity you know well—basketball, playing a musical instrument, painting, or whatever you choose. Then use what is now the third sentence as a conclusion.

> To excel in any skill, it is not enough just to be talented. Every kind of skilled activity has its special techniques that have to be learned by practice. What is needed is both talent and technical proficiency.

Your paragraph will then have the TRIT structure introduced on page 65.

ORDER

So far in this chapter we have considered unity and completeness in paragraphs. Now we come to the third major requirement, *order,* which deals with the sequence of the sentences within a paragraph. In a well-constructed paragraph the sentences follow a consistent order. As you saw in the paragraph on Pompeii (page 95), sentences that go in various directions are likely to bother readers by making it difficult for them to see the relationship among the sentences.

Order in a paragraph is like organization in an essay. But because paragraphs are smaller in scope, it may be simpler to consider order as *direction of movement.* In expository paragraphs the most usual directions are from *general to particular,* from *particular to general,* from the *whole to its parts,* and from *question to answer* or *effect to cause.* In the following pages we will explain and illustrate each of these orders.

General to particular   A common order in expository paragraphs is one that moves from a general statement, often a topic sentence, to specific explanation or illustration of that statement. The function of the paragraph is to make clear to a reader the meaning of the general statement. That meaning becomes increasingly clear as the paragraph progresses. You saw this kind of clarification in the paragraphs on gun control and the prenatal development of babies. In both these paragraphs the direction of movement was from a general statement to a particular explanation of that statement. The simplest prescription for a general-to-particular paragraph is

1.   begin with a general statement of the topic idea to be developed, and

2.   follow it with enough specific information to explain or illustrate the meaning of the opening statement.

Here is an additional example, which is also an example of the TRIT structure. Can you mark in the margin the symbol that is appropriate for each part of the paragraph? Notice the wealth of examples in the part you mark *I.*

Seven is an especially powerful number. Wherever superstition involving numbers exists—and that includes the entire world—seven plays an important part. In East India, for instance, the natives refuse to work six days and rest on the seventh. They believe that would be calamitous. Instead, they work seven days and rest on the eighth, missionaries notwithstanding. To the Hebrews seven was a sacred number. The Bible is full of the number seven. God made the Earth in six days and rested on the seventh. Likewise, there were seven years of plenty and seven years of famine; Jacob served Laban seven years for Leah and seven for Rachel, and his children mourned him for seven days at this death. There was a whole complex of sevens in the fall of Jericho—on the seventh day the city was encompassed seven times by seven priests bearing seven trumpets. Balaam demanded seven altars, with seven bullocks and seven rams; and Elisha healed Naaman of leprosy by making him wash seven times in the Jordan. The Greeks, too, considered seven lucky as did (and do) many other races. Indeed, there seems to be a universal belief that seven is no ordinary number, but a potent, perfect, and even magical number.

Particular to general   A particular-to-general order is the reverse of the one we have been studying. A paragraph written in this order begins with specific information and leads to a general conclusion, as in the following example:

> From 1959 to 1964, the public was clamoring for excellence in science and mathematics, and teachers were supposed to guide pupils in learning these disciplines by discovery, induction, and sheer ingenuity. From 1965 to the early 70's, the curriculum stressed compassion for the children of the socially and economically depressed minorities. "Relating" was the goal of the curriculum and the criterion of good teaching. Now the stress has shifted from excellence for the elites and compassion for the unfortunate to basics for everyone. The schools have been called upon to change directions radically about every five years. No wonder last year's college graduates are confused. (Harry S. Broudy, "A New Voice for the Schools," *Today's Education*)

This paragraph moves through three specific trends in education to a general conclusion drawn from all of them. Had the author chosen, he could have followed a general-to-particular order, beginning with "The schools have been called upon to change directions radically about every five years" and following that general statement with the three changes mentioned. But he preferred to lead up to his conclusion rather than to begin with it.

Whole to parts   Sometimes the function of a paragraph is not to explain an idea but to show the parts or divisions of a topic. Here is an example of this third kind of order taken from an earlier paragraph in this chapter:

> To be effective, a topical paragraph must meet four requirements. First, it must discuss one topic only; that is, it must have unity of subject matter. Second, it must say all that a reader needs to know about the topic; that is, it must be complete enough to do what it is intended to do. Third, the sentences within the paragraph must follow some reasonable order that a reader can recognize and follow. Fourth, the sentences within a paragraph must have coherence; that is, they must be so tied together that a reader can read the paragraph as a unit, not as a collection of separate sentences.

Such an order is often called *partitive* or *enumerative*. The opening sentence announces the number of parts of the topic, and the rest of the paragraph identifies and defines each of these parts in turn. You can easily use the paragraph above as a model to develop the following sentences into paragraphs:

The continental United States is divided into four time zones.

The composition process can be divided into three stages: prewriting, writing, and rewriting.

I have two main objections to the proposal.

A partitive or enumerative paragraph is useful to introduce the headings under which a topic is to be discussed. It is often used in argument, either as an introduction to identify the issues that will be considered or as a conclusion to sum up what has been done. If it is used in the middle of an essay, however, its lack of detail can lead to incomplete development. For example, the model paragraph about the four requirements of a topical paragraph may be adequate as an introduction, but it would be incomplete if that were all that the writer had to say about unity, completeness, order, and coherence.

Question to answer, effect to cause   A paragraph may begin with a question and give the answer, or with an effect and explain the cause. Such a paragraph may have no specific topic sentence beyond the opening question or effect. The answer or cause is given by the rest of the paragraph.

The following paragraph goes from question to answer:

> Should we make clones of human beings—copies of a beautiful mother, perhaps, or a clever father? Of course not. My view is that diversity is the breath of life, and we must not abandon that for any single form which happens to catch our fancy—even our genetic fancy. Cloning is the stabilization of one form, and that runs against the whole current of creation—of human creation above all. Evolution is founded in variety and creates diversity; and of all animals, man is most creative because he carries and expresses the largest store of variety. Every attempt to make us uniform, biologically, emotionally, or intellectually, is a betrayal of the evolutionary thrust that has made man its apex. (J. Bronowski, *The Ascent of Man*)

In the next paragraph the first sentence states an effect, the "immunity gap." The rest of the paragraph shows what causes that effect. You have seen this order earlier in this chapter, particularly in the paragraph showing the process of disintegration that led to the fall of the Roman Empire (page 95).

> The hard fact is that a wide "immunity gap" exists in our population between younger people and those fifty and over. The gap comes about in this way: the influenza virus, like other viruses, carries as part of its protein coating certain antigens that stimulate our immune systems to produce specific antibodies against it; because the swine type of influenza virus has not been in circulation for more than fifty years, people under fifty—and some above fifty as well—lack these protective antibodies and thus would be susceptible if such a virus were to become active again. (Jonas Salk, "The Ultimate Flu Vaccine," *Saturday Review*)

The summary table on page 104 provides a quick review of the four common orders discussed in this chapter.

Summary of Main Orders of Paragraph Movement

General to particular Opening general statement or topic sentence followed by illustration or details of explanation or proof. This is the TRI order and may conclude with a restatement of the topic sentence.

> Topic sentence followed by supporting details.
> Concluding statement optional.

Particular to general From a series of detailed statements to a conclusion drawn from them. If there is a topic sentence, it occurs at or near the end of the paragraph.

> Explanatory details or illustrations leading to conclusion or topic sentence.

Whole to parts Paragraph begins with an introductory statement about the number of parts and then explains each part; often a first, second, third order.

> Opening statement
> 1. _____
> 2. _____
> 3. _____

Question to answer, or *effect to cause* Paragraph begins with question or effect, then answers the question or shows the cause.

> Question or effect followed by answer or cause.

COHERENCE

The fourth requirement of an effective paragraph is *coherence.* Literally, the word means "sticking together." A paragraph is coherent when the sentences are woven together in such a way that the reader can move easily from one sentence to the next and read the paragraph as an integrated whole, rather than as a series of separate sentences.

A writer with a clear general plan is not likely to have serious trouble with coherence. Most incoherent paragraphs come from thinking out the implications of the topic one sentence at a time, without considering the relationships among the sentences. A writer who works this way will write one sentence, stop, think a minute, write a second sentence, stop, and continue in a series of spurts and pauses. Paragraphs written this way are likely to lack coherence, for the writer is starting afresh at every sentence. The sense of continuity between sentences is lost, and as a result the writing becomes jerky.

A paragraph that lacks orderly movement will not be coherent, since a reader who does not see how two sentences are related cannot go easily from one to another. But though inconsistent order is a major cause of lack of coherence, it is not the only one. Anything that keeps the reader from making clear and quick connections between the sentences in a paragraph or between successive paragraphs interferes with the transfer of ideas from writer to reader.

Here is an example of incoherent writing that does not come from faulty order. A student is writing a paper to show that Thomas Jefferson's writing is characterized by careful research and independent thinking. At one point in his paper he wants to illustrate that thesis by citing Jefferson's book *The Life and Morals of Jesus of Nazareth.* The student has the material he needs in his notes, from which he writes the following paragraph:

> Jefferson could read Greek, Latin, French, and English, so he pasted texts of the New Testament in these languages side by side. He thought that the Bible should be read critically, like any other book; so he accepted those stories about Jesus which agreed with natural laws, and rejected those that did not. He kept the teachings of Jesus but rejected the miracles. He also rejected anything that had to be explained by revelation. "I think," he wrote in a letter to Adams, "that every Christian sect gives a great handle to atheism by their general dogma that, without revelation, there would not be sufficient proof of the being of God." Jefferson considered Christianity the purest system of morality known.

Although this paragraph does develop the material in the notes into an orderly sequence of sentences, it has several weaknesses that could be removed in revision. Consider the following points:

1.   What is the purpose of the paragraph? We know from the description of the assignment that the writer wants to illustrate Jefferson's habits of careful research and independent thinking. The information does illustrate these habits, but its significance would be clearer if the individual sentences were clearly related to a topic sentence that would bind them together. Without such a topic sentence a reader may wonder why Jefferson examined the New Testament in four languages and may have difficulty in seeing any connection between the first sentence and the second.

2.   What is the relationship between this paragraph and the one that preceded it? You know that it is another illustration of the thesis of the paper, because we gave you that information. But the paragraph does not make that relationship clear. It needs some kind of introductory statement to show that this is another illustration.

3.   Although the repetition of *he* provides some natural coherence within the

paragraph and so ties the sentences together by giving them a common subject, the monotonous structure tends to emphasize the separateness of each sentence. The passage seems more like a collection of sentences than the development of a single idea.

4. The last sentence seems to have no relation to what has gone before. If it is not a digression, its function should be indicated.

Now consider the following revision:

Jefferson's book on Jesus of Nazareth provides another illustration of his careful collection and comparison of the evidence, and of his acceptance or rejection of it on the basis of reason rather than authority. To compare the evidence, Jefferson pasted texts from the New Testament in Greek, Latin, French, and English in columns side by side. As he was proficient in all four languages he felt he could come closer to the true meanings of the words by reading them in this way. To ensure that reason rather than the authority of tradition would guide him, he followed his own advice that the Bible should be read critically, like any other book. Accordingly, he accepted those parts which revealed the teachings of Jesus and rejected stories of miracles. He also rejected those passages which had to be supported by revelation. "I think," he wrote to Adams, "that every Christian sect gives a great handle to atheism by their general dogma that, without revelation, there would not be sufficient proof of the being of God." The result was a work which emphasized what Jefferson considered the purest system of morality known and toned down or omitted incidents which required a supernatural explanation.

Notice:

1. the topic sentence, which states the purpose of the paragraph (and so gives point to all that follows) and also relates this paragraph to the thesis of the paper.

2. the explanation of why Jefferson pasted the four different texts side by side. This explanation is necessary to illustrate the thoroughness of his working habits.

3. the clearer explanation of his selection and rejection of material ("To ensure that reason rather than the authority..."). This explanation helps to bind together four sentences that in the unsatisfactory version were connected only by a common subject.

4. the concluding sentence, which not only shows the pertinence of what previously looked like a digression but also, by showing Jefferson's emphasis, sums up the content of the whole paragraph.

5. the more pleasing effect obtained by slight but significant variations in the basic sentence pattern.

This contrast of the original and revised paragraphs shows how an unsatisfactory piece of writing can be improved by providing the connecting links that bring out the relationships among the sentences. In the revised paragraph these links were pieces of information that bridged the gaps in the original version and thus made the whole paragraph a fuller and clearer expression of the main idea, now stated as a topic sentence. Another way of linking sentences together into a coherent paragraph is to use such connective devices as *pronouns, repetitive structure, contrast,* and *transitional markers,* all of which are discussed in the following pages.

Coherence through pronoun reference Because it refers to an antecedent, a pronoun points back and gives a simple and natural connection. Notice how the pronoun *it* ties the last four sentences of the following paragraph to its antecedent, the kudzu vine:

> Kudzu may or may not control erosion, but people who planted the vine found they had difficulty controlling it. It leaped fences and raced freely over embankments into forests and fields. By the time cultivation of kudzu had ceased, it had run wild. Now it has a permanent grasp on the land. It squats on the countryside and vacant city lots like an obese potentate. (Larry Stevens, "King Kong Kudzu, Menace to the South," *Smithsonian*)

The constant pointing back of the pronoun *it* to the subject *kudzu vine* connects all five sentences and provides a consistent development of the main idea of the paragraph. The pronoun ties each sentence to the one preceding it and thus keeps a common subject running through the paragraph.

DISCUSSION PROBLEM

One of these paragraphs is a revision of the other. Which is the revised paragraph, and what weaknesses is it trying to remove?

(1) Although the writing of a research paper is a difficult assignment, many students make it more difficult than it needs to be because of inefficient procedures. (2) The work on the paper is too often postponed until it is too late to do a respectable job of it. (3) Failure to find out at the beginning whether sufficient material is available in the library often invites serious difficulty. (4) Many students tackle the topic in detail before they have formed a general notion of the

(1) Although the writing of a research paper is a difficult assignment, many students make it more difficult than it needs to be because of inefficient procedures. (2) Often they postpone work on the paper until it is too late to do a respectable job of it. (3) Sometimes they invite trouble by failure to find out at the beginning of the study whether sufficient material is available in the library. (4) Instead of getting a general notion of the topic before tackling it in detail, they begin

topic. (5) It is unwise to begin reading the first book available and to plunge into fine points before the student has learned to understand the topic as a whole. (6) The habit of taking notes too soon is inefficient. (7) Students should postpone note-taking until they have decided what information they need. (8) It is also a mistake to quote a paragraph in its entirety. (9) The notes should consist of factual information taken from the paragraph.

with the most convenient book and plunge into fine points before they see the topic as a whole. (5) They take more notes than necessary because they begin to take notes before they have decided what kind of information they need, and because they do not pick out factual information in a paragraph but quote the paragraph in its entirety.

Coherence through repetitive structure   Although unintended repetition is to be avoided, deliberate repetition of key words, phrases, or sentence patterns can connect sentences into a coherent paragraph. In the following paragraph every sentence after the first has the same kind of structure and the same opening words, "There is nothing." This kind of repetitive structure, which will be discussed as *parallelism* in the next chapter, ties the sentences together as a consistent development of the topic sentence.

America, the richest and most powerful nation in the world, can well lead the way in this revolution of values. There is nothing to prevent us from paying adequate wages to schoolteachers, social workers and other servants of the public to insure that we have the best available personnel in these positions which are charged with the responsibility of guiding our future generations. There is nothing but a lack of social vision to prevent us from paying an adequate wage to every American citizen whether he be a hospital worker, laundry worker, maid or day laborer. There is nothing except shortsightedness to prevent us from guaranteeing an annual minimum—and *livable*—income for every American family. There is nothing, except a tragic death wish, to prevent us from reordering our priorities, so the pursuit of peace will take precedence over the pursuit of war. There is nothing to keep us from remolding a recalcitrant status quo with bruised hands until we have fashioned it into a brotherhood. (Martin Luther King, Jr., *Where Do We Go from Here: Chaos or Community?*)

In the following paragraph the repetition of the pronouns *its* and *whose* combines with parallel sentence structure to provide effective links between the sentences. Can you identify the parallel or repetitive structures?

Those of us who came to know baseball when there was little television and no big-time professional football or basketball talked its language, heard its lore, and were taken with its special sense before we had ever played an organized game or pondered its beautiful mystery. There were giants on the field, men of legend whose voices we had never heard, whose faces we knew only from newspaper photographs or from the murky images on our bubble-gum cards, and whose records—batting average, home runs, runs batted in—suggested meaning beyond anything we understood. "Facts" supported myth, and myth magnified the facts on which it was supposed to be based. (Peter Schrag, "The Age of Willie Mays," *Saturday Review)*

Coherence through contrasted elements   When the topic sentence calls for comparison or contrast, the pairing of contrasted or compared elements gives some coherence. In the following example successive contrasts between past and present relations of husbands and wives connect individual sentences and relate them all to the topic sentence:

Many men also find it hard to adjust to the stark contrasts between the new ways and the old. Their mothers stayed home. Their fathers made all the important decisions. In an argument, the father's word was final. And the mother cooked, sewed and cleaned up in silence. It can therefore be very unsettling for men to suddenly find that their wives are discovering activities and ideas so different from their mothers'. "My husband and I got along just fine until I went back to work," said a woman from Atlanta. "Then, suddenly, he started wanting to have people for dinner, take long vacations and have his undershorts ironed—issues that never came up when my time belonged more to him. It's really been a hassle. He keeps talking about the way his mother was with his father. I tell him times have changed. He answers, 'But *I* haven't.'" (Linda Bird Francke, "Do Strong Women Frighten Men?" *Ladies' Home Journal)*

Topic sentence
Contrast 1
Contrast 2

Topic sentence restatement in more specific form

Contrast 3

Contrast 4

Coherence through transitional markers   *Transitional markers* are words or phrases often placed at or near the beginning of a sentence or clause to signal the relationship between a new sentence and the one before it. The commonest markers are the conjunctions *and, or, nor, but,* and *for.* Others—sometimes called *transitional connectives*—also indicate the direction the new sentence is about to take. The commonest transitional connectives are used as follows:

1.   to introduce an illustration: *for example, for instance, to illustrate*

2.   to add another phase of the same idea: *second, in the second place, then, furthermore, next, moreover, in addition, similarly, again, also, finally*

3.   to point up a contrast or qualification: *on the other hand, nevertheless, despite this fact, on the contrary, still, however, conversely, instead*

4.   to indicate a conclusion or result: *therefore, in conclusion, to sum up, consequently, as a result, accordingly, in other words*

EXERCISES   **A.**   Using whatever means you choose, rewrite the following passage to make it a coherent paragraph:

(1) I was accepted and started work. (2) My experience had been derived chiefly from books. (3) I was not prepared for the difficult period of adjustment. (4) I soon became discouraged with myself. (5) I was dissatisfied with my job. (6) I was on the point of quitting. (7) My employer called me into his office. (8) He talked to me about the duties of my position. (9) He talked about the opportunities for advancement. (10) I realized there was nothing wrong with me or the job. (11) I decided to stay.

B.   Use the revised Jefferson paragraph (page 106) as a model to convert this collection of sentences into a coherent paragraph. The purpose of the paragraph is to answer the question whether it ever gets too cold to snow. First write a topic sentence that will state a general answer to that question and thus suggest a focus for the information provided in the numbered sentences. Then work that information into a coherent paragraph.

1.   Snow particles form when the temperature falls below 32 Fahrenheit.

2.   At this temperature the particles are wet.

3.   Wet particles mat together to form flakes.

4.   As the temperature falls still lower, the air dries out.

5.   Dry snow does not flake but becomes powdery.

6.   At temperatures below zero, snow changes to fine, glittering ice-dust.

7.   At temperatures below zero, a heavy fall of snow is rare, but it can occur.

8.   The air is usually too dry to produce snow at subzero temperatures.

Coherence through connections between paragraphs   Coherence is necessary, not only within a paragraph, but also between the several paragraphs of an essay. On pages 58–59 you saw that in a well-organized outline, main headings clearly point back to the thesis, and subheadings point back to their main headings. This interlocking of the parts of an outline is carried into the writing of the paper, so that a reader can usually see how any paragraph is related to those that have come before.

The following selection illustrates this coherence among paragraphs. The thesis is stated in the first paragraph and is developed under two main headings: physical changes and intellectual changes. Each of these is explained by giving evidence–the physical changes in the second paragraph, and the intellectual changes in the third and fourth. The relations within and among the paragraphs are shown by connecting lines.

Disgruntled souls who shake their heads and mutter that young people aren't what they used to be are, as a matter of fact, absolutely correct. Young people have changed appreciably, and not just in the more publicized and superficial ways.
Thesis

Physically, young people are larger and healthier than they were fifty years ago. Girls and boys are about three inches taller and ten pounds heavier than they were in 1920, principally because of advances in nutrition and medicine. Childhood diseases that used to stunt and maim, and even fill the cemeteries, have been wiped out. (The chief cause of death for persons under 21 is now accidents, primarily automobile accidents.) These same advances in nutrition and medicine have caused adolescents to mature physiologically much earlier than in the past. In the United States the onset of puberty for girls has dropped from an average of 14 in 1920 to 12.4 today, and, for boys, from 15 to 13.5.
I. First main heading

A
Evidence for A

B

Evidence for B

Today's young people differ intellectually as well as physically. Kenneth Keniston of Yale, among others, has noted that the average American sixteen-year-old has had five years more schooling than his counterpart in 1920. A recent U.S. Census Bureau study reveals that the number of young adults with high school diplomas has doubled since 1940, while the number with college degrees has tripled.
II. Second main heading
A

Evidence for A

The average student today scores approximately one standard deviation above the student of a generation ago on standardized tests of intellectual achievement. A level of performance that places a student in the middle of his graduating class today would probably have placed him in the top 15 per cent thirty years ago. Or, to put it another way, in achievement, a teenager today is approximately one grade ahead of his parents when they were his age. (Ernest L. Boyer and George C. Keller, "The Big Move to Non-Campus Colleges," *Saturday Review*)
B

Explanation for B

The interconnections that link these paragraphs clearly suggest that one good way to get coherence in an essay is to plan it in prewriting. An essay written from a careful outline is likely to have built-in coherence. Knowing what each paragraph is supposed to do will help the writer to develop the paragraphs in a logical, coherent, and consistent way.

In the following selection coherence among the three paragraphs is achieved by repeated reference to two terms in the thesis. Show this coherence, first by underlining the thesis and circling the two terms, and then by drawing connecting lines between these terms and the statements that refer to them.
EXERCISE

A common myth about the nature of mathematical ability holds that one either has or does not have a mathematical mind. Mathematical imagination and an intuitive grasp of mathematical principles may well be needed to do advanced research, but why should people who can do college-level work in other subjects not be able to do college-level math as well? Rates of learning may vary. Competency under time pressure may differ. Certainly low self-esteem will get in the way. But where is the evidence that a student needs a "mathematical mind" in order to succeed at learning math?

Consider the effects of this mythology. Since only a few people are supposed to have this mathematical mind, part of what makes us so passive in the face of our difficulties in learning mathematics is that we suspect all the while we may not be one of "them," and we spend our time waiting to find out when our nonmathematical minds will be exposed. Since our limit will eventually be reached, we see no point in being methodical or in attending to detail. We are grateful when we survive fractions, word problems, or geometry. If that certain moment of failure hasn't struck yet, it is only temporarily postponed.

Parents, especially parents of girls, often expect their children to be nonmathematical. Parents are either poor at math . . . or, if math came easily for them, they do not know how it feels to be slow. In either case, they unwittingly foster the idea that a mathematical mind is something one either has or does not have. (Sheila Tobias, "Who's Afraid of Math, and Why?" *The Atlantic*)

SPECIAL PARAGRAPHS

So far in this chapter we have been dealing with topical paragraphs, those that develop the topic or some part of it. These are the main paragraphs in an essay. But certain other paragraphs have special functions. They are used to *introduce* or *conclude* an essay or to *mark a transition* from one main unit to another.

INTRODUCTORY PARAGRAPHS

The function of an introductory paragraph is to lead your readers into your essay. In effect it directs their attention to what is to come and so makes it easier for them to adjust themselves to the demands you, as a writer, are going to make on them. Usually introductory paragraphs tend to be one of two types or a combination of both: they are suggestions of what you intend to do in the essay, or they are attention-getting devices that capture your readers' interest and make them want to see what you have to say.

The first of these types is often a short paragraph that states the thesis of an essay, usually with a brief explanation. Such an introduction may be called a *thesis paragraph.* Here are some thesis paragraphs from essays presented earlier in this book:

> I have thought seriously about role-playing since our discussion in class last week, and while I fought the idea for a while, feeling that it cut down my image of myself, I finally had to admit it's true. I do play roles. I guess we all do. And now that I've admitted it, I think I understand myself a little better, and maybe other people too. (Page 15)

(The first sentence is background for the thesis, which is stated in the next two sentences.)

> Birds reared in isolation from their kind do not generally know what species they belong to: that is to say, not only their social reactions but also their sexual desires are directed towards those beings with whom they have spent certain impressionable phases of their early youth. Consequently, birds raised singly by hand tend to regard human beings, and human beings only, as potential partners in all reproductive activities. (Page 64)

(The thesis is stated in general terms in the first sentence up to the colon and restated in restricted form in the rest of the paragraph.)

> As Edward T. Hall points out in *The Silent Language,* attitudes toward time are conditioned by cultural habits: what is a long time in the United States may be a short time in other cultures. (Page 67)

(This paragraph has the same form as the one above it—a general statement of the thesis in the first sentence up to the colon, and a more restricted restatement in the remainder of the paragraph.) The following paragraph arrives at its thesis after a summary of the conditions that led to a downgrading of fraternities:

> During the turbulent changes of the 1960's college students began to question the value of traditions and organizations on their campuses. As a result, activities that had once been respected fell into disrepute. Homecoming parades, beauty contests, campus proms, and pep rallies before football games began to seem trivial to students who prided themselves on their maturity. In this reversal of values fraternities took a beating, and fraternity membership declined all over the country. It is my contention that rejection of fraternities ignores the valuable contributions they make to the social development of undergraduate men.

(This opening paragraph sets the stage for a defense of fraternities. In effect, the writer reviews the causes of what he considers a hasty and unwise effect, and so both introduces his defense and justifies it.)

As these examples show, the thesis may or may not start the introductory paragraph. Usually a good rule of thumb is: first lead up to the thesis, then state it, then clarify it.

Experienced writers usually avoid beginning with "In this paper I will show . . ." or "The purpose of this paper is to . . . ," but if such bald statements will get you started, put them in your first drafts and reconsider them during revision. These statements often strike readers as being too abrupt and mechanical, but at least they have the merit of telling your readers, and perhaps yourself, what you intend to do in the paper.

The second type of introductory paragraph is intended to catch the readers' attention and thus lure them into the essay. Journalists and scriptwriters call this kind of introduction to catch reader interest a "hook." Often it is a dramatic example pulled out of its normal place and set at the beginning as bait to entice the reader into going on. Sometimes it is an analogy that points up the real subject of a paper. Occasionally it is a question that challenges readers or arouses their curiosity. A good example is the introductory paragraphs of the paper on the stop-and-frisk law (page 20).

Here are some examples of the introductory hook:

1.   a question introducing an essay on the costs of eliminating pollution

   Do you honestly believe that people, including you, want a pollution-free environment badly enough to pay the costs? Before you answer that question, consider what these costs are.

2.   examples to introduce an article making fun of what the author considers our mania for excessive bathing

   Just on the market at $6,600 is a somewhat egg-shaped washing machine in which a human being reclines, to be flushed with hot water, massaged by rubber spheres and dried under infrared rays. In Texas, a student claims the world sluicing record—169 hours in the shower. Meanwhile, in Palm Springs, a well-heeled decorator has designed a $22,500 bathroom. It's so sumptuous that, he says, once inside, "I'm so thrilled to be there that I hate to go out." And in Tokyo, there's a hotel with a solid-gold bath available at 1,000 yen a quick dip, in the local belief that a two-minute dunk will add three years to your life. (Patrick Ryan, "Compulsive cleanliness may send us down the drain," *Smithsonian*)

3.   an introductory example intended to arouse readers' curiosity about the people who served as President before George Washington and about the conditions under which they occupied that office

   On January 20, 1977, Jimmy Carter took the oath of office as the 39th President. By another calculation, he is actually the 54th. It depends on whether you count from the first election of a President under the Constitution, from the first President under the Articles of Confederation, or from the start of the United States as an independent nation. (Richard B. Morris, "Hail to 14 forgotten Chiefs! Meet the men who were President before Washington," *Smithsonian*)

4. an introductory analogy in an essay showing the difficulties under which a social scientist must work

(1) In discussing the relative difficulties of analysis which the exact and inexact sciences face, let me begin with an analogy. (2) Would you agree that swimmers are less skillful athletes than runners because swimmers do not move as fast as runners? (3) You probably would not. (4) You would quickly point out that water offers greater resistance to swimmers than the air and ground do to runners. (5) Agreed, that is just the point. (6) In seeking to solve their problems, the social scientists encounter greater resistance than the physical scientists. (7) By that I do not mean to belittle the great accomplishments of physical scientists who have been able, for example, to determine the structure of the atom without seeing it. (8) That is a tremendous achievement; yet in many ways it is not so difficult as what the social scientists are expected to do. (9) The conditions under which the social scientists must work would drive a physical scientist frantic. (10) Here are five of those conditions. (11) He can make few experiments; he cannot measure the results accurately; he cannot control the conditions surrounding the experiments; he is often expected to get quick results with slow-acting economic forces; and he must work with people, not with inanimate objects. (12) Let us look at these conditions more closely. (Donald L. Kemmerer, "Are Social Scientists Backward?" *AAUP Bulletin*)

This paragraph is especially effective as an introduction to a long paper. It captures readers' attention by an analogy introduced as a question and so leads into the thesis in the sixth sentence. Then it restates the thesis in the eighth and ninth sentences and follows that restatement by enumerating the five conditions that make the social scientist's work difficult. It not only "hooks" readers into the paper; it also gives them a preview of the five difficulties the paper will discuss. It both introduces the thesis and announces the organization of the essay.

TRANSITIONAL PARAGRAPHS

A transitional paragraph is a signal of a change in content. Through transitional paragraphs writers announce that they have finished one main unit and are moving to the next, or that they are turning from a general explanation to examples or applications. In their simplest form such signals may be as brief as the following:

So much for the woodwinds. We come now to the brasses.

Let us see how this theory operates in practice.

A few examples will make this explanation clear.

I know of course that all this sounds vague. But don't worry. From this point on we are getting down to brass tacks. (Rudolph Flesch, *The Art of Plain Talk*)

Sometimes a writer supplements the bare signal with a concise summary of what has been done or with a hint of what is to come, as the next two examples show:

In this section of the book we move from planning a paper to writing it. So far you have been dealing with the problems of deciding what you wanted to do with your subject, what kind of material you needed, and how best to organize it into a plan. Now you will be dealing with the problem of developing your plan into a finished essay. In general, these problems are of four kinds: how to express your ideas in complete and consistent paragraphs; how to get clarity, emphasis, and variety in your sentences; how to choose the words that best convey your meaning to your reader; and how to achieve and maintain an appropriate style.

Each of these "faces" has been symbolic of the multifaceted nature of New York. Each, in its own way, has made or "remade" sections of the city. There is emerging now a new, fourth face—New York, the cultural city. (Daniel Bell, "The Forces Shaping the City: The Four Faces of New York")

CONCLUDING PARAGRAPHS

Contrary to popular student belief, not every paper needs a concluding paragraph. If an essay has adequately developed its thesis, nothing more is necessary. For example, the Lorenz passage about birds that are sexually confused (page 64) needs no concluding paragraph, because the conclusion is implied in the thesis. All that essay needs to do is to explain its thesis. Similarly, the contrast between different concepts of time (page 67) is complete without a concluding paragraph. There would be nothing wrong with adding a concluding paragraph to these essays, *provided that it strengthened the message.* But a merely mechanical conclusion that took the form "Thus we see that . . ." would be just a wordy anticlimax.

Yet an effective concluding paragraph can make a positive contribution by bringing the whole paper to a climax, by summing up the discussion in a few sentences that leave readers with the feeling, "Yes, that is what it is all about." Such a concluding paragraph gives the writer one final chance to drive the message home. Here are three examples of effective concluding paragraphs:

1.   a paragraph that emphasizes main points in a summary

The last three chapters have granted that at times language can be confusing, illogical, and infuriating; that it can play tricks on both speaker and listener; that though all human beings belong to the same species, they do not categorize their experience in any mutually intelligible way; that a mere flicker of the eyelids can sometimes belie the most carefully structured and grammatical utterance. In view of all this, can we regard the language game as an honest one? Yes, we can—despite the flaws. The flaws and limitations in language are a reflection of the flaws and limitations in our species, and an understanding of these will allow us to function within the boundaries of language with greater freedom and understanding than heretofore. (Peter Farb, *Word Play*)

2.   a paragraph that draws a conclusion from preceding paragraphs

   Therefore, if you want to gain weight, you must do either of two things: eat more calories (units of heat, therefore energy), or use less through inactivity. If you want to lose weight, you do the reverse: decrease your input of calories or increase the amount of energy you spend. There is no other way. Gaining or losing weight is always a relation between intake and output of potential energy.

3.   a paragraph that evaluates what has been done

   The procession which marked the conclusion of the ten-month Constitutional Convention set a symbolic seal on the long process and thus had the effect which many public ceremonies have of making it all seem a real and believable event. In the words of Benjamin Rush, the Philadelphia physician and signer of the Declaration of Independence, " 'Tis done. We have become a nation."

Each of these paragraphs leaves a reader with a sense of completeness, a conviction that the point has been made and that nothing more needs to be said. And each makes a contribution to the essay that could not be made by a "Thus I have shown . . ." conclusion.

DETECTING WEAKNESSES IN PARAGRAPHS

Before you can revise your own paragraphs, you have to see why they need revision. You know that a topical paragraph should be unified, complete, orderly, and coherent. But when it comes to checking your own paragraphs for these qualities, you are likely to run into a difficulty every writer has, that of seeing one's own work as a reader will see it. To some extent the ability to recognize weaknesses in your own writing can be acquired by close reading of the first draft, a reading in which you concentrate on examining the relation of sentences to each other and to the topic sentence.

The exercises in this section will give you practice in such close reading. They will do so by giving you contrasted examples of good and unsatisfactory paragraphs. You will be asked to decide which of a pair is the better paragraph and why, or to point out the means by which an inferior paragraph was improved.

EXERCISES   **A.**   This exercise offers an experience in reading closely in order to examine the structure of paragraphs, especially the order in which sentences appear. Two versions of an essay are given. Both versions develop the same thesis: "Democracy is both the easiest and most difficult form of government." Both develop that thesis through two paragraphs, the topic sentences of which are underlined. The question to be decided is: Which version better develops the thesis? Do the exercise in the following stages:

1.   Begin with the first paragraph of the left-hand version and read it carefully to see whether the topic sentence clearly relates to the thesis and whether each succeeding sentence shows a clear relation to the topic sentence. If you encounter any sentence that does not seem to belong in the paragraph, place a question mark before it.

2.   Follow the same procedure for the second paragraph. Does the topic sentence clearly relate to the thesis, and do all of the sentences clearly relate to the topic sentence?

3.   Summarize the structure of both paragraphs by writing the *number* of each topic sentence and, under it, the number of each sentence that develops it. Place a question mark before any number that, in your opinion, does not belong in a paragraph or seems out of order.

4.   Repeat stages 1 through 3 for the right-hand version.

5.   Using the evidence provided by your two summaries, decide which is the better version and write a paragraph justifying your decision.

(1) <u>Democracy is the easiest form of government because it permits all citizens a high degree of freedom.</u> (2) In a democracy, more than in any other form of government, they are free to think, talk, and worship as they please and, within wide limits, are free to engage in whatever kind of profession or career they are fitted for.

(1) <u>Democracy is the easiest form of government because it allows everyone to think and speak as he pleases.</u> (2) In a democracy voters have to make a choice between rival political candidates and the policies they stand for. (3) To do this they must be well informed on the issues. (4) They can choose any occupation

(3) <u>But democracy does not merely grant privileges; it also makes demands.</u> (4) It places on people the responsibility of being continually informed of the country's needs. (5) It requires them to decide which of several conflicting policies will best meet these needs. (6) It demands that they distinguish between the interests of special groups and the general welfare. (7) It insists that they learn to observe the will of the majority without ignoring the rights of minorities. (8) And it constantly imposes the difficult task of sensing the effect that present policies will have in the lives of their children.

they want, and can join any church, or none at all. (5) <u>But they must do what is best for the country, not just for their own benefit or for some special area or interest.</u> (6) In a democracy people have more freedom than in any other country. (7) They need a good education to know what is right, not only for them but for their children as well. (8) Democracy is the most difficult form of government because it makes great demands on people. (9) A good citizen must respect the rights of others, but he must obey the will of the majority, because that is what democracy is: government of the people by the people.

B. Following are two contrasted paragraphs. The one at the right is a revision of the one at the left, made to obtain greater coherence. First, contrast the two versions sentence by sentence, and make notes on each change in the revised paragraph. Then, group your notes into major types of changes. Finally, write a short paper that explains the reason for the major changes.

(1) On Bourbon Street in the French Quarter of New Orleans there are a fifty-cent peep show and a theater that shows pornographic movies. (2) Pictures painted by talented artists are for sale in a shop down the street. (3) Canned music blares through doors held partly open by hustlers of strip-joints. (4) There is a concert hall with no doors and no admission fee, where the crowd is entertained by jazz musicians. (5) In some places there are "dancing girls" who just walk across the stage and do "bumps" in what is supposed to be a dance routine. (6) Sometimes there is a young woman who dances gracefully. (7) She has mastered the techniques that the better burlesques made popular in earlier years.

(1) Bourbon Street in the French Quarter of New Orleans is a contrast of vulgarity and art. (2) Just a few doors down the street from a fifty-cent peep show and a theater that presents pornographic movies is a shop displaying for sale paintings by talented artists. (3) At strip-joints canned music blares out from doors kept ajar by hustlers seeking to entice passers-by; yet not far away is a concert hall with no admission fee, where musicians play first-rate jazz. (4) Even the "dancing girls" offer a sharp contrast: most limit themselves to a slow walk across the stage, interrupted by exaggerated "bumps"; but a few gracefully demonstrate the techniques that once made burlesque dancing at its best an art form.

6

SENTENCES:
PATTERNS
OF
EXPRESSION

As you have seen in the last chapter, the sentences in a paragraph are not isolated statements. They are related to what has gone before and to what follows. Although it is traditional to call sentences units of composition, they are units chiefly in the grammatical sense that each sentence has its own subject and predicate and is not part of another sentence. In this chapter we will consider how sentences are constructed and revised to make them effective expressions of ideas. We will begin with three types of sentences: *standard, balanced,* and *periodic.*

THE STANDARD SENTENCE

The standard sentence, sometimes called the "loose" or "cumulative" sentence, is considered standard partly because it is by far the most common, and partly because all other types are derived from its basic subject-predicate pattern. The core of a standard sentence is its main clause expressed in its simplest form. This core or basic sentence consists of a subject and predicate. The predicate may be a complete verb or a verb that needs something to complete it. For example, in the first of the following sentences the italicized verb is complete in itself; in the other two the verb needs something to make a complete predicate:

The dog + *barked.*

The dog + *bit* + the letter carrier.

The dog + *was* + vicious.

EXPANDING BASIC SENTENCES

All such basic sentences can be expanded by three grammatical processes (called *modification, subordination,* and *coordination*) that will be explained in the following pages.

Modification   Any element in a basic sentence may be modified by adjectives, adverbs, phrases, or clauses that describe or limit the words being modified. In the following sentences the modifiers are in parentheses and are connected by arrows to the words they modify:

(Stray) dogs are becoming a (serious) nuisance (in our neighborhood.)

(About two o'clock in the morning) we were awakened by a (loud) quarrel (between a man and a woman) (in the next motel room.)

By modifying any part or all of a main clause, a writer can enrich a sentence by specific details. You saw earlier in this book that such details improve the quality of writing by making it less general and more specific. This kind of specification can be introduced into sentences by modification, as the italicized modifiers in the following sentences show:

Somehow my strongest memories of San Francisco are of me in a rented sedan *roaring up hills or down hills, sliding on and off the cable-car tracks.* (Tom Wolfe)

I debated whether I should join a sorority *so early in the term before I knew what college would be like for a small-town girl who was relatively unsophisticated.*

The drug companies, *usually operating through private physicians with access to the prisons,* can obtain healthy human subjects *living in conditions that are difficult, if not impossible, to duplicate elsewhere.* (Jessica Mitford)

. . . Few travelers will find a better-appointed airport than Amsterdam's Schiphol—*clean, white, modern, uncrowded, and equipped with one of the best-appointed, free-port shopping areas in the world.* (Horace Sutton)

In sentences like these, the effect comes not from the main clause, which is too general to provide specific communication, but from the information provided in the italicized modifiers. This can easily be seen by isolating the main clauses from the italicized detail in the fully developed sentences above:

My strongest memories of San Francisco are of me in a rented sedan.

I debated whether I should join a sorority.

The drug companies can obtain healthy human subjects.

Few travelers will find a better-appointed airport than Amsterdam's Schiphol.

It is important to recognize that the modifying statements in the fully developed sentences are not merely extras tacked onto the main clause during the writing. They are essential parts of what the writers wanted to say. For example, a significant part of Tom Wolfe's memory of San Francisco was the way his car slid on and off the cable-car tracks; the student's debate about joining a sorority included the question whether it was wise for a girl like her to join so early in the term; Horace Sutton's satisfaction with the airport at Amsterdam was based on the details he listed. These sentences illustrate that modification is a way of thinking. The modifications had to occur in the writers' thinking before they could appear in the sentences. In a standard sentence we first state a general idea in the main clause and then refine it through modification into a complete expression of our thought.

The following sentences illustrate this procedure by italicizing the main clause and putting a double slash between successive modifiers.

Mr. Tanimoto is a small man, // quick to talk, laugh, and cry. (John Hersey)

A cat can forecast rain, // according to an old story, // by sitting with its back to the door // or lying on its back with the top of its head flat on the floor.

The world's sentimental attachment to the Danube is vicarious, // through a waltz that is lilting and haunting // sweet and bittersweet: // in a word, enduring.

EXERCISE   The following sentences are incomplete communications. Unless the context in which they occurred made them clear, they would say little to a reader. Make them more informative by expanding them to include answers to the parenthetical questions. The first sentence illustrates the method.

1.   His attitude is indefensible. (Which attitude and why?)

His attitude toward women's rights is indefensible, because he either cannot or will not re-examine his nineteenth-century stereotypes about men and women and their relationships in a modern society.

2.   By Super Bowl time, professional football has become boring. (Why?)

3.   Memories made me homesick. (What kind?)

4.   College students should be given more responsibility. (For what?)

5.   Some people charge that beauty contests are sexist. (Why?)

6.   I am very hopeful about the outcome. (What outcome and why?)

7.   There is a double standard on this campus. (What kind?)

8.   He walked toward me. (How?)

9.   The CBS (or NBC or ABC) evening news program is the best of its kind. (Why?)

10.   The illusion was broken. (What illusion and how broken?)

Subordination   Subordination is a way of reducing one sentence to a clause or a phrase so that it can be included as part of another sentence. For example, the second of the two basic sentences

We left early. We had work to do.

may be included in the first as a subordinate clause:

We left early *because we had work to do.*

Or a basic sentence may be reduced to a phrase, as happens when we change

The man was evidently in great pain. He was taken to a hospital.

to

The man, *evidently in great pain,* was taken to a hospital.

As these examples show, subordination combines the information of two sentences into one by embedding one sentence in the other. Clearly the revised sentence contains more information than either of the original sentences alone. We say it is "denser," which is simply a short way of saying that it contains more information.

Within limits, the ability to convey more information within a sentence comes with maturity. Investigators have discovered a correlation between the length of sentences and the age of the writer. In one study, for example, the average length of sentences written by fourth-grade students was found to be 13.5 words, compared with 16.9 words for twelfth graders and 24.7 words for adults writing in such magazines as *Harper's.** This comparison does not mean that all short sentences are necessarily immature, since adult writers, including professionals, often use them for emphasis and variety. But the consistent use of basic sentences in a sustained piece of writing is more common among children than among adults.

The following example illustrates the conversion of four immature sentences into one mature sentence through subordination:

1.   Last summer I camped for a week in Canada.
2.   Three friends were with me.
3.   We camped on the shore of a small lake.
4.   The lake was fifty miles from the nearest settlement.

Last summer three friends and I camped for a week on the shore of a small Canadian lake fifty miles from the nearest settlement.

The original four sentences took 32 words; the revised sentence expresses exactly the same information in 24 words, thus saving one-quarter of the space and getting rid of the monotony of the immature sentences. These results were achieved by subordinating sentences 2, 3, and 4, by making them phrases and embedding them in the first sentence.

EXERCISES

A.   To get practice in building denser sentences through subordination, reduce each of the following sets of sentences to a single sentence without omitting any of the information.

1.   We bought a sturdy old farmhouse.

   I had always wanted the rustic country life.

   The house was a mile out of town.

2.   State University won the Valley Tournament.

   State University's Karl Winster scored 35 points.

   He is all-conference.

   The game went into overtime.

   The score was 98–94.

   The game was played last night.

* Kellogg W. Hunt, *Grammatical Structures Written at Three Grade Levels* (National Council of Teachers of English, Research Report No. 3, 1965), p. 56.

3.   A railroad signal was faulty.

An express ploughed into the rear of a freight train.

The accident happened last night.

Five people were killed and fifty were injured.

B.   Take any paper you have written and see whether you can improve it by combining several short sentences that appear in it into denser ones.

Coordination   Coordination is the combining of similar elements into pairs or series. Instead of writing

Wire-tapping is one kind of invasion of privacy. Breaking-and-entering is another.

we can combine the two sentences into one by compounding the subjects and giving them a common predicate.

Wire-tapping and breaking-and-entering are both invasions of privacy.

Instead of writing

At the army surplus sale a shovel could be bought for a dollar. A compass cost a dollar. A dollar would buy a trench knife.

we can combine the subjects in a series and give them all the same predicate.

At the army surplus sale a shovel, a compass, and a trench knife could be bought for a dollar each.

EXERCISES   **A.**   Reduce each of the following groups of sentences to a single sentence by combining parts through coordination:

1.   Many young people cannot afford college tuition.

The expense of living away from home also keeps them from going to college.

2.   Energy consumption is a major problem in this country.

Inflation also causes us much trouble.

3.   Journalism is an overcrowded field just now.

Currently there are more licensed secondary school teachers than there are positions.

The legal profession is overcrowded.

4. The camp director warned us against trying to shoot the rapids.

   Our class sponsor reminded us of the danger involved.

   A native of the area told us the same thing.

5. The prisoner lost 65 pounds by fasting.

   Then he escaped from his cell through a small skylight.

   After that he fled the state.

B. Using either subordination or coordination, reduce the following nine sentences to not more than three without omitting any of the information:

Last night the Minnesota Twins and the Boston Red Sox were playing a baseball game at the Twins' park.

An unidentified person phoned the police.

He reported that a bomb had been placed under the stands.

In the middle of the fourth inning the game was stopped.

An announcement of the bomb report was made to the crowd.

The police cleared the stands and searched for the bomb.

They did not find one.

The fans were allowed to return to their seats.

The game was resumed after a total delay of 45 minutes.

COMBINING SENTENCES

In combining basic sentences into denser patterns through coordination and subordination, you have a wide choice of combinations and should choose those that best suit your purpose. Suppose you have the following pieces of information:

a. Small foreign cars could be produced at less cost than the larger cars made in the United States.

b. Foreign-made cars captured a significant share of the American market.

c. American manufacturers began to produce compacts to compete with the foreign cars.

d. In 1972 the U.S. dollar was devalued on the international exchange.

e. The price of a foreign car to an American buyer rose proportionately.

f. Compacts made in the United States could now be sold for less than small foreign cars.

If you want to show the process by which the automobile industry responded to foreign competition, you can reduce *a* to a subordinate clause and embed it in *b,* thus getting the sentence:

Because small foreign cars could be produced at less cost than the larger cars made in the United States, they captured a significant share of the American market.

You can now add to what you have, with a slight change in word order.

To compete with foreign cars, American manufacturers began to produce compacts.

You can repeat a similar procedure with *d, e,* and *f* to get the sentence:

When in 1972 the U.S. dollar was devalued on the international exchange, the price of a foreign car to an American buyer rose proportionately, and the American compacts could now be sold for less than the foreign ones.

But if your purpose is to show how devaluing the dollar affected the American domestic market, you can combine the original sentences as follows:

The 1972 devaluation of the U.S. dollar on the international exchange caused foreign-made products to cost more in the United States and thus gave American manufacturers an advantage over their foreign competitors. For example, the small foreign economy cars, the low price of which previously had forced American car-makers to produce the compact, now had to be sold in the United States at prices higher than those of compact cars made in America.

In this version the material of the original is rearranged to form a two-sentence paragraph, of which the first sentence is the topic sentence and the second an illustration. The emphasis is no longer on the steps of a process but on the effect of devaluation. The means of achieving that emphasis are still subordination and coordination.

The three devices we have been studying—modification, subordination, and coordination—can be thought of as techniques for processing material into mature sentences. Organizing ideas into efficient form is just as important in a sentence as in an outline or a paragraph. In immature sentences each idea is stated separately; the writer sets down one idea after another but does nothing to combine them into a denser, more coherent pattern. The ideas may all be there, but the relationships among them are not as clear as they should be. Moreover, immature sentences do not provide purposeful emphasis, since they do not distinguish between more and less important information: everything is treated as if it were equally important. By subordinating the less important to the more important, or by showing the equality of ideas through coordination, mature sentences give appropriate emphasis. They not only reduce monotony by providing more variety in the sentence structure, but they often provide better coherence.

USING PARALLEL STRUCTURES

When two or more coordinate elements have the same form, we say they have *parallel structure.* Parallel structures may occur unnoticed in any sentence, but when the parallelism is conspicuous the whole sentence may be called a *parallel sentence.* Thus, "He was without a job, without money, without opportunity, and without hope" is a parallel sentence in which the four phrases have the same form (they all start with *without*) and the same grammatical function (they all complete the verb *was*).

This sort of repetition of parallel elements can be effective in either a sentence or a paragraph. Consider these contrasted sentences:

I am in favor of equal economic rights for women. Women should be able to compete with men for jobs for which they are both qualified. The pay should be the same for the same jobs. There should be the same opportunities for promotion.	I am in favor of equal economic rights for women: the right to compete with men for jobs for which they are both qualified, the right to get the same pay for the same job, and the right to equal opportunities for promotion.

Both versions assert the same three rights. The version at the left advances these assertions through four sentences, each of which has a different subject. The version at the right states all three rights in one sentence and focuses the reader's attention on rights by the repetition of the phrase "the right to" throughout the sentence. The parallel structure of the second version gives it a unity, a coherence, and an emphasis that the first version lacks.

Parallel elements always have the same form and grammatical function. They may be single words, phrases, or clauses; they may act as subjects, objects, verbs, or adverbial or adjectival modifiers. But in a pair or series of coordinate elements all members must be of the same kind. We cannot coordinate nouns with adjectives, verbs with infinitives, or phrases with clauses. Any such attempt would break the parallelism that coordinate structures require and would thus disappoint the reader's expectation and result in awkwardness.

For example, in each of the following sentences the italicized element breaks the parallelism of the sentence by switching from one grammatical form to another:

The children were laughing, squealing, and *danced.*

(The sentence requires an *-ing* form, *dancing.* The switch from *laughing* and *squealing* to *danced* breaks the parallelism of the sentence.)

My two ambitions are to own my own business and *having* enough money to give my children a good education.

(Parallelism requires *to have* to go with *to own.*)

My parents taught me such things as honesty, faith, *to be fair,* and *having patience.*

(The first two elements in the series are nouns, the third is an infinitive, the fourth is a participle. Parallelism with the first two elements would be maintained by the nouns *fairness* and *patience.*)

The diagrams in the following sentences set off the parallel structures to show their similarity in form and function:

1. parallel predicates

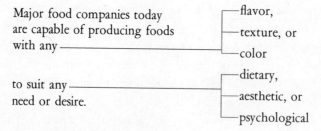

2. a series of nouns followed by another series of adjectives

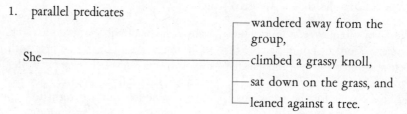

3. a series of prepositional phrases

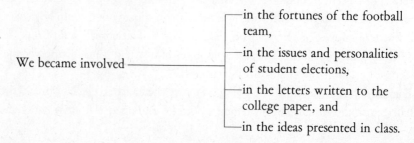

4. a series of compound prepositional phrases

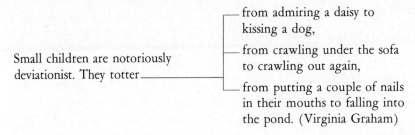

Small children are notoriously deviationist. They totter

- from admiring a daisy to kissing a dog,
- from crawling under the sofa to crawling out again,
- from putting a couple of nails in their mouths to falling into the pond. (Virginia Graham)

5. a series of objects of the preposition *of*

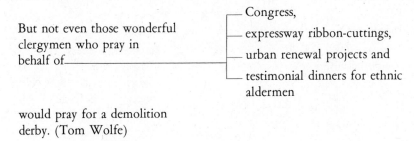

But not even those wonderful clergymen who pray in behalf of

- Congress,
- expressway ribbon-cuttings,
- urban renewal projects and
- testimonial dinners for ethnic aldermen

would pray for a demolition derby. (Tom Wolfe)

6. parallel subordinate clauses as objects of the infinitive *to realize*

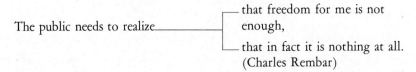

The public needs to realize

- that freedom for me is not enough,
- that in fact it is nothing at all. (Charles Rembar)

7. a series of infinitive phrases followed by a series of participial phrases

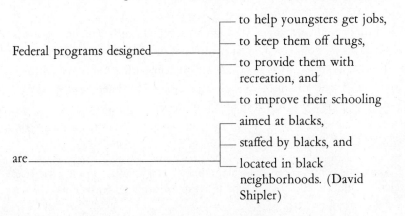

Federal programs designed

- to help youngsters get jobs,
- to keep them off drugs,
- to provide them with recreation, and
- to improve their schooling

are

- aimed at blacks,
- staffed by blacks, and
- located in black neighborhoods. (David Shipler)

EXERCISES   The following exercises will give you practice in recognizing and using parallel sentences.

A.   To identify and point up the parallelism in the following sentences, diagram the parallel elements as shown in the examples above.

1.   We hold these truths to be self-evident: that all men are created equal, that they are endowed by their Creator with certain unalienable Rights. . . .

2.   The book is full of stories of sinking ships and burning towns, of killing cold and windlashed waves, and of reckless men engaged in dangerous pursuits.

B.   Organize the following notes into parallel sentences by coordinating the notes in series.

1. **Big cars**	but	**Small cars**
More powerful		Repairs cost less
Comfortable		Easy parking
Prestigious		Purchase price relatively low
Safer in a crash		Better gas mileage

2.   **Watching football on TV**
　　　Close-up of details of action
　　　Expert commentators
　　　Explanations of what happened
　　　Replays
　　　Comfort

C.   Using the notes in B2 as a model, list the advantages of watching football in the stadium; then using B1 as a model, write a parallel sentence that contrasts the relative advantages of watching a football game on television and in the stadium.

D.   To get additional practice in writing parallel sentences, write three or four such sentences on subjects of your own choosing.

When parallelism is extended through a paragraph, each sentence becomes an element in a series. You have seen an example of such a series of parallel sentences in the paragraph on page 108 in which Dr. Martin Luther King carried through the paragraph a series of sentences, each beginning with "There is nothing. . . ." It was pointed out then that this kind of deliberate repetition provides the coherence that ties the individual sentences into a repetitive whole. Here is another example. Do you recognize conspicuous parallelism in it?

H. G. Wells continues to be a biographer's dream and a book reviewer's waltz. His life stretches very nearly from Appomattox to Hiroshima. He was one of the world's great storytellers, the father of modern science fiction, an autobiographic novelist of scandalous proportions, a proselytizer for world peace through brain power, an unsurpassed popular historian, a journalist and inexhaustible pamphleteer, the friend and worthy adversary of great men and the lover of numerous beautiful and intelligent women. (R. Z. Sheppard, *Time*)

THE BALANCED SENTENCE

A *balanced sentence* is one in which two parallel structures are set off against each other like the weights on a balance scale. In each of the following sentences the italicized parts illustrate the balance:

Many are called but *few are chosen.* (Matthew 22:14)

Beauty without grace is *the hook without the bait.* (Ralph Waldo Emerson)

We undertook this project *to promote intercollegiate debate,* not *to kill it.*

The test of our progress is not whether we add more to the abundance of those who have much; it is whether we provide enough for those who have too little. (Franklin D. Roosevelt)

In reading these sentences aloud, one tends to pause between the balanced parts. That pause is marked often by a coordinating conjunction (*and, but, or, nor, yet*), sometimes by *not* (as in the third sentence), and sometimes by punctuation alone (as in the fourth sentence). Whatever the marker, it serves as the fulcrum, the point at which the two parts balance against each other, as the following diagram shows:

but

| When a man dies on shore, his body remains with his friends, and the "mourners go about the streets," | when a man falls overboard at sea and is lost, there is a suddenness in the event . . . which gives it an air of awful mystery. (Richard Henry Dana) |

Here the similarity of thought and sentence structure on both sides of the conjunction sets up an equilibrium between the parts.

Although the balanced sentence is not limited to establishing a contrast, that is its most frequent use. It is an effective structure to use when, as in an alternating comparison, two subjects are being contrasted within the same sentence. It was used this way in the diagrammed example above, where the balanced structure points up the contrast.

THE PERIODIC SENTENCE

A *periodic sentence* is one that builds up, often through two or more parallel constructions, to a climactic statement in the final main clause. The italicized sentence below will introduce the structure:

> Just before I went away to college, my father took me aside, as I had expected, and said, as I had not expected, *"Now, Son, if a strange woman comes up to you on a street corner and offers to take your watch around the corner and have it engraved, don't do it."* (Eric Lax)

The father's remarks lead up to the advice of the final main clause—"don't do it"—which provides a climax, like the punch line of a joke. All the rest of the sentence has been preparation for that statement.

Here is another, more serious, example written by a student, in which the main clause is preceded by a long participial phrase ("Having reached . . .") that includes a subordinate clause.

> Having reached the murky grass flats of Tampa Bay, that place where under the hot sun and in rain squalls my father had so patiently taught me the unity of pain and beauty, I climbed over the side of the boat and scattered his ashes over the water.

One more example:

> Unless we maintain the pure traditional meaning of the word [*freedom*], unless we can understand in common and as a nation that the only opinion established in this country by the Constitution is the opinion that a man is free to hold *any* opinion, unless we can agree among ourselves that by freedom we mean *precisely* freedom, we may end by finding ourselves "free" in the sense in which the Russians now find themselves "democratic." (Archibald MacLeish)

The structure of this sentence consists of three parallel subordinate clauses followed by the main clause, which contains a subordinate clause. The full revelation of the meaning is withheld until the final comparison. The sentence says, in effect, "Unless this and this and this happen, this will happen."

A standard sentence usually begins with a main clause; a periodic sentence ends with one. In this sense the periodic sentence reverses the standard order. But the difference between them is more than a change in order. There are also differences in procedure and effect. In a standard sentence a writer may work out the sentence while writing it, starting with the main clause and clarifying it by adding necessary modifications. But in a periodic sentence the writer must know from the beginning how it will end. For example, the writer of the following sentence is moving toward his main clause through a series of *if* clauses that successively deal with life, liberty, and the pursuit of happiness, and what he has to say about each of these subjects must be chosen for its contribution to the idea of the main clause.

> But if life hardly seems worth living, if liberty is used for subhuman purposes, if the pursuers of happiness know nothing about the nature of their quarry or the elementary techniques of hunting, these constitutional rights will not be very meaningful. (Aldous Huxley)

As these examples show, a periodic sentence allows a writer to put unusual emphasis on the main clause by holding it off until the end.

In the following sentence the main idea Norman Mailer wants to communicate is that Marilyn Monroe was a complex individual whose apparent inconsistencies were a reflection of her complexity. That purpose requires him to construct a brief argument in which selected inconsistencies are resolved as effects of an underlying cause—her complex but integrated personality.

> The boldness with which she could parade herself and yet never be gross, her sexual flamboyance and bravado which yet breathed an air of mystery and even reticence, her voice which carried such ripe overtones of erotic excitement and yet was the voice of a shy child—these complications were integral to her gift. (Norman Mailer)

Mailer could have written this sentence in standard order, starting with the main clause and following it with the series of apparent inconsistencies. But had he done so, the force of the main clause would have been weakened. A reader would have left the sentence, not with a statement about integrated complexity, but with a series of contrasting details about Marilyn Monroe's sexuality and innocence. By using a periodic rather than a standard structure, Mailer could put his conclusion where it would have the greatest force, at the end of the sentence. If you doubt this statement, try writing the sentence in standard order; or observe the difference in effect when the following sentence is written in standard order:

> From breakfast to lunch, from lunch to dinner, from dinner to midnight snack, he is thinking of only one thing, the next meal.

EXERCISE   To test your ability to recognize and write periodic sentences, write a paragraph in which, in your own words, you explain the structure of a periodic sentence and illustrate it by examples that you yourself have written.

REVISING SENTENCES

So far in this chapter we have been concerned with the structure of different types of sentences and with techniques for increasing the density of sentences through modification, coordination, and subordination. In this section we will deal with the practical problem of revising sentences to make them more effective expressions of the ideas they are intended to convey. Much of the time, of course, a writer revises sentences while writing them. The process of shaping ideas into sentences is a learning process, and writers will make changes in sentence structure and wording as they grope toward a satisfactory statement of their ideas. But here we will be dealing with sentences that have already been written and will be trying to see how to improve them. The revisions we will stress are those that improve the *clarity, emphasis, economy,* and *variety* of the writing.

Because of the difficulty of seeing your own writing objectively as a reader will see it, we suggest that while you are revising your first draft, you think of yourself as an editor, as someone who is not expressing his or her own ideas but is examining someone else's writing to see how it can be improved. In this section we will be editing sentences by first detecting their weaknesses and then removing them. The experience you gain from this practice should make it easier for you to edit your own sentences.

REVISION FOR CLARITY

Lack of clarity can be a result of faulty grammar or punctuation, misleading pronoun reference, vague or ambiguous wording, or confusing sentence structure. Since we are dealing with sentence structure here, we will emphasize the lack of clarity that sometimes occurs when a writer tries to pack too much information into one sentence. The following example will introduce this problem:

Last month while I was visiting the federal buildings in Washington on a guided tour, we went to the National Art Gallery, where we had been for an hour when the rest of the group was ready to move on to the Treasury Building and I told a friend with the group that I wanted to stay in the Art

Gallery a while longer and I would rejoin the group about half an hour later, but I never did, even though I moved more quickly than I wanted to from room to room, not having seen after about four hours all that there was to see.

As written, this sentence of 106 words consists of three main clauses and eight subordinate clauses. This involved structure is hard going for both writer and reader. The revision should seek to simplify the structure by reducing the number of clauses per sentence. This can be done by either or both of two methods: by distributing the clauses into two or more sentences, or by omitting material not necessary to the statement. The second method depends on the writer's view of what is necessary.

There are several ways of revising the sentence. Let us consider two.

While I was visiting the National Art Gallery with a tour group last month, I decided to stay longer when the group left after an hour, and so I told a friend that I would rejoin the group at the Treasury Building in about half an hour. I moved from room to room much more quickly than I wanted to, but after four hours I still had not seen all there was to see. I never did rejoin the tour group that day.

This revision distributes all the original material into three sentences and makes the passage easier to read. In addition, the revision saves twenty-three words, a reduction of 20 percent.

The following revision cuts the original drastically by leaving out material not considered significant:

While visiting the National Art Gallery with a tour group last month, I stayed for four hours after the group left. Even then I did not see all I wanted to.

This version reduces the original eleven clauses to four and condenses the 106-word sentence to 31 words in two sentences.

Both revisions are clearer than the original. The first revision may be considered minor, since it makes little change in content. The second revision is major, since it selects and reorganizes the content. Between these minor and major revisions, others are possible. Try a few variations to see which you prefer.

Notice that the revisions above reduce the amount of information in the original sentence. This statement may seem to contradict what was said earlier about combining sentences to increase their density. But there is no contradiction. Some sentences should be combined to achieve greater density; others should be simplified by rewriting one sentence as two or three. The decision to combine or to separate, to enrich or to simplify, depends on the material and the writer's best judgment of how to present it to the reader.

EXERCISE   Simplify the structure of the following sentences to make them easier to read:

1. His sister, who had been living in Springfield, where she had been directing a child-service program that screened reports of child abuse and made referrals to case workers, having been appointed to a position in the Department of Health, Education, and Welfare, because she had performed so ably at the local level, has recently moved to Washington.

2. For several years controversy has centered upon a commonly used herbicide called 2-4-5-T, with producers insisting that it is not harmful to humans but with independent researchers saying there is evidence that it can contribute to miscarriages and development of cancer, among other problems, in people exposed to it, and the controversy has been highly publicized recently because the herbicide is similar in its chemical make-up to the defoliant used by the American military in Vietnam that is now suspected of causing cancer and other serious diseases in people who were exposed to it there.

3. My father has a friend who insists that he is dirt poor and I suppose that in a sense he is because he invests almost all of his extra income in land, since he says he can't afford to put it in the bank because inflation decreases the value of his money more than interest increases it and he doesn't want to be bothered with the problems that go along with rental property and he isn't interested in stocks and bonds, all of which causes him to buy land on the theory that no more land is being made and that the only way its value can go is to keep rising.

REVISION FOR EMPHASIS

Emphasis is a reflection of a writer's purpose and helps make that purpose clear to readers. There are usually several ways of expressing any idea, and if one way gives greater emphasis than others to what a writer wants to stress, that is the best way. Three ways of obtaining purposeful emphasis are *emphatic word order* (including *climactic order*), *emphatic repetition,* and *emphatic voice.*

Emphatic word order   The way word order is used for emphasis in a sentence depends on two considerations: What does the writer wish to emphasize? And what positions within a sentence provide the most emphasis? In an English sentence, both the beginning and the end are emphatic positions. The most important material is put in these positions, and less important material is placed in the middle. If unimportant details pile up at the end of a sentence, they may get more emphasis than they deserve, and readers may feel that the sentence is "running down" because they expect important information at the end and do not get it.

Notice the difference between the following statements:

Unemphatic order	Emphatic order
On July 31, 1973, a plane crash which killed 88 people and which was the first fatal crash for Delta Airlines in 95 billion passenger miles occurred at Boston's Logan International Airport.	Eighty-eight people were killed in a plane crash at Boston's Logan International Airport on July 31, 1973, the first fatal crash for Delta Airlines in 95 billion passenger miles.

The version at the left puts the date and place in the most emphatic positions in the sentence (the beginning and the end) and the number killed and Delta's impressive safety record in the least emphatic position. The version at the right puts the most significant information where it will get the greatest emphasis and fills in the middle with the place and date.

Here is another example:

Unemphatic order	Emphatic order
Much debate focused on the effect that the Supreme Court's Bakke decision would have on affirmative action programs in years to come.	The Supreme Court's Bakke decision caused much debate about the future of affirmative action programs.

The two parts of the sentence that deserve most emphasis are "Supreme Court's Bakke decision" and "affirmative action programs." Unlike the version at the left, the version at the right places these two phrases in the most emphatic positions in the sentence, the beginning and the end.

Revise the following sentences by changing the order to emphasize the parts you think important: **EXERCISE**

1. He said that the UN had failed in its chief function, to preserve peace, although it had done much of which it could be proud and was still performing valuable services in many areas.

2. It is entirely possible that morality consists chiefly in the courage of making a choice, I sometimes think.

3. A decision that has caused much concern about censorship is the one about pornography that the Supreme Court made recently.

4.   A problem that is important to our environment, noise pollution, is one that we have only recently given much attention to.

5.   He was accused of cheating and was expelled from college by the Disciplinary Committee yesterday afternoon at a meeting.

6.   The governor said that he had considered the arguments for and against a stay of execution and was in favor of mercy when everything was taken into account.

7.   The doctor told me I could eat anything I pleased except animal fats while I was on this diet.

8.   Thomas Marshall, Vice President under Woodrow Wilson, expressed our traditional neglect of the men in that office when he said, "If you're not coming in, throw me a peanut," to visitors looking curiously through his doorway.

9.   In 1978 Proposition 13, which served as a stimulus for a nationwide concern about reducing taxes, was approved by the voters of California.

10.   We can be sure that a reduction in taxes is what most political candidates will promise.

11.   Though he hit the ball to the right-field wall, Pete Rose was called "Out!" after he rounded first and second and dived into third base in a head-first slide.

12.   The situation faced by hundreds of American travelers stranded at the London airport was, because of the decreased value of the dollar, a quite serious one.

Climactic order   Climactic word order is a form of emphatic order that arranges the material of a sentence so as to build up to a major idea. We have seen that the force of the periodic sentence comes from this order, but climax may also be used in standard sentences. The following examples contrast anticlimactic and climactic order. Study both versions of each sentence and explain what changes were made in the revisions.

Anticlimactic order

Near the end of *A Separate Peace,* Dr. Stanpole says to Gene that he must tell him that his best friend Finny is dead, the sort of news that the doctor fears the boys of Gene's generation will hear much of.

In a magnificent stretch run the favorite overtook six horses and won by a nose, thrilling the crowd.

Climactic order

Near the end of *A Separate Peace,* Dr. Stanpole tells Gene that he must give him the sort of news he fears the boys of Gene's generation will hear much of, that Gene's best friend Finny is dead.

In a magnificent stretch run that thrilled the crowd, the favorite overtook six horses and won by a nose.

The prosecution asked in its summing up that the jury bring in a verdict of guilty, which was the only possible verdict considering the violence of the crime and the lack of provocation.	In summing up, the prosecution asked the jury to consider the violence of the crime and the lack of provocation and then bring in the only possible verdict—guilty.

Emphatic repetition   More often than not, unintentional repetition weakens a sentence, as the following examples show:

> Psychotic patients suffering from psychoses are sometimes hospitalized in hospitals operated especially for them.

> The writer who wrote the novel that won the prize for the best novel of the year did not attend the awards ceremony.

> The disappointing results were all the more disappointing because we were sure that the experiment would be a success, and so were disappointed in the results.

Intentional repetition, by contrast, can produce a desired emphasis. We have seen that repeated key words can help knit a paragraph together (page 108) and that the repetition of sentence structure through parallel and balanced elements creates desirable emphasis (page 129). Deliberate repetition, therefore, can be effective. Consider the following:

> If at first you don't succeed, *try, try* again.

> And this hell was, simply, that he had never in his life owned anything—*not* his wife, *not* his house, *not* his child—which could not, at any instant, be taken from him by the power of white people. (James Baldwin)

> It is easy to find scapegoats for the pollution problem: to *blame* the industrialist, to *blame* the scientist, to *blame* advertising or capitalism, or in one comprehensive condemnation, to *blame* society; but everyone who drives a car or burns electricity or flushes a toilet has a share of the *blame;* it is not *blaming* that is needed, but a conscientious and consistent attempt to make *blame* unnecessary.

Emphatic voice   It is common in composition courses to urge students to use verbs in the active rather than the passive voice. This advice is generally sound, because the active voice is usually more natural and the so-called weak passive sometimes leads to wordiness and awkward shifts in structure.

Weak passive	**More emphatic active**
Fashion design majors modeled the outfits that had been made by them during the term.	Fashion design majors modeled the outfits they had made during the term.

The length of the lake was swum by the six candidates for life-saving certificates.

The six candidates for life-saving certificates swam the length of the lake.

Thirty miles of rough road had been traveled before we realized that the tent had been forgotten.

We had traveled thirty miles of rough road before we realized that we had forgotten the tent.

EXERCISE   Revise the following sentences by changing passive verbs to the active voice:

1.   Once the danger was gone, the safety precautions that had been so carefully observed by us were abandoned.

2.   An almost perfect game was pitched by Vida Blue.

3.   It was estimated by the garage mechanic that $200 would be needed for the repairs.

4.   A local women's club was spoken to by Gloria Steinem about the feminist movement.

5.   The path to the bottom of the canyon was descended by everyone in our group.

6.   Gun control laws have been persistently opposed by the National Rifle Association.

7.   A touchdown was scored by each of our running backs during the game.

8.   He was not prepared for the test and so only half of the questions were answered.

9.   The instructor said the papers would be graded and returned by him within three days.

10.   It must surely be recognized by the American Hospital Association that such costs cannot be afforded by many families.

But there are situations in which the passive voice is more emphatic than the active. The beginning of a sentence is, as we have seen, a position of stress, and putting an unimportant word or phrase there tends to emphasize it—sometimes unwisely. For example:

The letter carrier delivers mail twice a day.

A person cannot smoke in this section of the plane.

People should expect some delay in these circumstances.

Someone stole her car from the parking lot.

The doctor performed the emergency surgery under battery-operated lights.

In these sentences the stress should not fall on the grammatical subjects, which are of almost no interest. Passive constructions, ignoring these subjects entirely, give more accurate emphasis:

Mail is delivered twice a day.

Smoking is prohibited in this section of the plane.

In these circumstances some delay is to be expected.

Her car was stolen from the parking lot.

The emergency surgery was performed under battery-operated lights.

The choice between active and passive is like any other choice a writer has to make. It is to be judged by the results: which form will give the emphasis the writer wants? But because misuse of the passive voice often results in an awkward or ungrammatical sentence, it is wise to choose the active voice unless there is a clear gain from using the passive.

REVISION FOR ECONOMY

Economy is a relation between the number of words used and the amount of meaning they convey. A sentence is not economical because it is short, or wordy because it is long. The test is not the number of words but the amount of information they convey. Consider these two statements:

I should like to make it entirely clear to one and all that neither I nor any of my associates or fellow workers had anything at all to do in any way, shape or form with this illicit and legally un-justifiable act that has been committed.	I want to make it clear to everyone that neither I nor any of my associates had anything to do with this illegal act.

The version at the left takes forty-six words to say what is more clearly said at the right in twenty-four. The extra words do not add any significant information; they merely make reading more difficult and annoy the reader by useless repetition of the same idea in different words.

Now contrast the following statements:

His defense is not believable.	His defense is not believable: at points it is contradicted by the unanimous testimony of other witnesses, and it offers no proof that that testimony is false; it ignores significant facts about which there can be no dispute, or evades them by saying that he does not recollect them; it contains incon-sistencies that he is unable to resolve, even when specifically asked to do so.

The version at the right contains over ten times as many words as the one at the left, but its greater length is justified by the greater information it provides. Both versions share a common judgment, but the second goes on to show the reasons for that judgment. If these reasons are necessary, it would be foolish to omit them simply to get a shorter sentence. Decisions about economy must always be made in relation to meaning.

Wordiness—the opposite of economy—is common in student writing. When a whole essay is wordy, the trouble may lie in scanty prewriting or in a monotonous style that could be tightened up by better use of coordination and subordination. Revision of these weaknesses requires complete rewriting. Here, however, we are considering only wordiness *within* a sentence, and revision is relatively easy. The two most common methods are cutting out useless words and substituting more economical expressions for wordy ones. Both methods are illustrated below.

Cutting out a useless introductory phrase

By way of response, He said he would think about it.

With reference to your question, I think we should accept the invitation.

It goes without saying that they certainly need help.

It seems unnecessary to point out that I was in Chicago at that time.

Cutting out useless words within the body of a sentence

As we walked in the direction of home, I felt as if I had never been happier.

The task of English teachers is to help students develop the ability to understand and communicate in their native language.

She looked as though she was angry.

The truth of the matter is/ to call a spade a spade/ that he is afraid of her.

Richard Wright was a person who became disillusioned with the Communist Party that was operating in America because of the fact that he felt that it was not sufficiently sensitive to the problems of most of the black Americans.

Substituting an economical statement for a wordy one

We find the situation that exists at the moment *present* intolerable.

I think the time has come for us to be leaving. *It is time to leave.*

The modern trend
~~The idea of communication has led the vanguard of the "New English." The~~
is to emphasize
~~emphasis now placed on~~ the teaching of linguistics ~~ties into the importance~~
as an aid to effective communication.
~~implied in teaching children to communicate effectively.~~
preceding the withdrawal of
The years ~~which preceded the~~ time ~~when~~ American troops ~~were withdrawn~~
of
from Vietnam were a time ~~when there was~~ much social and political unrest
~~among the people~~ in this country.

Revise the following sentences to reduce wordiness:

EXERCISE

1.   Often the words that he uses do not convey the meaning that he intends.

2.   She looked as though she was feeling indisposed.

3.   As far as the average citizen is concerned, it is probable that most people are not greatly concerned about the scandals of politicians.

4.   When we studied defense mechanisms, which we did in psychology class, I discovered that I use most of the mechanisms that are discussed in the textbook.

5.   Just before the time when World War I broke out, Alsatians who were of French descent were outraged by the act of a German soldier's slapping a cobbler who was lame across the face with a sword.

6.   Concerning the question of whether men are stronger than women, it seems to me that the answer is variable, depending on how one interprets the word *stronger.*

7.   When, after much careful and painstaking study of the many and various problems involved, experts in charge of the different phases of our space flight programs made the decision to send a rescue ship to bring back the astronauts who were in space in Skylab II, about a thousand people set to work at Cape Kennedy, each with his or her own duties to perform, to get the rescue ship ready to fly into space and bring back the astronauts.

REVISION FOR VARIETY

Logically, a discussion of variety in sentence structure belongs in a chapter on the paragraph, since variety is a characteristic not of single sentences but of a succession of sentences. But because we get variety through modification, coordination, subordination, and word order, we have postponed this discussion until this point in the sentence chapter.

Consider the following series of sentences:

1. Maxwell Perkins was born in 1884 and died in 1947.
2. He worked for Charles Scribner's Sons for thirty-seven years.
3. He was head editor for Scribner's for the last twenty of these thirty-seven years.
4. He was almost certainly the most important American editor in the first half of the twentieth century.
5. He worked closely with Thomas Wolfe, Scott Fitzgerald, and Ernest Hemingway.
6. He also worked closely with a number of other well-known writers.

These sentences are all of similar length (10, 9, 14, 17, 11, and 11 words respectively), and they are all standard sentences of the same basic structure (subject + predicate). Their lack of variety becomes monotonous.

Now contrast the same passage revised for variety:

> Maxwell Perkins (1884–1947), head editor of Charles Scribner's Sons for the last twenty of his thirty-seven years with that company, was almost certainly the most important American editor in the first half of the twentieth century. Among the many well-known writers with whom he worked closely were Thomas Wolfe, Scott Fitzgerald, and Ernest Hemingway.

The revision combines the original material into two sentences of thirty-seven and eighteen words respectively and results in greater economy (fifty-five words instead of seventy-two), greater density, and less monotony. These results were obtained by the following operations:

(1) Sentences 1, 2, 3, and 4 of the original were combined in the first revised sentence by

a. making Maxwell Perkins the subject of the new sentence.
b. placing his dates in parentheses.
c. reducing sentences 2 and 3 to a phrase in apposition with the subject of the new sentence.
d. making sentence 4 the complement of the new sentence.

(2) Sentences 5 and 6 of the original were combined by

a. having them share a common verb, *were.*
b. making sentence 6 the subject of that verb, and sentence 5 the complement.

Other revisions are possible. For example:

> Maxwell Perkins (1884–1947), who as head editor for Charles Scribner's Sons for twenty years worked closely with such well-known writers as Thomas Wolfe, Scott Fitzgerald, and Ernest Hemingway, was almost certainly the most important American editor in the first half of the twentieth century.

This version reduces the original to a single sentence by making the statement about Perkins's importance the main clause and embedding the rest in a subordinate clause between the subject and predicate of the main clause. Still other revisions are possible. The point is not that one revision is better than another, but that subordination and coordination can get rid of the obvious weakness of the original—its lack of variety.

EXERCISE

As an exercise in using the procedure above, first consider the possible revisions that follow the paragraph about Henry V. Then decide which of these possibilities you want to use in rewriting the paragraph. It is not necessary to use all the possibilities. Use those that give you the best paragraph.

For ease of reference the sentences are numbered.

> (1) Shakespeare's chronicle history of *Henry the Fifth* is a drama of kinghood and war. (2) It is essentially a play about a young king's coming of age. (3) Henry V had been an irresponsible young prince before his accession to the throne. (4) He had to prove his worthiness as king by leading his army in war. (5) He invaded France and captured Harfleur, and then tried to withdraw his troops to Calais. (6) He and his men were confronted by a numerically superior French army at Agincourt. (7) In a famous passage in Shakespeare's play, Henry urges his soldiers on to an incredible victory. (8) The superior mobility and firepower of the English proved too much for the heavily armored French.

The possible revisions

1. Combine 1 and 2 by omitting *is* in 1 and, with necessary punctuation, omitting *It* at the beginning of 2, thus making "a drama of kinghood and war" a phrase within the combined sentence. Write the sentence so formed.

2. Combine 3 and 4 by inserting a comma + *who* after *Henry V,* substituting a comma for the period at the end of 3, and omitting the *He* in 4. Write the sentence so formed.

3. Reduce the first half of 5 to a phrase, "After invading France and capturing Harfleur," and substitute *he* for *and then.*

4. Join 6 with 5 by *but* and change the *He* of 6 to *he*. Write the sentence thus revised.

5. Combine 8 and 7 by inserting *in which* after *victory* and making the necessary change in capitalization. Write the revised sentence.

6. Now, using any of these revised sentences, or any revisions of your own, rewrite the complete paragraph.

Here are three pieces of advice on sentence variety. First, *don't overdo it*. It is neither necessary nor wise to construct every sentence differently or to pack too much material into individual sentences. On the one hand, sentences that are too dense are hard to read. On the other hand, those not dense enough are monotonous and may seem immature. The main thing is to be sure you have *some* variety in sentence structure within your paragraphs. Most of your sentences will probably be standard sentences averaging about twenty words. But within a paragraph individual sentences may range from ten words or fewer to thirty or more, and may include balanced or periodic structures. As the writer, you control the choice of length and structure. Knowing how to vary sentences helps you make intelligent choices.

Second, *postpone revision for variety until you have written your first draft*. Then you can read the draft aloud and hear whether the sentence structure is monotonous. You can even *see* unvaried sentences by noticing that they all take about the same number of lines.

Third, *be aware of the effect that sentence length has on readers*. In general, long sentences slow down the reading, and short ones speed it up. Short sentences are often effective as topic sentences because they state a general idea simply, but longer sentences will often be needed to develop that idea through the paragraph. Short sentences are excellent for communicating a series of actions, emotions, or impressions; longer sentences are more likely to be appropriate for analysis or explanation. Short sentences are closer to the rhythms of speech and are therefore suitable when the style is conversational and the writer is adopting an intimate tone. The more formal the style, the more likely a writer is to use long and involved sentences. But all these statements are relative to the particular kind of material being presented to a particular kind of reader: as in all writing, the choice comes back to the writer's purpose.

REVIEW EXERCISES

A. As a final demonstration of your ability to revise a collection of sentences into an effective, coherent paragraph, use all the information given below to write a paragraph on lobbyists.

1. The most successful lobbyists working in state capitals are experts in legislative strategy.

2. They are highly paid.

3. They know more about the legislative process than do most state legislators.

4. They are skillful, professional workers.

5. They are available to almost any group with sufficient funds to pay for their services.

6. Lobbyists today are not likely to apply the old-fashioned direct pressure to politicians.

7. They are likely to try to persuade legislators' constituents to apply the pressure.

8. A pressure group wants something, and the public wants something.

9. Lobbyists hope to convince legislators that these are the same.

B. Edit the following paragraph into a more effective statement. First read the paragraph as a whole. Then go over it sentence by sentence, making whatever changes you think desirable. Finally rewrite the paragraph in its revised form.

> One of the conceptions not founded in fact that many people have about the nature of language is that it is one of those things that will "hold still" and refuse to change. And many of those who know that this English language of ours has changed through the years, and continues to the present time to change, have the suspicion that there is something that is not good about this change from the status quo. You may have heard someone express his or her regret about the fact that our language is in this day and age no longer the "grand old language of Shakespeare." The person who would express that regret would be surprised to become cognizant of the fact that Shakespeare was one of those people who were denounced for corrupting and polluting the English language. But change in the language that we speak and write is not to be deplored: it is simply a fact that is with us in our lives.

7

DICTION:
THE
CHOICE
OF
WORDS

As you think your way through a sentence, you are inevitably concerned with finding the words that best convey your thought. Sometimes, especially when you are quite clear about what you want to say, the words come so easily that you are hardly aware of choosing them. At other times you find yourself scratching out one choice after another as you search for the word that will best convey the meaning you want. Such revisions are not necessarily a sign of indecision. Often it is the best writers who worry most about diction; and perhaps they are the best writers partly because they take pains to choose the right word.

But words are not right or wrong in themselves. In a dictionary one word is as good as another. What makes a particular word right for you is the effect it has in your sentence or paragraph. Readers do not read isolated words; they read words in a context provided by other words, and that context affects their response to any particular word. For example, they will respond quite differently to the word *disorderly* when it is used to describe a mob than they will when it is used to describe a house. Your choice of words must therefore take into account the context in which the selected word is to appear. Whatever words you use must be appropriate to the context. We will return to the subject of appropriateness in a few pages, but first we must make a distinction between two kinds of meaning.

DENOTATION AND CONNOTATION

The most familiar use of words is to name things—trees, cars, games, people, stars, oceans. When words are used this way, the things they refer to are called their *denotations*. The word *chair* most commonly denotes a piece of furniture for sitting on. The denotation of *Detroit* is the city of that name.

But words acquire *connotations* as well as denotations. Connotations are attitudes that we associate with particular words. When we call an action "courageous" or "foolhardy," we are not only describing it; we are expressing, and inviting a reader to share, an attitude toward it. Connotations are sometimes called *implicit* meanings, as contrasted with the *explicit* meanings of denotations, because they imply or suggest attitudes that they do not state outright.

In each of the following sentences the writer is implying different attitudes toward similar events:

> Our troops *routed* the enemy from the hill. The next day they made a *strategic withdrawal* from the same position.

> Some of the stockholders charged that the corporation was *operating in the red,* but the chairman of the board explained that it was actually *achieving a programmed deficit.*

> The difference between a *boyish prank* and an *act of vandalism* depends on whose child does the mischief.

> When the principal announced that the teachers were *implementing a child-centered curriculum,* one disgruntled parent said they were *mollycoddling the kids.*

> When our men started on *reconnaissance patrol,* they came across an enemy squad *sneaking behind our lines.*

Within each contrast in these sentences the choice is not between denotations and connotations but between favorable and unfavorable connotations. "Boyish prank" is just as connotative as "act of vandalism" but implies a different attitude toward the event. "Operating in the red" and "achieving a programmed deficit" refer to the same financial situation; but whereas the first phrase will create unfavorable associations, the second may win approval from the stockholders.

Whatever words you choose should support your purpose. If you wish to report objectively what you saw or heard, you will choose words that imply no attitude. Thus you will prefer "reconnaissance patrol" to "sneaking behind the lines." If you wish to convey a tolerant or approving attitude, you will use words that invite such a response—"a boyish prank," "a strategic withdrawal," "a child-centered curriculum." But if you wish to suggest disapproval, you will select words with unfavorable connotations—"an act of vandalism," "mollycoddling the kids."

THREE QUALITIES OF GOOD DICTION

What we mean by good diction is the choice of words that best allows you to communicate your meaning to your readers. That choice is always made with reference to a particular sentence. For this reason no dictionary will give you *the* right word. All a dictionary can do is to tell you what meanings a word generally has. It is up to you to decide which, if any, of these meanings meets your needs. But, as background for that decision, it will be useful to consider three qualities that should be taken into account: *appropriateness, specificity,* and *imagery.*

APPROPRIATENESS

Words are appropriate when they are suited to the writer's purpose, which includes the writer's analysis of the situation and of the audience for which the writing is intended. Imagine a doctor explaining to a patient the damage done by a heart attack, and the same doctor reporting on the same subject at a medical convention. The subject is the same, but the situation and the audience are so different that they will affect the content, the manner, and the language of the speaker. Differences in audience and situation affect the whole treatment of a subject and include choices that go beyond diction. We will discuss these differences in the next chapter. Here we limit ourselves to their effect on the writer's choice of words.

"Al, you're a sweetheart. Listen, gotta run. Call me Friday for a quick bite. Beautiful! Love to Fern and the kids. Ciao!"

First published in *Esquire* Magazine.

One of the major choices a writer has to make is how formal to be in a given situation. You know that in social situations the clothes you choose to wear depend on the occasion: a formal gown would be conspicuously inappropriate to the classroom; jeans and a shirt would not do for a formal dance. The same thing is true of diction. Some words are appropriate to some situations but not to others. We can best show this distinction by considering four types of words: *learned, popular, colloquial,* and *slang.*

Popular and learned words   In English, as in other languages, a great part of the total vocabulary consists of words that are common to the speech of educated and uneducated speakers alike. These words are the basic elements of our language. They are indispensable for everyday communication, and by means of them people of widely different backgrounds are able to speak a common language. These are called *popular words;* they belong to the whole populace.

Contrasted with these are words that we read more often than we hear, and write more often than we speak—words more widely used by educated than by uneducated people, and more likely to be used on formal than on informal occasions. These we call *learned words.*

The distinction between learned and popular words is illustrated in the following list, which contrasts the members of some pairs of words that have roughly the same meaning:

Popular	Learned	Popular	Learned
agree	concur	lying	mendacious
beggar	mendicant	make easy	facilitate
behead	decapitate	near (in time)	imminent
break	fracture	prove	verify
clear	lucid	secret	cryptic, esoteric
end	terminate	surrender	capitulate
fat	corpulent	truth	veracity
hairdo	coiffure	wordy	verbose

Colloquialisms   The term *colloquial* is defined by *The American Heritage Dictionary* as "characteristic of or appropriate to the spoken language or to writing that seeks its effect; informal in diction or style of expression." Colloquialisms are not "incorrect" or "bad" English. They are the kinds of words that people, educated and uneducated alike, use when they are speaking together quite informally. In writing they are used to give the impression of talking directly and intimately with the reader. To achieve this effect the writer is likely to use contractions—*don't, wasn't, hasn't*—and *clipped words*, like *taxi, phone*, which are shortened forms of longer words. The list below illustrates typical colloquialisms:

awfully (for *very*)	fix (for *predicament*)	over with (for *completed*)
back of (for *behind*)	it's me	party (for *person*)
cute	kind of; sort of (for	peeve (for *annoy*)
exam	*somewhat*)	plenty (as an adverb)
expect (for *suppose*)	a lot of; lots of	movie (for *film*)
fellow	mad (for *angry*)	sure (for *certainly*)

Slang   The *Oxford English Dictionary* defines *slang* as "language of a highly colloquial type." Notice that the adjective is *colloquial*, not *vulgar* or *incorrect*. Slang is used by people in all walks of life, though those with well-stocked vocabularies tend to use it less than those whose vocabulary range is limited. As with other types of words, the appropriateness of slang depends on the occasion. A college president, for example, would usually avoid slang in a public address but might well use it in many informal situations.

Slang satisfies a desire for novelty of expression. Much of it is borrowed from the special vocabularies of particular occupations or activities: *zero in* (gunnery), *on the beam* (aerial navigation), *behind the eight ball* (pool), *raise the ante* (poker), *pad* (rocketry), *offbeat* (music), *tuned in* and *turned off* (radio). Some of it comes from the private languages of the underworld or the underground: *snow, grass, joint, mainliner, stoned.* Many slang expressions are words borrowed from the standard vocabulary and given new meanings: *flipped, split, cool, cat, soul, rap, high, trip, spaced out, wheels, bread, vibes.* Some slang proves so useful that it passes into the popular vocabulary, but most is a thing of the moment and soon dies.

These four types of diction can be arranged on a scale showing decreasing formality.

	Learned	Popular	Colloquial	Slang	
Most formal					*Least formal*

In most of the expository essays you write in college the degree of formality you use will be closer to the middle of this range than to either extreme. In general, therefore, your best choices will be popular words. Unfortunately, some students have the mistaken idea that in an English class formality is a virtue and that big, fancy words are preferred to short, common ones. This error is compounded when these students cannot maintain the formality. Then the style of their writing becomes obviously inconsistent.

The following passage provides a humorous illustration of this kind of inconsistency. It is taken from George Bernard Shaw's play *Pygmalion,* perhaps better known by its musical and film versions as *My Fair Lady.* In this scene Liza Doolittle, a Cockney flower girl who is being taught by Professor Higgins to talk like a lady, meets her first test at a small party at the home of Mrs. Higgins, the professor's mother. Notice the contrast between Liza's first speech and her last.

> Mrs. Higgins: Will it rain, do you think?
> Liza: The shallow depression in the west of these islands is likely to move slowly in an easterly direction. There are no indications of any great change in the barometrical situation.
> Freddy: Ha! Ha! How awfully funny!
> Liza: What is wrong with that, young man? I bet I got it right.
> Freddy: Killing!
> Mrs. Eynsford Hill: I'm sure I hope it won't turn cold. There's so much influenza about. It runs right through our whole family regularly every spring.
> Liza: My aunt died of influenza: so they said. . . . But it's my belief they done the old woman in. . . . Why should *she* die of influenza? She come through diphtheria right enough the year before. I saw her with my own eyes. Fairly blue with it, she was. They all thought she was dead; but my father he kept ladling gin down her throat 'til she came to so sudden that she bit the bowl off the spoon. . . . What call would a woman with that strength in her have to die of influenza? What become of her new straw hat that should have come to me? Somebody pinched it; and what I say is, them as pinched it done her in.

Here the obvious switch from a formal to a highly colloquial style is justified by Shaw's purpose, which is to show Liza in a transitional stage at which she cannot yet maintain the pose of being a well-educated young woman. She does not see that her learned comment on the weather is inappropriate in this situation and therefore has no idea what Freddy is laughing at. Then when the subject changes to influenza, she forgets she is supposed to be a lady and reverts to her natural speech—which incidentally is much more expressive and colorful than her phony formality. Her inconsistency is amusing, as Shaw meant it to be.

But most inconsistencies in student writing are not introduced for humorous effect. They slip in when writers are not in control of *how* they want to say *what* they want to say. They may start off like Liza, hoping to make a good impression, but their natural voice asserts itself and the final result is something that is neither formal nor informal, but an embarrassing mixture of both. The inconsistencies may, of course, be caught in revision. But it is better to avoid them in the first place by choosing words consistently appropriate to the situation.

DISCUSSION
PROBLEMS

A.   The following passage was spoken by a man on trial for murder and taken down by a member of the jury. As written here it is a harmonious statement, since every word adds up to a consistent picture of the speaker. What happens if we try to refine it by "correcting" the language—for example, changing *goan* to *are going to* and substituting more formal diction such as *perceived* for *seen,* *ensnared* for *trapped,* and *prevaricating* for *tellin' lies?*

> One time I seen a fly that was trapped in a spider's web and watched it suffer. These people that been tellin' lies to frame me goan suffer like that fly did. They goan lay awake at night worryin' 'bout it and it goan be with them in the mo'nin'. They goan live with their lies every day wonderin' when they goan be framed, or their chilren, or their friens and neighbors. On the Last Day they goan have to face Him with it, and I'm goan have a clean heart, 'cause I ain't done nuthin' wrong.

B.   In the following paragraph the diction is inconsistent because some of the words are too informal for the context. Identify them and provide acceptable substitutes.

> One serious rap that has been made against pressure groups is that they wield power without corresponding responsibility. Because they do not have to stand the test of power by winning elections, they are able to make beefed-up claims about the clout the people they represent give them. If these claims are made confidently, timid members of Congress are likely to be impressed. Some people think that this susceptibility of politicians to being hoodwinked is increased by the failure of the great political parties to support their members against the pressure groups. Others feel that Congress itself is too wishy-washy about propagandists. Whatever the cause, the irresponsibility of pressure groups has fostered rip-offs that distort their legitimate function to tip off legislators concerning public policy.

Another kind of inconsistency is the choice of a word that does not fit the writer's intent. Usually in revision an obviously wrong word, like *urban* for *rural* or *figment* for *fragment,* is easy to detect and change. Implied meanings are more troublesome. While few of us would write *skinny wench* in a context that called for *slender girl,* we can easily miss subtle distinctions and choose a word that does not exactly convey our meaning. For example, *admonish, rebuke,* and *scold* all have the same general meaning, but in context they can have different effects. An employee would rather be admonished than rebuked by a supervisor, and rebuked rather than scolded. The supervisor would rather be considered a constructive critic than a faultfinder.

The choice of implied meanings should consistently support your purpose. Ideally you know what effects you want your words to produce and will make the right choices. But under the pressure of writing you may overlook shades of meaning not suitable to your purpose, and thus introduce inconsistencies. The best time to catch these is in revision, when you are free to concentrate on particular words and to ask, "Is this exactly what I mean?" In the following sentences the blank may be filled with any of the words in parentheses, but each choice will change the meaning. The right choice is the one that best fits what you intend the sentence to mean.

1. She was a _____ reader.   (compulsive, critical, perceptive)

2. The children were _____.   (sleepy, exhausted, weary)

3. The candidate gave a(n) _____ answer.   (judicious, ambiguous, cautious)

4. It was an _____ insult.   (intentional, unmistakable, implied)

5. He was in a(n) _____ mood.   (faultfinding, quarrelsome, irritable)

The only basis for choosing one of these parenthetical alternatives is its appropriateness in the context of the writing. Each right choice supports those that have gone before and strengthens the reader's interpretation. Each wrong choice introduces undesirable associations and creates at least momentary uncertainty in the reader. If there are enough wrong choices, the work will be so inconsistent that the reader will not know what to make of it.

SPECIFICITY

Specific and *general* are opposite terms. Words are said to be specific when they refer to individual persons, objects, or events: *Brooklyn Bridge, the Boston Massacre, Joe's mother, the next intersection, the girl sitting nearest to the door.* Words are general when they refer not to individual things but to groups or classes—*bridge, massacre, mother, intersection, girl.* As these examples show, a general term may be made specific by a modifier that restricts the reference to a particular member of the group.

Specific and *general* are also relative terms, since a word may be specific compared with one other word, and general compared with a second, as the accompanying diagram shows.

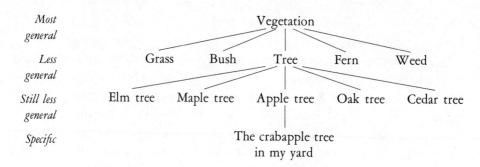

EXERCISE   For each set of terms below, show the gradation from general to specific by putting the most general term at the left and the most specific at the right, thus:

matter, food, fruit, citrus fruit, orange

1.   football player, quarterback, Roger Staubach, athlete
2.   Labrador retriever, quadruped, bird dog, animal, dog
3.   member of the CBS news staff, TV newsman, anchor man, Walter Cronkite
4.   senator, legislator, politician, Senator Edward Kennedy
5.   vacation spot, St. John Island, West Indies, U.S. Virgin Islands
6.   bush, rosebush, plant, decorative bush, Tropicana rosebush
7.   the man who stole my wallet, criminal, pickpocket, thief

Neither specific nor general words are good or bad in themselves. There are purposes that require generalities. A President's inaugural address cannot deal with specifics; it can be only a general statement of policy or intention. But for the kind of writing you do in college, it is generally the best policy to be as specific as the situation permits. Notice how the specific language at the right communicates meaning not conveyed by the general diction at the left:

The child has a contagious disease.	The child has measles.
She was born in Europe.	She was born in France.
His grades last term were poor.	Last term he received two F's and a D.
After the strenuous activities of the day, I did not feel like dancing.	After playing twenty-seven holes of golf, I did not feel like dancing.

The term *concrete* is often used for some kinds of specific diction. *Concrete* is the opposite of *abstract*. Words are said to be concrete when they refer to particular things that can be perceived by our senses: details of appearance, sound, smell, touch, and taste. They are said to be abstract when they refer to qualities that many things seem to share: newness, width, size, shape, value, joy, and anger, for example. These qualities are not objects that we perceive directly by observation; they are concepts that we infer from what we see.

In the following paragraph the author provides concrete illustrations of the abstract opening sentence. The sensory details are so clear that, if you were an artist, you could paint the marshes turning pink, lilac, and golden green at sunset, the beach at low tide, a girl sliding down the sandhills on her bloomers, the lone sneaker beneath the sofa, and the shoes and towels in the closet. But you could not paint the "physical," the "appetite," or the "summertime" of the topic sentence.

> The memories of Beach Haven run all to smells and sounds and sights; they are physical, of the blood and appetite, as is natural to summertime. At the west end of Coral Street the marshes began, turning soft with color at sunset, pink and lilac and golden green. The ocean beach at low tide lay hard underfoot, wet sand dark below the waterline. On the dunes—we called them sandhills—we played King of the Castle or slid down on our bloomer seats, yelling with triumph and pure joy. The floors of Curlew Cottage, the chairs, even the beds were sandy. Always a lone sneaker sat beneath the hall sofa; by August our city shoes were mildewed in the closets, and towels were forever damp. (Catherine Drinker Bowen, *Family Portrait*)

As the preceding paragraph illustrates, some words refer to sensory experiences: to what we see, hear, touch, taste, and smell. Because these words call up sensory images, they are particularly effective in description. Some of the words in the following list could fit into more than one sensory category:

Touch chill, clammy, cold, corrugated, grainy, gritty, harsh, jarring, knobby, moist, nubby, numb, plushy, rough, satiny, slimy, slithering, smooth, sting, tingle, tickly, velvety

Taste bland, biting, bitter, brackish, briny, metallic, minty, nutty, peppery, salty, sour, spicy, sweet, tainted, vinegary, yeasty

Smell acrid, fetid, greasy, mouldy, musky, musty, pungent, putrid, rancid, rank, reek, stench, sulphurous, woodsy

Sound bellow, blare, buzz, chatter, chime, clang, clatter, clink, crackle, crash, creak, gurgle, hiss, hum, murmur, pop, purr, rattle, rustle, screech, snap, splash, squeak, swish, tinkle, whine, whisper

Sight blaze, bleary, bloody, burnished, chalky, dappled, ebony, flame, flash, flicker, florid, foggy, gaudy, glare, glitter, glossy, glow, golden, grimy, haze, inky, leaden, lurid, muddy, roiled, sallow, shadow, smudged, spark, streak, tawny, turbid

EXERCISES   **A.** As a demonstration of your ability to recognize concrete and specific diction, read the following passage and pick out the words or phrases that seem most concrete. Do you see any relation between the words being used and the writer's observation of the scene? Which came first, the observations or the words?

> The scullery was a mine of all the minerals of living. Here I discovered water—a very different element from the green crawling scum that stank in the garden tub. You could pump it in pure blue gulps out of the ground; you could swing on the pump handle and it came out sparkling like liquid sky. And it broke and ran and shone on the tiled floor, or quivered in a jug, or weighted your clothes with cold. You could drink it, smell it, draw with it, froth it with soap, swim beetles across it, or fly it in bubbles in the air. You could put your head in it, and open your eyes, and see the sides of the bucket buckle, and hear your caught breath roar, and work your mouth like a fish.
> (Laurie Lee, *The Edge of Day)*

B. The following pairs of contrasted statements deal with the same subject. From each pair choose the one that you think is more concrete and justify your choice.

In the past, girls in rural communities had no facilities for bathing except those offered by some neighboring stream. In such circumstances a bathing suit was not always a necessity, but if one was worn it was likely to consist of nothing more than some discarded article of clothing tailored to fit the occasion.

Forty years ago, if the farmer's daughter went swimming she swam in the crick below the pasture, and if she wore a bathing suit, which was not as customary as you may think, it was likely to be a pair of her brother's outgrown overalls trimmed with scissors as her discretion might suggest.

Suddenly I felt something on the biceps of my right arm—a queer light touch, clinging for an instant, and then the smooth glide of an oily body. I could feel the muscles of the snake's body slowly contract and relax. At last I saw a flat, V-shaped head, with two

Suddenly I felt the snake moving over my arm. I felt the contraction of its muscles as it moved. Then I saw its ugly head and its evil-looking eyes. All the time its tongue kept moving in and out, making a kind of hissing noise.

glistening, black, protruding buttons.
A thin, pointed, sickening yellow
tongue slipped out, then in,
accompanied by a sound like that of
escaping steam.

C. For practice in using specific and concrete diction, recall some scene that impressed you vividly, or remember how you felt on some occasion; then describe your experience so that a reader can share it with you. Do not choose a large subject but think instead of something that can be treated fully in a substantial paragraph. Do not be in a hurry to start writing. Concentrate on the subject until you have the details clearly in mind. Then translate the experience into words.

IMAGERY

As applied to diction, *imagery* has two general meanings: the images or pictures that concrete words sometimes suggest, and figures of speech such as similes and metaphors. The first meaning includes the pictorial quality we saw in the last section in such phrases as "green crawling scum," "pure blue gulps," "quivered in a jug." It is with the second meaning, the figurative use of language, that we are concerned here.

The chief element in all figures of speech we will discuss is an imaginative comparison in which two dissimilar things are described as being alike in some way significant to the writer. Here is an example:

The moon was a ghostly galleon tossed upon cloudy seas. (Alfred Noyes)

The basic comparison in this line of poetry is of the moon and a sailing ship. Now in most ways the moon is quite unlike a ship. But as the poet watches it alternately emerging from behind the clouds and disappearing into them again, it reminds him of the way a ship disappears from view as it goes down into the trough between two waves and then comes into view again as it rises on the next crest. In his imagination the moon is being *tossed* by the clouds the way a ship is tossed by the waves, and in this respect the moon and the ship resemble each other. The resemblance can be set up as a proportion.

$$\frac{\text{moon}}{\text{clouds}} = \frac{\text{ship}}{\text{waves}} \text{, in respect to the tossing motion}$$

The figures of speech most commonly used are *simile, metaphor, analogy, person-ification,* and *allusion.* Each of these makes some kind of comparison, but each has its own characteristic form and use.

Simile   A simile compares two things—A and B—by asserting that one is *like* the other. A simile usually contains the word *like, as,* or *so,* and is used to transfer to A the qualities or feelings we associate with B. Thus in

> . . . there was a secret meanness that clung to him almost like a smell (Carson McCullers)

the abstract word *meanness* (A) is made concrete by likening it to a smell (B) that "clings" to the man the way tobacco smoke might permeate his clothing.
Here are other similes:

> She crouched like a fawning dog. (John Steinbeck)
>
> Records fell like ripe apples on a windy day. (E. B. White)
>
> His face was as blank as a pan of uncooked dough. (William Faulkner)
>
> Laverne wasn't too bad a dancer, but the other one, old Marty, . . . was like dragging the Statue of Liberty around the floor. (J. D. Salinger)
>
> The Hovercraft looked like a single-decker bus fixed to the top half of a whale. (Anthony Bailey)
>
> What the ad fails to mention is that smoking Carltons is like sucking air through a straw.
>
> As the crowd left the scene of the accident, all that remained was a sprinkling of broken glass that shone like tears in the moonlight.

Metaphor   A metaphor compares two things by identifying one with the other. It does not say that A is *like* B, but instead states that A *is* B. Thus when the Greek playwright Sophocles wrote,

> Sons are the anchors of a mother's life

he was suggesting that a son gave stability to a woman's life the way an anchor held a ship in place, that in the culture of ancient Greece a woman without a son had nothing to hold her secure within the family.
Here are other metaphors:

> California is the flashy blonde you like to take out once or twice. Minnesota is the girl you want to marry. *(Time)*

Elliot Erwitt/Magnum Photos

The President is asking Congress to join him in a crash landing, and the reason this presents difficulty is that they were not brought in on the take-off. (Eric Sevareid)

Europe was a heap of swords piled as delicately as jackstraws; one could not be pulled out without moving the others. (Barbara Tuchman)

I've climbed that damned ladder of politics, and every step has been rough. I've slipped many times and almost fallen back.... That top rung is never going to be mine. My fingernails are scraping it, but I don't have a grip. (Hubert Humphrey)

Good families are fortresses with many windows and doors to the outer world. (Jane Howard)

The script was more than four hundred pages long—overrich, repetitious, loaded with irrelevant, fascinating detail and private jokes, of which we loved every one. We spent two more weeks going through the pages with machetes—hacking away, trimming, simplifying, clarifying its main dramatic lines and yelling at each other all the time. (John Houseman)

Many words and phrases no longer thought of as figures of speech were originally metaphors or similes. Thus "foil" and "parry" derived from the sport of fencing; "checkmate" was a metaphor from chess; "rosy red" and "sapphire blue" were similes, as were "dirt cheap" and "silver hair." "At bay" once described a hunted animal when it finally turned to face the baying hounds; a "crestfallen" cock was one that had been humbled in a fight. Many other expressions retain their metaphorical appearance although we no longer think of them as figures of speech—expressions such as the "mouth" of a river, the "face" of a clock, the "front" (originally "forehead") of a house, the "brow" of a hill. These are often called, metaphorically, *dead* or *frozen metaphors*. They are so common in the language that it would be hard to write a paragraph without one.

Analogy   An analogy is a metaphor or simile extended through one or more paragraphs to explain a difficult idea or to persuade a reader that because two things are alike, a conclusion drawn from one suggests a similar conclusion from the other. In the following analogy the injury done to the soul of a black person is compared to a callus on the foot:

> ... The Negro has a callus growing on his soul and it's getting harder and harder to hurt him there. That's a simple law of nature. Like a callus on the foot in a shoe that's too tight. The foot is nature's and that shoe was put on by man. The tight shoe will pinch your foot and make you holler and scream. But sooner or later, if you don't take the shoe off, a callus will form on the foot and begin to wear out the shoe.

It's the same with the Negro in America. That shoe—the white man's system—has pinched and rubbed and squeezed his soul until it almost destroyed him. But it didn't. And now a callus has formed on his soul, and unless that system is adjusted to fit him, too, that callus is going to wear out that system. (Dick Gregory)

As this analogy illustrates, a figure of speech is an effective way to make the abstract concrete. Abstractly stated, the argument is that the Negro has become inured to the white man's injustice, which has bruised his soul, but also strengthened it, so that in time it will force a change in the system. The analogy with the callus pictorializes the argument by likening the process to something every reader will both understand and feel. There is therefore an emotional impact in the analogy that is lacking in the abstract argument.

Personification   Personification is a figure of speech by which abstractions and nonanimals are given human or animal characteristics. Thus winds are said to "roar" or "bite"; flames "eat hungrily" at a house on fire and may even "devour" it; a tree may "bow meekly" before a gale or in fair weather "lift its leafy arms to pray"; truth or virtue emerges "triumphant"; and justice is "blind." In all these examples, the writer imagines a resemblance between the actions being described and those of an animal or a person.

Such implied comparisons are often effective, but they should be used with restraint. If they seem to a reader exaggerated or far-fetched (as in "The waves roared their threat to the listening clouds while the palm trees nodded their approval"), a reader is likely to reject them as far-fetched or as a mistaken attempt to be "literary."

Allusion   An allusion is a reference to some historical or literary event or person seen by the writer to resemble in some way the subject under discussion. When the Prudential Insurance Company urges people to "own a piece of the rock," it is inviting the comparison that it is as solid and permanent as the Rock of Gibraltar, which it uses as its symbol. Or when a political scandal is called another Teapot Dome or Watergate, it is being likened to the most notorious political scandals in our history.

A successful allusion provides a flash of wit or insight and gives the reader the pleasure of recognition. But if readers do not recognize an allusion, it can mean nothing to them. Therefore the writer must be reasonably sure that the allusion is suited to the audience. Likening an uncomfortable cot to the bed of Procrustes will be received as a humorous exaggeration only by readers who know that Procrustes used to stretch or shorten his guests to fit the bed. If the allusion is not likely to be understood, what is the point of using it?

EXERCISES   As a review of what has been said about specific words and imagery, follow the directions for A and B.

A.   In each of the three selections that follow, underline whatever examples of specificity and imagery seem to you especially effective.

When wild ducks or wild geese migrate in their season, a strange tide rises in the territories over which they sweep. As if magnetized by the great triangular flight, the barnyard fowl leap a foot or two into the air and try to fly, . . . and a vestige of savagery quickens their blood. All the ducks on the farm are transformed for an instant into migrant birds, and into those hard little heads, till now filled with humble images of pools and worms and barnyards, there swims a sense of continental expanse, of the breadth of seas and the salt taste of the ocean wind. The duck totters to the right and left in its wire enclosure, gripped by a sudden passion to perform the impossible and a sudden love whose object is a mystery. (Antoine de Saint Exupéry, *Wind, Sand and Stars)*

The word is terracide. As in homicide, or genocide. Except it's terra. Land.
It is not committed with guns and knives, but with great, relentless bulldozers and thundering dump trucks, with giant shovels like mythological creatures, their girdered necks lifting massive steel mouths high above the tallest trees. And with dynamite. They cut and blast and rip apart mountains to reach the minerals inside, and when they have finished there is nothing left but naked hills, ugly monuments to waste, stripped of everything that once held them in place, cut off from the top and sides and dug out from the inside and then left, restless, to slide down on houses and wash off into rivers and streams, rendering the land unlivable and the water for miles down-stream undrinkable.
Terracide. Or, if you prefer, strip-mining. (Skip Rozin, "People of the Ruined Hills," *Audubon)*

Smoke was rising here and there among the creepers that festooned the dead or dying trees. As they watched, a flash of fire appeared at the root of one wisp, and then the smoke thickened. Small flames stirred at the trunk of a tree and crawled away through leaves and brushwood, dividing and in-creasing. One patch touched a tree trunk and scrambled up like a bright squirrel. The smoke increased, sifted, rolled outwards. The squirrel leapt on the wings of the wind and clung to another standing tree, eating down-wards. Beneath the dark canopy of leaves and smoke the fire laid hold on the forest and began to gnaw. Acres of black and yellow smoke rolled steadily toward the sea. At the sight of the flames and the irresistible course of the fire, the boys broke into shrill, excited cheering. The flames, as though they were a kind of wild life, crept as a jaguar creeps on its belly toward a line of birch-like saplings that fledged an outcrop of the pink rock. They flapped at the first of the trees, and the branches grew a brief foliage of fire. The heart of flame leapt nimbly across the gap between the trees and then went swinging and flaring along the whole row of them. Beneath the capering boys a quarter of a mile square of forest was savage with smoke and flame. The separate noises of the fire merged into a drum-roll that seemed to shake the mountain. (William Golding, *Lord of the Flies*)

B.   Which of the following versions of the same scene do you prefer, and why?

He entered the tavern and took a seat comfortably back from the potbellied wood stove around which the regular customers sat drinking beer and exchanging the local gossip. The room was unevenly lit by two suspended bulbs that swayed in the draft each time the door was opened, causing the shadows to swing eerily around the walls.

He entered the tavern and sat near the stove around which people were drinking and talking. The room was lit by two electric bulbs. Outside the wind was blowing, and every time the door opened it caused shadows to move around the walls.

REVISING DICTION

In a sense we have been concerned with revising diction through most of this chapter. In considering the qualities of good diction, we were comparing effective and ineffective ways of expressing ideas, and that comparison included a good deal of revision. But now we are changing the emphasis from good to bad qualities. When you are revising your first draft, you are not trying to find out what is good; you are looking for parts that are unsatisfactory and trying to improve them. Therefore we will take up four major weaknesses in diction and suggest how they may be removed. These are *vagueness, jargon, triteness,* and *ineffective imagery.*

ELIMINATING VAGUENESS

Words are vague when, in context, they do not convey to a reader one specific meaning. Consider this sentence:

I could tell by the funny look on her face that she was mad.

Words like *funny* and *mad* can have quite specific meanings, but not in this context. What does *mad* mean here? Certainly not "insane," which it might mean in another sentence. "Angry," then, or "annoyed," "irritated," "offended"? A reader cannot be sure. But the writer can remove any doubt by using more specific diction:

I could tell *by the way her face stiffened* that she was *offended.*

Words like *funny* and *mad* belong to a group called *utility words.* These, as their name implies, are useful. In ordinary speech, which does not usually permit deliberate choice and gives little chance of revision, they are common and often pass unnoticed. In writing they may be adequate if the context limits them to one clear interpretation. But because they are often left vague in student writing, they deserve a special caution here. The following list shows some of the most common utility words:

affair	fierce	lovely	proposition
aspect	fine	marvelous	regular
awful	freak	matter	silly
business	funny	nature	situation
circumstance	gadget	neat	smooth
condition	glamorous	nice	stuff
cool	goods	organization	terrible
cute	gorgeous	outfit	terrific
factor	great	peculiar	weird
fantastic	line	pretty	wonderful

In revising your papers, be sure that the meaning of a utility word is clearly implied by its context. Consider this:

In Bill's *situation* I would quit school.

If this sentence occurs in a context that clearly shows that Bill's problem is caused by low grades, lack of money, or family troubles, the sentence will present no difficulty. But if the context does not clarify the meaning of *situation,* the sentence should be rewritten to specify the intended meaning, as in

If I had Bill's grades, I would quit school.

Usually the simplest way to clarify a vague utility word or phrase is to substitute a specific word or phrase, as in the following examples:

It was a ~~peculiar~~ *puzzling* statement.

Such scandals ~~are bad business for~~ *weaken confidence in* politicians.

seriously ill.

He is ~~in bad shape~~.

alarming.

The news tonight is ~~terrible~~.

Other substitutions could have been made. The problem is to choose the one that specifies the intended meaning.

Assuming that the italicized words are not made clear by the context, substitute more specific diction for the utility words to give a precise meaning.   **EXERCISE**

1.   He is a doctor, but I don't know what his *line* is.

2.   Our *organization* is opposed to Brenda Ames for student president.

3.   It was a *smooth* party—*nice* people, *lovely* food, and *marvelous* conversation.

4.   What a *terrific* surprise to meet so many *cool* people at the same *affair*.

5.   The actors gave a *swell* performance.

6.   The judge said the *matter* was *peculiar* but she would take it under advisement.

7.   Mother is *fussing* about Jean's moving into her own apartment; she really is *fierce* about it.

8.   One *aspect* of the *proposition* is its effect on prices.

9.   I thought that the new TV series was *sort of cute,* but it got *awful* ratings.

10.   The price they are charging for steak is *something else.*

Vagueness is not limited to unclear utility words. Any word or phrase that is more general than the intended meaning should be revised. The substitutions in the following sentences make the information more specific:

Antigone.

The class was discussing ~~a Greek play~~.

terminal cancer.

Her father has ~~an incurable disease~~.

getting along with other students.

Jim has difficulty ~~adjusting to his peers~~.

In the paragraph below, choose the more specific expression in each parenthesis.   **EXERCISE**

   The whole surface of the ice was *(a chaos—full)* of movement. It looked like an enormous *(mass—jigsaw puzzle)* stretching away to infinity and being *(pushed—crunched)* together by some invisible but irresistible force. The impression of its *(titanic—great)* power was heightened by the unhurried deliberateness of the motion. Whenever two thick *(pieces—floes)* came together, their edges *(met–butted)* and *(moved–ground)* against one another for a time. Then, when neither of them showed signs of yielding, they rose *(uncertainly–quiveringly),* driven by the *(implacable–tremendous)* power behind them. Sometimes they would stop *(altogether–abruptly)* as the unseen forces affecting the ice appeared mysteriously to lose interest. More frequently, though, the two floes–often ten feet thick or more–would continue to rise, *(rearing up–tenting up)* until one or both of them toppled over, creating a pressure ridge.

ELIMINATING JARGON

Jargon originally meant meaningless chatter. It later came to mean the specialized language of a group or profession, as in "habeas corpus" (law), "top up the dampers" (British for "fill the shock absorbers"), and "stand by to come about" (sailing). A third meaning is suggested by the following definition from *Webster's Third New International Dictionary,* which says jargon is "language vague in meaning and full of circumlocutions and long high-sounding words."

It is in this third sense that we use the word here. There is no valid objection to the use of learned and technical terms for audiences and situations to which they are appropriate, but using them unnecessarily when addressing a popular audience is a violation of the basic rule that the style should fit the writer's purpose and audience. Jargon in informal writing is pretentious in the writer and frustrating for the reader. The following contrast will illustrate this charge. The version at the left comes from the King James translation of the Bible; that at the right is George Orwell's translation of it into modern jargon.

I returned and saw under the sun, that the race is not to the swift, nor the battle to the strong, neither yet bread to the wise, nor yet riches to men of understanding, nor yet favor to men of skill; but time and chance happeneth to them all.	Objective considerations of contemporary phenomena compel the conclusion that success or failure in competitive activities exhibits no tendency to be commensurate with innate capacity, but that a considerable element of the unpredictable must invariably be taken into account.

Although the Biblical version is more than three hundred years old, it makes more sense and is easier to read than the "translation," which destroys the simplicity and clarity of the original by smothering the meaning under a blanket of vague, polysyllabic words. As Orwell points out:

The first contains forty-nine words but only sixty syllables, and all of its words are those of everyday life. The second contains thirty-eight words of ninety syllables; eighteen of its words are from Latin roots, and one from

Greek. The first sentence contains six vivid images, and only one phrase ("time and chance") that could be called vague. The second contains not a single fresh, arresting phrase, and in spite of its ninety syllables it gives only a shortened version of the meaning contained in the first. ("Politics and the English Language," *Shooting an Elephant and Other Essays)*

The three chief characteristics of jargon are

1. highly abstract diction, often technical, showing a fondness for "learned" rather than "popular" words: "have the capability to" for "can," "facilitate" for "make easy," "implementation of theoretical decisions" for "putting a theory to use," "maximize productivity" for "increase production," and "utilization of mechanical equipment" for "use of machinery."

2. excessive use of the passive voice. If machines break down, they "are found to be functionally impaired." If a plan does not work, "its objectives were not realized." If management failed to consider the effects of certain changes on the workers, the error is reported as: "With respect to employee reactions to these changes, management seems to have been inadequately advised." If more than half the students in a class did not make an outline before writing an essay, "It was discovered that, on the part of a majority of the class population, the writing of the essay was not preceded by the construction of an outline."

3. conspicuous wordiness, as illustrated in the examples given above.

These three characteristics combine inappropriateness, vagueness, and wordiness into one consistently unintelligible style. Most students have enough sense to avoid this kind of writing. Those who fall into jargon do so because they believe that ordinary language is not good enough for an English class. Like Liza Doolittle, they are trying to make a good impression. The best way to make a good impression in an English class is to have something to say and to say it clearly.

The only way to revise jargon is to rewrite to get rid of it. Leaving it in only forces readers to do the rewriting that the author should have done, and readers may not be sure what it means. As an exercise in revising jargon, let us take an example and see what we can do with it. Read the following paragraph to get a general impression of the difficulty it presents to a reader:

(1) The innermost instincts of the infantryman, that unsung hero of the soldiery entrusted to wage our country's altercations, provide him with some of his fundamental feelings relevant to his fortune in war. (2) He lends more credibility to his instincts than he does to the reasoning faculties of his intellect. (3) The forefront of the field of battle is not a place where one intellectualizes rationally with maximum ease. (4) Indeed, a foot soldier is

not desirous of contemplating the vicissitudes of his condition logically, for there are too many infelicities that the hazards of war may foist upon his person. (5) But though a human being can decline to reason intellectually, he cannot be inattentive to his instincts. (6) He was not instrumental in the formulation of these feelings of his inner self, and it is not within his capacity to deactualize them. (7) They are particles of his very essence, and he must coexist with them.

Now, let us take the paragraph sentence by sentence and see what the writer was trying to say.

Sentence 1.   There are two ideas in this sentence: that an infantryman's instincts provide him with his feelings about war, and that he gets little credit for his service. In the context of the whole paragraph the second idea does not seem to be important and might better be left out. But, assuming the writer thought it important, we can rewrite the sentence as follows: *The instincts of the indispensable but unappreciated infantryman determine his feelings about his conduct in battle.*

Sentence 2.   This sentence means that *he trusts his instincts more than his reasoning.*

Sentence 3.   *The front line is no place for reasoning.*

Sentence 4.   *A foot soldier does not want to think logically about his condition because there are too many unknowns that may affect him.*

Sentence 5.   *But though he can refuse to reason, he cannot ignore his instincts.*

Sentence 6.   *He did not create his instincts and he cannot stop them.*

Sentence 7.   *His instincts are an inseparable part of him.*

If we simply string these italicized revisions together, we get a version that says all that the original was trying to say, and says it more clearly and in fewer words—84 instead of 152. But we might get a still better revision by combining some sentences and making some slight subtractions and additions.

In battle an infantryman uses instinct rather than logic. There are too many unknowns in a battle to make logical reasoning either possible or trustworthy. So he acts on his instincts. He does what he feels he must do under the conditions that exist for him at the moment.

In this version, we have said nothing that was not said in the italicized revision above. But we have sharpened the focus of the paragraph by giving it a clear topic sentence and then explaining that sentence. In the process we have got rid of all the pomposities of the original version and have communicated its meaning in one-third the space.

Following the procedure illustrated above, rewrite this student paragraph: EXERCISE

(1) While on duty one evening, a colleague, who was interested in weightlifting, allowed me to peruse a book on the subject entitled *Big Arms,* by Bob Hoffman. (2) Not yet having realized my latent interest in athletic endeavors, I was surprised at the manner in which the book held my interest. (3) This I only realized after a while. (4) It was that book which stimulated me to make a purchase of a weightlifting set and, despite the inhibiting influences of long work hours, little sleep, and irregular meals, to exercise in my free moments.

ELIMINATING TRITENESS

The terms *trite, hackneyed, threadbare,* and *cliché* are used to describe expressions, once colorful and apt, which have been used so much that they have lost their freshness and force. Like outdated slang, trite expressions once called up original images and conveyed a sense of excitement and discovery. But the very qualities that make a phrase striking when it is new work against it when it has been used too much. Here are a few examples of triteness:

apple of her eye	hook, line, and sinker
birds of a feather	lock, stock, and barrel
black sheep	mountains out of molehills
blind as a bat	raining cats and dogs
budding genius	sober as a judge
cool as a cucumber	teeth like pearls
diamond in the rough	thick as thieves
fly in the ointment	water over the dam

Trite diction blocks thought. Writers who use ready-made phrases instead of fashioning their own soon have no thought beyond the stereotyped comment that the trite diction conveys. Consequently, their ideas and observations follow set patterns: any change in personnel becomes a "shakeup"; all hopes become "fond," "foolish," or "forlorn"; standard procedure for making a suggestion is to "drop a hint"; defeats are "crushing"; changes in the existing system are "noble experiments" or "dangerous departures"; unexpected occurrences are "bolts from the blue"; and people who "sow wild oats" always have to "pay the piper" even though they are "as poor as church mice." As these examples suggest, the use of trite phrases is habit-forming.

"Mr. Manning, my mother wants to know if she may borrow a well-turned phrase?"

John Ruge. Reprinted from *Saturday Review.*

Whenever it can be recognized, triteness should be removed in revision. Unfortunately, what is recognized as trite by an instructor may seem original to some students. They may have had just enough experience with a cliché to think it sounds impressive, and not enough to realize that, like "water over the dam," it has been repeated so often by so many people that it is thoroughly stale. How, then, do they learn to detect and avoid triteness in their own writing?

The only way to learn is by experience. One way to get that experience is to recognize triteness in the speech and writing of others. Note the italicized clichés in the following paragraph from a student essay:

> *Money doesn't grow on trees* and how well I've learned that. What a *rude awakening* when I finally realized that all the odd change I used to ask for at

home wasn't available at school. I had thought my allowance was enormous and, before I knew it, it was gone. College has taught me that *"A penny saved is a penny earned."* I have learned to live within my allowance and even to *save something for a rainy day.* What I have learned in college is *not all in the books.* I have also learned to *shoulder responsibility.*

How many of these phrases do you recognize as ready-made expressions that the writer did not invent but simply borrowed from the common stock of trite expressions? Many of them are like prefabricated units that can be fitted into any kind of structure. By using them, this writer did not have to shape her own ideas; she found them ready at hand. All we said earlier about the uniqueness of each student essay is denied by this kind of writing. If you can see that triteness reduces a writer's comment to a parroting of stock remarks, you are more likely to avoid it in your own writing.

Read the following paragraph and discuss in class the question, "Does the writer provide any new insight into the value of football, or is he just repeating clichés that other people have used over and over again?" Support your judgments by reference to the text.

> Wherever the gridiron game is played in the United States—on a sandlot, a high school field, or in a college or professional stadium—the players learn through the school of hard knocks the invaluable lesson that only by the men's blending together like birds of a feather can the team win. It is a lesson they do not forget on the gridiron. Off the field, they duly remember it. In society, the former player does not look upon himself as a lone wolf on the prowl who has the right to do his own thing—that is, to observe only his individual social laws. He knows he is a part of the big picture and must conduct himself as such. He realizes that only by playing as a team man can he do his share in making society what it should be—the protector and benefactor of all. The man who has been willing to make the sacrifice to play football knows that teamwork is essential in this modern day and age and that every citizen must pull his weight in the boat if the nation is to prosper. So he has little difficulty in adjusting to his roles in family life and in the world of business and to his duties as a citizen in the total scheme of things. In short, his football training helps make him a better citizen and person, better able to play the big game of life.

Do *one* of the following:

1. As a result of the class discussion, rewrite the paragraph about football to get rid of the major objections to it made in class.

2.   Choose as your general subject the values of any college activity that interests you. Restrict that general subject to the one value that you think is most important to students, and write a substantial paragraph supporting your judgment. Then proofread it to catch any trite language you may have used.

ELIMINATING INEFFECTIVE IMAGERY

You have seen that an effective figure of speech can lend concreteness to writing. But a figure that is trite, far-fetched, or confused is worse than useless, since it calls unfavorable attention to itself and distracts the reader. *Mixed metaphors*—metaphors that try to combine two or more images in a single figure—are especially ineffective.

Consider the following example:

The mayor decided to test the political temperature by throwing his hat into the ring as a trial balloon.

This sentence mixes three different images, all of them so overused that no imagination is required to write them. "Testing the temperature" has a literal meaning in cooking and bathing, and a figurative use when extended to politics. "Throwing one's hat into the ring" comes from the old days of bareknuckle prize fights, when this was a conventional way of issuing a challenge. "Trial balloons" were originally sent up to determine the direction and velocity of the wind. Each of these images can be adapted to a political situation, but fitting all three of them into one consistent figure of speech is impossible. The writer of the sentence should abandon the metaphor entirely and simply say, "The mayor decided to get a better sense of his chances of being re-elected by announcing his candidacy."

The lesson to be learned from the mixed metaphor given above is that a poor figure of speech is worse than none at all. The pictorial quality is ruined if no consistent picture is possible, and a device that is intended to strengthen communication actually weakens it. For this reason, it is wise to test every figure of speech by "seeing" the picture it presents. If you will visualize what your words are saying, you will have a chance to catch any ineffective images and revise them before they reach your reader.

EXERCISE   The following sentences try unsuccessfully to combine inconsistent images in the same figure of speech. Visualize the images they suggest and then revise each sentence either by providing an acceptable figure or by stating the idea in literal language.

1. A host of students flocked into the corridor like an avalanche.

2. You people have been selected for this program so that we can retread the cream of the crop.

3. The defense attorney expressed confidence that the real facts of the case would come out in the wash.

4. The President's ill-advised action has thrown the ship of state into low gear and unless the members of Congress wipe out party lines and carry the ball as a team, it may take months to get the country back on the track.

5. Some of the things that policeman said would make your flesh stand on end. (Archie Bunker in "All in the Family")

8

TONE
AND
STYLE

In the last two chapters we dealt with sentence structure and diction separately. Now we want to consider their joint effect on the *tone* and *style* of a piece of writing. You are generally familiar with these terms. You know what is meant when someone says, "Don't speak to me in that tone," or "The style of this book is unnecessarily difficult." But in this chapter *tone* and *style* are technical terms that require explanation.

TONE

Tone may be defined as *the sum of those characteristics that reveal the author's attitudes toward the subject and the readers.* These attitudes are usually determined in the prewriting. For example, the student who wrote "Why We Need More Westerns on Television" (page 17) decided before she began to write that she was going to make fun of westerns by pretending to praise them. That decision gave her her real subject: of all the things she might say about TV westerns, she would limit herself to those that would make fun of them. In making this decision she established an attitude toward her subject. Since that attitude required her to count on her readers to see what she was doing and so join in the fun, she was also adopting an attitude toward them as partners in the spoof. These two attitudes combined to set the tone of her essay.

INFORMATIVENESS AND AFFECTIVENESS

One of the decisions about tone that will come out of your purpose is the degree to which your writing will be informative or affective—that is, the extent to which it will try to explain something to your readers (inform them) or to influence them in some way (affect them). We can best explain these two emphases by looking at an extreme example of each.

> Siemens, the big German electrical equipment maker, has become the latest bidder for the business of cleaning up automobile emissions. Siemens researchers in Erlangen, Bavaria, have developed a cigar-box-sized device that replaces the carburetor and, they claim, allows today's piston engine to run essentially pollution-free without use of complex and bulky devices to clean up the exhaust after it leaves the engine.
>
> The device, called a "crack carburetor," uses a catalytic process to break down, or crack, gasoline into gaseous components, primarily methane, hydrogen, and carbon monoxide. These gases are mixed with air and burned in the engine. Automotive engineers have long known that gaseous fuels, such as liquid petroleum gas or natural gas, give very clean exhausts, but their adoption has been blocked by problems of distribution and on-board storage. Siemens gets around that by allowing the car to carry gasoline as its fuel and produce its own combustion gases. *(Business Week)*

We can observe the following things in this sample:

1.   The writer is principally concerned with giving readers information about the subject. In writing for *Business Week,* a magazine sold chiefly to people who want to keep up with what is going on in the business world, the writer assumes that the readers will be interested in an invention that may reduce pollution, but that they

do not know what a "crack carburetor" is. The writer's chief concern, therefore, is to explain to these readers the process by which Siemens hopes to get rid of harmful waste products. This is the real subject, and it establishes the writer's view of both the subject and the readers of *Business Week.*

2.   The writing is completely *objective*—that is, the writer's own judgments and feelings and personality are not allowed to show in the writing. The readers are not assured that the invention will be successful, since that would require a judgment on the part of the writer. The article reports that the company *claims* the device will reduce pollution, but says nothing that would either support or cast doubt on that claim. As far as it is possible to do so, the writer stays out of the writing.

3.   As a result of this procedure the tone of the writing is informative, factual, and impersonal.

Now contrast this sample with the one that follows.

> You can also forget about *Guess Who's Coming to Dinner.* It's a comedy about a nice liberal family whose daughter decides to marry a black man (Sidney Poitier) who is so noble and wonderful that the issue of interracial marriage is completely blunted.
>
> I feel a sadness bordering on anger that Mom and Dad were played by Katharine Hepburn and Spencer Tracy. It is infuriating that these two graceful people and glorious actors should have to make their last appearance together in such a heavy-handed, message-burdened vehicle. It's a travesty of the pictures they had previously—perhaps immortally—done. I think it's close to a moral act to avoid this dreadful work. It is an affront not only to movie art but to the difficult issue it pretends to examine. (Richard Schickel, "A Critic's Guide to Movies on TV," *Redbook*)

Our observations of this sample are quite different:

1.   This piece is short on information. It tells us that Katharine Hepburn played Mom, Spencer Tracy played Dad, and Sidney Poitier played the black man who is going to marry their daughter. It does not tell who played the white girl or the black parents, although these three had important roles in the movie. Nor does it say anything about the conflicts among these people that made up the whole plot and theme of the story.

2.   Instead, it is almost entirely concerned with the reviewer's personal reaction to the film. The review is an unfavorable judgment, presented without evidence in highly emotional language. The writer's attitude toward the subject is hostile; his attitude toward his readers is authoritative: Don't waste your time on this movie: it's dreadful.

3.   The writing is almost completely *subjective*—that is, it deals chiefly with how

the writer *feels* about the movie. Not only does he say, "I think," "I feel," but the diction reflects his annoyance: "infuriating," "heavy-handed, message-burdened," "travesty," "dreadful work," "affront . . . to movie art"—these are all emotionally loaded terms that reveal his attitude to the subject. Another reviewer might be equally emotional in praise of the film: "It's a great movie, dealing in a sensitive way with an important social problem, and superbly acted. You leave it feeling some hope that the level-headedness of the younger generation will finally triumph over the stupidity of their parents." That is just as subjective a judgment as the first. The purpose of such reviews is not to inform readers about the movie but to affect their attitudes toward it.

We can place the two quoted passages on a scale going from informative to affective.

Informative ——————————————————————————————— *Affective*
(Siemens article)   (Movie review)

Between the extremes we could place other samples showing varying degrees of informativeness and affectiveness, with those in the middle about equally balanced between the two.

In your writing you will have to decide how informative or affective you want to be. Certain assignments, such as reports of experiments, summaries of books or events, and essay examinations, usually require an informative treatment. Persuasive essays, which are intended to get a reader to believe or to do something, are usually affective. But most expository essays combine informative and affective elements. For such essays your choice will depend on the situation and your purpose. The essay about the stop-and-frisk law in Chapter 1 was intended to change the readers' attitude toward that law. Yet most of the second half, in which the writer was explaining the law, was informative, because the writer felt that whatever objections the audience had to the law would be reduced if they knew the facts.

Students sometimes believe that the way to be objective is to avoid using the pronoun *I.* That rule of thumb may be true in some situations, but, as a general rule, it is misleading in two respects. First, when you are writing about your own experiences, ideas, and feelings, there is no reasonable objection to the use of *I.* Second, avoiding *I* will not in itself guarantee an objective treatment of the subject. The statement "I saw the car run through a red light" is more objective than "The crazy fool drove through a red light," even though the first contains *I* and the second does not.

Whether the tone is informative or affective is a conclusion from *all* the evidence in the writing. If the writing emphasizes an objective description of the subject, the tone can be called informative. If the writing seems designed to influence the reader's response by emphasizing the writer's feelings and opinions, the tone can be called affective. If the writing seems to preserve an even balance between fact and opinion, the tone falls midway in the scale between informative and affective.

To what extent do you judge the following passages to be informative or affective? Where would you place each passage on the informative-affective scale? On what evidence do you base your judgment? (Hint: On these questions some difference of opinion is to be expected. Do not merely label the passage, but examine it closely so that you can support your judgment by specific reference to details.)

DISCUSSION
PROBLEM

Passage 1

Our church was built on brick pillars and stood about thirty inches from the ground. No lattice work fenced off the area under the church and, consequently, hogs chose that spot for their family bedroom, especially in winter. Sometimes there would be an argument among members of the hog family during the sermon. One of the hogs, possibly, would want to turn over and sleep on the other side for a while—this to the inconvenience of the others. Then we could hear a considerable oinking and squealing above the minister's voice. Sometimes the backs of the larger hogs would strike against the floor joists with such force that we could feel vibrations inside the church.

Hogs bred fleas in their under-the-floor beds, and the fleas came through cracks between the floor planks and into the church, seemingly seeking tender flesh. A prim young lady sitting in the choir in full view of everybody in the church could not reach handily under many layers of long skirts to get at the flea. She had to be dignified. So fleas bit at will. I heard women members of the choir complain of this. (Virgil Conner, *Life in the Nineties,* an unpublished dissertation)

Passage 2

It is a miracle that New York works at all. The whole thing is implausible. Every time the residents brush their teeth, millions of gallons of water must be drawn from the Catskills and the hills of Westchester. When a young man in Manhattan writes a letter to his girl in Brooklyn, the love message gets blown to her through a pneumatic tube—*pfft*—just like that. The subterranean system of telephone cables, power lines, steam pipes, gas mains and sewer pipes is reason enough to abandon the island to the gods and the weevils. Every time an incision is made in the pavement, the noisy surgeons expose ganglia that are tangled beyond belief. By rights New York should have destroyed itself long ago, from panic or fire or rioting or failure of some vital supply line in its circulatory system or from some deep labyrinthine short circuit. Long ago the city should have experienced an insoluble traffic snarl at some impossible bottleneck. It should have perished of hunger when food lines failed for a few days. It should have been wiped out by a plague starting in its slums or carried in by ships' rats. It should have been overwhelmed by the sea that licks at it on every side. The workers in its myriad cells should have succumbed to nerves, from the fearful pall of smoke-fog that drifts over every few days from Jersey, blotting out all light at noon and leaving the high offices suspended, men groping and depressed, and the sense of world's end. (E. B. White, *Here Is New York*)

Passage 3   I have lost friends and relatives through cancer, lynching and war. I have been personally the victim of physical attack which was the offspring of racial and political hysteria. I have worked with the handicapped and seen the ravages of congenital diseases that we have not yet conquered because we spend our time and ingenuity in far less purposeful wars. I see daily on the streets of New York, street gangs and prostitutes and beggars; I know people afflicted with drug addiction and alcoholism and mental illness; I have, like all of you, on a thousand occasions seen indescribable displays of man's very real inhumanity to man; and I have come to maturity, as we all must, knowing that greed and malice, indifference to human misery and, perhaps above all else, ignorance—the prime ancient and persistent enemy of man—abound in this world.

I say all of this to say that one cannot live with sighted eyes and feeling heart and not know and react to the miseries which afflict this world. (Lorraine Hansberry, *To Be Young, Gifted, and Black*)

DISTANCE

Another element of tone is *distance*. In a discussion of tone the word is used to measure the impression of distance between writer and reader.

Consider a professor lecturing to a large audience. She is separated from her listeners by her position on the platform. She cannot speak to each member of the audience individually, though she may try to create the illusion of doing so. The situation requires her to speak more slowly, more loudly, more formally than if she were conferring with a student in her office. In the lecture room she is forced to be both physically and stylistically farther away from her audience than she would be in her office. Or contrast the distance in a statement in a printed syllabus that "Students are expected to hand in assignments on the date stipulated" and an instructor's after-class remark, "Joe, you've got to get your papers in on time." In the first statement the writer is impersonal and remote; in the second the speaker is personal and close.

The following selections further illustrate the difference between writing that tries to get close to the reader and writing that addresses the reader from a distance:

It's Friday afternoon, and you have almost survived another week of   *Example 1*
classes. You are just looking forward dreamily to the weekend when the
English instructor says: "For Monday you will turn in a five-hundred word
composition on college football."

Well, that puts a good big hole in the weekend. You don't have any
strong views on college football one way or the other. You get rather
excited during the season and go to all the home games and find it rather
more fun than not. On the other hand, the class has been reading Robert
Hutchins in the anthology and perhaps Shaw's "Eighty-Yard Run," and
from the class discussion you have got the idea that the instructor thinks
college football is for the birds. You are no fool, you. You can figure out
what side to take. (Paul Roberts, *Understanding English*)

The distance between writer and reader here is very slight. The writer gives the
impression of speaking personally to an individual reader, whom he addresses as
"you." The conversational tone, the diction, and the kinds of comments made
about the subject suggest a close identification of writer and reader.

White lies, first of all, are as common to political and diplomatic affairs as   *Example 2*
they are to the private lives of most people. Feigning enjoyment of an
embassy gathering or a political rally, toasting the longevity of a dubious
regime or an unimpressive candidate for office—these are forms of politeness
that mislead few. It is difficult to regard them as threats to either individuals
or communities. As with all white lies, however, the problem is that they
spread so easily, and that lines are very hard to draw. Is it still a white lie for a
secretary of state to announce that he is going to one country when in reality
he travels to another? Or for a president to issue a "cover story" to the effect
that a cold is forcing him to return to the White House, when in reality an
international crisis made him cancel the rest of his campaign trip? Is it a
white lie to issue a letter of praise for a public servant one has just fired?
Given the vulnerability of public trust, it is never more important than in
public life to keep the deceptive element of white lies to an absolute minimum, and to hold down the danger of their turning into more widespread
deceitful practices. (Sissela Bok, *Lying: Moral Choice in Public and Private
Life*)

This paragraph is addressed not to any particular reader, but to all readers. The
writer makes no attempt to address her readers as "you" or to appeal to their
special interests. She is more interested in what she has to say than to whom she is
saying it. Therefore she makes no attempt to get close to her readers. The whole
tone suggests much greater distance between writer and reader than was implied in
the preceding passage.

This impression of distance comes chiefly from sentence structure and diction, and we will discuss these linguistic bases of tone under "Style." All we want to show here is that tone depends partly on the decision writers make about what distance, or degree of separation, to maintain between themselves and their readers. This is not an arbitrary decision. It is related to the writers' decision about attitude toward the subject, and is consistent with the total purpose.

STYLE

The word *style* has many meanings, ranging from one's "lifestyle" to the latest fashion in clothes. Even when limited to writing, it can refer to anything from the writer's philosophy to the choice of words or sentence structure. It is a useful word, but it can be used with precision only when the context clearly implies its meaning. In this chapter we will define style as it applies to writing, discuss its chief components, and give some practical advice about how the style of your papers may be improved.

STYLE DEFINED

The American Heritage Dictionary defines style as "the way in which something is said or done, as distinguished from its substance." In writing, *substance* means "what is said"—the message or content. The definition assumes that what is said can be examined apart from how it is said. But this assumption is not always true. In many subtle ways a change in the style of a statement may change its meaning. For example, if we change "Please go!" to "Get lost!" the change in tone causes a change in the message. Only with this reservation can we accept the dictionary definition as a starting point and say, "Style is the way it is written."

But how do we describe the way something is written? Consider the following passage from *The Adventures of Huckleberry Finn.* Huck is staying with the Grangerfords after his raft has been wrecked. He has been reading a "poem" written by the youngest daughter, now dead. The poem is so bad that it is amusing. But it is supposed to be a sad poem about a young man who fell into a well and drowned. Huck thinks it is very good. After reading it, he says:

> If Emmeline Grangerford could make poetry like that before she was four-teen, there ain't no telling what she could a done by-and-by. Buck [her younger brother] said she could rattle off poetry like nothing. She didn't

ever have to stop and think. He said she would slap down a line, and if she couldn't find anything to rhyme with it she would just scratch it out and slap down another one, and go ahead. She warn't particular; she could write about anything you choose to give her to write about just so it was sadful. Every time a man died, or a woman died, or a child died, she would be on hand with her "tribute" before he was cold. She called them tributes. The neighbors said it was the doctor first, then Emmeline, then the undertaker— the undertaker never got in ahead of Emmeline but once, and then she hung fire on a rhyme for the dead person's name, which was Whistler. She warn't ever the same, after that; she never complained, but she kinder pined away and did not live long.

We can notice the following things about this passage:

1. Mark Twain is having fun with the subject. He knows the poem is sentimental to the point of being ridiculous, and he expects the reader to see that, too.

2. Huck himself is serious. Twain is getting the humorous effect by letting Huck talk about the poetry. Huck is the narrator in the scene, who says what a boy like him, but not a man like Twain, would say. In other words, even though Twain is the writer, the *voice* we hear is that of Huck Finn. Twain creates an ironical situation in which everything Huck says about Emmeline's poetry will produce a quite different judgment in the readers.

3. The diction is appropriate to the speaker. The effect would be lost if Huck were made to speak like a sophisticated adult. He must speak in his own voice.

4. All these elements are so interrelated that a change in any one of them would spoil the total effect. They all add up to a consistent piece of irony that is making fun of extreme sentimentality.

Even so small a sample suggests that the decision on "how it is written" includes such considerations as (1) the writer's attitude toward the subject, (2) the writer's relationship with the readers, and (3) the language the writer uses to express his or her ideas. The first two of these considerations can be included in the general term *tone*. We can therefore expand our starting definition as follows:

> The *style* of a piece of writing is the pattern of choices the writer makes in developing his or her purpose. If the choices are consistent, they create a harmony of tone and language that constitutes the style of the work. A description of the style of any piece of writing is therefore an explanation of the means by which the writer achieved his or her purpose.

This definition relates purpose and style as cause and effect. We said in Chapter 1 that your purpose as a writer is your awareness of what you want to do and how you want to do it for the readers you are addressing.

In subsequent chapters we emphasized that a clear sense of purpose guides you through all the choices you must make from planning your paper to revising it. If these choices are consistent with your purpose, your writing will show a harmonious pattern. This pattern is the style of your work. When we are describing the style of a paper, we are not dealing with some vague literary quality; we are generalizing a common pattern from all the particular choices the writer has made.

LANGUAGE AND RANGE OF STYLES

Style, of course, finally rests on language. So now we look closely at the sentence structure and diction of selected passages to see what generalizations we can draw from them.

Example 1

You're going to paint that picturesque old barn. All right. One vertical line (better use charcoal) will place the corner of the barn, another line the base. A couple of lines for the trunk of the tree, and maybe a branch or two. Then a line to indicate the horizon—whatever divides the sky from whatever meets it (tree, barn, hill). That's all! No leaves, doorknobs, cats, mice, or daffodils. It's the painting that's fun, and any time wasted in getting into a mess of details is to be deplored. As we start to paint, anything resembling a real drawing on our canvas is purely accidental. . . .

Now squeeze out little blobs of color on your palette, and a big blob of white. And take a look at that sky. It is, let's say, cloudless. And it really is blue. Still not as blue as Uncle Ed's shirt. Take a half of a butter ball of white on your palette knife and plaster it on the front of your palette. Careful now! Just a pinch of blue and mix with the white until there are no streaks. Not blue enough? All right, just a tiny bit more—but easy! Satisfied? Dip your brush in the turpentine, then in the paint and slap it on! Boldly—never mind if you slop over the barn a bit. (Joseph Alger, "Get in There and Paint," *Recreation*)

Analysis of example 1:
Sentence Structure

The twenty-two sentences of this passage average only ten words in length, and over half of them are fragments. Most of the complete sentences consist of a main clause or two compound main clauses. There are no inverted constructions or periodic sentences, and few parallel structures. The sentences usually follow a straight subject-verb-object order, and most of them are commands.

Diction

In the whole passage there are fewer than a dozen words—about 5 percent—more than two syllables long. *Picturesque, accidental,* and *turpentine* are the most notable. Except possibly for *palette,* there are no "learned" words. Contractions are numerous—*you're, that's, it's, let's.*

Tone

The writer's attitude toward the subject is enthusiastic and subjective. His attitude toward the reader is both informative and affective, since he is trying to influence the reader's conduct by giving information and telling the reader how to use it. The distance between writer and reader is exceptionally slight: the writer creates the impression of standing beside the reader and giving advice on every move. The voice we hear is that of a teacher eager to share his knowledge, a little bossy in a friendly way, but encouraging and helpful.

All these components blend into a consistent style that aims at ease and clarity through simple sentences and diction. The writer gives the impression of talking in print. The diction and the rhythms of the sentences are those of informal conversation. In the last chapter we used the word *colloquial* to describe diction of this sort. Now we can expand that term to cover the whole style. Such an obviously colloquial style is not common in college writing, but it is by no means an uneducated style, and it can be used—as it is here—when it suits the writer's purpose.
Summary

Now contrast the following example with the one you have just studied:

> From those high storied shelves of dense rich bindings the great voices of eternity, the tongues of mighty poets dead and gone, now seemed to speak to him out of the living and animate silence of the room. But in that living silence, in the vast and quiet spirit of sleep which filled the great house, amid the grand and overwhelming stillness of that proud power of wealth and the impregnable security of its position, even the voices of those mighty poets dead and gone now seemed somehow lonely, small, lost and pitiful. Each in his little niche of shelf securely stored—all of the genius, richness, and whole compacted treasure of a poet's life within a foot of space, within the limits of six small dense richly-garnished volumes—all of the great poets of the earth were there, unread, unopened, and forgotten, and were somehow, terribly, the mute small symbols of a rich man's power, of the power of wealth to own everything, to take everything, to triumph over everything—even over the power and genius of the mightiest poet—to keep him there upon his little foot of shelf, unopened and forgotten, but possessed. (Thomas Wolfe, *Of Time and the River*)
Example 2

This paragraph has only three sentences. There are no fragments, and the sentences are long—38, 55, and 104 words respectively, or an average of 66 against 10 in the preceding example. All the sentences are involved; none of them is simple; none starts with the subject. Subjects and verbs are often separated—sometimes widely—by intervening modifiers. The last sentence, as the punctuation shows, is extremely involved. Throughout the paragraph parallel and periodic structures are used for rhythmic and other effects.
Analysis of example 2: Sentence Structure

About 10 percent of the words are more than two syllables long, and there is a smaller proportion of monosyllables than in example 1. The diction is less concrete, and there are more learned words—*animate, impregnable, niche, compacted,*
Diction

garnished, mute. Several phrases have a lofty, poetic ring—"high storied shelves," "great voices of eternity," "living and animate silence," "proud power of wealth," "the mute small symbols of a rich man's power," "unopened and forgotten, but possessed."

Tone The attitude toward the subject is clearly affective: the author is expressing his indignation about people who reduce great books to mere symbols of their wealth. The distance between writer and reader is great; the emphasis is on the subject, not on the reader. The tone is impersonal, dignified, and eloquent.

Summary As in the first example, all these components blend into a consistent style. But what a different style! This one aims at eloquence, not ease or familiarity. It is not the kind of style that one would use to give directions, explain a process, answer an examination, or report a story in a newspaper. We could call it a *grand* style, but the usual name for it is *formal*.

Example 3 Conant was the first Harvard president to recognize that meatballs [identified by the author as "commuting Irish, Jewish, and Italian youngsters from Greater Boston"] were Harvard men, too, and so he set apart a ground floor room at Dudley Hall where we could bring our lunches in brown paper bags and eat at a table, or lounge in easy chairs between classes. . . .

Dudley Hall was plowed regularly by Harvard's intellectual upper-class Communists, who felt that we were of the oppressed. Occasionally such well-bred, rich or elite Communist youngsters from the resident houses would bring a neat brown-paper-bag lunch and join us at the round tables to persuade us, as companions, of the inevitable proletarian revolution. . . . Most of us, largely Boston Latin School graduates, knew more about poverty than anyone from Beacon Hill or the fashionable East Side of New York. We hated poverty; and meant to have no share in it. We had come to Harvard not to help the working classes but to get out of the working classes. We were on the make. And in my own case, the approach to Harvard and its riches was that of a looter. Harvard had the keys to the gates; what lay behind the gates I could not guess, but all that lay there was to be looted. Not only were there required courses to be attended, but there were courses given by famous men, lectures open to all, where no one guarded the entry. I could listen. There were museums to be seen, libraries and poetry rooms of all kinds to tarry in—and stacks and stacks and stacks of books. It was a place to grab at ideas and facts, and I grabbed at history. (Theodore H. White, *In Search of History)*

Analysis of example 3: All the sentences in this passage follow the standard pattern: subject–verb–
Sentence Structure object, each with its modifiers, and with subordinate clauses following their main clauses. There are no conspicuous parallel or periodic sentences and no sentence fragments. Sentences vary in length from 3 words to 48 and average 21, as contrasted with 10 in example 1 and 66 in example 2.

In this example there is only one learned word *(proletarian).* Slang words occur *Diction*
twice *(meatballs* and *on the make).* All the rest, including *grab,* are popular words.
About 7 percent of the words contain more than two syllables.

The attitude toward the subject is serious and subjective. The author is describ- *Tone*
ing his Harvard experience as he knew it, and what he has to say is influenced by
his personal point of view. His attitude toward his readers, most of whom are
probably college graduates, is mainly informative. The distance between writer and
reader is greater than in example 1 but less than in example 2.

The style does not call attention to itself as do the styles of the other examples. *Summary*
The sentence structure is neither so simple as that of example 1 nor so involved as
that of example 2. It contains none of the fragments that were so frequent in the
first example and none of the conspicuous parallelism of the second. The average
sentence length is between that of example 1 and example 2. This is an in-between
style. We call it a *moderate* style.

If we represent these three styles on a scale that extends from most to least
formal, their respective positions can be shown as follows:

Formal	Moderate	Colloquial
∧	∧	∧
Example 2	Example 3	Example 1

This diagram is intended to suggest three things.

1.   The scale measures degree of formality, from most to least; it does not
measure degree of excellence, from good to bad. There is certainly no suggestion
that a formal style is necessarily better than a moderate one, or that moderate is
necessarily better than colloquial. All three are standard English styles, and each is
appropriate in some situations. It is our opinion that the most appropriate style for
most freshman compositions is the moderate style and that students would be well
advised not to try to cultivate a too-formal or a too-colloquial style in college
expository writing.

2.   Each stylistic classification is itself a range. Within the formal range a particular sample may be more or less formal than others. For example, in many ways a
legal contract is more formal than the Wolfe paragraph.

3.   There is no rigid dividing line between these styles. The overlapping shown in
the diagram is intended to suggest that the moderate style has such a broad range
that it can include some formal and some colloquial elements. These inclusions,

Summary of the Formal, Moderate, and Colloquial Styles

	Formal	Moderate	Colloquial
Sentences	Relatively long and involved; likely to make considerable use of parallel, balanced, and periodic structures; no fragments.	Of medium length, averaging between fifteen and twenty-five words; mostly standard structure but with some parallelism and occasionally balanced and periodic sentences; fragments rare.	Short, simple structures; mainly subject-verb-object order; almost no use of balanced or periodic sentences; fragments common.
Diction	Extensive vocabulary, some use of learned and abstract words; no slang; almost no contractions or clipped words.	Ranges from learned to colloquial but mostly popular words; both abstract and concrete diction; occasional contractions and clipped words; may contain some inconspicuous slang.	Diction limited to popular and colloquial words, frequent contractions and clipped words; frequent use of utility words; more slang than in moderate style.
Tone	Always a serious attitude toward an important subject; may be either subjective or objective and informative or affective; no attempt to establish closeness with reader, who is almost never addressed as "you"; personality of the writer not conspicuous; whole tone usually dignified and impersonal.	Attitude toward subject may be serious or light, objective or subjective, informative or affective; relationship with reader close but seldom intimate; writer often refers to himself or herself as "I" and to reader as "you"; but the range of moderate style is so broad that it can vary from semiformal to semicolloquial.	Attitude toward subject may be serious or light but is usually subjective; close, usually intimate, relation with reader, who is nearly always addressed as "you"; whole tone is that of informal conversation.
Uses	A restricted style used chiefly for scholarly or technical writing for experts, or for essays and speeches that aim at eloquence or inspiration; a distinguished style, but not one for everyday use or practical affairs.	The broadest and most usable style for expository and argumentative writing and for all but the most formal of public speeches; the prevailing style in nontechnical books and magazines, in newspaper reports and editorials, in college lectures and discussions, in all student writing except some fiction.	Light, chatty writing as in letters to close friends of the same age; on the whole, a restricted style that is inappropriate to most college writing except fiction.

however, must be consistent with the purpose and context of the paper. Theodore White was justified in using *meatballs* in example 3, because that was what brown-bagging Harvard men were called when he was in college.

The table on page 194 will give you a more complete summary of these three styles than it is possible to derive from a single example of each.

Working individually, rate the styles of the following lettered paragraphs by placing the letter under the appropriate number on the scale. Then discuss your ratings in class.

EXERCISE

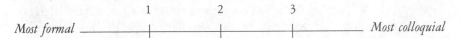

Most formal ——————————————————— *Most colloquial*

What I have been talking about is knowledge. Knowledge, perhaps, is not a good word for this. Perhaps one would rather say my *Image* of the world. Knowledge has an implication of validity, of truth. What I am talking about is what I believe to be true: my subjective knowledge. It is this image that largely governs my behavior. In about an hour I shall . . . leave my office, go to a car, drive down to my home, play with the children, have supper, perhaps read a book, go to bed. I can predict this behavior with a fair degree of accuracy because of the knowledge which I have: the knowledge that I have a home not far away, to which I am accustomed to go. The prediction, of course, may not be fulfilled. There may be an earthquake, I may have an accident with the car on the way home, I may get home to find that my family has been suddenly called away. A hundred and one things may happen. As each event occurs, however, it alters my knowledge structure or image. And as it alters my image, I behave accordingly. *The first proposition of this work, therefore, is that behavior depends on the image.* (Kenneth Boulding, *The Image*)

Paragraph a

This isn't the kind of thing you hear about during your orientation period, partly because of the national aversion to history, partly because there are many more pressing matters. The prospect for a winning football season. What the kids are wearing. What the lowdown is on the local Greeks, or activists, or literati, or jocks, whatever's your crowd. The food in the cafeteria. How to get into the dorm after hours. Where the john is in the library. With all this to assimilate, who has time or patience to consider the nature of the institution to which you've entrusted the next four years of your life? (Leonard A. Greenbaum and Rudolph B. Schmerl, *Course X: A Left Field Guide to Freshman English*)

Paragraph b

Paragraph c   I have, myself, full confidence that if all do their duty, if nothing is neglected, and if the best arrangements are made, as they are being made, we shall prove ourselves once again able to defend our island home, to ride out the storm of war, and to outlive the menace of tyranny, if necessary for years, if necessary alone. At any rate, that is what we are going to try to do. That is the resolve of His Majesty's Government—every man of them. That is the will of Parliament and the nation. The British Empire and the French Republic, linked together in their cause and in their need, will defend to the death their native soil, aiding each other like good comrades to the utmost of their strength. Even though large tracts of Europe and many old and famous States have fallen or may fall into the grip of the Gestapo and all the odious apparatus of Nazi rule, we shall not flag or fail. We shall go on to the end. We shall fight in France, we shall fight on the seas and oceans, we shall fight with growing confidence and growing strength in the air, we shall defend our island, whatever the cost may be. We shall fight on the beaches, we shall fight on the landing grounds, we shall fight in the fields and in the streets, we shall fight in the hills; we shall never surrender, and even if, which I do not for a moment believe, this island or a large part of it were subjugated and starving, then our Empire beyond the seas, armed and guarded by the British Fleet, would carry on the struggle, until, in God's good time, the new world, with all its power and might, steps forth to the rescue and the liberation of the old. (Winston Churchill, *Blood, Sweat, and Tears*)

SOME PRACTICAL ADVICE
ABOUT STYLE

So far in this chapter we have examined other writers' styles in the belief that by analyzing sample passages you can acquire a background that will help you see what kinds of considerations are involved in style. Now we want to apply what you have learned to your own writing. What we say here will give the gist of the preceding chapters in seven main points. Since this is a summary, it will not introduce new ideas, but it will give you, in compact form, the chief considerations to keep in mind in all your writing.

1.   *Let your purpose be your guide.* We have repeatedly pointed out that a clear sense of purpose acts as a control over all the choices you make at every stage of composition. Style is the result of that control. It is not some kind of literary covering that can be put on writing the way a coat of paint is added to a house. It must grow out of and reflect the writer's purpose. Indeed, style is so dependent on purpose that it makes little sense to talk about style apart from purpose. We are

tempted to say, "Take care of your purpose and your style will take care of itself." This does not mean that you need not bother about style; it means that the best way to bother about it is to know what you are trying to do and to trust that knowledge as a guide. All that we have to say on the other six points is implied in this first one.

2. *Generally, choose a moderate style.* There is nothing wrong with either a formal or a colloquial style when it is appropriate, and there are times when each is right for a particular purpose. But these times are rare in college writing or in most of the writing you will do after you graduate. The trouble with unnecessary formality in college writing is that it often leads to pretentiousness and wordiness; the student tries too hard to be impressive and literary when it would be enough just to be clear. The trouble with a colloquial style is that, if used for serious treatment of a subject, it can easily degenerate into slovenliness and work against a serious purpose. The best general policy is to aim at something near the middle of the range between formal and colloquial. You can then be objective or subjective, informative or affective, and your writing is likely to seem more natural than at either extreme. The broad range of the moderate style gives you all the leeway you need.

3. *Keep your style consistent.* Probably the worst defect in style is inconsistency. A piece of writing that is completely inconsistent will have no discoverable purpose and therefore no discoverable style. But usually inconsistency occurs in particular paragraphs, sentences, or words and can be removed in revision.

a. Inconsistency in tone. Conspicuous inconsistency in tone is likely to jar a reader. The inconsistency will be most obvious when colloquial elements appear in a formal style, or formal elements in a colloquial one. Because a moderate style can range from semiformal to semicolloquial, it can tolerate usages that would be more conspicuous in the extreme styles.

b. Inconsistency in diction. As early as the first paragraphs of an essay, you commit yourself to a recognizable approach to your subject and to your reader. Your thesis announces what idea you are going to develop, and the opening sentences establish the tone. A reader senses these commitments and expects you to honor them.

If your choices of words are harmonious, they will build to a consistent style; but unconsidered choices may make it difficult for a reader to see any pattern in your writing. Your choice of words should suit the style you have already established. Words that clearly suggest an undesired meaning are relatively easy to detect in revision. You are most likely to go wrong by choosing words that are close, but not close enough, to your intended meaning. Do you want *insensitive, naive, thoughtless,* or *undiscriminating* in a particular sentence? The answer, of course, depends on the context. It is not a question of which is the "best" word, but of which is the best word for your purpose at this point in your paper.

4.   *Try to see your writing as your reader will see it.* Of all the advice given here, this is the hardest to follow. We all tend to assume that what is clear to us will be equally clear to others. Common experience should tell us that this assumption does not always work. Even in ordinary conversation we often ask and are asked, "What do you mean by that?" Usually the speaker can explain, but the point is that explanation is necessary. Clarity is even more necessary in writing, for the reader usually cannot ask for an explanation. As far as possible, try to anticipate your reader's difficulties.

Despite your best efforts to be clear, you may still get papers back with "Meaning?" in the margin. This is evidence that at least one reader had trouble understanding. A stock response is, "Oh, you know what I mean!" But this response is an evasion, a cop-out. The marginal question identifies a trouble spot at which the reader is asking for clarification. It is your responsibility as writer to provide it. If you cannot see what is causing the trouble, you can ask for advice.

5.   *Be as specific as you can.* Language is often a difficult medium. What makes it so is its abstractness. The word *apple* is more abstract than any apple you ever ate or saw, because it leaves out most of our actual experience with apples—their shape, size, color, texture, and taste. The farther we get from the names of common objects, the more abstract language becomes. When we are talking about truth and beauty and justice, we are referring not to things but to highly abstract concepts.

The common problem of all writers is to make the abstractions of language concrete enough so that readers will get some clear image or idea from written statements. There are two common ways of doing this: one is to illustrate the meaning of a general statement by examples or details; the other is to choose words that are reasonably specific.

Try always to pin down your general statements by examples or details. If you do not have the details in mind, you are not ready to make the general statement, for generalizations are inferences drawn from details of observation and can be explained or supported only by reference to these details. The realization that you are not ready to be specific may force you to study your subject in greater depth, and this will contribute to your understanding of it.

The second way of avoiding abstractness in language is to use words that specify the meaning you want. Don't write "an *unsuccessful* attempt" if *abortive, blundering, botched, fruitless,* or *half-hearted* comes closer to your meaning. Don't write "walked," if *limped, lurched, sauntered,* or *strode* describes more accurately the kind of walking you have in mind. If you must use a utility word such as *mess,* restrict its general meaning by a specifying adjective, such as *cluttered, gooey,* or *untidy,* whichever describes the particular kind of mess you are writing about. But use sparingly adjectives that are themselves too general to be helpful—words like *awful, beautiful, grand, lovely, nice, terrible.*

6. *Avoid wordiness.* In Chapter 6 we discussed wordiness as a relation between the number of words used and the amount of meaning conveyed. Any time you add explanatory or descriptive details, you add more words to your paper; but as long as those words also add meaning, they improve communication. It is only when writers conspicuously use words that add no meaning that we call them wordy. The techniques for removing wordiness were discussed on pages 143–145.

7. *Revise and proofread.* Throughout this book we have stressed revision as a necessary stage in the composition process. How much revision you need to do will vary with different papers. In general, a paper carefully prewritten will need less revision than one not prewritten at all. But prewriting promises only a sound plan and a consistent approach. Revision of individual paragraphs and sentences may still be necessary, whether done during or after the first draft. But before you type the finished draft, you should read the whole paper carefully, preferably more than once, to see what further changes occur to you.

Proofreading is a careful reading of the final version to catch and correct any errors in grammar, spelling, and punctuation that may have survived the revision or been made in the final copy. This reading should be done slowly, preferably aloud. Doing it thoroughly can sometimes mean the difference of one grade or more in the instructor's evaluation of your paper.

As a review of what you have learned about style in this chapter, write a substantial comment on the style of the following student paper. In preparation for your comment, consider the following questions and provide specific evidence for your answers.

REVIEW EXERCISE

1. What is the writer's attitude toward her subject—serious or light, subjective or objective, informative or affective?

2. What is the writer's attitude toward her readers? Specifically, what kind of reader does she seem to have in mind? Is the distance between writer and readers close or remote?

3. On the evidence of sentence structure and diction, would you classify the style as chiefly formal, moderate, or colloquial?

4. Is the style appropriate to the writer's purpose?

5. What is your final judgment of the effectiveness of the paper?

You Are What You Smoke

Have you ever seen in *any* magazine a cigarette ad that was smaller than the whole page? I'll bet you a Cricket lighter you haven't. Well, there are two—an occasional ad for Lucky 100's printed in red and black, cramped against the outer edge of a page, and on the opposite edge of the adjacent page an almost identical green and black ad for Iceberg 100's, Lucky's menthol twin. They look like two garish Christmas-colored bookends. Now who do you know that smokes Luckies or Icebergs? Nobody, right? Who have you ever even *seen* smoking those brands? Nobody but nobody. That's easy enough to understand: the quality of the ad suggests that they're 90% alfalfa, and regardless of financial status, most people aren't cheap enough to be seen with a pack that is actually as tacky as it looks in print.

Much less offensive but still not quite visually attractive are the full-page ads for the ever-booming market of low tar and nicotine cigarettes. These ads seem straightforward enough—they feature a package of the brand in question and explain its advantages. Yet who's going to take the time to read a whole page of print? An interested and concerned person, that's who. Obviously the low tar smoker is rational, intelligent, and somewhat of a stoic—qualities to be proud of—for he is not only protecting his health and prolonging his lifespan, but also sacrificing the pleasure of a stronger brand. The most prestigious of the low tar brands is Carlton. "Nobody's lower than Carlton"; you can even check out that claim by comparing "the latest U.S. government figures" in a conveniently provided graph. What the ad fails to mention is that smoking Carltons is like sucking air through a straw.

Undaunted by the save-your-health campaign, the stronger brands emerge as the most effectively advertised of all cigarettes. Comprised of merely a few simple words and a pleasing photograph, these ads induce the eye to stop, linger, savor, absorb—proving once again that a picture is worth a thousand words. Surrounded by lush greenery in the open countryside, a soft, gently feminine woman enjoys the peacefulness of nature and the nearby babbling brook while her gentleman-friend hovers in the background. "Lady be Kool." The women may be different, but all the Kool ads convey the same mood of blissful relaxation in the out-of-doors. If the men feel rejected from the Kool world, they can travel to Marlboro Country and experience the rugged, solitary existence of a rancher astride his faithful horse. Those who are still concerned about health have the option of choosing Marlboro Lights. You don't get the real-life photograph; instead you get an artist's sketch of a cowboy which at least offers "the *spirit* of Marlboro in a low tar cigarette."

But what if you're not the outdoors type? Well, there's Winston, for one. Winston ads focus on people, not environment. Winston smokers are strong and silent individuals. The men are virile and masculine enough to unabashedly flaunt necklaces on their hairy chests; the women are ice-goddesses. These people look out at the world with an I-don't-take-bull-from-anyone expression. But then, "Winston wasn't my first cigarette. I learned about smoking by trying different cigarettes." Yes, these people are experienced. *You* may not be ready for Winston yet, but "when your taste grows up, so should your cigarette."

If the Winston personality seems too severe, do not fear. There's still Salem, the true pleasure cigarette. "I don't let anything get in the way of my enjoyment." Apparently not. Female Salem smokers casually sit on a green turf, legs spread apart, necklines plunging exposingly downward, arms receptively open. The well-built mature-looking men smile seductively and the women seem to bask in a post-orgasmic blush.

Ah, the poor, lost consumer souls of America! Are we so insecure that we need to define ourselves by others through association, so immature that we need to identify with prefabricated images? I, for one, needn't stoop so low. Because, well, my uncle knows Paul Newman.

9

PERSUASION

The emphasis in the preceding seven chapters was on the explanation of ideas. When we move to persuasion, the emphasis will be on trying to get readers to accept some belief or opinion. The examples will still use explanation, but now the explanation will be not an end in itself, but a means of persuading readers.

Persuasion, as we are considering it, is *verbal communication that attempts to bring about a voluntary change in judgment so that readers or listeners will accept a belief they did not hold before.* The purpose of persuasion is to cause a change in thinking. That change may be simply the substitution of one belief for another, or it may result in action, such as voting for A instead of B, giving up smoking, or buying a product. As we are defining persuasion, the change of opinion must be voluntary: the people being persuaded must be free to accept or reject the belief or proposal. If they accept it, they do so because, all things considered, they want to. Finally, persuasion must cause a change in belief. No persuasion is needed to make people believe what they already believe.

CHANGING THE READER'S IMAGE

On page 195 you read a paragraph in which Kenneth Boulding explained what he meant by *image*. As he was using it, *image* meant the view or set of beliefs we have learned to accept. That view, or image, controls our behavior. If our image of democracy is associated with the right of people to choose their political leaders by secret ballot, to speak openly for or against their policies while they are in power, and to vote them out of office when their conduct is unsatisfactory, we will respond favorably to any proposal that is consistent with that image and reject any that seems to oppose it. Thus we will generally assume that democracy, as we understand it, is "good" and that communism and fascism are "bad." Our image of democracy becomes the standard by which we judge competing systems of government.

If in defining persuasion we substitute *image* for *belief,* we can say that the purpose of persuasion is to change the reader's image of something. To do this requires two kinds of knowledge: the writer has to know (1) what the reader's image is and (2) how it may be changed. The first requires a realistic understanding of one's readers; the second requires familiarity with the principal means of persuasion. Only insofar as a writer meets these requirements will he or she be persuasive. Failure to realize this often results in arguments that, however logically constructed, have no effect because they do not reach the image that controls the reader's behavior.

Images are shallow-rooted or deep-rooted. A shallow-rooted image can be removed or changed without any drastic effect on the person who holds it. Many beliefs based on reason are of this kind. People can be persuaded to do things they would prefer not to do, such as submit to an operation, when the evidence leads them to conclude that the action is necessary or beneficial. Provided the reasons given are convincing, they can change their accustomed conduct without much trouble.

But some images are so deeply embedded in the personality that one cannot give them up. To abandon them would be to deny something essential to one's self-respect, to one's sense of integrity as a person. A reader who believes that creation is an act of God and that a child is created at the moment of conception must view deliberate abortion as murder and cannot give up that image without denying a basic article of faith. This image will not be changed by any argument that a woman has a right to decide whether she wishes to bear a child, because acceptance of that belief would be an admission that a woman has a right to commit murder. The image is so deeply rooted that it cannot be removed without tearing out a cluster of beliefs essential to the reader's view of his or her own character.

A writer who understands the nature of deep-rooted images will respect them and will not dismiss a reader who holds them as "stupid" or "stubborn." The writer will not assume that these images can be changed in any one essay. Direct attack on them will only intensify resistance. Ridiculing them will create antagonism and may alienate other readers who are not committed to these images but resent the writer's insensitivity. The writer's best course is to follow three steps:*

1.   to recognize that he or she is confronted by a deep-rooted image that can be changed only by the reader, and then only when the emotional commitment given to the original image can be transferred to the new image

2.   to show understanding of the reader's position by restating it in terms acceptable to the reader

3.   to explore possible compromises between the reader's position and the writer's.

Even if the writer does not succeed in this third step, this procedure will help in at least three ways. First, it will reduce antagonism: the reader will feel less threatened and more inclined to listen to what the writer has to say. Second, the concessions made by the writer may encourage concessions by the reader: no longer forced to defend an image, the reader may be willing to consider some modification of it, and so move closer to the writer. Third, even if no acceptable compromise is possible, the writer's fairness will impress other readers and so be

* This discussion is indebted to Anatol Rapoport's "Ethical Debate" in his *Fights, Games, and Debates* (Ann Arbor: University of Michigan Press, 1960).

persuasive for them. We will later discuss this third advantage under the heading "Trustworthiness."

FITTING THE PERSUASION TO THE AUDIENCE

The more you understand your readers, the better chance you have of persuading them. Readers of course vary. But even though you may not know them all individually, you can know where they, as a group, are likely to stand on the question you are dealing with. You can estimate what they already know about the subject, what opinions and attitudes about it they now have, what issues they are most concerned with, and what kind of evidence will be most influential with them. Out of this knowledge you decide what kinds of appeals will best help you to persuade them. Making this decision is a major part of your prewriting. The following advice will help:

1. *Have specific readers in mind.* Whom are you trying to persuade—your parents, your instructor, your classmates, the readers of your college newspaper, or others? An essay written for one of these will not necessarily be persuasive to the others. A paper addressed to the world in general is not aimed at anybody in particular. You will write more purposefully if you begin prewriting by defining the particular set of readers for whom you are writing.

2. *Identify with your readers.* Once you have identified your readers, you can begin to identify *with* them. In this sense, *identify* means putting yourself imaginatively in their place and seeing the problem from their point of view. If persuasion is necessary, your readers do not at present share your beliefs. Your purpose is to lead them toward these beliefs. In order to lead them, you must start where they are. Only by understanding their present attitudes can you hope to change them. This kind of initial identification with the reader is not a trick; you are not pretending to be something you are not. You are simply trying to establish an area of agreement that you intend to broaden.

You have already seen a good example of how a writer leads an audience to a new point of view in the stop-and-frisk essay, "Three Points of View," on page 20. There the student author began by identifying with the attitude he assumed his classmates would take, that of an innocent citizen subjected to the indignities of the stop-and-search procedure. Then he asked them to look at the situation through the eyes of the officer making the search, and in so doing he led them to modify their original attitude. Finally he combined both views in a larger one that would be acceptable not only to the citizen and the officer but to all fair-minded people. In all this there was no trick and no dishonesty. The student was simply following a strategy designed to lead his audience to the conviction that, when conducted by a capable officer, the stop-and-search procedure protects everybody's legitimate interests.

3. *Be careful about the tone of your writing.* As you saw in Chapter 8, the tone reveals an attitude toward the readers. Your tone should help strengthen your identification with your readers; it should certainly avoid anything that will increase the distance between you and them. You can be angry or indignant about the situation you are trying to change or about those who allow that situation to exist. But you cannot be angry or indignant with your readers, not if you want their agreement. Nor can you talk down to them. You are trying to establish a partnership with them. Such a partnership requires mutual respect, and anything in your tone that lessens that respect will work against your purpose.

4. *Provide the evidence your readers need to accept your beliefs.* If you respect your readers, you will not ask them to accept your unsupported opinions, any more than a businessman would expect his partner to take his word for it that a proposed investment will be profitable. Normally both partners would go over the evidence in detail until both were satisfied. As a writer you have an obligation to spell out in detail why you think a reader should accept your conclusions. It is not enough that the writer believes the argument is sound. It is the reader who must be persuaded.

5. *Make your paper easy to read.* When you are asking your readers to agree with you, make their job as easy as possible. Highly complex arguments, confused structure, technical terminology, abstract diction, complex statistics—all these make communication difficult. Since the writer leads the reader, you should do everything you can to make it easy for the reader to follow your writing.

MEANS OF PERSUASION

In general a writer has three means of being persuasive: winning the trust of readers, appealing to their emotions, and convincing them through the logic of argument. These means are not separate; a writer may use them together in the same essay so that each supplements the others. But we can deal with them here only by taking them one at a time.

"Thank you for not smoking."

TRUSTWORTHINESS

Trustworthiness is the kind of persuasion that comes from the character or personality of the persuader. When writers seem trustworthy, readers have confidence in them and are inclined to agree with their arguments. This confidence may be a result of the writer's reputation, or it may be a response to what a writer does in a particular essay. In either case, the reader's trust is based on the belief that the writer is *knowledgeable* and *fair.*

Knowledgeability   To be judged knowledgeable a writer must appear to be fully and accurately informed on the subject. The standard of knowledgeability is relative. In medicine, specialists are usually considered more knowledgeable about their specialties than general practitioners would be, but outside of their specialties they may be less well informed. The knowledgeability of a student writer is usually measured in relation to that of other students. A student who has carefully studied a subject and shows familiarity with the pertinent facts will be considered more knowledgeable than another who has only a superficial grasp of the subject and is often wrong on significant details. The best way to be considered knowledgeable on any subject is to study it thoroughly.

When a piece of writing relies on information from printed sources, the writer's trustworthiness depends in part on the reliability of these sources. If they are questionable, the writer's trustworthiness suffers, because the ability to distinguish between reliable and unreliable sources is part of the test of knowledgeability. It is often hard to assess the reliability of printed sources, but the following advice will help:

1.   If certain information is important to an argument, your readers will want to know where you got it. If you cannot or do not identify your source, you may raise a doubt about your knowledgeability. If you can identify your source, do so, either in the text of your paper or in a footnote.

2.   Distinguish between primary and secondary sources. A *primary source* is the original source of the information; a *secondary source* is a report based on the primary one. Thus a television speech by a public figure or the text from which it was read is a primary source. Some newspapers, such as the *New York Times,* usually print the complete text of important speeches, and in this sense newspapers, too, may be considered primary sources. A newspaper report that summarizes the speech is, by contrast, a secondary source. It may or may not be accurate. If you are going to quote the speaker, it would be better to quote directly from the primary source. If that source is not available, you may have to quote and identify the newspaper report.

3.   When using a secondary source, see whether it specifically identifies the primary source. Many reliable publications do. Be cautious about such vague identifications as "It was learned from usually reliable sources," or "Sources close to the President say. . . ." These are deliberate devices to conceal the primary source, either to protect the informant or to give the report credibility it may not deserve. The 1973 investigations of the Watergate affair were frequently confused by testimony identified as coming from "the highest levels at the White House." Investigators could not determine who these "highest levels" were.

The main point to remember in this discussion of knowledgeability is that if you want a reader to trust you enough to accept your opinions, you must be sure of the facts on which these opinions are based. If you are not sure, check your information in some reliable source. Certainly do not trust your memory on historical information. A student who writes "John F. Kennedy, twenty-first President of the United States, was assassinated in Houston, Texas, on November 16, 1963," makes three misstatements of fact that could easily have been corrected by checking any of several reliable yearbooks or almanacs. Even a dictionary would identify John F. Kennedy as the *thirty-fifth* President. The effect of such carelessness on a reader is to raise doubts whether any factual statement the writer makes can be trusted.

Fairness   Any obvious unfairness will weaken a writer's trustworthiness. The most common kind of unfairness appears when writers are so committed to their own views that they cannot see the question objectively, and so read into opposing arguments motives and inferences that are products of their own bias. Common signs of unfairness are *distortions of opposing views, slanting, quoting out of context,* and *name-calling.*

Distortion is misrepresentation of an opposing view by inaccurate reporting. A common trick is to exaggerate the view and then attack it in its exaggerated form. Here is an example:

> MR. A: With all the things that have to be taught in English, there is not much point in devoting a great deal of class time to questions of disputed usage. The distinction between *shall* and *will,* the use of *like* as a conjunction, saying *data is* for *data are*—these are not choices between educated and uneducated speech, since both forms are used by educated people. A teacher may prefer one form to the other and may encourage students to follow that preference. But it is a waste of valuable class time to teach over and over again a distinction which, whatever its historical justification, is no longer a fact of English usage. We have more important things to do.
>
> MR. B: The difference between Mr. A and me is that I respect the purity of the English language, and he does not. If we permit *will* instead of *shall* and

data is for *data are,* where do we draw the line? Mr. A says that the incorrect forms become correct because educated people use them. I say that no one who says *data is* is an educated person. What Mr. A is doing is advocating the philosophy of "anything goes." Many of our troubles come from the adoption of that philosophy in various walks of life—in business, in government, in personal morality. It is a philosophy which reduces the conventions of educated speech to the level of gutter talk, and I think anyone who has any regard for the purity of his native tongue should stand up against the corruptive effects of this false philosophy.

Mr. A did not say "anything goes," nor did he advocate that educated speech should be reduced to the level of gutter talk. He did not even say teachers should accept usages they disapprove of. All he said was that there is not much point in devoting class time to usages that are common in the language of educated people. Mr. B is entitled to oppose that opinion. He is not entitled to distort it by misrepresenting it. In persuasion it is often necessary to attack a statement one thinks unwise or even quite wrong, but the attack should be directed at the statement actually made, not at an unfair exaggeration of it. To avoid the temptation or the suspicion of misrepresenting an opponent's statement, it is good policy and good manners to quote the statement fully and accurately before attacking it.

Slanting is the practice of selecting facts favorable to one's opinion and suppressing those against it. The result is a distorted and unfair view. For example, a writer who says there can be no real poverty in a country where the average annual income is more than $10,000 ignores two facts: that this average includes incomes of a million dollars or more, and that great numbers of people do not have anywhere near the average income. The omitted facts are just as pertinent to the question of poverty as is the average figure. The evidence is slanted to support a conclusion that would seem less true if the omitted facts were given.

A third kind of distortion is *quoting a statement out of context* and so making it mean what it was not intended to mean. You probably know that by deleting certain parts of a taped speech and then recording the edited tape, one can greatly distort the original speech. This may be amusing when done as a joke. It would be thoroughly dishonest if offered as evidence of what someone actually said. Yet writers sometimes produce similar effects by deliberately or carelessly omitting significant parts of a context. In reviewing a play, a critic writes: "The plot of this play is fascinating in a strange way: you keep waiting for something to happen, but nothing does. The characters never come close to greatness, and the few witty lines seem out of place among the platitudes of the dialogue." An advertisement based on this review reads: "Fascinating plot . . . characters close to greatness . . . witty lines." Even though some omissions are indicated, the effect of the advertisement is to distort what the critic said.

Name-calling is an attempt to discredit an opponent through the use of labels or descriptive words with highly unfavorable connotations. Examples are *male chauvinist pig, commie-lover, radical, reactionary, charlatan.* Within limits it is reasonable in persuasion to use connotations that advance the writer's purpose. But when emotional language is carried to the point of name-calling, it provokes an unfavorable response from intelligent readers, especially when name-calling is substituted for logical argument. A writer does not have to call opponents names. It is enough to show that they are mistaken, or that what they propose is not in the readers' best interests.

Distortion, slanting, quoting out of context, and name-calling do more harm to the users than to their opponents. These devices are clear signs of unfairness, and readers resent them. Writers who create such resentment hurt their chances of being persuasive.

EXERCISE   The following excerpt is from an article written by a famous journalist about William Jennings Bryan. Bryan had been three times the Democratic candidate for President, had served as Secretary of State under Wilson, and had been one of the prosecution lawyers in the Scopes trial in Dayton, Tennessee. At that trial Scopes, a biology teacher, was found guilty of breaking a state law by teaching the theory of evolution.

Study the diction in this excerpt. Do you find it persuasive or objectionable? Support your judgment by reference to particular words or phrases. What conclusions do you draw about the writer's fairness?

> This talk of sincerity, I confess, fatigues me. If the fellow was sincere, then so was P. T. Barnum. The word is disgraced and degraded by such use. He was, in fact, a charlatan, a mountebank, a zany without shame or dignity. His career brought him into contact with the first men of his time; he preferred the company of rustic ignoramuses. It was hard to believe, watching him at Dayton, that he had traveled, that he had been a high officer of state. He seemed only a poor clod like those around him, deluded by childish theology, full of an almost pathological hatred of all learning, all human dignity, all fine and noble things. He was a peasant come home to the barnyard. Imagine a gentleman, and you have imagined everything that he was not. What animated him from end to end of his grotesque career was simply ambition—the ambition of a common man to get his hands upon the collar of his superiors, or, failing that, to get his thumb into their eyes. He was born with a roaring voice, and it had the trick of inflaming half-wits. His whole career was devoted to raising those half-wits against their betters, that he himself might shine. (H. L. Mencken, *Prejudices: Fifth Series*)

EMOTIONAL APPEAL

Some people think of emotional appeal as an unworthy kind of persuasion. The term suggests to them a writer stampeding readers into thoughtless action by causing their feelings to overrule their judgment. This does happen, but abuses of emotional appeal do not negate the need for it. Readers feel as well as think, and to be thoroughly persuaded they must be both intellectually and emotionally involved. The need for emotional appeal is greatest when a writer is trying to persuade readers that the present situation is bad and something must be done about it. Since any action takes effort, people are not likely to act until they feel a compelling need to do so. Emotional appeal creates that need. Once they are emotionally persuaded that something must be done, they will be willing to consider possible solutions and choose the one that seems best. Someone has said that emotional appeal is the starter and logical argument the steering wheel. We do not choose between them. Both are necessary.

The strongest emotional appeals usually dramatize a need through examples. Agencies seeking money to provide food, shelter, clothing, and medical care for suffering children often choose one child as typical and appeal for sympathy with a picture of that child. In the accompanying advertisement the real problem is not so much the plight of the child in the picture as the negligence of parents. The statistics in the advertisement may be persuasive to people who take the trouble to think about them. But it is the picture of the crippled child that gets their attention and makes them start thinking about the high risk of polio, diphtheria, and other preventable diseases among young children. The example personalizes the problem. From any parent who has not had a child vaccinated, it is likely to provoke the response, "That could be *my* child!" Once parents have identified their own children with the child in the picture, they are more likely to take protective action.

In using emotional appeal in your own writing, you will have almost no opportunity of presenting pictures; you must provoke the desired response through words alone. Your best means will probably be narration or description or a combination of both. If you want to show that a serious evil exists, dramatize that evil by showing it happening to somebody. If you want to show that the present situation is shocking, describe it in specific detail. The following paragraph combines both example and description:

> As I sit in my jail cell in Santa Fe, capital of New Mexico, I pray that all poor people will unite to bring justice to New Mexico. My cell block has no daylight, no ventilation of any kind. After 9 P.M. we are left in a dungeon of total darkness. Visiting rules allow only fifteen minutes per week on Thurs-

If you forget to have your children vaccinated, you could be reminded of it the rest of your life.

There's no gentle way of putting it.

Parents who don't have their children immunized against polio are risking a senseless tragedy. We only raise the point here because that's exactly what many parents seem to be doing.

In 1963, for example, 84% of all preschoolers had three or more doses of polio vaccine. Ten years later the number had plummeted to 60% — which is simply another way of saying that 2 out of every 5 children have not been immunized against polio.

And polio isn't the only childhood disease people seem to be ignoring.

Immunization against diphtheria has been so neglected that not long ago there was an epidemic of it in Texas.

In 1974, reports show there were 57,407 cases of mumps, 22,085 of measles, 94 of tetanus, and 1,758 of whooping cough — all preventable.

What about your children? Are they protected against these diseases?

The best way to make sure is to see your family doctor. He can help you check on which immunizations your children may have missed, and then see that your children get them.

Of course, one of the best weapons

in preventing any disease is knowledge. So to help you learn about immunization in greater detail, we've prepared a booklet. You can get it by writing: "Immunization," Metropolitan Life, One Madison Avenue, New York, N.Y. 10010.

Our interest in this is simple. At Metropolitan Life, literally everything we do is concerned with people's futures. And we'd like to make sure those futures are not only secure, but healthy and long.

✳ Metropolitan Life
Where the future is now

Carl Fischer for Metropolitan Life

days from 1 to 4 P.M. so that parents who work cannot visit their sons in jail. Yesterday a twenty-two-year-old boy cut his throat. Today, August 17, two young boys cut their wrists with razor blades and were taken unconscious to the hospital. My cell block is hot and suffocating. All my prison mates complain and show a daily state of anger. But these uncomfortable conditions do not bother me, for I have a divine dream to give me strength: the happiness of my people. (Reies Lopez Tijerina, "A Letter from Jail," *We Are Chicanos*)

DISCUSSION PROBLEM

The following article appeared in *Ms.*, a magazine addressed to women. It views the husband-wife relationship through the eyes of a woman and argues that a wife is such a useful companion that even a *wife* would want one. Its persuasiveness for an audience of both sexes partly depends on whether the "husband" and "wife" in the article are typical. What do you think? Discuss the article with special attention to trustworthiness and emotional appeal.

I Want a Wife

I belong to that classification of people known as wives. I am a Wife. And, not altogether incidentally, I am a mother.

Not too long ago a male friend of mine appeared on the scene fresh from a recent divorce. He had one child, who is, of course, with his ex-wife. He is obviously looking for another wife. As I thought about him while I was ironing one evening, it suddenly occurred to me that I, too, would like to have a wife. Why do I want a wife?

I would like to go back to school so that I can become economically independent, support myself, and, if need be, support those dependent on me. I want a wife who will work and send me to school. And while I am going to school I want a wife to take care of my children. I want a wife to keep track of the children's doctor and dentist appointments. And to keep track of mine, too. I want a wife to make sure that my children eat properly and are kept clean. I want a wife who will wash the children's clothes and keep them mended. I want a wife who is a good nurturant attendant to my children, who arranges for their schooling, makes sure they have an adequate social life with their peers, takes them to the park, the zoo, etc. I want a wife who takes care of the children when they are sick, a wife who arranges to be around when the children need special care, because, of course, I cannot miss classes at school. My wife must arrange to lose time at work and not lose the job. It may mean a small cut in my wife's income from time to time, but I guess I can tolerate that. Needless to say, my wife will arrange and pay for the care of the children while my wife is working.

I want a wife who will take care of *my* physical needs. I want a wife who will keep the house clean. A wife who will pick up after me. I want a wife who will keep my clothes clean, ironed, mended, replaced when need be, and who will see to it that my personal things are kept in their proper place so that I can find what I need the minute I need it. I want a wife who cooks the meals, a wife who is a *good* cook. I want a wife who will plan the menus, do the necessary shopping, prepare the meals, serve them pleasantly, and then do the cleaning up while I do my studying. I want a wife who will care for me when I am sick and sympathize with my pain and loss of time from school. I want a wife to go along when our family takes a vacation so that someone can continue to care for me and my children when I need a rest and change of scene.

I want a wife who will not bother me with rambling complaints about a wife's duties. But I want a wife who will listen to me when I feel the need to explain a rather difficult point I have come across in my course of studies. And I want a wife who will type my papers for me when I have written them.

I want a wife who will take care of the details of my social life. When my wife and I are invited out by my friends, I want a wife who will take care of the babysitting arrangements. When I meet people at school that I like and want to entertain, I want a wife who will have the house clean, prepare a special meal, serve it to me and my friends, and not interrupt when I talk about the things that interest me and my friends. I want a wife who will have arranged that the children are fed and ready for bed before my guests arrive so that the children do not bother us. I want a wife who takes care of the needs of my guests so that they feel comfortable, who makes sure that they have an ashtray, that they are passed the hors d'oeuvres, that they are offered a second helping of the food, that their wine glasses are replenished when necessary, that their coffee is served to them as they like it.

And I want a wife who knows that sometimes I need a night out by myself.

I want a wife who is sensitive to my sexual needs, a wife who makes love passionately and eagerly when I feel like it, a wife who makes sure that I am satisfied. And, of course, I want a wife who will not demand sexual attention when I am not in the mood for it. I want a wife who assumes the complete responsibility for birth control, because I do not want more children. I want a wife who will remain sexually faithful to me so that I do not have to clutter up my intellectual life with jealousies. And I want a wife who understands that *my* sexual needs may entail more than strict adherence to monogamy. I must, after all, be able to relate to people as fully as possible.

If, by chance, I find another person more suitable as a wife than the wife I already have, I want the liberty to replace my present wife with another one. Naturally, I will expect a fresh, new life; my wife will take the children and be solely responsible for them so that I am left free.

When I am through with school and have a job, I want my wife to quit working and remain at home so that my wife can more fully and completely take care of a wife's duties.

My God, who wouldn't want a wife? (Judy Syfers, *Ms.*)

EXERCISE

Choose any situation either on or off campus that you think is bad and ought to be changed. Then in two or three pages write an emotional appeal designed to make your readers feel as you do about the problem. You need not propose any specific changes. Your purpose in this paper is simply to make your readers feel that the situation is intolerable and thus make them willing to consider whatever changes are later proposed.

ARGUMENT

In addition to trustworthiness and emotional appeal, a third means of persuasion is argument. Argument is first of all a way of thinking. We observe something and draw a conclusion from it; the relation between the observation and the conclusion is an argument. Once we have convinced ourselves that the conclusion is sound, we can use the argument to persuade others.

The Structure of Argument　In its simplest form an argument consists of two statements, one of which is a conclusion from the other.

> Mary's temperature is 104 degrees.
> She ought to go to the infirmary.

Here the second statement is a *conclusion* from the first. The first statement is what tends to make us believe the second. In this chapter we will call it a *premise.* The two statements taken together constitute an argument.

In Chapter 2 you learned that an inference is a thought process that moves from an observation through some knowledge or belief to a conclusion. Since anyone who concludes that Mary should go to the infirmary must believe that a person with a temperature of 104 degrees needs medical attention, the argument is an inference. *All arguments are inferences in which the conclusion is inferred from the premise.* The statement that

> Mary's temperature is 104 degrees.
> Her mother must be a lawyer.

is not an argument, since there seems to be no logical connection between her temperature and her mother's profession. We say that there is no *premise-conclusion relation* between the two sentences.

Now consider these two statements:

> Mary's temperature is 104 degrees.
> She must have appendicitis.

The only reader who will accept the second statement as a conclusion from the first is one who believes that appendicitis is the *sole* cause of such a temperature. Few readers, if any, hold such a belief; therefore we must say that there is no premise-conclusion relation between the sentences and that the statements do not constitute an argument.

The difference between statements that are related as premise and conclusion and those that are not may be further illustrated by the examples below. Each pair of sentences at the left consists of a premise and an italicized conclusion. In the pairs at the right there is no premise-conclusion relation, since no reader can reasonably infer one sentence as a logical conclusion from the other solely on the information given.

Premise-conclusion relationship	No premise-conclusion relationship
These men and women are doing the same job. *They should get the same pay.*	These men and women are doing the same job. Some of them are married.
Professor Jones is a tough grader. A check of his grades for the past five years shows that less than 5 percent of his students got A's, and 20 percent got F's.	Professor Jones is a tough grader. He has a Ph.D. degree.
Unless you arrive on campus before eight o'clock, it is impossible to find a parking space. *Something ought to be done about the campus parking situation.*	This morning I had to park half a mile from campus. Students cannot afford to park in a metered area.

The arguments at the left are not necessarily convincing. Some readers might want additional premises before accepting the conclusion. But whether convincing or not, the paired sentences at the left are related as those at the right are not. We can make that relationship more obvious by inserting *because* before the premise or *therefore* before the conclusion. But no sentence at the right can be inferred as a conclusion from the sentence paired with it. If you disagree, first add *because* before the premise or *therefore* before the conclusion, and explain what a reader would have to believe in order to accept the conclusion.

EXERCISE   Which of the following pairs of statements are related as premise and conclusion and are therefore arguments? At this time do not worry about whether the argument is convincing. We are concerned only with your ability to recognize premise-conclusion relations.

Final examinations cause unnecessary hardships for both students and instructors. Final examinations are traditional ways of evaluating student performance.

Final examinations cause unnecessary hardships for both students and instructors. Final examinations should be abolished.

John Jones is the most politically experienced candidate for the Senate. He has served in the House of Representatives and in his state legislature.

John Jones is the most politically experienced candidate for the Senate. He has five children, all of whom have college degrees.

No woman should be penalized because of her sex. Some people are kept in inferior jobs just because they are female.

No woman should be penalized because of her sex. In a democracy women are absolutely indispensable.

Students have the right to disagree with their instructors. It is only through disagreement that they learn how to evaluate opinions.

Students have the right to disagree with their instructors. Some students are more disagreeable than others.

So far we have been considering arguments of the simplest structure—a single premise and a single conclusion. Many arguments are more complex. The next paragraph has five premises in sentence 3.

(1) But busing hasn't worked. (2) After almost a decade, it seems clear that the principal mistake was to assume that we could create a more socially responsible society by putting the problem on wheels and expecting it to arrive at a daily solution. (3) The evidence is substantial that busing is leading away from integration and not toward it; that it has not significantly improved the quality of education accessible to blacks; that it has lowered the standard of education available to whites; that it has resulted in the exodus of white students to private schools inside the city or to public schools in the comparatively affluent suburbs beyond the economic means of blacks; and, finally, that it has not contributed to racial harmony, but has produced deep fissures within American society. (Norman Cousins, *Saturday Review*)

Do you recognize this as a TRI paragraph such as you studied in Chapter 4? The first sentence is the topic sentence (*T*); the second explains the topic sentence and therefore can be marked (*R*); the third sentence gives five illustrations of the topic sentence and so can be labeled (*I*). These illustrations are the premises for the conclusion stated in the first two sentences.

"It was the only thing to do after the mule died."

Three years back, the Hinsleys of Dora, Missouri, had a tough decision to make.

To buy a new mule.

Or invest in a used bug.

They weighed the two possibilities.

First there was the problem of the bitter Ozark winters. Tough on a warm-blooded mule. Not so tough on an air-cooled VW.

Then, what about the eating habits of the two contenders? Hay vs. gasoline.

As Mr. Hinsley puts it: "I get over eighty miles out of a dollar's worth of gas and I get where I want to go a lot quicker."

Then there's the road leading to their cabin. Many a mule pulling a wagon and many a conventional automobile has spent many an hour stuck in the mud.

As for shelter, a mule needs a barn. A

bug doesn't. "It just sets out there all day and the paint job looks near as good as the day we got it."

Finally, there was maintenance to think about. When a mule breaks down, there's only one thing to do: Shoot it.

 But if and when their bug breaks down, the Hinsleys have a Volkswagen dealer only two gallons away.

Copyright 1972, Volkswagen of America, Inc.

DISCUSSION PROBLEM The text of this advertisement contains five premises for a conclusion that is unstated but hinted at in the statement immediately under the picture. See if you can agree in converting the ad into a premise-conclusion outline in which the conclusion is followed by five premises.

In a still more complex argument a conclusion from one or more premises may become a premise for another conclusion, as one unit of the argument is built on another. In the following outline of a student paper the marginal and parenthetical notations show the premise-conclusion relations among the parts of the argument:

Thesis: Teen-age marriages are not advisable. (Conclusion from I, II, III—the main premises—below)   *Conclusion*

  I. The divorce rate for teen-age marriages is high. (First main premise for thesis, but also a conclusion from A and B below)   *Main premise*

    A. Dr. Laura Singer, president of the New York Division of the American Association of Marriage Counselors, says that two out of three teen-age marriages end in divorce. (First subpremise for I)   *Subpremise*

    B. Dr. Harold Christensen, the author of many articles on marital adjustment, says that the younger the age of marriage, the higher the percentage of divorces. (Second subpremise for I)   *Subpremise*

  II. Teen-age marriage is especially difficult for students. (Second main premise for thesis, but also a conclusion from A and B below)   *Main premise*

    A. Unless they are subsidized by their parents, married teen-agers have to divide their time between school and part-time jobs and have both academic and financial difficulties. (First subpremise for II)   *Subpremise*

    B. In a recent study of married college students, Dr. Ruth Hoeflin of Ohio State University found that often either the husband or the wife had to drop out of school and work in order to meet expenses, and that between work and school they had little time to spend with their spouses. (Second subpremise for II)   *Subpremise*

  III. Teen-age marriages restrict individual development. (Third main premise for thesis, but also a conclusion from A and B below)   *Main premise*

    A. Early marriage deprives both partners of the maturing influences of travel, wide social acquaintances, independent decision-making, and development of a sense of selfhood. (First subpremise for III)   *Subpremise*

    B. A person who goes directly from responsibility to parents to responsibility to a spouse never has the experience of being responsible only to himself or herself. (Second subpremise for III)   *Subpremise*

This outline shows the structure of an argument in which the thesis states the conclusion, and the premises provide support for that conclusion. The whole argument breaks into three smaller arguments, any one of which a writer could develop into a separate paper by making a main premise the thesis. In its present form this argument will be persuasive to any reader who believes that the three main premises with their supporting subpremises establish the soundness of the conclusion. When this happens, we say that the premises *prove* the conclusion.

But proof is seldom as precise in argument as it is in mathematics. In Euclidean geometry we can prove that, without exception, the square on the hypotenuse is equal to the sum of the squares on the other two sides. But we cannot prove conclusively that teen-age marriages are *never* advisable. All we can do is show that they are *generally* inadvisable. We can do this only when a reader accepts the premises and the conclusion drawn from them. Usually, therefore, what we mean by *proof* in an argument is *acceptance of the reasoning.*

EXERCISES   **A.**   The following·three-part exercise should be done individually; then, if your instructor wishes, the final results may be discussed in class.

1.   The following statements may be outlined as two main premises for the conclusion "In practice we are not able to define *heredity* or *environment* with precision." One of the premises has two subpremises; the other has none. Outline the argument to show all premise-conclusion relations.

a. Some inherited characteristics of fruit flies appear only when the environment encourages their appearance.

b. We are not able to define *heredity* except in terms of characteristics that may have been influenced by environment.

c. An acorn will never grow into anything but an oak tree, but whether it becomes an oak tree depends on environmental conditions.

d. The environment of individuals in a society is so complex that we cannot define it precisely.

2.   The following statements can be outlined as three main premises for the conclusion "We cannot experimentally study heredity and environment apart from each other." Each main premise has one subpremise. Outline the argument to show all premise-conclusion relations.

a. We cannot do this with newborn babies.

b. We cannot do it with ordinary (fraternal) twins.

c. A boy twin has a different environment than a girl twin.

d. Identical twins come from the same egg and thus have the same inheritance, but we cannot be sure that they have had the same environment while growing up.

e. Newborn babies have had nine months of prenatal environment.

f. We cannot do it with identical twins.

3.   Combine 1 and 2 into a larger argument, first by outlining the whole argument as in the outline on teen-age marriages (p. 221), then by writing the conclusion or thesis that your outline proves.

B. As a practical test of your ability to construct a sound argument, choose any question about which you are concerned and informed, and prepare a one-page outline showing your final conclusion and the premises and subpremises proving that conclusion.

COMMON TYPES OF ARGUMENTS

As we have seen, arguments are reasoning processes in which a conclusion is inferred from premises. Here we will consider common types of arguments by identifying common kinds of premises and inferences.

TYPES OF PREMISES

The most common types of premises are *statements of fact, judgments,* and *expert testimony.*

Statements of fact   Statements of fact may be verified by checking them against the facts they report. If the statement corresponds to the facts, it is "true"; if it does not, it is "false." Statements of fact make the most reliable premises. Among intelligent people the authority of facts is likely to be decisive; hence the common saying, "The facts speak for themselves." This is something of an exaggeration, since different conclusions can sometimes be inferred from the same factual premise, but controversies tend to dissolve when they are reduced to questions of fact. For this reason, the best preparation for argument is a diligent search for the facts.

Judgments   Judgments are conclusions inferred from facts. You saw that in the student outline on teen-age marriages the main premises were conclusions (judgments) from the subpremises beneath them. These judgments then became premises for the conclusion shown in the thesis. This procedure is common in complex arguments. For example, a doctor trying to find out what is causing a patient's symptoms may early in the examination make a tentative diagnosis that the symptoms are caused either by tuberculosis or by a tumor. If laboratory tests eliminate tuberculosis, the patient has a tumor, in which case it may be malignant (cancerous) or benign. That question can be decided only by surgery, and the facts revealed by the operation will determine the final conclusion. An outline of the doctor's reasoning would show the following steps:

1. *The symptoms are caused by either tuberculosis or a tumor.* This hypothesis, or tentative conclusion, is a judgment based on knowledge of the two diseases.

2. *It is not tuberculosis.* This conclusion is based on the laboratory tests.

3. *The patient has a tumor,* a conclusion based on an inference from 1 and 2 above.

4. *The tumor is benign and therefore the patient does not have cancer.* This is a further conclusion based on the operation.

If the first three steps in the doctor's reasoning are put in this form—

1. It is either tuberculosis or a tumor.

2. It is not tuberculosis.

3. Therefore, it is a tumor.

—the two premises from which the final conclusion is reached are judgments, since each is a conclusion inferred from the facts. A three-step argument in this form is called a *syllogism.* The doctor deduces or discovers the conclusion by making a logical inference from the two premises. Whether this syllogism is a sound argument or not will depend on whether the premises are true. For example, if the symptoms could be caused by a third disease—say emphysema—the first premise will be false, and the conclusion that the patient has a tumor cannot be accepted.

Expert testimony   Expert testimony is a statement by a person presumed to be an authority on the subject. The statement may be factual, as when a doctor describes the conditions revealed by an autopsy; or it may be a judgment, as when a psychiatrist testifies that in her opinion a defendant is insane. Since expert testimony is always a statement of fact or a judgment, it could be dealt with under those two categories. It is here considered separately (1) because factual statements by an expert are often extremely difficult for a nonexpert to verify (for example, ordinary citizens cannot usually check the facts to determine whether a swimmer's death was caused by heart failure or by drowning); and (2) because the qualifications of the expert require special consideration.

Expert testimony is often abused. It is too easy to assume that the testimony of any prominent person is reliable, though most of us—if we stop to think—realize that a person may be distinguished in one field but not in another, or may be expert in one phase of a subject and still know little about another phase of it. To be trustworthy, expert testimony must meet two requirements: the expert must be an authority on the particular subject, and there must be no reasonable probability of bias.

The following material consists of four arguments in favor of simplified spelling.* For each argument mark the conclusion *C* and the premise *P.* Then identify the premise as a statement of fact, testimony, or judgment. Finally, decide for each argument whether the premises persuade you to accept the conclusion. If they do not, what would the writer have to do to get you to accept the conclusion?

E X E R C I S E

1.   There is a tremendous lack of agreement between pronunciation and spelling in English. The sound of *a* in *ale* may also be spelled *ae* in *maelstrom, ai* in *bait, ay* in *day, e* and *ee* in *melee, ea* in *break, eigh* in *weigh, et* in *beret.*

2.   The same letter may be used for different sounds. The letter *a* has different pronunciations in *sane, chaotic, care, add, account, arm, ask,* and *sofa.*

3.   English is full of silent letters. It is estimated that two-thirds of all the words in the Merriam-Webster unabridged dictionary have at least one silent letter.

4.   The cost of typing, printing, and proofreading illogical English spellings is high. George Bernard Shaw, who in addition to being a great playwright was a powerful advocate of simplified spelling, repeatedly stated his opinion in the *London Times* that by adopting simplified spelling Britain could have saved enough money to pay the costs of World War II.

TYPES OF INFERENCES

In this section we will discuss three major types of inferences and one minor one. The major types are *generalization, causal relation,* and a combination of these two called *causal generalization;* the minor type is *analogy.*

Generalization   A generalization is the type of reasoning that draws a conclusion about a whole class from a study of some of its members. The members used are called a *sample,* and the conclusion infers that what is true of the sample will be true of the whole class. Well-known examples are questionnaires that attempt to describe public opinion on an issue by polling a sample and extending the results to the whole population.

* Much of the material in this exercise is from Falk Johnson, "Should Spelling Be Streamlined?" in *The American Mercury* for September, 1948.

Obviously a generalization based on a small sample is riskier than one based on a large sample, but the typicality of the sample is more important than its size. A sample is believed to be typical when there are good reasons for assuming that what is true of the sample will also be true of the unexamined part. For example, the butterfat content of a twenty-gallon can of homogenized milk will be the same in all parts of the can; therefore one part is as good a sample as another. Since there is no probability that increasing the size of the sample would increase the accuracy of the test, a single cupful—perhaps a few spoonfuls—would be a typical sample. But if the milk is not homogenized, the cream will rise to the top, and a sample taken from the top of the can will exaggerate the butterfat content, while one taken from the middle or bottom of the can will be lower in butterfat. In this case there is no typical sample.

It is important to understand this distinction, because *the hasty assumption that a sample is typical is the chief cause of unsound generalizations.* It is often very diffi-cult—sometimes impossible—to be sure that a sample is typical, and much useful reasoning is based on samples that can only be presumed so. But for any serious generalization, all possible care should be taken to see that the samples are probably typical. Any sample that tends to be "loaded"—that is, more likely to be true of part of a class than of all of it—should be rejected. Both the following samples are loaded:

> a study of all members of a fraternity to answer the question, "Do fraterni-ties help incoming students adjust to college life?"

(This sample consists of students who have already answered this question in the affirmative and excludes those who have already answered it negatively. The sample is too biased to be typical of all male undergraduates. Even if all fraternities on campus were polled, the sample would still not be typical.)

> a study of college hospital records to determine how many days a semester a student is likely to be sick

(This sample will exaggerate the amount of sickness because it ignores the health-iest part of the college population—those who did not need hospitalization.)

The commonest safeguard against loading is to choose samples at random. A random sample is one in which the examined members are chosen by chance, as in a lottery, or by some other procedure so arbitrary that it is almost the same as a chance selection. The assumption behind this kind of selection is that any inference made from the sample is likely to be typical, since there is no reason for believing that the sampling procedure is likely to be loaded.

You will generally be safer with a large sample than with a small one. A conclusion about the advisability of teen-age marriages based on the testimony of eight teen-age couples you know would be a *hasty generalization,* one based on too small a sample to warrant any conclusion. In contrast, Dr. Christensen's testimony cited in the student outline on page 221 was based on 15,000 teen-age marriages. His sample may or may not have been typical, but its size would help to make it persuasive.

One way to avoid hasty generalizations is to be suspicious of any statement about *all* of a group or class—all women drivers, all teen-agers, all college professors. Such statements imply that your samples are typical and that the judgment is true without exception. Your generalization may be true of *many* or of *some* members of the class. If so, say so. Do not use *all* unless you are ready to prove that there are no exceptions. If you overstate the generalization, you invite doubts about your own trustworthiness. Notice that even if a generalization does not include the word *all,* it may still mean *all.* To say that college professors are absent-minded implies *all* college professors.

A. Rate the acceptability of the lettered generalizations below, marking them by the following key:

EXERCISES

3. True in all cases
2. True in most cases
1. True in some cases

Discuss your answers.

a. Athletes are not interested in the arts.
b. People who play slot machines a great deal lose more money than they win.
c. Qualified lifeguards are better-than-average swimmers.
d. The English have better manners than Americans.
e. Stockbrokers are experts on the economy.
f. College graduates earn more money in their lifetime than do noncollege workers.
g. Artists have low moral standards.
h. Advertising insults the public's intelligence.
i. Clothing sold in high-priced department stores is of the best quality.

B. The following selection from an article attempts to find an answer to the question posed in the first paragraph. Read it and discuss the questions following it.

Why is America, blessed with the finest medical schools, the most extensive research facilities, the largest drug laboratories, the best-equipped hospitals and the highest-paid doctors, a "second-rate" country in the distribution of health care? That verdict doesn't come from Ralph Nader. It's the view of the nation's ranking public-health official, Dr. Roger O. Egeberg, Special Assistant to the Secretary for Health Policy of the Department of Health, Education and Welfare. . . .

Why is this so? My search for answers began in a utilitarian one-bedroom apartment awash in dirty hospital uniforms and copies of the *New England Journal of Medicine*. Slumped in the middle of her Levitz sofa, just off night-shift duty at one of the nation's major community hospitals, was a nurse, coughing badly from a cold, compliments of her patients. She was talking about a millionaire surgeon on her hospital staff. This physician, who specialized in diseases of the rich, was adored by high-society patients. His friends blessed him for finding imaginary breast masses on their wives and then subjecting them to needless mastectomies. Hardly a week passed when he didn't take out a normal stomach or a healthy uterus.

The nurse, still wearing her hospital whites and hacking steadily, went on for several hours about the outrages she had seen performed at the hands of this surgeon. The physician had tried to cure a woman's diarrhea with three totally unrelated surgeries: hysterectomy, thyroidectomy, and hemorrhoidectomy. The diarrhea did not abate. Another woman plagued by vaginal bleeding from her I.U.D. ended up with a hysterectomy (when the doctor simply should have removed the I.U.D.). After performing an appendectomy on one man, he closed the patient up before the pus could drain; he was in a hurry to make a baseball game with his son. The patient went downhill and the surgeon returned to pronounce him beyond hope. Several of the nurse's colleagues were so distraught they appealed to the chief of staff, persuading him to bring in other doctors, who drained the pus and saved the man's life. . . .

I remember feeling haunted by her stories when I drove home that night. I had read about such outrages in magazines and newspapers but somehow always managed to associate them with poor people who couldn't afford good medical care. Her firsthand accounts of this surgeon's work at the expense of his high-society patients jolted me. Now, dozens of hospitals and clinics later, the surgeon seems like a footnote to what I saw and heard during my travels about America's medical empire. I found:

> Patients denied admission to hospitals who dropped dead on their way home.
>
> Hospitals that falsify medical-committee-meeting minutes to win accreditation.
>
> In 1972, the head of California's hospital-licensing division openly admitted that she would not feel safe in some hospitals licensed by her own office.
>
> A state contracting with medical groups to provide prepaid health-care services at hospitals specifically disapproved by inspectors from that same state's medical association.

A surgeon walking out in the middle of a hysterectomy because the nurse said something he didn't like (the anesthetist completed the operation).

A medical-board-certified cardiovascular surgeon with impeccable medical credentials and a lengthy bibliography who has butchered a number of patients straight into their graves.

Chiropractors, optometrists, and dentists handling emergency-room patients.

Nurses who can't discriminate between live and dead patients.

(Roger Rapoport, "It's Enough to Make You Sick," *Playboy*)

1.   Before answering the following questions, record your general response to the selection. Did you find it persuasive?

2.   Insofar as it is persuasive, is the emotional appeal of the examples a significant factor in your response?

3.   How satisfied are you that the examples are typical?

4.   Which of the following seems to you a reasonable conclusion from the selection? If none of these satisfies you, state your own conclusion.

a. The medical profession is a disgrace.

b. Most doctors are incompetent and greedy.

c. Some doctors are guilty of malpractice.

Causal relation   Another common type of reasoning is the search for causes and results. We want to know whether cigarettes really do cause lung cancer; we want to know what causes malnutrition, the decay of cities, the decay of teeth. We are equally interested in effects: what is the effect of alcohol on the formation of unborn infants, of sulphur or lead in the atmosphere, of mercury in tunafish, of oil spills and raw sewage in rivers and the sea, of staying up late on the night before an examination?

Causal reasoning may go from cause to effect or from effect to cause. Either way, we reason from what we know to what we want to find out. Sometimes we reason from an effect to a cause and then on to another effect. Thus, if we reason that because the lights have gone out the refrigerator won't work, we first relate the effect (lights out) to the cause (power off) and then relate that cause to another effect (refrigerator not working). This kind of reasoning is called, for short, *effect to effect*. It is quite common to reason through an extensive chain of causal relations. When the lights go out we might reason in the following causal chain: lights out–power off–refrigerator not working–temperature will rise–milk will sour.

In other words, we diagnose a succession of effects from the power failure, each becoming the cause of the next.

Causes are classified as necessary, sufficient, or contributory. A *necessary* cause is one that must be present for the effect to occur, as combustion is necessary to drive a gasoline engine. A *sufficient* cause is one that can produce an effect unaided, though there may be more than one sufficient cause of a given effect: a dead battery is enough to keep a car from starting, but faulty spark plugs or an empty gas tank will have the same effect. A *contributory* cause is one that helps to produce an effect but cannot do so by itself, as running through a red light may help cause an accident, though other factors—pedestrians or other cars in the intersection—must also be present.

In establishing or refuting a causal relation, it is usually necessary to show the process by which the alleged cause produces the effect. Such an explanation is called a *causal process*. The following selection refutes an alleged cause and suggests a more plausible one by examining the process between cause and effect. You saw the first paragraph on page 100; this is a more complete version.

> What we know of prenatal development makes such attempts [attempts made by a mother to mold the character of her unborn child by studying poetry, art, or mathematics during pregnancy] seem utterly impossible. How could such extremely complex influences pass from the mother to the child? There is no connection between their nervous systems. Even the blood vessels of mother and child do not join directly. They lie side by side and the chemicals are interchanged through the walls by a process that we call osmosis. An emotional shock to the mother will affect her child, because it changes the activity of her glands and so the chemistry of her blood. Any chemical change in the mother's blood will affect the child—for better or worse. But we cannot see how a liking for mathematics or poetic genius can be dissolved in blood and produce a similar liking or genius in the child.
>
> In our discussion of instincts we saw that there was reason to believe that whatever we inherit must be of some very simple sort rather than any complicated or very definite kind of behavior. It is certain that no one inherits a knowledge of mathematics. It may be, however, that children inherit more or less of a rather general ability that we may call intelligence. If very intelligent children become deeply interested in mathematics, they will probably make a success of that study.
>
> As for musical ability, it may be that what is inherited is an especially sensitive ear, a peculiar structure of the hands or of the vocal organs, connections between nerves and muscles that make it comparatively easy to learn the movements a musician must execute, and particularly vigorous emotions. If these factors are all organized around music, the child may become a musician. The same factors, in other circumstances, might be organized about some other center of interest. The rich emotional equipment might find expression in poetry. The capable fingers might develop

skill in surgery. It is not the knowledge of music that is inherited, then, nor even the love of it, but a certain bodily structure that makes it comparatively easy to acquire musical knowledge and skill. Whether that ability shall be directed toward music or some other undertaking may be decided entirely by forces in the environment in which a child grows up. (William H. Roberts, *Psychology You Can Use*)

The most common errors in causal reasoning are

1. *assuming that A causes B because A always precedes B.* Although it is true that a cause always precedes its effect, a mere time order is not necessarily a causal order. Night always follows day, and it is just as true that day follows night. But neither one causes the other. Each is caused by the rotation of the earth toward or away from the sun. The time order between A and B may suggest a causal relation, but that relation must be supported by other evidence, preferably an explanation of the causal process by which the effect is produced.

2. *mistaking an effect for a cause.* Since a cause may produce more than one effect, two effects may be obvious at the same time. Getting rid of one effect will not necessarily get rid of the other. For example, certain medicines may remove a cough without curing the cold that causes the cough and other symptoms. But because effects are more obvious than causes, it is easy to assume that one effect is the cause of the other.

3. *mistaking a contributory cause for a sufficient cause.* A tailgating driver who explains a crash by saying that the car ahead stopped suddenly is confusing contributory cause with sufficient cause. It is perhaps true that had the car ahead not stopped suddenly the tailgater would not have run into it. But without the tailgating, the stopping of the car ahead would not have resulted in an accident.

4. *failing to recognize that the cause may be not a single event but a complex of causes.* This kind of oversimplification is probably the most common error in causal reasoning. We tend to think that every effect has *a* cause, and so we look for *the* cause. But the more complex the question is, the more causes may be at work. War, inflation, depression, a decline in the value of the dollar, and similar effects usually have a number of related causes. Even such a relatively simple event as losing one's temper may grow out of an accumulation of irritations. Failure to realize this often results in a superficial analysis of a problem. A wife who blows up when her husband asks, "Isn't dinner ready yet?" may be responding not to his question but to a whole series of frustrations that occurred earlier. His question is not the cause; it is just the last straw.

Causal generalization The kind of causal analysis we have been considering works best when we are dealing with events in which all possible causes can be isolated and tested independently of each other. Many problems do not permit such a procedure. We cannot, for instance, test the hypothesis that fluorides prevent tooth decay by eliminating all other possible factors affecting decay—heredity, prenatal environment, diet, and so forth. All we can do is to contrast the amount of tooth decay in people who use fluoridated toothpaste or drink fluoridated water with the amount in people who do neither, and draw a conclusion from the contrast. Basically, we are generalizing from contrasted samples and making a causal-relation inference from the generalization. We are thus combining generalization and causal relation in a *causal generalization*.

The following selection is a causal generalization. The writer is reporting the results of a study to determine the effect of alcohol on Orientals. The generalization is a conclusion from the effect of alcohol on two groups of people. The causal relation is an attempt to establish a connection between race and the drinking of alcoholic beverages.

Orientals and Alcohol

Upon being offered the traditional one for the road, a Japanese will more likely than not decline with a polite *"Kao akaku naru"* (My face will get red). If he does accept the drink, he may feel uncomfortable after downing it. In any event, he—like most Asians—will probably never become an alcoholic. That fact has long been a puzzle to hard-drinking Westerners. The difference is often explained away by Oriental cultural or social traditions, like the strong Chinese taboo against public drunkenness. But now a group at the University of North Carolina has given new weight to a more recent explanation: the East-West drinking disparity may be primarily caused by genetic differences.

To check earlier findings by Boston psychiatrist Peter H. Wolff that Orientals blush more easily in response to alcohol than Westerners, the North Carolina team selected 48 test subjects, 24 Americans of European extraction and 24 Orientals, mostly Japanese, Chinese, Taiwanese and Koreans. All of them lived in central North Carolina, mostly around the college town of Chapel Hill, and were modest to moderate drinkers.

The North Carolina team, led by psychiatrist John Ewing, gave laboratory cocktails of ginger ale and ethyl alcohol, measuring the amount of alcohol so that each subject drank an amount proportionate to his body weight. The volunteers were then questioned and tested for two hours to gauge the effect of the cocktail. The tests revealed a striking difference. After drinking, the Westerners tended to feel relaxed, confident, alert and happy; the Orientals were more likely to experience muscle weakness, pounding in the head, dizziness and anxiety.

Other test results were equally conclusive. Seventeen of the 24 Orientals became deeply flushed, some within minutes of drinking; that was established visually and by a special device that records pulse pressure of the earlobe. Only three of the Westerners blushed, none as heavily. Blood pressure dropped more sharply and heartbeat quickened more in Orientals than in Westerners. In addition, the alcohol tended to produce a higher level of acetaldehyde, a chemical with anesthetic and antiseptic properties, in the blood of the Oriental subjects. Ewing suspects that the production of this chemical may be partly responsible for the disagreeable reaction that the Orientals experienced.

Ewing's conclusion: "The general level of discomfort in drinking small amounts of alcohol would seem to offer protection to many Orientals from overusing alcoholic beverages as a psychological escape mechanism." He suspects that genetic differences may also account for the drinking habits of other ethnic groups. To check his theory, the North Carolina team has begun carrying out similar tests on blacks, Jews and other groups that tend to use alcohol sparingly. *(Time)*

Analogy On pages 166–167 we discussed analogy as illustration in the form of extended metaphor. It can also be considered as argument based on similarities. From the premise that two very different things are alike in some significant way, the argument concludes that an inference about one will also apply to the other. The following famous Shakespearean analogy illustrates this type of inference:

> I am a Jew. Hath not a Jew eyes? Hath not a Jew hands, organs, dimensions, senses, affections, passions?–fed with the same food, hurt with the same weapons, subject to the same diseases, healed by the same means, warmed and cooled by the same winter and summer as a Christian is? If you prick us, do we not bleed? If you tickle us, do we not laugh? If you poison us, do we not die? And if you wrong us, shall we not revenge? If we are like you in the rest, we will resemble you in that. (Shylock, in *The Merchant of Venice*)

We can see the structure of this analogy better if we set up the compared characteristics in parallel columns, matching each characteristic of a Christian with a similar characteristic of a Jew. The whole combines to form a series of premises leading up to the conclusion that, like the Christian, the Jew will seek revenge if wronged.

	Christian		**Jew**
	1. Has hands, organs, dimensions, etc.	→	1. Has hands, organs, dimensions, etc.
P	2. Is affected in specific ways by food, weapons, disease, etc.	→	2. Is affected in the same specific ways by food, weapons, disease, etc.
	3. If pricked, bleeds.	→	3. If pricked, bleeds.
	4. If tickled, laughs.	→	4. If tickled, laughs.
	5. If poisoned, dies.	→	5. If poisoned, dies.
C	6. If wronged, seeks revenge.	→	6. If wronged . . .

In argument analogy can be both useful and misleading. It is helpful in suggesting hypotheses for further investigation. For example, if we have found that the best protection against one virus disease is to isolate the virus and prepare an immunizing serum from it, we can predict that the same method will work with another virus disease. If the prediction proves true, the analogy has helped to solve the problem. If the prediction proves false, the suggested solution will be quickly rejected and no great harm will have been done.

When analogy is used as the sole proof of a conclusion, it should be examined very closely. It may be more persuasive than it should be and lead us to a conclusion that is not valid, for a single difference can make a whole analogy false. The test of an analogy is the question, "Are the two things analogous for the purpose for which the analogy is being used?" They may have many differences that are unimportant to the inference based on the analogy. But they must not be different in any detail essential to that inference. Thus the analogy that a motherless baby ape could be reared by feeding it as if it were a human baby would be sound because, despite many differences, young apes and human babies have similar digestive systems. But to reason that because two varieties of mushrooms look alike both will be good to eat is a dangerous analogy, since the possibility that one is poisonous would be more important than all their similarities.

EXERCISE   Study the following analogies and judge their persuasiveness. First, consider whether the alleged similarities offer a reasonable comparison. Then consider whether there is any difference that would cause you to reject the analogy no matter how similar are the things being compared. Finally, write a short critique of each analogy to show specifically why you accept or reject it.

Passage 1   Impeaching a President is like major surgery. It is an act that should not be done hastily nor emotionally, and only when it is necessary to restore the well-being of the patient, in this case the government of the nation. The purpose of surgery is not to punish the diseased organ; neither is the purpose of impeachment to punish a President. In both situations the only legitimate purpose is to remove a source of serious trouble and re-establish a healthy condition.

A surgeon does not initiate the decision to operate. Before he has been called into the case, the patient has been examined by a physician who must satisfy himself by the evidence of laboratory tests and x-rays that an operation may be necessary. When the surgeon is consulted, he reviews the evidence and makes the final decision. A similar procedure is followed in impeachment. The House first studies the question, seeks all pertinent evidence, and then decides whether the matter should go to the Senate. The Senate reviews the evidence and makes the final decision. The whole process of deciding what to do in either surgery or impeachment may take many months.

Both surgery and impeachment are periods of stress for everybody involved. And just as the patient may suffer post-surgical shock, so may the political body suffer from the shock of impeachment. In view of the possible consequences, neither should be undertaken unless there is no satisfactory alternative. But when the patient's health depends on cutting out the source of infection, failure to act, in both surgery and impeachment, may have serious consequences.

Passage 2*

I believe that we all accept the principle that an affluent society must do what it can to prevent hunger and misery, and also to provide equality of opportunity to those who have been denied it. But how far can a society go in the redistribution of wealth without changing the very nature of society? I think this is a problem that we've got to face. I do not think that a majority in Congress are trying to face it, or realize that it is a problem, because so many of them are still hard at work at this business of redistributing income.

All that reminds me of what happened in the universities during the 1960's and 1970's—events that I witnessed from a ringside seat. During this period we had a fashion of giving A's to every student—there were no failures. The effect on academic life was devastating. When illiterate or lazy students could get an A average, good students stopped studying. The result was a profound change in academic life: formerly dropouts were those who failed in their studies; in the 1960's and 1970's most of the dropouts were the most gifted and brilliant students, who found that college had become meaningless.

What happens in the schools is not unlike what happens in society at large when the penalties of improvidence, laziness, or ignorance are not just softened, but removed. When there is no such thing as failure, there is no such thing as success either. Motivation, the desire to excel, the urge to accomplishment—all these disappear. The dynamism of society is lost.

This, I'm afraid, is the direction in which our society has been going steadily for many years. The biggest losers are the brightest and most capable men and women. But the average person is a loser too. Faced with no challenge, assured of a comfortable living whether they work or not, such persons become willing dependents, content with a parasitical relationship to the rest of society.

What is significant in our time is that there is a whole class of people interested in encouraging this parasitism. Many welfare officials and social workers are threatened with a loss of their power if there is a marked reduction in the number of their clients, so they are motivated to increase rather than decrease welfare dependency.

Politicians, too, have flourished by getting increased federal grants for this or that disadvantaged group. They go back to their constituents and say, "Look what I've done for you," and get reelected. These are the officeholders who are far more interested in being reelected than in doing what is good for people, good for the economy, good for the nation.

If everybody is rewarded just for being alive, you get the same sort of effect as you do when you reward every student just for being enrolled. You destroy not only education, you destroy society by giving A's to everyone. This is a philosophical consideration that bothers me very much as I sit in the United States Senate and see its great budget allocations going through. (S. I. Hayakawa, "Mr. Hayakawa Goes to Washington," *Harper's)*

REFUTING FALLACIES

A *fallacy* is any error in the reasoning process that makes an argument unreliable. The following discussion will identify the most common fallacies and suggest how to refute them if your purpose requires you to deal with them in a paper.

IGNORING THE BURDEN OF PROOF

It is a general rule in argument that *he who asserts must prove.* An *assertion* is a statement offered as a conclusion without a supporting premise. Since argument has been defined as a logical relation between a premise and a conclusion, an assertion is not an argument. You, as writer, must assume responsibility for making your reasoning acceptable to the reader. The least you can do is to give the premises on which you base your conclusion. The standard response by a reader to an unsupported assertion is to ask, "What is the evidence for that assertion?" Assuming that your assertions are true unless the reader can disprove them is *shifting the burden of proof.* It is the writer's job, not the reader's, to prove the truth of an assertion.

Example

College students spend four years of their lives and thousands of dollars of their parents' money trying to get as little as possible out of their college education, provided only that they get their coveted diplomas.

Analysis

This assertion is a generalization, but what is the evidence on which it is based? The writer gives none. If the evidence were given, the reader could evaluate the generalization and would probably dismiss it as a hasty one. The best refutation is to expose the argument as an assertion and ask for the evidence.

"All in all, then, I think we're agreed. We leave liquor alone and go for tea. After all, who's going to object to a few pennies' taxation on tea?"

BEGGING THE QUESTION

A question is "begged" when part of what has to be proved is assumed to be true. The best defense against this fallacy is to show how the begging takes place.

Example

In taking the position that persons accused of a crime cannot be interrogated without their lawyers being present, the Supreme Court is showing more concern for the protection of the criminal than for the protection of society. The laws were made to protect law-abiding citizens, not those who defy the law. A criminal loses the rights of a citizen on committing a crime. It is the duty of the police to get at the truth, and they have a right to question an accused person as long as they don't use force.

Analysis

This argument begs the question by assuming that anyone being interrogated by the police has defied the law and is a criminal. But this is what has to be proved. An accused person is innocent until found guilty by a judge or jury. Until then the accused is a "law-abiding citizen" and is entitled to the protection of the law.

Sometimes question-begging takes the form of a *circular argument*, one that goes from conclusion to unproved assertion and back to conclusion again.

Example

Much of this talk about spending millions for slum clearance is based on the fallacy that if we provide fine homes for people who live in the slums, they will suddenly become responsible and productive citizens. This argument puts the cart before the horse. The basic trouble is with the people who live in the slums. These people are shiftless and irresponsible. The conditions under which they live prove this. If they had any initiative or industry, they would not be living in slums.

Analysis

In this argument the conclusion that slum dwellers are responsible for slums is supported by the unproved assertion that anyone who lives in a slum must be shiftless and irresponsible. That assertion begs the question, and the argument goes around in the following circle: "Slums are caused by shiftless tenants; this is true because shiftless tenants cause slums." The way to refute this argument is to show the circularity of the reasoning and the question-begging assumption about the nature of slum dwellers.

ARGUMENTUM AD HOMINEM

The Latin phrase *argumentum ad hominem* means "argument against the man" and names the fallacy of attacking the person instead of the argument. Such an attack is legitimate when someone presents no argument except his or her own unsupported testimony. The device is frequently used in courts to discredit witnesses who are testifying as experts. If it can be shown that they are not experts or that their testimony cannot be relied on because of their characters, their trustworthiness as witnesses is seriously challenged. But if an argument rests on evidence and reasoning, it should be judged accordingly.

Example	Analysis
No, I haven't read the bill. I don't need to. It's being supported by Congressman Blank, and there isn't a worse scoundrel in the country. If Blank's in favor of this bill, I'm against it.	*The bill should be considered on its own merits. If Blank is a scoundrel, that would be a factor in considering his trustworthiness, but Blank is not the issue here. It is the bill that should be attacked or defended.*

EXTENSION

Extension is the device of distorting an argument by exaggerating it. A college professor states that some high school graduates enter college inadequately prepared in English and mathematics. An opponent then charges that the statement belittles high school teaching. This charge greatly extends and exaggerates the original remark. If the professor makes the mistake of accepting the extension and of trying to show that high school instruction *is* bad, she falls into the trap and must defend a much weaker position. Her best response is to go back to her original statement and point out that, first, her statement was about *some* students, not *all;* second, it was about *two* high school subjects, not *all;* third, it did not place the blame for the students' deficiencies on the teachers. If the extension is not deliberate, the charge will be withdrawn. If it is deliberate and is not withdrawn, it will damage the accuser more than the accused. This fallacy is sometimes called the *straw man fallacy,* because the extension creates a "straw man" that is easier to demolish than a real one.

RED HERRING

In hunting, a strongly scented object drawn across a trail will distract hounds and cause them to follow the new scent. In rhetoric, a *red herring* is a false issue used to lead attention away from the real one. Usually the false issue arouses an emotional response that creates a digression. The best defense is to show that the false issue is not pertinent to the discussion and then to refuse to follow it.

Example

As long as we're talking about whether women should be paid at the same rate as men for similar work and have equal chances of promotion, we should also be asking whether women want to be equal with men and still retain preferred treatment on social occasions, such as having men pay the expenses of a date, open doors for women, light their cigarettes, and so on. It seems to me that what women want is to have equal and preferred treatment at the same time.

Analysis

The question of how women should be treated socially is a red herring. The real issue is one of economic equality. How men treat women on social occasions has nothing to do with this issue. The best way to deal with this question is to show that it is irrelevant. Whatever courtesies a man extends to a woman on a date are social, not legal, practices. The best defense is to show that the question is irrelevant to the issue.

UNJUSTIFIABLE EMOTIONAL APPEAL

Ideally, emotional appeal supplements logical argument. When it is used as a substitute for argument, the test of its acceptability is the question, "Does it contribute to the best interests of the audience?" An emotional appeal to someone to give up an injurious habit is justifiable. One used in the sole interest of the persuader is not.

For example, if a politician is accused in the media of accepting bribes from companies seeking government contracts, it is in the public interest that these charges be investigated fully and fairly. An emotional appeal by the politician that he is being victimized by the media may prevent such an investigation and thus put the interests of the politician above those of the public.

HASTY GENERALIZATION

Any generalization drawn from an obviously small sample or one not likely to be typical is a hasty generalization.

Example

Women just aren't any good at logic. Although there are twelve women to ten men in our logic section, the four highest scores on the final exams were made by men and the four lowest by women.

Analysis

In the first place, what would make us believe that what is true of twelve women in one class will be true of all women? In the second, are the top four and bottom four scores typical of the scores in the class? Even as a comparison for this class alone, the sample is faulty. It would be better to take the median score of the women and compare it with the median score of the men. If the comparison favored the men, it would justify the conclusion that women in this class did less well than men in this class on an examination in logic. That is a less impressive conclusion than the one offered in the original argument.

STEREOTYPE

A *stereotype* is a standardized mental image that pays too much attention to characteristics supposedly common to a group and not enough to individual differences. We begin with a number of individuals who have one thing in common (let us say that the individuals are women who have married children); we group them in a class (mothers-in-law); we develop an attitude toward that class (mothers-in-law are interfering) based on a hasty generalization; then we apply that attitude to individual mothers-in-law without waiting to see whether they actually are interfering.

To help us avoid this fallacy some students of language advise us to use index numbers after the class names to remind us that each member of a group has personal characteristics—that $German_1$ is not $German_2$, that college $professor_A$ is not college $professor_B$, that $freshman_{1980}$ is not $freshman_{1960}$. Whether we write these index numbers or merely think them, they are useful reminders not to assume that individuals with a common class name will be alike in all respects.

EITHER-OR FALLACY

The either-or fallacy is the fallacy of ignoring possible alternatives. When we say we must either do this or do that, we are assuming that there are no other alternatives. This assumption may be right, in which case there is no fallacy. But if we have ignored alternatives, our reasoning is faulty. The way to refute an either-or fallacy is to show the alternatives that have been ignored.

Example

John's grades are not satisfactory. Either he lacks the ability to do college work or he is loafing.

Analysis

There are other possibilities. John may have an outside job that is using up much of his time and energy; he may be so concerned about some problem at home that he cannot keep his mind on his studies; he may be ill. These possibilities should be checked before any conclusion is drawn.

OVERSIMPLIFIED CAUSE

The two most common oversimplifications of a causal relation are mistaking a contributory cause for a sufficient one, and recognizing only one of several causes of an effect.

Example

The reason why so many people cannot find employment is that they do not have a college education.

Analysis

The lack of a college education may be a sufficient cause for unemployment in those jobs that require a college degree. But it does not explain why people without a degree cannot get other jobs. The suggested cause may contribute to unemployment, but it offers only a partial explanation.

The reason for the oil shortage is that the big oil companies are holding back on production so that they can make higher profits.

Even if it were proved that the oil companies are holding back production, there are many other factors that would have to be taken into account to explain the shortage, including the greatly increased demand for oil in an expanding economy all over the world, the use of oil as a political weapon in the Middle East, and the extravagant use of oil and electricity by Americans generally.

UNEXAMINED ANALOGIES

As we pointed out earlier, an analogy should be carefully examined to be sure the things being compared are alike in ways essential to the conclusion being drawn. The fact that they are alike in *some* ways is not enough. If there is one difference that would cause rejection of the conclusion, the analogy is fallacious.

Example

We can send people to the moon and communicate with them while they are there. Surely we can learn to communicate with one another here in our own country and so live together harmoniously.

Analysis

There is an essential difference in the type of communication between astronauts and the space administration on the one hand, and the discussion of economic, political, and social issues on the other. Astronauts in flight limit themselves to matters of fact that can be quickly checked. Living together harmoniously requires sensitivity to other people's images and needs, and

*tolerance of opposing points of view. It is
probable that astronauts have as much
difficulty communicating at this level as
other people do.*

The following arguments contain various kinds of fallacies. Evaluate each and explain clearly what is wrong with it. Do not be content with naming the fallacy. The skill you are trying to develop is not identification, but analysis. It is more important to explain the errors than to name them.

1. Of course he's guilty. If he were innocent, he would have disproved these charges long ago.

2. Dad, I think you will be making a mistake if you take out a big insurance policy now. The mortality tables show you have a life expectancy of sixty-nine and you are only forty-four. That means you have a reasonable expectation of living twenty-five years more. In four years both Madge and I will be through college and self-supporting. If you postpone the insurance until then, we won't have to skimp to pay the premiums.

3. Careful research shows that the most successful people have the largest vocabularies. This proves that one way to be successful is to develop a large vocabulary.

4. Teen-agers are not mature enough to get married. They have the highest divorce rate of any age-group. If they were mature, they would make a go of their marriages.

5. We can recognize that athletes who participate in major sports must be given special consideration within our grading system, or we can let the university sink into athletic oblivion.

6. Bill, you're a superb mechanic; you seem to have a natural talent for detecting what the trouble is and remedying it. Surely, then, you can analyze the rough drafts of your papers and turn them into polished essays.

7. Students here are rude. Last night the fellows in the room next to mine played their radio at full blast until two in the morning, and as I was on my way to class this morning a bicyclist almost ran me down.

8. The only reason the human race has survived is that human flesh is less palatable than that of other animals. A beast of prey will dash right past a defenseless human being to kill a gazelle or an impala.

9. A: When Thomas Wolfe was at his best, he was very good, but too often he was painfully verbose.

   B: You have no appreciation of the sort of spontaneity and lyricism Wolfe was capable of. I suppose you also think that Faulkner was no good and that

DISCUSSION
PROBLEM

Flannery O'Connor and Carson McCullers were decadent writers. What have you got against the South?

10.   I went to a women's lib meeting last night. The speakers were about as homely a group of women as I've ever seen. No wonder they hate men. A man would have to be pretty desperate to want to have anything to do with them.

11.   It comes down to this: either NATO should require the European countries to finance and man the European part of the program or the United States should pull out.

12.   The reason for the epidemic of violent student demonstrations in the sixties was that these students had been brought up under Dr. Spock's permissive theories of child-rearing.

13.   I don't know what the colleges are teaching nowadays. I have just had a letter of application from a young man who graduated from the state university last June. It was a wretched letter—badly written, with elementary errors in spelling, punctuation, and grammar. If that is the kind of product State is turning out, it does not deserve the tax support it is getting.

14.   The argument that football is a dangerous sport is disproved very simply by showing that the death rate—not total deaths, but deaths per thousand—among high school, college, and professional players combined is much less than the death rate of the total population.

15.   According to the newspapers, venereal disease is rising at an alarming rate among children in their early teens. If this is true, it raises a serious question about the wisdom of teaching sex-education in junior high schools.

16.   All right-thinking people will support the board of education's decision to destroy novels in the school libraries which are offensive to the moral standards of the community. If there were an epidemic of typhoid, the health authorities would be expected to do everything in their power to wipe it out. Pornography is worse than typhoid, since it corrupts the minds and morals of the young, not just their bodies. The school board is to be applauded for its prompt action in wiping out this moral disease.

17.   I dined in a London restaurant last summer, and the filet of sole was almost inedible. What's more, a friend of mine traveled on a British liner, and she said the menus were boring—too much roast beef and Yorkshire pudding. The English seem to have no talent for cooking.

18.   The fundamental problem in a democratic society is education. In a democracy the citizens are continually faced with alternatives. Whether they choose wisely or not will depend on how well educated they are. It is for this reason that each state must support public education generously. The better the support, the

better the educational system; and the better the educational system, the wiser the citizens and thus the state.

A. Suppose that you are one of the judges who are to determine the most persuasive essay in a student contest and that the choice has been narrowed down to the two following essays. Select the winner and justify your judgment in a paper. Since your paper will itself be an example of persuasion, make your reasons as complete, clear, and convincing as you can.

REVIEW EXERCISES

A New Look at an Old Myth

The U.S. Department of Labor statistics indicate that there is an oversupply of college-trained workers and that this oversupply is increasing. Already there is an overabundance of teachers, engineers, physicists, aerospace experts, and other specialists. Yet colleges and graduate schools continue every year to turn out highly trained people to compete for jobs that aren't there. The result is that graduates cannot enter the professions for which they were trained and must take temporary jobs which do not require a college degree. These "temporary" jobs have a habit of becoming permanent.

On the other hand, there is a tremendous need for skilled workers of all sorts: carpenters, electricians, mechanics, plumbers, TV repairmen. These people have more work than they can handle, and their annual incomes are often higher than those of college graduates. The old distinction that white-collar workers make a better living than blue-collar workers no longer holds true. The law of supply and demand now favors the skilled worker.

The reason for this situation is the traditional myth that a college degree is a passport to a prosperous future. A large segment of American society equates success in life with a college degree. Parents begin indoctrinating their children with this myth before they are out of grade school. High school teachers play their part by acting as if high school education were a preparation for college rather than for life. Under this pressure the kids fall in line. Whether they want to go to college or not doesn't matter. Everybody should go to college, so of course they must go. And every year college enrollments go up and up, and more and more graduates are overeducated for the kinds of jobs available to them.

One result of this emphasis on a college education is that many people go to college who do not belong there. Of the sixty per cent of high school graduates who enter college, half of them do not graduate with their class. Many of them drop out within the first year. Some struggle on for two or three years and then give up. Some of these may return after a time and complete their degree requirements, but the mortality rate is high. For many students their exposure to college was an expensive mistake, expensive in money, time, and blasted hopes.

High schools should be more open-minded about alternatives to college. A step in the right direction is the implementation of work-study programs which allow students to get firsthand experience at an appropriate job in their field of interest. Even if students eventually want to go to college, there is no reason why they must go directly from high school. They could work for a year or two and perhaps get some kind of realistic understanding of their own abilities and interests. But because many guidance departments in high school have a built-in bias toward a college education, they discourage delay as procrastination. They have a now-or-never complex about going to college.

There are many viable alternatives to college that can lead to satisfying and even creative vocations. Vocational-technical schools, fine-arts schools, union-sponsored apprentice programs are examples. If a college education were viewed as just one of a number of acceptable possibilities, the stage would be set for a sounder assessment of career choices. Unfortunately these alternatives are hard to fit into the American myth. They lack glamour and prestige. They don't have football teams or fraternities or Homecomings. It takes more maturity than most eighteen-year-olds have to prefer West End Vocational to State U.

The trauma of a student's flunking out will continue to increase as long as society perpetuates a myopic view of college education. There is nothing sacred about college. It is not the Promised Land. In fact, it is a worthless experience to some people. The availability of alternative choices must be continually held out if the rising number of dropouts is to be stopped.

DDT Should Be Banned from All Use

Silence . . . Total, barren silence. No signs of life can be seen. Cities and towns are completely deserted and an eerie death-like stillness seems to encompass the entire earth. Nothing remains but silence—endless, boundless silence.

Perhaps this depicts the view of a pessimistic observer who is attempting to paint a picture of the not-too-distant future on planet Earth. Or could it possibly be the view of a realist? We have been destroying our environment by pollution for so long that the pollutants will eventually destroy humanity.

One of these pollutants is DDT (dichloro-diphenyl-trichloroethane). DDT is a colorless, synthetic chlorinated hydrocarbon which is known primarily for its use as a pesticide. Although it was first invented in 1874, it did not go into widespread use until after World War II. Once it became available to the public, its popularity increased immensely, and by 1967 over 103 million pounds were being released annually into the environment. The inventors had failed, however, to take into consideration the possible long-term effects on our environment.

One catastrophic effect that was never considered concerns a scientific process called biological magnification. As DDT is injected into the environment, it is dispersed throughout the atmosphere, landing not only on the specified pests but also on trees, grasses, and plants. The herbivores feeding on these plants accumulate the chemical within their bodies and pass it on to the carnivores that feed on them. Moreover, as it is passed through each level of the food chain, the amount of DDT is intensely magnified. As you can see, by the time it reaches the top carnivores, such as eagles and hawks, it has acquired a high degree of concentration. This concentration not only has the ability to destroy individual animals, but is also capable of wiping out the entire species. For example, just since the recent widespread use of DDT, scientists have noticed a definite decrease in the thickness and calcium content of the egg shells of carnivorous birds. Weak egg shells make it impossible for the young to withstand environmental problems during incubation, and they are eventually destroyed. Lacking subsequent generations to replace the parents, the entire species soon becomes extinct.

Now, since humans occupy the top level of the food chain, they are most exposed to DDT accumulation. It has been reported that in the United States all human foods, with the exception of a few beverages, contain chlorinated carbons such as DDT. They have even been detected in human milk. The average breast-fed baby ingests .02 milligrams of DDT-derived materials each day, which is twice the acceptable intake allowed by the World Health Organization. The effects of this amount have not yet been determined because of the limited extent of the study. But the admission that the effects have not yet been evaluated does not imply that DDT is harmless. It merely means that we have not yet had time to examine the long-term exposure problem. It should be noted, however, that serious results have been discovered in laboratory animals. Not only has DDT produced cancer in these animals; it has also caused birth defects and deformities in their offspring.

The only justification for the use of DDT is its effectiveness as a pesticide. Let us consider this claim. Granted, DDT has saved perhaps millions of lives by reducing the spread of malaria. And, by cutting crop losses, it has proved to be a major aid in reducing the universal hunger problem. But its effectiveness is gradually diminishing. Pests are not only acquiring extraordinary powers of resistance, but are also developing new species on which the pesticide has no effect. By 1967, for example, resistance had developed in 224 species of insects. The more resistance these pests are able to develop, the greater is the amount of DDT required to destroy them. So every year we have to expose ourselves to more and more DDT contamination in order to kill fewer and fewer insects.

Since its widespread use, DDT has destroyed much of our wildlife. If allowed to continue, it will eventually destroy the matrix in which life exists—our environment. As intelligent and conscientious individuals, we must not allow this to happen. It is not enough to *restrict* the use of DDT. We must ban it from *all* use—now! We must act before it is too late, not only for our plants and animals, but for the very survival of life itself.

B. Write an editorial for your college newspaper in which you advocate that some change should be made. Begin with a paragraph or two in which you stress the evils of the present system; then explain clearly the change you want made; then present an argument proving the advantages of your proposal.

PART

3

SPECIAL

ASSIGNMENTS

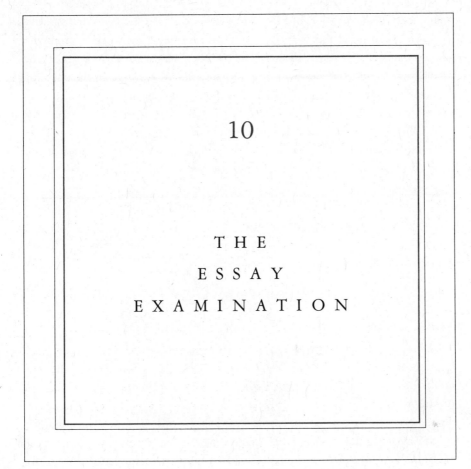

10

THE
ESSAY
EXAMINATION

The essay examination is one of the most practical of all composition assignments. By asking you to compose in one or more paragraphs an answer to a specific question, it calls on most of the skills the composition course tries to develop. It also tests your ability to read carefully and to write purposefully within a rigidly limited time.

Instructors often complain that students write their worst on essay examinations. Of course, the pressure of an examination hardly encourages stylistic polish. But the chief weakness of examination answers is not that they are unpolished or ungrammatical or awkward, but that they are not composed at all. Many students do not first plan what they want to say and then develop their intention into an adequate answer. Too often they begin to write without a clear purpose and assume that as long as they are writing they are somehow answering the question. The result is often an answer that is irrelevant, inadequate, unclear, and even self-contradictory.

This chapter attempts to improve the quality of essay answers through applying to them the principles of purposeful writing discussed in earlier chapters of this book. We cannot, of course, teach subject matter here. But many weaknesses in examination papers are caused not by ignorance of the subject matter, but by carelessness, haste, or panic. The recommendations in the sections that follow should help you avoid such weaknesses.

READ THE QUESTION CAREFULLY

Before beginning to answer any part of an examination, read the question carefully to see what it asks you to do. If you misinterpret the question, your whole answer may be off the point, even if it shows detailed knowledge of the subject and is otherwise well written. So before you begin to write, ask yourself, "What does this question require me to do?" Notice especially whether it asks you to explain, summarize, discuss, evaluate, or compare. These are often key words in an essay question. If you are asked to *evaluate* a paragraph or a poem, a *summary* or an *explanation* of the paragraph or a *paraphrase* of the poem will not satisfy the requirement. If you are asked to *compare* two characters in a play, a *description* of each character may not develop a comparison. Presumably, the wording of the question has been carefully thought out, and you will be expected to follow the directions it implies. *Never begin to write until you have a clear idea of what kind of answer is asked for.*

To see how a student can drift into a bad answer by not reading the instructions carefully and seeing clearly what they require, study the following question and the two answers to it.

> Using Le Corbusier's Savoye House and Frank Lloyd Wright's Kaufmann House as typical examples, contrast the architectural styles of these two men as expressions of their beliefs of what a house should be.

Answer 1:
Thesis stating basic
contrasting views

The major differences in the architectural styles of Le Corbusier and Wright came from their different views of what a house should be. For Le Corbusier a house was "a machine for living" which should be efficient and attractive; for Wright a house should integrate the needs of its owners with its surroundings. The Savoye House and the Kaufmann House are good illustrations of the results of this fundamental difference.

Four characteristics of the Savoye House are typical of a Le Corbusier residential design. First, the emphasis is on the house itself; its environment is just the location on which it is built, and a similar house could be constructed in a different place. Second, it is built on three levels, each of which meets a different need of the family. The ground level is an open space which can serve as a garage; the middle level, which is raised from the ground on piers and cantilevered out from the ground level, is the living area; the top level, the flat roof, is a recreational area with a space for sunbathing and a small garden. Third, the different levels are painted in different colors to emphasize their different uses. Fourth, the whole structure is built of steel and cement in a harmonious arrangement of horizontal and vertical lines relieved only by the curved cement windbreak around the roof garden. The major emphasis throughout is on utility. The whole effect is one of efficient regularity in an attractive design.

Topic sentence of enumerative paragraph showing characteristics of Savoye House

Summary statement

Frank Lloyd Wright referred to such buildings as "structures on stilts." He saw the machine as a potential enemy of modern man and, through his houses, he rebelled against it. In designing a house he started with the family needs and the environment, and he sought to unite these two elements in the building. This makes it more difficult to identify any one Wright house as "typical," since each house is designed for a different set of conditions. The Kaufmann House, named *Falling Water,* is a good example of this uniqueness. Because the Kaufmanns were fond of their natural waterfall, Wright designed the house to be built partly over it. Indeed, he made the house a vertical extension of the waterfall by projecting two massive cement cantilevers which, in effect, added two stories to the falls. The house proper was designed to blend into the environment. Its basic materials were wood and a native stone that harmonized with the surrounding colors. To increase this color-blending, Wright sometimes mixed local dirt with cement. The house itself is built into a hillside and is on several levels which merge into the surrounding landscape through a series of porches and terraces. This identification of the house with its environment, achieved through structure and materials, is what Wright calls his "organic architecture."

Topic sentence stating Wright's view

Summary statement

This is an excellent response to the examiner's directions. It first establishes in the introductory paragraph the basic contrast between the two architects' views from which the specific differences follow. Then it examines each house to show how it illustrates the architect's objectives. Every detail of the second paragraph adds to the theme that a Le Corbusier house is "a machine for living." Every detail in the third paragraph supports the relation between house and environment in a Wright design. No digressive details are allowed in the answer. The writer knows

LES HEURES CLAIRES, Le Corbusier Villa Savoye, Poissy-sur-Seine, France, 1929–31

Photograph, Courtesy The Museum of Modern Art, New York

FALLING WATER, Kaufmann House, Frank Lloyd Wright, 1936–37

Photograph by Ezra Stoller © ESTO

what the directions demand. That determines her purpose, which in turn controls what she has to say.

Answer 2   The Savoye House is a rectangular building. Its main part, the living area, is raised above the ground, and the space under it can be used for a combination garage and open basement. On top of the living quarters is a flat roof on which there is a small garden almost surrounded by a curving wall. The rest of the roof is vacant, except for some vents and a pipelike metal chimney.

Around the middle level is an almost continuous band of windows, so the living quarters are well lighted. There are no windows on the lower level, since that is completely open, except for the supports on which the rest of the house stands. The exterior of the house is made of painted concrete with a different color for each level. This helps to break the monotony of the rectangular structure.

The Kaufmann House is one of Frank Lloyd Wright's most famous creations. It has an unusual setting because it was built over a waterfall. The base of the house consists of three great cement slabs. Two of these project over the waterfall like huge diving boards. Rising above these slabs is a large chimney that looks like the funnel of a ship. As a matter of fact the whole building makes you think of a battleship.

Frank Lloyd Wright calls this kind of architecture "organic." This means that he uses chiefly organic materials like wood and stone, where other architects would use steel and cement. There is quite a lot of cement in the Kaufmann House, but mostly in the slabs. The house itself is made chiefly of stone. It is a one-level house, but the big slabs give it the appearance of several stories.

Even though it shows good observation of details, answer 2 is unsatisfactory, chiefly because it does not respond directly to the question. The purpose imposed by the directions was *to show the differences between the architectural styles of Le Corbusier and Wright* by contrasting two representative examples of their work. Answer 2 does not achieve this purpose. It simply describes each house separately, paying almost no attention to what the descriptions were supposed to illustrate. Except for the definition of "organic architecture" (which is incomplete), it fails to relate the observed details to a contrast of architectural styles. From this answer a reader learns what each house looks like but is not told the major differences between the styles of Le Corbusier and Wright.

The composition of these answers is a practical application of the A + B contrast discussed in Chapter 4. The structure of answer 1 is similar to that of the essay contrasting the American concept of time with the time concept of other cultures (page 67): an introductory paragraph identifying the two elements of contrast (A and B), followed by a paragraph illustrating A and another illustrating B. In the discussion following that essay, the warning was given that "A simple description of two unlike houses, for instance, is not necessarily a contrast. It becomes one only when it points up dissimilarities implied in a thesis." The thesis of answer 1 is clearly expressed in its introductory paragraph. But answer 2 has no thesis, and the reason it has no thesis is that the writer has not made up his mind what basic contrast his answer should establish. By ignoring the final part of the directions and plunging too soon into descriptive details, he fails to answer the question satisfactorily. Since the first answer would probably be graded at least two full grades higher than the second, the writer of answer 2 would pay a stiff price for his failure to apply a principle established in Chapter 4.

THINK OUT YOUR ANSWER BEFORE WRITING

Think out your general answer before you begin to develop it. Since there is almost no chance of rewriting in an essay examination, your answer must be correctly planned the first time. If you have your thesis or topic sentence clearly in mind, explanatory and illustrative details will suggest themselves as you write. But if you have not decided what you want to say before you begin, you may veer away from the question or write a series of unrelated sentences that do not add up to a unified answer. For some questions, it may be wise to jot down on a separate sheet of paper the information you want to work into your answer; for others, framing a topic sentence will be preparation enough. This advice repeats what was said in earlier chapters, but the advice becomes even more important in an examination because there is so little chance to revise.

The answer given below shows a carefully planned response to the following question:

> Just before he dies, Laertes says to Hamlet, "Mine and my father's death come not on thee, nor thine on me." In view of the facts of the play, how do you interpret this statement?

The student thinks over the question and the facts of the play and frames a general answer thus:

> Laertes' statement fits some of the facts but not all of them and is best understood as a request to let bygones be bygones.

This is the topic sentence or thesis of his answer. It requires him to do three things: (1) to show that Laertes' statement fits some of the facts, (2) to show that it does not fit other facts, and (3) to explain what he means by interpreting the statement as a request to let bygones be bygones. Notice how he satisfies his own intention and the requirements of the question.

Answer 1   Laertes' statement fits some of the facts but not all of them and is best understood as a request to let bygones be bygones. True, Hamlet is not responsible for Laertes' death, because Hamlet thought he was engaging in a friendly bout with blunted swords. When he picked up Laertes' sword in the mix-up he did not know it was poisoned. Since Laertes deliberately put the poison there, he was responsible for both Hamlet's death and his own. Hamlet killed Polonius by mistake, thinking that the person behind the curtain was the king. To that extent it was an accidental killing, but a killing nevertheless. I think Laertes' statement is not intended as a literal description of the facts but as a reconciliation speech. I interpret the statement as meaning: "We have both been the victims of the king's treachery. Forgive me for your death, as I forgive you for mine and my father's."

This answer is an excellent example of purposeful writing in a paragraph: topic sentence, followed by supporting details, followed by a restatement of the topic idea in a concluding statement. The structure of the paragraph is implied in the topic sentence. Since the student thought out his whole answer before beginning to write, he controls the content of the paragraph. He knows that he must document his topic sentence from the facts of the play.

Contrast that answer with one by a student who has not thought out his general answer and plunges into a summary of the facts without considering how they relate to the question he is supposed to be answering.

Answer 2   Laertes returns from France and learns that his father has been killed by Hamlet. He is almost mad with grief and rage and in a stormy scene with the king he demands revenge. He and the king conspire to arrange a duel between Laertes and Hamlet in which Laertes will use a poisoned sword. The duel takes place after Ophelia's funeral, and Laertes cuts Hamlet with the poisoned sword. Then, in a scuffle, their swords are knocked from their hands and Hamlet picks up Laertes' sword and wounds him. Meanwhile the king has put poison in a goblet of wine he intended for Hamlet, but the queen drinks it instead. When Hamlet sees she is dying he kills the king; then both Hamlet and Laertes die.

This paragraph does not answer the question asked. It does not interpret Laertes' final speech. It simply summarizes the action of the play from the time of Laertes' return from France until his death in the duel. Since the question assumes that the facts of the play are known to everyone in the class, the answer contributes nothing.

Failure to read the question carefully enough to see what it asks and failure to prewrite your answer are related faults. If you know the subject, careful reading of the question suggests an answer, and prewriting the answer gives you a check against the wording of the question. A student who misses the first step will probably miss the second also. The sensible thing is to postpone the writing until you know what you are trying to say, and why.

WRITE A COMPLETE ANSWER

Unless the directions specify a short answer, do not write a one- or two-sentence answer in an essay examination. This advice requires you to distinguish between a short-answer test and an essay examination. A short-answer test tests knowledge of the facts. Accordingly, the questions can be answered satisfactorily in one or two minutes. Usually there are from twenty to thirty such questions in a fifty-minute quiz. An essay examination, by contrast, requires a *discussion* of the question to show the student's ability to select and organize information to support a thesis. Since such an answer needs one or more paragraphs, the examiner assumes it will take from fifteen to thirty minutes. Sometimes the directions specify how much time to allow for an answer. But if they do not, the number of questions asked indicates the average time for each. Therefore, the student should know from the situation how much time to allow for each question.

A complete answer is one that deals with the subject as fully as possible within the time limits. An answer that is complete for a short-answer test will be inadequate for an essay examination. For example, the second sentence of the first answer on the styles of Le Corbusier and Wright

> For Le Corbusier a house was "a machine for living" which should be efficient and attractive; for Wright a house should integrate the needs of its owners with its surroundings.

would be complete for a short-answer test, but it would be inadequate for an essay examination because it lacks the detailed contrast of the two houses that the directions required.

The following answers further illustrate the difference between a complete and an incomplete answer in an essay examination. Here is the question:

> *Explain the real issue behind Alexander Hamilton's bargaining with Pennsylvania, Maryland, and Virginia on the site of the projected national capital.*

Answer 1   The real issue was whether Alexander Hamilton's desire to have a strong central government would prevail. To enlist support for this idea Hamilton proposed that the federal government should assume responsibility for the existing state debts. This won over the heavily indebted states but was opposed by those states that were relatively free of debt. Hamilton knew that the vote would be a close one and that the votes of the delegates from Pennsylvania, Maryland, and Virginia (who all wanted the capital to be in their state) might be decisive. After considerable negotiation with the delegates from these states he arranged a compromise that Philadelphia should be the temporary capital for ten years while Washington was being built on the Potomac on land ceded by Maryland and Virginia. In return, the delegates from these three states would vote for federal assumption of state debts. This compromise worked. The advocates of assuming state indebtedness won, and the arrangement for the location of the capital was ratified by Congress.

Answer 2   Alexander Hamilton bargained with Pennsylvania, Maryland, and Virginia, and finally worked out a plan making Philadelphia the temporary capital for ten years while Washington was being built between Maryland and Virginia.

Answer 2 is incomplete for two reasons: it leaves out Hamilton's motivation and the issue of the federal government's assumption of the state debts; and by doing so it does not explain the real issue behind the bargaining but merely states some of the results. The answer is not appropriate to the situation for which it was written, though it would have been adequate as a short answer to the question, "What compromise did Alexander Hamilton arrange to get Pennsylvania, Maryland, and Virginia to agree to the location of the national capital?"

Completeness in an examination essay is no different from completeness in paragraphs, which we discussed in Chapter 5. The topic sentence of a paragraph or the thesis of an essay is necessarily a general statement. To make that statement clear and convincing to a reader, the writer must develop it in specific detail. This is especially true when the examination question calls for a judgment. That judgment is only a topic sentence until it is developed into a complete answer by the evidence needed to support or explain it. If the writer of answer 1 on Laertes' statement had stopped with the general answer, "Laertes' statement distorts the facts. It is not an accurate report of what happened. He is rationalizing his own guilt and that of Hamlet by blaming Claudius," he would have written an incomplete answer. It is the explanatory details he offers that make his answer complete.

DO NOT PAD YOUR ANSWER

Padding an answer is more likely to hurt than help. A student who pads an answer with wordiness, repetition, or irrelevant detail draws attention to the fact that he or she has little to say and is trying to conceal this lack of knowledge. It is naive to think that a grader will accept padding as a contribution to the answer. There is a relationship between length and content, because presenting content takes space. For example, the good answers in the preceding pages could not have been reduced in length without losing significant content. But no experienced grader equates mere length with content. Graders are not easily persuaded that an answer is good just because it is long. They are more likely to be annoyed at having to spend time to separate a few kernels of wheat from a bushel of chaff. It is the student's responsibility to select and present what is relevant to the question.

The essay on page 262 is a padded response to the question on the bargaining by which the site of the national capital was decided. The grader's comments identify the two major weaknesses of the answer—failure to explain the reason for Hamilton's negotiations with the delegates from Pennsylvania, Maryland, and Virginia; and the useless repetition of the content of the first paragraph in the second. It is obvious that the student was not prepared to answer the question and that she said in the first paragraph all she could say. But she seemed to feel that saying it over again in the second paragraph would somehow make her answer acceptable. Notice the irritation the grader expresses in both the crossed-out paragraph and the marginal comments. However harsh this criticism may seem to a student, it is the kind of response that conspicuous padding may provoke. Even if a grader does not so openly express irritation, it will be a factor in deciding the grade given to the answer.

For each of the following paired answers choose what you think is the better one and discuss your reasons in class. The first pair is for a course in library science, the second for a course in psychology, and the third for a course in humanities. Even though you may not be familiar with the subjects being discussed, you should be able to decide which answer better satisfies the requirements of the directions.

DISCUSSION PROBLEM

1. Discuss the contribution of William Morris to book design, using as an example his edition of the works of Chaucer.

Question 1

William Morris's *Chaucer* was his masterpiece. It shows his interest in the Middle Ages. The type is based on medieval manuscript writing, and the decoration around the edges of the pages is like that used in medieval books. The large initial letters are typical of medieval design. Those letters were

Answer 1

The bargaining that led to the establishment of the U.S. capital in Washington, D.C., was an example of how important political decisions are made in a democracy. Whatever state the capital was located in would get prestige and political influence by having the capital located in that state. So many states were eager to get ~~this prestige and political influence by having~~ the capital in that state that there was bound to be jealousy no matter which state won. The only logical solution was to have the capital in no state but in a separate area called the District of Columbia which was governed by the federal government, not by a state government.

But what was the bargaining— who bargained with whom about what, and why?

The bargaining that led to this decision was an attempt to find a solution that would avoid state jealousies by treating every state the same. If no state had the national capital, there would be no need to be jealous of any one state. Therefore all states would be likely to support this proposal, because every state would feel that the next best thing to having the capital within their boundaries would be to let no state have the capital. This was done by setting up the District of Columbia as an independent area under the control of Congress. In that way the capital was in no state but belonged to the whole country.

This ¶ merely restates what was said in ¶ 1 and does not give further information about the nature of the bargaining.

Not only does the second paragraph repeat the content of the first, but neither paragraph gives any detailed explanation of the bargaining between Hamilton and the delegates of Pennsylvania, Maryland, and Virginia. The independence of the District of Columbia was not an issue in that bargaining, but assumption of state debts was.

printed from woodcuts, which was the medieval way of printing. The illustrations were by Burne-Jones, one of the best artists in England at the time. Morris was able to get the most competent people to help him because he was so famous as a poet and a designer of furniture (the Morris chair) and wallpaper and other decorative items for the home. He designed the furnishings for his own home, which was widely admired among the sort of people he associated with. In this way he started the arts and crafts movement.

Morris's contribution to book design was to approach the problem as an artist or fine craftsman, rather than as a mere printer who reproduced texts. He wanted to raise the standards of printing, which had fallen to a low point, by showing that truly beautiful books could be produced. His *Chaucer* was designed as a unified work of art or high craft. Since Chaucer lived in the late Middle Ages, Morris decided to design a new type based on medieval English script and to imitate the format of a medieval manuscript. This involved elaborate letters and large initials at the beginnings of verses, as well as wide borders of intertwined vines with leaves, fruit, and flowers in strong colors. The effect was so unusual that the book caused great excitement and inspired other printers to design beautiful rather than purely utilitarian books.

Answer 2

2. *Explain the chief differences between neurosis and psychosis.*

Question 2

The chief differences between neurosis and psychosis are the extent to which a person is alienated from reality and his chances of making a workable adjustment to normal living. The boundary between the two cannot be precisely drawn; therefore the differences are best illustrated at their extremes.

Answer 1

A person suffering from neurosis may feel serious anxieties but still be able to handle the ordinary activities of daily living. For example, a woman may have a phobia about being left alone with a red-headed man because a male with red hair once assaulted her. But as long as she avoids that particular situation, she is able to conduct her domestic and business duties in a normal manner. Through psychiatric counseling she may learn to understand the cause of her phobia and either get rid of it or control it. Fears of heights and crowds are other examples of neuroses. They are not central to the way one organizes his life and can be alleviated either by counseling or by avoidance of situations in which the neurotic response is likely to occur.

But a psychotic person is so divorced from reality that in severe cases, like paranoid schizophrenia, he lives in a private world which has little relation to the real one. A man who thinks he is Moses and feels a divinely granted right to punish those who break any of the Ten Commandments has reorganized experience around a delusion that makes life bearable for him. His delusion is necessary to his continued existence. In a sense he has found a therapy that works for him. He will resist psychiatric help because he thinks he no longer has any problem: it is the sinners who have problems. Such a person may be helped to some degree by specialized, institutional care, but the chances of a complete recovery are slim.

Between these extremes are conditions which may be classified as either neurosis or psychosis. In such cases psychiatrists may disagree in their diagnoses.

Answer 2   Because there is some neurosis in all of us, we all utilize defense mechanisms against our frustrations. For that matter, a psychotic person may also use such defenses, but he is less likely to be aware of what he is doing. We may repress our frustrations—simply refuse to think about them. Or we may defend by consciously developing characteristics the opposite of those we disapprove of. For example, a person who is troubled by his tendency toward greediness may force himself to be generous in giving away possessions he wants to keep. We can also escape frustration and low self-esteem by projection of our faults, blaming them on other people. Or we can use rationalization by devising excuses to justify our behavior. Finally, we may save our pride by fantasizing. That is, a young man may imagine that the girl who has declined to date him is cheering wildly in a basketball gymnasium while he sets a new school scoring record and that she will be waiting for him with bated breath at the locker-room door.

Neurotic people may need the help that defense mechanisms can give them, but excessive use of such devices can make a problem worse. And if a neurotic condition becomes so serious that the person is out of touch with the real world and locked into his private world, he is psychotic. As I think back over my answer it seems to me that a psychotic person would be more likely to use some of these mechanisms than he would others.

Question 3   3. *To illustrate the differences between early and late Renaissance painting, contrast Fra Filippo Lippi's* Madonna with Child *with Raphael's* Sistine Madonna.

Answer 1   Fra Filippo's picture is a good example of early Renaissance naturalism. The Madonna—his own wife—is wearing a stylish gown, which is painted in faithful detail. Her hair is dressed in the mode of the time. She is seated—as though in her own home—on an elaborately carved chair, with a framed painting of a landscape serving as the background. Her pose and expression are calm, perhaps devout, but neither exalted nor humble. She is an ordinary worldly mother with a chubby baby, who is being lifted to her rather ungracefully by a saucy angel. The entire scene is intimate, personal, and joyous, but hardly reverent. Filippo, pleased with the new-found technical mastery of his age, is content to paint what he sees.

Raphael was able to get above his technique and make it expressive of lofty emotion. The figures in the *Sistine Madonna* are monumental and stand out against a subdued background. The Madonna, her feet resting weightlessly on a cloud, wears an expression of sublime dignity. She holds with graceful ease the Child, whose sober eyes reveal the portent of His future.

MADONNA WITH CHILD, Filippo Lippi, 1406–1469

Scala/Editorial Photocolor Archives

SISTINE MADONNA, Raphael, 1483–1520

Scala/Editorial Photocolor Archives

The figures wear classic robes, whose flowing lines give a wonderful, circling movement to the painting. A cloud of tiny cherubs' heads, peeping through the effulgence surrounding the Virgin, completes the heavenly setting. Where Filippo's work is mere copying, Raphael's is imaginative and spiritual. This loftiness of conception combined with grace of design and beauty of execution is the flower of the High Renaissance.

Filippo's picture is simply designed, and the figures are naturalistic. The Madonna is sweet, gracious, and human, dressed in the mode of the times. The Bambino is a natural, playful child. He is being lifted up by two older boys—undoubtedly Fra Filippo's family posed for the picture. The background is a stylized landscape of rocks and streams, bounded by a frame. The Madonna is seated in a chair with an elaborately carved arm which stands out in the foreground.

Answer 2

Raphael designed the Sistine Madonna in a pyramid with the Madonna herself at the apex. She carries the curly-haired Child, and although she is standing still, her garments swirl as in a strong wind. One's eye is first caught by the figure of Pope Sixtus at the lower left and, through the folds of his garment and his uplifted eyes, drawn toward the central figure of the Virgin. Her garments, billowing to the right, draw the eye downward again to the figure of St. Barbara, kneeling on a cloud. Her eyes are cast down, and the glance follows hers to discover two jaunty cherubs leaning on the lower frame. They look upward, thus deflecting the eyes of the beholder up again, completing the movement of the design.

Take from your file any essay examination you have previously written, preferably an unsatisfactory one, and review it to see how it could be improved.

EXERCISE

11

THE
CRITICAL
ESSAY

A critical essay is one that attempts to analyze, interpret, and evaluate its subject. The word *critical* in this context does not mean "fault-finding." Its Greek root means "to separate, discern, or choose," and a critical essay is chiefly an exercise in analysis, interpretation, or evaluation. It may deal with any subject worthy of serious study—a book, a film or television program, a painting, a building, a political or social movement. But since the favorite subject for critical essays in an English class is literature, this chapter will be limited to that subject.

PREWRITING
THE CRITICAL ESSAY

The procedure for prewriting a critical essay is similar to that for other papers. You will discover your purpose through prewriting and then will select, organize, and develop your material to show a reader what the work means to you, or how you respond to it. Much of what you do will involve persuasion; so you will have the same concern for trustworthiness and logical argument that you learned in Chapter 9.

The chief difference is that more than in any other kind of paper your writing will depend on reading. The first stage in the prewriting of a critical essay is a careful, sometimes a repeated, reading of the novel, short story, play, or poem you are writing about. Since everything depends on a sound knowledge of the work, your prewriting will be more efficient if you know what to look for in your reading. Accordingly, we begin by examining the basic elements that you will be concerned with in reading literature. These are *situation, character, plot, dramatic conflict, theme, structure, symbol, irony, point of view,* and *voice.* In any particular work some of these elements will be more important than others. Which one or what combination of them you want to emphasize will be part of your decision about your real subject.

To illustrate these elements, we will use a short story, Ralph Ellison's "King of the Bingo Game," as our chief source and will supplement it by references to other works.

King of the Bingo Game
by Ralph Ellison

The woman in front of him was eating roasted peanuts that smelled so good that he could barely contain his hunger. He could not even sleep and wished they'd hurry and begin the bingo game. There, on his right, two fellows were drinking wine out of a bottle wrapped in a paper bag, and he could hear soft gurgling in the dark. His stomach gave a low gnawing growl. "If this was down South," he thought, "all I'd have to do is lean over and say, 'Lady, gimme a few of those peanuts, please ma'm,' and she'd pass me the bag and never think nothing of it." Or he could ask the fellows for a drink in the same way. Folks down South stuck together that way; they didn't even have to know you. But up here it was different. Ask somebody for something, and they'd think you were crazy. Well, I ain't crazy. I'm just broke, 'cause I got no birth certificate to get a job, and Laura 'bout to die 'cause we got no money for a doctor. But I ain't crazy. And yet a pinpoint of doubt was focused in his mind as he glanced toward the screen and saw the hero stealthily entering a dark room and sending the beam of a flashlight along a wall of bookcases. This is where he finds the trapdoor, he remembered. The man would pass abruptly through the wall and find the girl tied to a bed, her legs and arms spread wide, and her clothing torn to rags. He laughed softly to himself. He had seen the picture three times, and this was one of the best scenes.

On his right the fellow whispered wide-eyed to his companion, "Man, look a-yonder!"

"Damn!"

"Wouldn't I like to have her tied up like that . . ."

"Hey! That fool's letting her loose!"

"Aw, man, he loves her."

"Love or no love!"

The man moved impatiently beside him, and he tried to involve himself in the scene. But Laura was on his mind. Tiring quickly of watching the picture he looked back to where the white beam filtered from the projection room above the balcony. It started small and grew large, specks of dust dancing in its whiteness as it reached the screen. It was strange how the beam always landed right on the screen and didn't mess up and fall somewhere else. But they had it all fixed. Everything was fixed. Now suppose when they showed that girl with her dress torn the girl started taking off the rest of her clothes, and when the guy came in he didn't untie her but kept her there and went to taking off his own clothes? *That* would be something to see. If a picture got out of hand like that those guys up there would go nuts. Yeah, and there'd be so many folks in here you couldn't find a seat for nine months! A strange sensation played over his skin. He shuddered. Yesterday he'd seen a bedbug on a woman's neck as they walked out into the bright street. But exploring his thigh through a hole in his pocket he found only goose pimples and old scars.

The bottle gurgled again. He closed his eyes. Now a dreamy music was accompanying the film and train whistles were sounding in the distance, and he was a boy again walking along a railroad trestle down South, and seeing the train coming, and running back as fast as he could go, and hearing the whistle blowing, and getting off the trestle to solid ground just in time, with the earth trembling beneath his feet, and feeling relieved as he ran down the cinder-strewn embankment onto the highway, and looking back and seeing with terror that the train had left the track and was following him right down the middle of the street, and all the white people laughing as he ran screaming . . .

"Wake up there, buddy! What the hell do you mean hollering like that! Can't you see we trying to enjoy this here picture?"

He stared at the man with gratitude.

"I'm sorry, old man," he said. "I musta been dreaming."

"Well, here, have a drink. And don't be making no noise like that, damn!"

His hands trembled as he tilted his head. It was not wine, but whiskey. Cold rye whiskey. He took a deep swoller, decided it was better not to take another, and handed the bottle back to its owner.

"Thanks, old man," he said.

Now he felt the cold whiskey breaking a warm path straight through the middle of him, growing hotter and sharper as it moved. He had not eaten all day, and it made him light-headed. The smell of the peanuts stabbed him like a knife, and he got up and found a seat in the middle aisle. But no sooner did he sit than he saw a row of intense-faced young girls, and got up again, thinking, "You chicks musta been Lindy-hopping somewhere." He found a seat several rows ahead as the lights came on, and he saw the screen disappear behind a heavy red and gold curtain; then the curtain rising, and the man with the microphone and a uniformed attendant coming on the stage.

He felt for his bingo cards, smiling. The guy at the door wouldn't like it if he knew about his having *five* cards. Well, not everyone played the bingo game; and even with five cards he didn't have much of a chance. For Laura, though, he had to have faith. He studied the cards, each with its different numerals, punching the free center hole in each and spreading them neatly across his lap; and when the lights faded he sat slouched in his seat so that he could look from his cards to the bingo wheel with but a quick shifting of his eyes.

Ahead, at the end of the darkness, the man with the microphone was pressing a button attached to a long cord and spinning the bingo wheel and calling out the number each time the wheel came to rest. And each time the voice rang out his finger raced over the cards for the number. With five cards he had to move fast. He became nervous; there were too many cards, and the man went too fast with his grating voice. Perhaps he should just select one and throw the others away. But he was afraid. He became warm. Wonder how much Laura's doctor would cost? Damn that, watch the cards! And with despair he heard the man call three in a row which he missed on all five cards. This way he'd never win . . .

When he saw the row of holes punched across the third card, he sat paralyzed and heard the man call three more numbers before he stumbled forward, screaming,

"Bingo! Bingo!"

"Let that fool up there," someone called.

"Get up there, man!"

He stumbled down the aisle and up the steps to the stage into a light so sharp and bright that for a moment it blinded him, and he felt that he had moved into the spell of some strange, mysterious power. Yet it was as familiar as the sun, and he knew it was the perfectly familiar bingo.

The man with the microphone was saying something to the audience as he held out his card. A cold light flashed from the man's finger as the card left his hand. His knees trembled. The man stepped closer, checking the card against the numbers chalked on the board. Suppose he had made a mistake?

The pomade on the man's hair made him feel faint, and he backed away. But the man was checking the card over the microphone now, and he had to stay. He stood tense, listening.

"Under the O, forty-four," the man chanted. "Under the I, seven. Under the G, three. Under the B, ninety-six. Under the N, thirteen!"

His breath came easier as the man smiled at the audience.

"Yessir, ladies and gentlemen, he's one of the chosen people!"

The audience rippled with laughter and applause.

"Step right up to the front of the stage."

He moved slowly forward, wishing that the light was not so bright.

"To win tonight's jackpot of $36.90 the wheel must stop between the double zero, understand?"

He nodded, knowing the ritual from the many days and nights he had watched the winners march across the stage to press the button that controlled the spinning wheel and receive the prizes. And now he followed the instructions as though he'd crossed the slippery stage a million prize-winning times.

The man was making some kind of a joke, and he nodded vacantly. So tense had he become that he felt a sudden desire to cry and shook it away. He felt vaguely that his whole life was determined by the bingo wheel; not only that which would happen now that he was at last before it, but all that had gone before, since his birth, and his mother's birth and the birth of his father. It had always been there, even though he had not been aware of it, handing out the unlucky cards and numbers of his days. The feeling persisted, and he started quickly away. I better get down from here before I make a fool of myself, he thought.

"Here boy," the man called. "You haven't started yet."

Someone laughed as he went hesitantly back.

"Are you all reet?"

He grinned at the man's jive talk, but no words would come, and he knew it was not a convincing grin. For suddenly he knew that he stood on the slippery brink of some terrible embarrassment.

"Where are you from, boy?" the man asked.

"Down South."

"He's from down South, ladies and gentlemen," the man said. "Where from? Speak right into the mike."

"Rocky Mont," he said. "Rock' Mont, North Car'lina."

"So you decided to come down off that mountain to the U.S.," the man laughed. He felt that the man was making a fool of him, but then something cold was placed in his hand, and the lights were no longer behind him.

Standing before the wheel he felt alone, but that was somehow right, and he remembered his plan. He would give the wheel a short quick twirl. Just a touch of the button. He had watched it many times, and always it came close to double zero when it was short and quick. He steeled himself; the fear had left, and he felt a profound sense of promise, as though he were about to be repaid for all the things he'd suffered all his life. Trembling, he pressed the button. There was a whirl of lights, and in a second he realized with finality that though he wanted to, he could not stop. It was as though he held a high-powered line in his naked hand. His nerves tightened. As the wheel increased its speed it seemed to draw him more and more into its power, as though it held his fate; and with it came a deep need to submit, to whirl, to lose himself in its swirl of color. He could not stop it now, he knew. So let it be.

The button rested snugly in his palm where the man had placed it. And now he became aware of the man beside him, advising him through the microphone, while behind the shadowy audience hummed with noisy voices. He shifted his feet. There was still that feeling of helplessness within him, making part of him desire to turn back, even now that the jackpot was right in his hand. He squeezed the button until his fist ached. Then, like the sudden shriek of a subway whistle, a doubt tore through his head. Suppose he did not spin the wheel long enough? What could he do, and how could he tell? And then he knew, even as he wondered, that as long as he pressed the button, he could control the jackpot. He and only he could determine whether or not it was to be his. Not even the man with the microphone could do anything about it now. He felt drunk. Then, as though he had come down from a high hill into a valley of people, he heard the audience yelling.

"Come down from there, you jerk!"

"Let somebody else have a chance . . ."

"Old Jack thinks he done found the end of the rainbow . . ."

The last voice was not unfriendly, and he turned and smiled dreamily into the yelling mouths. Then he turned his back squarely on them.

"Don't take too long, boy," a voice said.

He nodded. They were yelling behind him. Those folks did not understand what had happened to him. They had been playing the bingo game day in and night out for years, trying to win rent money or hamburger change. But not one of those wise guys had discovered this wonderful thing. He watched the wheel whirling past the numbers and experienced a burst of exaltation: This is God! This is the really truly God! He said it aloud, "This is God!"

He said it with such absolute conviction that he feared he would fall fainting into the footlights. But the crowd yelled so loud that they could not hear. Those fools, he thought. I'm here trying to tell them the most wonderful secret in the world, and they're yelling like they gone crazy. A hand fell upon his shoulder.

"You'll have to make a choice now, boy. You've taken too long."

He brushed the hand violently away.

"Leave me alone, man. I know what I'm doing!"

The man looked surprised and held on to the microphone for support.

And because he did not wish to hurt the man's feelings he smiled, realizing with a sudden pang that there was no way of explaining to the man just why he had to stand there pressing the button forever.

"Come here," he called tiredly.

The man approached, rolling the heavy microphone across the stage.

"Anybody can play this bingo game, right?" he said.

"Sure, but . . ."

He smiled, feeling inclined to be patient with this slick looking white man with his blue sport shirt and his sharp gabardine suit.

"That's what I thought," he said. "Anybody can win the jackpot as long as they get the lucky number, right?"

"That's the rule, but after all . . ."

"That's what I thought," he said. "And the big prize goes to the man who knows how to win it?"

The man nodded speechlessly.

"Well then, go on over there and watch me win like I want to. I ain't going to hurt nobody," he said, "and I'll show you how to win. I mean to show the whole world how it's got to be done."

And because he understood, he smiled again to let the man know that he held nothing against him for being white and impatient. Then he refused to see the man any longer and stood pressing the button, the voices of the crowd reaching him like sounds in distant streets. Let them yell. All the Negroes down there were just ashamed because he was black like them. He smiled inwardly, knowing how it was. Most of the time he was ashamed of what Negroes did himself. Well, let them be ashamed for something this time. Like him. He was like a long thin black wire that was being stretched and wound upon the bingo wheel; wound until he wanted to scream; wound, but this time himself controlling the winding and the sadness and the shame, and because he did, Laura would be all right. Suddenly the lights flickered. He staggered backwards. Had something gone wrong? All this noise. Didn't they know that although he controlled the wheel, it also controlled him, and unless he pressed the button forever and forever and ever it would stop, leaving him high and dry, dry and high on this hard high slippery hill and Laura dead? There was only one chance; he had to do whatever the wheel demanded. And gripping the button in despair, he discovered with surprise that it imparted a nervous energy. His spine tingled. He felt a certain power.

Now he faced the raging crowd with defiance, its screams penetrating his eardrums like trumpets shrieking from a jukebox. The vague faces glowing in the bingo lights gave him a sense of himself that he had never known before. He was running the show, by God! They had to react to him, for he was their luck. This is *me*, he thought. Let the bastards yell. Then someone was laughing inside him, and he realized that somehow he had forgotten his own name. It was a sad, lost feeling to lose your name, and a crazy thing to do. That name had been given him by the white man who ·had owned his grandfather a long lost time ago down South. But maybe those wise guys knew his name.

"Who am I?" he screamed.

"Hurry up and bingo, you jerk!"

They didn't know either, he thought sadly. They didn't even know their own names, they were all poor nameless bastards. Well, he didn't need that old name; he was reborn. For as long as he pressed the button he was The-man-who-pressed-the-button-who-held-the-prize-who-was-the-King-of-Bingo. That was the way it was, and he'd have to press the button even if nobody understood, even though Laura did not understand.

"Live!" he shouted.

The audience quieted like the dying of a huge fan.

"Live, Laura, baby. I got holt of it now, sugar. Live!"

He screamed it, tears streaming down his face. "I got nobody but YOU!"

The screams tore from his very guts. He felt as though the rush of blood to his head would burst out in baseball seams of small red droplets, like a head beaten by police clubs. Bending over he saw a trickle of blood splashing the toe of his shoe. With his free hand he searched his head. It was his nose. God, suppose something has gone wrong? He felt that the whole audience had somehow entered him and was stamping its feet in his stomach, and he was unable to throw them out. They wanted the prize, that was it. They wanted the secret for themselves. But they'd never get it; he would keep the bingo wheel whirling forever, and Laura would be safe in the wheel. But would she? It had to be, because if she were not safe the wheel would cease to turn; it could not go on. He had to get away, *vomit* all, and his mind formed an image of himself running with Laura in his arms down the tracks of the subway just ahead of an A train, running desperately *vomit* with people screaming for him to come out but knowing no way of leaving the tracks because to stop would bring the train crushing down upon him and to attempt to leave across the other tracks would mean to run into a hot third rail as high as his waist which threw blue sparks that blinded his eyes until he could hardly see.

He heard singing and the audience was clapping its hands.

> Shoot the liquor to him, Jim, boy!
> Clap-clap-clap
> Well a-calla the cop
> He's blowing his top!
> Shoot the liquor to him, Jim boy!

Bitter anger grew within him at the singing. They think I'm crazy. Well let 'em laugh. I'll do what I got to do.

He was standing in an attitude of intense listening when he saw that they were watching something on the stage behind him. He felt weak. But when he turned he saw no one. If only his thumb did not ache so. Now they were applauding. And for a moment he thought that the wheel had stopped. But that was impossible, his thumb still pressed the button. Then he saw them. Two men in uniform beckoned from the end of the stage. They were coming toward him, walking in step, slowly, like a tap-dance team returning for a third encore. But their shoulders shot forward, and he backed away, looking wildly about. There was nothing to fight them with. He had only the long black cord which led to a plug somewhere back stage, and he couldn't use that because it operated the bingo wheel. He backed slowly, fixing the men with his eyes as his lips stretched over his teeth in a tight, fixed grin; moved toward the end of the stage and realizing that he couldn't go much further, for suddenly the cord became taut and he couldn't afford to break the cord. But he had to do something. The audience was howling. Suddenly he stopped dead, seeing the men halt, their legs lifted as in an interrupted step of a slow-motion dance. There was nothing to do but run in the other direction and he dashed forward, slipping and sliding. The men fell back, surprised. He struck out violently going past.

"Grab him!"

He ran, but all too quickly the cord tightened, resistingly, and he turned and ran back again. This time he slipped them, and discovered by running in a circle before the wheel he could keep the cord from tightening. But this way he had to flail his arms to keep the men away. Why couldn't they leave a man alone? He ran, circling.

"Ring down the curtain," someone yelled. But they couldn't do that. If they did the wheel flashing from the projection room would be cut off. But they had him before he could tell them so, trying to pry open his fist, and he was wrestling and trying to bring his knees into the fight and holding on to the button, for it was his life. And now he was down, seeing a foot coming down, crushing his wrist cruelly, down, as he saw the wheel whirling serenely above.

"I can't give it up," he screamed. Then quietly, in a confidential tone, "Boys, I really can't give it up."

It landed hard against his head. And in the blank moment they had it away from him, completely now. He fought them trying to pull him up from the stage as he watched the wheel spin slowly to a stop. Without surprise he saw it rest at double zero.

"You see," he pointed bitterly.

"Sure, boy, sure, it's O.K.," one of the men said smiling.

And seeing the man bow his head to someone he could not see, he felt very, very happy; he would receive what all the winners received.

But as he warmed in the justice of the man's tight smile he did not see the man's slow wink, nor see the bow-legged man behind him step clear of the swiftly descending curtain and set himself for a blow. He only felt the dull pain exploding in his skull, and he knew even as it slipped out of him that his luck had run out on the stage.

SITUATION

The situation is the combination of circumstances, including the setting, out of which the action emerges. Much of what happens in "King of the Bingo Game" occurs because the main character is "up North," where he is a stranger, without a job and with little hope of getting one, and because his wife is "'bout to die 'cause we got no money for a doctor." To obtain the money to save his wife's life has become a compulsion with him. The only solution he can think of is to win the jackpot at the bingo game played in a local movie theater. To increase his chances of winning he has somehow acquired five bingo cards and has decided just how hard to spin the wheel to make it stop on the double zero.

This desperate need for money provides the immediate motive for his actions, but there is another element in the situation that is not made explicit. As a disadvantaged black, he has apparently been pushed around by whites and by events he could not control. He therefore has a psychological need to assert his dominance in the control of his own fate. Once he wins the bingo game and goes to the stage, this second motive becomes irresistible. What he is fighting for at the end of the story is not money but power. Much of what happens results directly from this dual-level situation.

In thinking about situation in whatever work you are dealing with, you may find the following questions helpful:

1.   What is the situation here? Be sure you have a clear understanding of it before you move on to more complex problems in analysis and interpretation.

2.   How is the situation revealed? Through description or explanation by the narrator? By dialogue? By historical information that the reader already possesses? In "King of the Bingo Game" it is chiefly revealed by an unnamed narrator who describes the situation and lets us see what the main character thinks of his plight.

3.   How important is the situation in the total work? In Ellison's story it is so important that it supplies the motivation for the man's actions throughout the story. In other works, it may be less important.

CHARACTER

The word *character* is used in two senses in literature: first, to identify the people who appear in the story, play, or poem; second, to describe the personality of any of these people, especially those traits that affect the development of the work. The second meaning is the important one in this chapter.

In "King of the Bingo Game" the main character's reaction to his frustrating situation is all-important. All his life he has reacted to other people; now they must react to him. Though he has temporarily forgotten his name and is confronted with the age-old question of identity (" 'Who am I?' he screamed"), he thinks that if he can just hold onto the power that accompanies the pressing of the button he can show his audience "how to win": "I mean to show the whole world how it's got to be done." He must instruct the "poor nameless bastards" who think he is crazy and laugh and applaud. He is, temporarily at least, a man with a mission: "I'll do what I got to do."

The minor characters may be essential to the main action of a story, or they may be introduced for some special purpose—to provide comic relief, to serve as narrator, to act as a mouthpiece for the author, or to provide a foil through which some quality of the major character is emphasized. The theater manager in "King of the Bingo Game" serves as a foil: he asks the right questions, makes the right comments, and takes the right action to show us the main character as we must see him if we are to have this story.

In thinking about the characters in a literary work, consider the following questions:

1.   Do you have a clear impression of the major characters? If so, how did you get it? Through what they do or say? Through what others say about them? Through the author's or narrator's comments?

2.   Do the characters change as the story proceeds—that is, do their experiences make them stronger or weaker, nobler or more corrupt, than they were at the beginning? If so, do you feel that the change is justified by what happens in the story?

3.   Does the dialogue ring true? Do characters speak in a way consistent with their regional and social backgrounds?

PLOT

The term *plot* is generally familiar. The plot is the sequence of actions that make up the core of the story. It is what the characters do or what is done to them as the story proceeds. Thus the plot of "King of the Bingo Game" is what happens to the main character in his attempt to win the money he needs.

DRAMATIC CONFLICT

Dramatic conflict occurs when opposing forces meet. The conflict may be physical, as in a fight; or it may be psychological, as in Huck Finn's difficulty in reconciling his friendship with Jim and his sense of guilt in aiding a runaway slave to escape. The conflict is likely to be resolved by decisions the characters make and by the actions they take or refuse to take.

In "King of the Bingo Game" the main character experiences several kinds of conflict. The most interesting is that between him and the wheel. He says of it, "This is God!" and he feels he must control this life-sustaining force if he is to save Laura. He shouts, "Live, Laura, baby. I got holt of it now, sugar. Live!" He feels that the wheel controls him, too, and that if he stops pressing the button, the wheel will stop and Laura will die. When he is subdued, the wheel does stop, ironically at double zero. His only victory is in having tried.

There are other conflicts, between him and the manager who tries to interfere with his plan, and with the audience who call him a "jerk" and taunt him until he feels as if "the whole audience had somehow entered him and was stamping its feet in his stomach."

THEME

In addition to showing characters in action or in conflict, a work may express a general idea or theme that gives unity to the action. Often the theme is not stated explicitly. For example, in much of *The Adventures of Huckleberry Finn* there is a contrast between Huck's sense of values and the values that the adults in the story proclaim or reveal. Mark Twain's criticism of society, as it is represented in Miss Watson, the Grangerfords, the King, and others, so permeates the story that it can be said to be the theme of the book. If what these adults stand for is "sivilization," Huck wants none of it. As he says at the end, "But I reckon I got to light out for the territory ahead of the rest, because Aunt Sally she's going to adopt me and sivilize me, and I can't stand it. I been there before." In "King of the Bingo Game" the author does not actually say that the man's attempt to control the symbolic wheel and thus assert his own power and save Laura is futile, but we can infer that theme from the facts of the story.

Sometimes there is a statement within a work that does state the theme explicitly. For example, Lieutenant Frederick Henry, the narrator of Hemingway's *A Farewell to Arms,* reflects on his days with Catherine Barkley and says:

> If people bring so much courage to this world the world has to kill them to break them, so of course it kills them. The world breaks every one and afterward many are strong at the broken places. But those that will not break it kills. It kills the very good and the very gentle and the very brave impartially. If you are none of these you can be sure it will kill you too but there will be no special hurry. (Ernest Hemingway, *A Farewell to Arms*)

When at the end of the story we see Catherine die giving birth to a stillborn child and watch Lieutenant Henry walk from the hospital out into the rain a broken man, we realize that the statement we read seven chapters earlier does indeed express the unifying idea of the novel.

STRUCTURE

The structure of a literary work is the pattern into which the parts fit so as to form a unified whole. In some kinds of writing the pattern is so common that we can speak of it as a conventional structure. For example, a five-act play is likely to proceed from (1) an explanation of the situation, to (2) the complication, to (3) the climactic action or decision, and then through a relatively brief (4) falling action to (5) the resolution, or final outcome. Most detective stories move through six stages: (1) the situation preceding the murder, (2) the murder, (3) identification of a number of suspects, (4) elimination of innocent suspects, often through *their* murders, (5) identification of the real murderer, (6) concluding explanations that resolve the mystery.

Each of these structures imposes certain limits on writers that influence what they can say and how they can say it. For example, in the conventional detective story the writer must conceal the identity of the murderer until the end, and must build a plausible case against each of the suspects before he or she is absolved of the crime.

In addition to the requirements imposed by conventional structures, writers can structure their work to suit their own purposes. "King of the Bingo Game" is organized in two scenes, the first of which is introductory to the second. The first scene shows the man in the theater audience, watching a movie he has seen three times before. He is paying more attention to the people eating and drinking around him than to the movie, and finally he checks his bingo cards as the numbers are called. The second scene, the main one, shows the man on the stage trying to win the jackpot. As the action develops, the man gets carried away by the power he attributes to the wheel and cannot let go of the button that controls it until he is wrestled to the floor and finally hit over the head. This two-scene structure is the author's choice. He could have started the story with the man's going up on the stage, but evidently he felt the introductory scene was necessary as background for the main action.

Within this two-scene structure "King of the Bingo Game" has smaller structural elements that contribute to the meaning of the story. For example, at the beginning the main character watches his favorite scene in the movie for the fourth time, a scene in which a woman bound on a bed is rescued by her lover. The melodramatic quality of the rescue foreshadows his equally unrealistic scheme for rescuing Laura, who is also bound to a bed by her illness. Another structural device is the use of two train scenes, one near the beginning and the other near the end of the story. These scenes "frame in" the view of a man always on the run from threatening forces, and emphasize his need to seize control of his fate. Such structural details tie different parts of the story together and so help us to see them in relation to some common theme. They are thus important clues to our interpretation of the story.

S Y M B O L

The simplest kind of symbol is one that stands for or represents something else, as two bars on an army officer's uniform are a symbol of the rank of captain. When the symbol can be interpreted in only one way, it is a *closed* symbol. The jerk of an umpire's thumb in a baseball game is a closed symbol; it means only one thing— the runner is officially out. A symbol is *open* when different people can interpret it in different ways. Thus our flag is a symbol of the United States, but it can mean much more than just the country; it can also suggest to different people different clusters of associations about the nation and its history.

In literature the most interesting symbols are open ones, because their ambiguity presents a challenge that makes interpretation more difficult but more satisfying. For most readers the realization that they can read into an open symbol a whole cluster of associations gives them a sense of discovery that more than compensates for the difficulty. Even though they may sometimes read into the text more than other readers would accept, the interpretation of an open symbol is a source of pleasure, because the readers add something of themselves to the work and so make their reading of it a personal experience. When this happens, we say the readers become involved in the work.

The most important symbol in "King of the Bingo Game" is the wheel of fortune, with its double zero and the attached cord and button. When the man first goes onto the stage, we learn that he considers the spinning of the wheel to be a ritual, and rituals are symbolic performances. As the story progresses, the wheel becomes much more than a device to decide whether the man will win the prize. It becomes a means of controlling fate, and confers the godlike power of deciding whether Laura will live or die. Anyone who controls the wheel controls the future. That is why the man cries excitedly, "This is God!" Clearly he associates the wheel with some supernatural or magical power.

There are other symbols in the story. The double zero is an ambiguous symbol within the symbol of the wheel. It can mean "jackpot" or it can mean "absolutely nothing." The two trains mentioned in the story are also symbols of the man's fantasy that he can escape from poverty, illness, and insignificance by some magical solution that gives him control over his destiny. Notice that the main character is never named. By standing for nobody, he can be a symbol of everybody. He can be a symbol of the frustration of blacks in a white-dominated world, or a symbol of the frustrations and delusions of all humankind.

IRONY

Irony is a stylistic device by which a writer conveys to readers a different meaning than would result from a literal interpretation of the words. You have already seen two examples of irony in "Why We Need More Westerns on Television" (page 17) and the quotation from *Huckleberry Finn* (page 188) in which Huck praises Emmeline Grangerford's poetry.

The plot of a story may develop ironically when the action seems to lead one way but actually leads another. In "King of the Bingo Game" the man's original strategy was to give the wheel "a short quick twirl" to make it stop at double zero and so win enough money to take care of all his problems. The reader's attention is focused on that event; it seems to be the culmination of the story. Then the man is caught up in the symbolic power of the wheel and tries to keep it running forever. When he is forced to let go of the button, the wheel stops, ironically, at double zero. But again, ironically, the winner gets nothing; he is hit on the head and dragged off the stage. Even if he had won the jackpot, it would have been of little use, since it came to only $36.90. That situation, too, is part of the irony of the story. Even the word *King* in the title is ironical. A bingo game is a small realm for a king. This king's rule lasted but a few minutes, and his fall from power was complete. At the end he, like the members of the audience, is just another "poor, nameless bastard."

POINT OF VIEW

Literally, a point of view is the position one occupies in viewing an object. Applied to literature, the phrase refers to the way an author views a subject or tells a story. Generally either an *omniscient* or a *limited* point of view can be used. With an omniscient view the author can know everything about the characters, and can tell not only what they do and say, but also what they are thinking. What happened in the past or will happen in the future can be reported, as well as what is happening at present. A limited point of view, by contrast, requires the author to tell the story as some one person knows it. That person may be one of the characters, or someone who witnessed the events but did not share in them, or even the author but without omniscience.

A third point of view combines the omniscient and the limited. This is the one Ellison uses in "King of the Bingo Game." The narrator is omniscient regarding the main character and so can say that the character thought of a terrifying train in a half-dream, that he felt the manager was making a fool of him, and that he knew "his luck had run out" when he "felt the dull pain exploding in his skull." But this narrator does not speak this way about other characters; he only reports what they say and do and *seem* to feel. His point of view is omniscient for the main character but limited for all the others.

VOICE

The term *voice* identifies the person or personality speaking in a literary work. The question "Who is speaking here?" is often important to the interpretation of a work. A story written in the first person need not be about the author or even represent the author's thinking. Huckleberry Finn is not speaking for Mark Twain when he says that people who behave as he has done—that is, who have helped a slave escape—go to hell. This is Huck's voice expressing ideas that he believes but Twain does not.

Sometimes a narrator speaks with a dual voice, as Ellison's narrator does. At times he speaks in the author's relatively detached standard English ("Tiring quickly of watching the picture he looked back to where the white beam filtered . . ."); at other times he speaks in the dialect of the main character ("Well, I ain't crazy. I'm just broke, 'cause I got no birth certificate to get a job . . ."). This duality in voice enables Ellison's narrator to move into the mind of the character and tell us convincingly in the man's own language what he is thinking, while still retaining the right to comment as narrator.

Your familiarity with these ten elements of imaginative writing can be useful when you choose your real subject for any paper you write on a literary work. You may decide to concentrate on one of the elements or on two or three of them. And you certainly will find yourself drawing on your knowledge of these elements as you analyze, interpret, or evaluate an entire work.

We will use William Saroyan's story "Snake" and the comments that follow it to demonstrate the prewriting of a critical essay. To make the demonstration as useful as possible, we have chosen a story that poses some problems of interpretation.

Snake

by William Saroyan

Walking through the park in May, he saw a small brown snake slipping away from him through grass and leaves, and he went after it with a long twig, feeling as he did so the instinctive fear of man for reptiles.

Ah, he thought, our symbol of evil, and he touched the snake with the twig, making it squirm. The snake lifted its head and struck at the twig, then shot away through the grass, hurrying fearfully, and he went after it.

It was very beautiful, and it was amazingly clever, but he intended to stay with it for a while and find out something about it.

The little brown snake led him deep into the park, so that he was hidden from view and alone with it. He had a guilty feeling that in pursuing the snake he was violating some rule of the park, and he prepared a remark for anyone who might discover him. I am a student of contemporary morality, he thought he would say, or, I am a sculptor and I am studying the structure of reptiles. At any rate, he would make some sort of reasonable explanation.

He would not say that he intended to kill the snake.

He moved beside the frightened reptile, leaping now and then to keep up with it, until the snake became exhausted and could not go on. Then he squatted on his heels to have a closer view of it, holding the snake before him by touching it with the twig. He admitted to himself that he was afraid to touch it with his hands. To touch a snake was to touch something secret in the mind of man, something one ought never to bring out into the light. That sleek gliding, and that awful silence, *was* once man, and now that man had come to this last form, here were snakes still moving over the earth as if no change had ever taken place.

The first male and female, biblical; and evolution. Adam and Eve, and the human embryo.

It was a lovely snake, clean and graceful and precise. The snake's fear frightened him and he became panic stricken thinking that perhaps all the snakes in the park would come quietly to the rescue of the little brown snake, and surround him with their malicious silence and the unbearable horror of their evil forms. It was a large park and there must be thousands of snakes in it. If all the snakes were to find out that he was with this little snake, they would easily be able to paralyse him.

He stood up and looked around. All was quiet. The silence was almost the biblical silence of *in the beginning*. He could hear a bird hopping from twig to twig in a low earthbush near by, but he was alone with the snake. He forgot that he was in a public park, in a large city. An airplane passed overhead, but he did not see or hear it. The silence was too emphatic and his vision was too emphatically focused on the snake before him.

In the garden with the snake, unnaked, in the beginning, in the year 1931.

He squatted on his heels again and began to commune with the snake. It made him laugh, inwardly and outwardly, to have the form of the snake so substantially before him, apart from his own being, flat on the surface of the earth instead of subtly a part of his own identity. It was really a tremendous thing. At first he was afraid to speak aloud, but as time went on he became less timid, and began to speak in English to it. It was very pleasant to speak to the snake.

All right, he said, here I am, after all these years, a young man living on the same earth, under the same sun, having the same passions. And here you are before me, the same. The situation is the same. What do you intend to do? Escape? I will not let you escape. What have you in mind? How will you defend yourself? I intend to destroy you. As an obligation to man.

The snake twitched before him helplessly, unable to avoid the twig. It struck at the twig several times, and then became too tired to bother with it. He drew away the twig, and heard the snake say, Thank you.

He began to whistle to the snake, to see if the music would have any effect on its movements, if it would make the snake dance. You are my only love, he whistled; Schubert made into a New York musical comedy; *my only love, my only love;* but the snake would not dance. Something Italian perhaps, he thought, and began to sing *la donna è mobile,** intentionally mispronouncing the words in order to amuse himself. He tried a Brahms lullaby, but the music had no effect on the snake. It was tired. It was frightened. It wanted to get away.

He was amazed at himself suddenly; it had occurred to him to let the snake flee, to let it glide away and be lost in the lowly worlds of its kind. Why should he allow it to escape?

He lifted a heavy boulder from the ground and thought: Now I shall bash your head with this rock and see you die.

To destroy that evil grace, to mangle that sinful loveliness.

But it was very strange. He could not let the rock fall on the snake's head, and began suddenly to feel sorry for it. I am sorry, he said, dropping the boulder. I beg your pardon. I see now that I have only love for you.

And he wanted to touch the snake with his hands, to hold it and understand the truth of its touch. But it was difficult. The snake was frightened and each time he extended his hands to touch it, the snake turned on him and charged. I have only love for you, he said. Do not be afraid. I am not going to hurt you.

---

* "Woman is fickle." The libertine Duke of Mantua in Verdi's opera *Rigoletto* sings a song entitled "La donna è mobile." One of the stanzas says, "Women are all the same—Never believe them! Love them and leave them—That's how to play the game!"

Then, swiftly, he lifted the snake from the earth, learned the true feel of it, and dropped it. There, he said. Now I know the truth. A snake is cold, but it is clean. It is not slimy, as I thought.

He smiled upon the little brown snake. You may go now, he said. The inquisition is over. You are yet alive. You have been in the presence of man, and you are yet alive. You may go now.

But the snake would not go away. It was exhausted with fear.

He felt deeply ashamed of what he had done, and angry with himself. Jesus, he thought, I have scared the little snake. It will never get over this. It will always remember me squatting over it.

For God's sake, he said to the snake, go away. Return to your kind. Tell them what you saw, you yourself, with your own eyes. Tell them what you felt. The sickly heat of the hand of man. Tell them of the presence you felt.

Suddenly the snake turned from him and spilled itself forward, away from him. Thank you, he said. And it made him laugh with joy to see the little snake throwing itself into the grass and leaves, thrusting itself away from man. Splendid, he said; hurry to them and say that you were in the presence of man and that you were not killed. Think of all the snakes that live and die without ever meeting man. Think of the distinction it will mean for you.

It seemed to him that the little snake's movements away from him were the essence of joyous laughter, and he felt greatly pleased. He found his way back to the path, and continued his walk.

In the evening, while she sat at the piano, playing softly, he said: A funny thing happened.

She went on playing. A funny thing? she asked.

Yes, he said. I was walking through the park and I saw a little brown snake.

She stopped playing and turned on the bench to look at him. A snake? she said. How ugly!

No, he said. It was beautiful.

What about it?

Oh, nothing, he said. I just caught it and wouldn't let it go for a while.

But why?

For no good reason at all, he said.

She walked across the room and sat beside him, looking at him strangely. Tell me about the snake, she said.

It was lovely, he said. Not ugly at all. When I touched it, I felt its cleanliness.

I am so glad, she said. What else?

I wanted to kill the snake, he said. But I couldn't. It was too lovely.

I'm so glad, she said. But tell me everything.

That's all, he said.

But it isn't, she said. I know it isn't. Tell me everything.

It is very funny, he said. I was going to kill the snake, and not come here again.

Aren't you ashamed of yourself? she said.

Of course I am, he said.

What else? she said. What did you think, of me, when you had the snake before you?

You will be angry, he said.

Oh, nonsense. It is impossible for me to be angry with you. Tell me.

Well, he said, I thought you were lovely but evil.

Evil?

I told you you would be angry.

And then?

Then I touched the snake, he said. It wasn't easy, but I picked it up with my hands. What do you make of this? You've read a lot of books about such things. What does it mean, my picking up the snake?

She began to laugh softly, intelligently. Why, she laughed, it means, it simply means that you are an idiot. Why, it's splendid.

Is that according to Freud? he said.

Yes, she laughed. According to Freud.

Well, anyway, he said, it was very fine to let the snake go free.

Have you ever told me you loved me? she asked.

You ought to know, he said. I do not remember one or two things I have said to you.

No, she said. You have never told me.

She began to laugh again, feeling suddenly very happy about him. You have always talked of other things, she said. Irrelevant things. At the most amazing times. She laughed.

This snake, he said, was a little brown snake.

And that explains it, she said. You have never intruded.

What the hell are you talking about? he said.

I'm so glad you didn't kill the snake, she said.

She returned to the piano, and placed her hands softly upon the keys.

I whistled a few songs to the snake, he said. I whistled a fragment from Schubert's Unfinished Symphony. I would like to hear that. You know, the melody that was used in a musical comedy called *Blossom Time*. The part that goes, *you are my only love, my only love,* and so on.

She began to play softly, feeling his eyes on her hair, on her hands, her neck, her back, her arms, feeling him studying her as he had studied the snake.

Your first reaction to this story may be puzzlement. What is it about? We can begin to find out by asking questions about the chief elements.

1. What is the situation here? There seem to be two: the scene between a man and a snake in a park, and another between the same man and a woman in a house. Since this is one story, the two scenes must be related. Obviously they are related

through the snake, which is the main subject of conversation between the man and the woman, and through the title, which suggests that the whole story is about a snake. But *what* about the snake? The answer to that question seems to be a major problem of interpretation.

2.   As we consider the story of a snake in a park (*park* can be used to include a garden), we need to remember another snake and another garden, which are part of the context of Saroyan's story. You can read the Biblical account in the second and third chapters of Genesis.

3.   Now look at the characters. Assuming that the snake is a character, we can say there are three, two in each scene. What does the man think about the snake? At the beginning he calls it "our symbol of evil." Later he says, "To touch a snake was to touch something secret in the mind of man, something one ought never to bring out into the light." Then he associates the snake with Adam and Eve and echoes that association with the statement, "In the garden with the snake, un-naked, in the beginning, in the year 1931." Adam and Eve were naked in the beginning; it was only after they met the snake that they were unnaked. It becomes increasingly clear that this is not just a little brown snake, but a symbol of some relationship between a man and a woman. What is the relationship? The Biblical snake is associated with both knowledge and sin. Is the man sexually attracted to the woman, and if so does he feel guilty because he thinks that to know her sexually would be sinful? Sex, Sin, and the Snake. Do they all go together?

4.   At first the man experiences "the instinctive fear of man for reptiles" and intends to kill the snake. That is his "obligation to man," though he sees that it is "a lovely snake, clean and graceful and precise." He starts to bash its head with a rock, "to destroy that evil grace, to mangle that sinful loveliness." But then he begins to feel sorry for the snake and says, "I see now that I have only love for you." He picks it up and finds it pleasant to the touch. He has been all wrong about the snake. Is his attitude toward the woman similar to his attitude toward the snake? Before you answer, reread the last part of the dialogue, beginning with "I'm so glad, she said. But tell me everything." What is the man likely to conclude about the woman on the basis of what he has learned about the snake?

5.   Consider carefully the dialogue that begins with the woman's asking "Have you ever told me you loved me?" and concludes with "I'm so glad you didn't kill the snake." She says here, "And that explains it." What explains what? If we can answer this question, we will have gained considerable insight into their relationship. What is there near this statement that will help us answer the question?

6.   Does the woman seem to be wiser than the man, or at least more perceptive about the nuances of his adventure with the snake? It is *he* who asks *her,* "What does it mean, my picking up the snake? . . . Is that according to Freud?" What does her answer reveal about her interpretation of the snake incident and about her relationship with the man? Is she happy or offended when, in the last paragraph, she begins to play the piano and feels him "studying her as he had studied the snake"?

7.   Consider what we do not know about these people—what they look like, how long they have known each other, even their names. Since the story is written from an omniscient point of view, Saroyan could have told us these things. Why didn't he? Are the characters themselves symbolic, so that they represent not particular people, but Man and Woman? Are they a twentieth-century Adam and Eve resolving through the snake the doubts and confusions of falling in love? Or are we simply meeting a neurotic young man who can profess his love to a snake but not to a woman?

8.   It is now clear that the snake is a symbol. Does the structure of the story bear this out? Consider how details in the second part echo details in the first: the man's wanting to kill the snake and leave the woman because he thinks they are both evil, his admission that he loves the snake, the woman's realization that he loves her, the song "You are my only love" referred to in both parts, and his studying the woman as he studied the snake. What at first seemed to be two situations not clearly connected are now blended into an integrated story.

Notice that this analysis of "Snake" follows the three-step method of interpretation presented in Chapter 2: first, observation of particular details; second, the recognition that these details can be related as partial interpretations (the man's attitude toward the snake, his attitude toward the woman, the parallelism by which the second part of the story echoes the first); finally, the inclusion of those partial explanations into a unified view of the whole story. We do not start with the belief that the two parts of the story are merged into a whole by the symbolism of the snake. That conclusion grows on us as it gradually emerges from our observations of specific details.

If, after this kind of close reading and thinking, you see what you want to write about, you have discovered your real subject and are in the second main stage of prewriting. You now know your purpose and probably have the information needed to develop it. If you have not already taken notes, you may wish to do so now. It will usually be wise, before beginning to write, to outline your paper and check your notes to see if you have all the information you need to do what your outline requires. At this stage much of the hard work of the paper has been done.

A.   As preparation for writing a paper on "Snake," first discuss in class in as much   EXERCISES
detail as you can the following questions:

1.   Suppose Saroyan had made the man kill the snake in the first part. How
would that change affect the structure of the story? Would there be a second part?
If so, what would it do? Would the man have to kill the woman at the end of the
story?

2.   Suppose Saroyan had identified the man as Joe Doakes, a used-car salesman,
and the woman as Jane Doe, a typist. How would this change affect the story?

3.   Why does the woman call the man "an idiot" on page 288, and what is it that
is "splendid"?

4.   If you agree with the partial interpretation of the story suggested in this
chapter, what additional information can you provide to support that interpretation?

5.   If you disagree with that interpretation, can you provide textual evidence to
support your disagreement?

B.   As a result of your discussions, choose any thesis you please about "Snake"
and write a paper supporting that thesis.

QUESTIONS OF EMPHASIS

A critical essay is likely to discuss one or more of the following three types of
concerns: *technical analysis,* or the methods used to achieve the effects revealed in
the work; *interpretation,* or what the work means; *evaluation,* or the essayist's
judgment of the effectiveness or significance of the work or of any part of it. These
three kinds of criticism are not independent of each other. Interpretation, as you
have seen in "Snake," sometimes depends on technical analysis, and evaluation
sometimes includes both technical analysis and interpretation. But in any one paper
a critic can emphasize the kind of criticism he or she is most concerned with. The
pages that follow will explain these three kinds of emphasis in some detail.

TECHNICAL ANALYSIS

Technical analysis is chiefly concerned with technique, with the means a writer
uses to develop situation, characters, theme, structure, or any of the ten elements
we considered earlier. Thus we were making a technical analysis of "Snake" when

we pointed out the relation between the man, the snake, and the woman, and when we observed the parallelism between the two parts of the story. In Chapter 8 we defined *style* as the way a work is written; technical analysis deals also with those stylistic features of a work that the analyst wishes to discuss.

The following extract from a student essay makes a technical analysis by showing how James Thurber handled contrasts and transition in his short story "The Secret Life of Walter Mitty." The subject of the story is a timid, incompetent man married to a domineering woman who constantly criticizes him for his shortcomings. To escape from his wife's henpecking, Mitty resorts to fantasies in which he can imagine himself a powerful, brave, resourceful, and confident hero who distinguishes himself in every imaginable situation.

What makes "The Secret Life of Walter Mitty" more than just another amusing short story is Thurber's unique and effective use of contrasts. Consider, for example, the first three paragraphs. Here the Walter Mitty of imagination is placed side by side with the Walter Mitty of reality. The contrast between the iron-hearted Naval Commander, bravely giving orders to his men, and the chicken-hearted Walter Mitty, timidly taking orders from his wife, is quite apparent. But the use of contrasts is by no means restricted to the beginning of the story. On the contrary, it is employed all the way through to the very last word. Compare the quick-thinking Doctor Mitty, famous surgeon, to the Walter Mitty who cannot park his car, remove his tire chains, nor readily remember to buy a box of puppy biscuits. Compare also the "greatest shot in the world" or the daring Captain Mitty, or the "erect and motionless, proud and disdainful Walter Mitty the Undefeated" with the Walter Mitty who seeks the quiet refuge of a big leather chair in a hotel lobby. Contrasts are effective tools for any writer, but the straightforward manner in which Thurber employs them enhances their effectiveness considerably.

After briefly skimming through the collection of contrasts that makes up "The Secret Life of Walter Mitty," one might feel that there is little connection between the paragraphs describing the imagined Walter Mitty and the Mitty of reality. However, closer observation reveals that Thurber does, by the use of suggestive words and phrases, cleverly establish links between the Mitty of fact and the Mitty of fancy. . . . Consider how Mrs. Mitty's mention of Doctor Renshaw and the event of driving by a hospital lead to a daydream in which Walter Mitty, a distinguished surgeon, assists Doctor Renshaw in a difficult operation. Take note also of how a newsboy's shout about the Waterbury trial initiates the trial of Walter Mitty in the following paragraph. Such skillful employment of transitions, by which an event in reality triggers an event in the imagination, is sound not only from the literary standpoint, but also from the psychological point of view.

This critic has not concerned himself with interpretation, for the meaning of Thurber's story—that a timid, insecure, and weak character can take refuge in heroic fantasies—is easily grasped by any perceptive reader. The critic has instead analyzed Thurber's method of conveying this meaning. First he treats the repeated use of contrasts in moving back and forth between the "real" world of Walter Mitty and the more satisfying life of his daydreams, and gives illustrations of this movement. Next he demonstrates that the opposing elements in any contrast have a subtle connection in thought or language.

The writer of the paper on pages 294–295 had the advantage of a group of study questions intended to help him analyze the poem "Hunting Song." Only after he had done the technical analysis as a prewriting exercise did he attempt to write his paper. Here are the poem, the analytical questions, and the paper:

Hunting Song   *The poem*
    by Donald Finkel

The fox came lolloping, lolloping,
Lolloping. His tongue hung out
And his ears were high.
He was like death at the end of a string
When he came to the hollow
Log. Ran in one side
And out of the other. O
He was sly.

The hounds came tumbling, tumbling,
Tumbling. Their heads were low
And their eyes were red.
The sound of their breath was louder than death
When they came to the hollow
Log. They held at one end
But a bitch found the scent. O
They were mad.

The hunter came galloping, galloping,
Galloping. All damp was his mare
From her hooves to her mane.
His coat and his mouth were redder than death
When he came to the hollow
Log. He took in the rein
And over he went. O
He was fine.

The log, he just lay there, alone in
The clearing. No fox nor hound
Nor mounted man
Saw his black round eyes in their perfect disguise
(As the ends of a hollow
Log). He watched death go through him,
Around him and over him. O
He was wise.

The questions the student used in analyzing the poem

1.   In what ways do *Log* (line 6 in each stanza) and *O* (line 7 in each stanza) draw your attention to the log?

2.   Read aloud the first sentence in each stanza. How does the poet rely on contrast in sound and rhythm to draw your attention to the log?

3.   Contrast the use of *death* in stanzas 1, 2, and 3 with its use in stanza 4. Observe the irony of the dead log's construing the live characters to represent death.

4.   Contrast the effect of the final word in stanzas 1, 2, and 3 with the effect of the final word in stanza 4.

5.   By now you see (1) that much in the poem says "Pay attention to the log," (2) that contrast and irony contribute to meaning, (3) that death is prominent in the theme, and (4) that the log's relationship to the action of the poem is different from that of any other "character."

The student's paper

The Detached Interpreter

Donald Finkel's "Hunting Song" speaks of a fox chase and of a hollow log's reaction to the chase. By watching the log carefully throughout the poem, by observing contrasts between the log and the other characters, and by being alert to ironical implications about the characters' proximity to death, the reader can discover what the poem says about the living and the dead.

There is much evidence that the reader must pay attention to the log. The word *Log* appears as the first word in line 6 of each stanza, even though it is the last word in its sentence. The word's being out of its normal position, the capital letter it normally would not have, the period that follows it even though it is the first word in the poetic line—all these draw attention to *Log.* So does the *O,* surely a representation of the end of a hollow log, which is conspicuous as the end word in line 7 of each stanza.

Contrast operates to draw the reader's attention to the log—contrast in cadence, for example. The first sentences of the first three stanzas are action statements:

The fox came lolloping, lolloping,
Lolloping.

The hounds came tumbling, tumbling,
Tumbling.

The hunter came galloping, galloping,
Galloping.

But the cadence in the log's stanza is different:

The log, he just lay there, alone in
The clearing.

Clearly the log is different from the rest in that it is not caught up in the action of the chase.

Another difference between the stanza about the log and the first three develops from the ironical use of *death*. The animate characters are very much alive; yet the fox "was like death at the end of a string," the hounds' "breath was louder than death," and the hunter's "coat and his mouth were redder than death." By the fourth stanza these characters are no longer compared with death; they *are* death. The log "watched death go through him, / Around him and over him." It is the log, so long dead that it is hollow, that can serve as the interpreter of the scene. On the figurative level the literally dead log is alive (his eyes are only disguised to look like the ends of a hollow log); the literally alive characters are representative of death.

If matters proceed as they are likely to, the fox will die within a few minutes. Before long the hounds will be dead and then the mare. A few years more and the man will be gone. The log lived and died long ago—so long that he is detached from the sound and the fury of the hunt. He knows that this chase and others like it will soon end and that the participants will experience the detachment of the dead rather than the involvement of the living.

Finally, while the fox is sly, the hounds are mad, and the hunter is fine, the log—this log so long dead that he is free from involvement in temporal matters and so can watch the chase with sublime detachment—is wise.

The writer of this paper has interpreted, but not without first engaging in careful analysis. Notice that the study questions do not ask for comment on what the poem says until an analysis has been completed. Only after we know *how* a literary work says, should we feel confident that we know *what* it says.

INTERPRETATION

An interpretation shows how the interpreter reads a work, what the work means to him or her. It is thus a personal response, and because it is personal, different readers may interpret a piece of literature in somewhat different ways. But to say that different interpretations may be possible is not to say that "anything goes" or that any one interpretation is as good as any other. To be acceptable to your readers, your interpretation must be consistent with all of the facts of the work. You may emphasize some facts more than others, but you cannot ignore significant facts just because they are not convenient to your interpretation. Thus no one can reasonably argue that "Snake" is a story about a man who falls in love with a snake and so abandons his fiancée. There is too much evidence in the story against that interpretation.

Students sometimes jump to a hasty interpretation of a poem because they fail to pay attention to all its details. They draw a hasty conclusion from some details and ignore others. The result is a slanted interpretation similar to the slanted arguments discussed in Chapter 9. The best defense against hasty interpretation is to follow the three-step method presented in Chapter 2: first, observe all the details; second, see how individual details fit into patterns; third, generalize these patterns into a unified view of the whole work. If you follow this procedure, your interpretation will be grounded on the facts and will develop from them.

Interpretation is never mere summary. Telling the story of a play or novel, or paraphrasing a poem, is not what is expected in a critical essay. The critical-essay assignment requires the student to discover a meaning in the work, but a summary does not interpret: it simply reports, or gives a statement of fact. A critical essay uses the facts to support a judgment about meaning, and is thus a statement of opinion based on facts.

DISCUSSION
PROBLEM

The following student paper about "Hunting Song" (page 293) was written as an exercise in analysis and interpretation. What details in the poem support the interpretation given in the paper? What details oppose it? What details does the interpretation ignore? What is commendable about the student's method of arriving at the interpretation? What is not commendable about the method? In view of your answers to these questions, how acceptable is the interpretation?

Symbolism in "Hunting Song"

The first reading of "Hunting Song" gave me a pleasant description of the fox hunt. This was evident particularly in the first three stanzas. The fourth stanza, with a definite change in tone, suggested a deeper meaning than a mere fox hunt. Donald Finkel very carefully chose a simple description to convey a significant and moving incident of religious belief.

If the poet's intent was to give a mere description of the fox hunt, the first three stanzas could be complete by themselves. But he doesn't stop here. He presents a fourth stanza which alters our image of the hunt. The words of this stanza give much deeper meaning to the poem. The rhythm becomes very slow and the tone calm; the hunt is over and all is quiet. ". . . he just lay there, alone in / The clearing." But what does it all mean?

To discover a meaning, I look to the title, "Hunting Song." Like "Song of Solomon," this conveys a religious feeling. To me it represents man's hunt, or search, for a reason to believe. The question becomes—Believe in what?

On reading the poem several more times I begin to see the symbols, not just the participants of a fox hunt. The fox becomes the redheaded Judas. "His tongue hung out / And his ears were high" as he lolled about awaiting the opportunity to betray. "He was like death at the end of a string" seems almost like a prediction of the fate, the hanging, which awaits Judas. The line "Ran in one side / And out of the other" indicates the sneaking movement of Judas to his master, the kiss of betrayal, and then his moving right along with the crowd.

Oh—he was sly.

In the second stanza we see the "hounds . . . tumbling." This symbolizes the soldiers and masses of people jumping about in a complete state of disorder. Some in the crowd were ashamed of their actions and stood with "their heads . . . low and their eyes . . . red." But for the majority, "The sound of their breath was louder than death" as they shouted a demand for action. They were in disorder only until "a bitch found the scent"—until someone let out a yell, "Crucify Him!"—and thereby set the direction of action for the masses to follow.

Oh—they were mad.

The third stanza brings us to the hunter. He is not alone; he is mounted. The mount is symbolic of his royal position, that of emperor. The hunter also wears the red coat of royalty, but his mouth is "redder than death" when he realizes the task before him. Rather than make a decision by himself, Pilate washes his hands to symbolize the purging from head to foot. This action is evident in the line "All damp was his mare [his royal position] / From her hooves to her mane." Pilate would not be guilty of such a crime; the people could decide and take the blame.

Oh—he was fine.

The fourth stanza gives the tone which is in great contrast to the preceding action. This is the end of the poem, but it portrays an unending scene. This is the verse which makes you reread the poem for deeper meaning. The log now becomes a symbol of the Cross of Crucifixion. Though he has "watched death go through him, / Around him and over him," Christ, now on the Cross "alone in the clearing," was not recognized by Judas, the masses, or Pilate as the true Son of God in the perfect disguise of man.

Truly—he was wise.

EVALUATION

In technical analysis you discuss the ways in which effects are achieved in a work of literature. In interpretation you show what the work means to you. In evaluation you judge the effectiveness or significance of the work. We have already pointed out that all three of these interests may be combined in a single paper, but here we want to limit ourselves to a paper that emphasizes evaluation.

The judgment you make in an evaluation may be favorable or unfavorable or may consider both merits and weaknesses. It may be a judgment about the whole work or about any important element of it, such as the characters, the plot, the theme, the structure, or any combination of these elements. The following evaluation by a professional critic is chiefly unfavorable and focuses on the main character:

In "A Perfect Day for Bananafish," the first of J. D. Salinger's remarkable short stories to attract widespread attention, a young veteran recovering from a nervous breakdown in Florida takes a little girl out swimming, in a charmingly described interlude, and then goes to his hotel room and shoots himself when he is confronted by his shallow wife. In "For Esmé—with Love and Squalor," one of the best and most moving of all his stories, an American soldier in Germany suffering from an extreme case of combat fatigue is brought back by a message from a little girl he had met in England. And in the climactic scene of his first novel, *The Catcher in the Rye,* the sixteen-year-old hero who has been wandering around New York alone for three days, ever since his expulsion from boarding school, in a state somewhere between reality and unreality, abandons his dream of running away to the West and goes home (and subsequently to a sanitarium) when his ten-year-old sister, whom he has met secretly, is clearly broken-hearted at the thought of his leaving.

In all three cases the children and the boy-men are exceedingly well done. In each case, despite the similarity of situation, they are quite different and distinct individuals. The final scene in *The Catcher in the Rye* is as good as anything that Salinger has written, which means very good indeed. So are a number of other episodes. But the book as a whole is disappointing, and not merely because it is a reworking of a theme that one begins to suspect must obsess the author. Holden Caulfield, the main character who tells his own story, is an extraordinary portrait, but there is too much of him. He describes himself early on and, with the sureness of a wire recording, he remains strictly in character throughout:

I shook my head. I shake my head quite a lot. "Boy!" I said. I also say "Boy!" quite a lot. Partly because I have a lousy vocabulary and partly because I act quite young for my age sometimes. I was sixteen then, and I'm seventeen now, and sometimes I act like I'm about thirteen. It's really ironical because I'm six foot two, and I have gray hair. I really do. The one side of my head—the right side—is full of millions of gray hairs. I've had them ever since I was a kid. And yet I still act sometimes like I was only about twelve.

In the course of 277 pages the reader wearies of this kind of explicitness, repetition and adolescence, exactly as one would weary of Holden himself. And this reader at least suffered from an irritated feeling that Holden was not quite so sensitive and perceptive as he, and his creator, thought he was. In any case he is so completely self-centered that the other characters who wander through the book—with the notable exception of his sister Phoebe—have nothing like his authenticity. *The Catcher in the Rye* is a brilliant tour de force,* but in a writer of Salinger's undeniable talent one expects something more. (Anne L. Goodman, "Mad About Children," *New Republic)*

The structure of this 500-word essay is worth a close look. It consists of three paragraphs. The first relates *The Catcher in the Rye* to two of Salinger's short stories. The second states the thesis of the essay ("the book as a whole is disappointing . . .") and presents the main evidence for the critic's judgment, the quotation from the book. The third offers a final explanation of the judgment contained in the thesis.

The position of the thesis—exactly in the middle of the essay—may seem a bit unusual, but the long introductory paragraph performs two important functions. First, by showing the critic's familiarity with some of Salinger's earlier stories and her appreciation of them, it establishes her credentials: she knows Salinger's work and likes it. That suggests to a reader that she is not predisposed to be hostile to *The Catcher in the Rye,* and helps to emphasize her "disappointment." Second, her comparison of the two stories and the novel lays the groundwork for her judgment that *Catcher* is "a reworking of a theme that one begins to suspect must obsess the author." This judgment is part of her reason for being disappointed in the book.

The second paragraph deals with her main point, that Holden's character is presented in such explicit detail that we get too much of him. Her readers need some evidence for this assertion, and Ms. Goodman gives it in the quotation. Whether or not you agree with her judgment, does the quotation show you why she finds Holden a bit tedious? That is what it is intended to do.

The final paragraph expands the criticism of Holden's character: not only is he wearisome, but the reader begins to doubt his sensitivity and perceptiveness. Yet, despite the irritation that Holden causes, Salinger succeeds in making him an authentic and unforgettable character. This is the tour de force that the critic speaks of, the triumph of Salinger's artistry in making such a character the hero of an immensely popular novel.

---

* *Tour de force:* literally, "a feat of skill or power"; in literature, a triumph of the author's artistry over the limitations of the subject.

WRITING THE PAPER

For two reasons, the actual writing of a critical essay needs only brief attention here. First, most of the work on this kind of paper is done in the prewriting, since once you have decided what you are going to say about the work you are discussing, the content of your paper has been established. Second, the writing of a critical essay is not significantly different from the writing of an expository or persuasive paper, both of which have been fully treated in earlier chapters. The advice that follows merely applies the principles of purposeful writing to this kind of assignment.

1. *Make clear to your readers what your real subject is.* The real subject, as explained on pages 10–14, identifies the particular view of the general subject you are going to deal with and thus provides the focus of your paper. Sometimes the real subject will be implied in the title; usually it is stated in an introductory paragraph containing a thesis. Such an introduction prepares your readers for what you are going to do. It also commits you to doing that, and so helps control the choices you will make during the writing. If you are bothered about how to start, review the discussion of introductory paragraphs on pages 112–115.

2. *Select and evaluate your material.* Your material will be the judgments you make about the work and the explanatory and persuasive details that support those judgments and so make your criticism acceptable to readers. The best way to be persuasive is to base your judgments on the facts of the text and, through quotations and descriptions, to show those facts, so that your readers will see why you say what you do. The basis for selecting your material is its pertinence to your real subject. If you know what you want to do, you should have no trouble choosing pertinent evidence. But, especially during revision, it will be wise to ask yourself, "Does this evidence clearly prove what I want it to prove?" If you have any doubt, remove it by choosing stronger evidence, or by establishing a clearer connection between the evidence and the judgment you are making from it, or by revising the judgment.

Especially be cautious when dealing with symbolism. If you think something is being used as a symbol, take pains to establish that belief. Notice how much evidence we gathered, as we investigated "Snake" through a series of questions, to support the belief that the snake in Saroyan's story is a sexual symbol, and how little evidence was used to support the assertions in "Symbolism in Hunting Song" that the hunter on his horse is a symbol of the emperor and that "all damp was his mare / From her hooves to her mane" is a symbol for Pontius Pilate's washing his hands. All of us have a right to see symbols wherever we want to; but if we expect other people to accept our interpretations, we must be prepared to defend them with more than unsupported assertions.

3. *Summarize the work when necessary.* One of the decisions you must make in writing a critical essay concerns summarizing. The best procedure is to summarize only when necessary and then only as much as necessary. But what is "necessary"? If your readers are not familiar with the work you are writing about, they will need some kind of background information to appreciate the pertinence and significance of your comments. It is therefore necessary to give them enough information about the content of the work so that they can readily follow you. If you are writing a criticism of a story or novel, do not let this necessity of providing enough information lead you into a retelling of the story, or of considerable parts of it. Select and summarize only that information that a reader will need in order to appreciate your criticism. More than that is a waste of space. But if your essay is a criticism of a poem, it is usually necessary to give the full text of the poem so that your readers can refer to it.

4. *Use quotations when they help, but do not overuse them.* An apt quotation from the work can be helpful in two ways: it can illustrate the point you are making, and it can provide evidence to make your judgments acceptable. The sample papers included in this chapter use quotations skillfully to make their comments clear and convincing. But the overuse of quotations may result in padding; so, in general, keep quotations short and to the point. It is customary to indent and single-space prose quotations of five lines or more, or two or more lines of a poem.

5. *Use source references if necessary.* If you refer only to the work you are writing about, you may include page numbers (line numbers of a poem) in parentheses within the text of your paper, thus: "(page 12)" or "(lines 5–6)." Unless a reader needs such references, however, they can be omitted; notice that very few of the student papers in this chapter use page or line references. But if you are writing a long paper that makes use of several sources, it is customary to cite these sources in a note either at the bottom of the page *(footnote)* or at the end of the paper *(endnote).* That note should identify at least the author, the title of the work, and the page number or numbers. The conventional forms of such notes are discussed and illustrated in Chapter 13 ("The Research Paper").

6. *Always proofread your finished essay carefully, preferably more than once.* This is standard procedure for all essays.

In this exercise you are asked to study two poems, on one of which you are to write a critical essay emphasizing interpretation. Do not try to interpret either of the poems as soon as you have read it. Instead, let your interpretation develop

EXERCISE

gradually as you write responses to the study questions. The questions are designed to enable you to employ the method for analyzing and interpreting that you have learned earlier—observing significant details and then fitting related details together into meaningful patterns.

Bring your prewriting notes on both poems to class to use in discussion. If you need to, revise your notes as a result of the discussion. Then decide which poem you will write about. Do your responses to the questions allow you to make a general interpretive statement about the poem? If so, you are ready to develop that statement in a paper. If not, you may want to write about the problems that prevent you from arriving at an interpretation in which you have confidence.

Bears
by Adrienne Cecile Rich

Wonderful bears that walked my room all night,
Where are you gone, your sleek and fairy fur,
Your eyes' veiled imperious light?

Brown bears as rich as mocha or as musk,
White opalescent bears whose fur stood out
Electric in the deepening dusk,

And great black bears who seemed more blue than black,
more violet than blue against the dark—
Where are you now? upon what track

Mutter your muffled paws, that used to tread
So softly, surely, up the creakless stair
While I lay listening in bed?

When did I lose you? whose have you become?
Why do I wait and wait and never hear
Your thick nocturnal pacing in my room?
My bears, who keeps you now, in pride and fear?

Questions 1.   In the first two stanzas the narrator speaks of the bears' "sleek and fairy fur," the "veiled imperious light" of their eyes, their being "as rich as mocha or as musk," and the "opalescent" effect of their fur. Is the narrator a child who admires the bears or an adult who is reflecting on the admiration she felt for them as a child?

2.   From what sources might a child's imagination have created the bears?

3.   Attempt to answer the narrator's questions "Where are you gone...?" (asked in stanza 1 and repeated in stanzas 3 and 5) and "When did I lose you?" (stanza 5).

4.   The narrator seems to wish that she could once again hear the bears treading on the stair and pacing in her room. Why does she have this wish?

5. The narrator wonders who keeps her bears. Offer her an answer.

6. If someone is keeping the bears "in pride and fear," what is the source of the pride? of the fear? (*Fear* is conspicuous for being the final word in the poem. Give it close attention.)

The Going Away of Young People*
   by Eleanor Ross Taylor

1

This was the day
The crumbs from last night's dinner
Lay all day on the table.

Your room filled only by sunlight
Is darkened by the late sleeper.

    You forgot your love.
    I'd mail it but
    There's the chore of string
    And paper and
The timbre of hi-fi turned off
Strings the psyche.
    Anyway it's stuff I'm used
    To stumbling over in various
    Recesses of my house
    Wondering why I haven't
    Given it away, put it
    To some use—
    But keep on hoarding it, ashamed.

2

And our sailers-away hang yet full sail
In our autumn windows,
The windows across the street
Becalmed of young people.
Grass infiltrates their marigolds.
The garage cries out.

3

I won't say goodbye.
But all leave-taking is a permanence.
We can't be sewed back up.
My mother's face at the window
Like a postage stamp
Hinges a faded September.

4

And over a drink my old friend fights tears,
Fights impatiently sympathy,
At her window cuts at the traffic
With her hand—"It was all woods!
Gone! And I've failed, too."

5

Windows between Septembers,
More and more windows,
Muffling, fogging over,
At last reflect only me
In car window, kitchen window,
Across-the-street windows,
This window I open over your bed
In case you should come back
For what you forgot.

Questions: Stanza 1 1. Why have the crumbs not been cleared from the table on this particular day?

2. Literally, the room is filled with sunlight. Why, then, does it appear to be darkened? Does your answer explain the term "late sleeper"?

3. What does the speaker have in mind when she considers mailing the forgotten love?

4. What is "the chore of string / And paper" that the speaker refers to? What is the "stuff I'm used / To stumbling over"?

5. Why and how does the "timbre of hi-fi turned off" affect the speaker?

6. In the light of your answers to these questions, can you describe briefly the state of mind of the speaker?

Stanza 2 This stanza contains a metaphor in which one house is likened to a ship under sail, the other to a ship becalmed.

1. Who are the "sailers-away"?

2. What are the signs that the house across the street is becalmed?

3. Why is the first house not becalmed?

4. Does this stanza suggest to you that in time the first house, too, will become becalmed? (If you cannot answer this question now, skip it and come back to it after you have answered all the other questions.)

5. Who is the speaker in stanza 2—the same person as in stanza 1, or somebody else?

6. Do you see any relation between the ideas expressed in stanza 2 and those expressed in stanza 1 and suggested by the title of the poem?

1.   Who is it who won't say goodbye: the same speaker as in stanza 1 or a   *Stanza 3*
different speaker?

2.   To what situation does the first line refer: (a) the same situation as in stanza 1,
(b) a situation that occurred much earlier, (c) both *a* and *b*? Explain your answer.

3.   Why "faded September"?

1.   Assuming that the person speaking in the first three lines is offering sympathy   *Stanza 4*
to a friend, what is the occasion for the sympathy?

2.   Why does the friend say, "I've failed, too"? Why "failed" and why "too"?

3.   Do you see any relation between this conversation and what has been said in
earlier stanzas?

1.   Why the emphasis on windows in this stanza? When windows have been   *Stanza 5*
mentioned earlier, what has been their function?

2.   Why do these windows finally "reflect only me"?

3.   Do the last three lines return the poem to the situation in stanza 1 and to
something forgotten there?

12

USING
THE
LIBRARY

A library is much more than a collection of books. It is a highly organized system for obtaining, classifying, and retrieving knowledge. As such, it is the most valuable educational agency on any college campus. The ability to use it efficiently is a prerequisite for success in most of the courses you will take during your college career. This chapter will help you to begin developing that ability by identifying the major resources of a library and showing you how to use them. If you need more specific assistance, two excellent sources are available. The first is Jean Key Gates's paperback, *Guide to the Use of Books and Libraries* (3rd edition; New York: McGraw-Hill, 1973). The second is your library staff, whose members will be glad to help you.

THE CARD CATALOG

Many libraries are now using automated cataloging systems to store information about their holdings. This information can be found by using computer terminals on which the patron can select from items displayed on a screen. It will be a while, though, before all libraries are using computer systems, and in the meantime the card catalog will remain the register of the materials in the library: books, manuscripts, pamphlets, microforms, recordings, newspapers, pictures, and films.

The set of catalog cards shown on page 309 consists of an *author card* produced by the Library of Congress and two copies on which new top lines have been typed by the purchasing library to make a *title card* and a *subject card* for the same book. The author card is filed under the surname of the author (Akers); the title card is filed under the first significant word in the title (omitting *a, an,* or *the*); the subject card is filed under the subject heading (Cataloging). The call number for the book is typed on all three cards in the upper left corner. In the new automated systems, three separate and complete imprinted cards are produced for each book, as shown on page 310.

In card catalogs there are also *cross-reference cards* to aid in finding works by subject. A "see reference" informs a user that the catalog does not contain a subject card for a particular topic, but that books on that topic are filed after another subject:

KNEE JERK   NUCLEAR ENERGY
See   See
REFLEXES   ATOMIC ENERGY

"See-also references" show additional headings under which similar materials are filed:

PHONOTAPES   TANK TRUCKS
See also   See also
TALKING BOOKS   CHEMICALS—TRANSPORTATION

CLASSIFICATION SYSTEMS

Many American academic libraries use the Library of Congress classification system for identifying and arranging materials on the shelves. The Dewey Decimal classification system is also widely used. Printed descriptions of these systems are available for reference in your library.

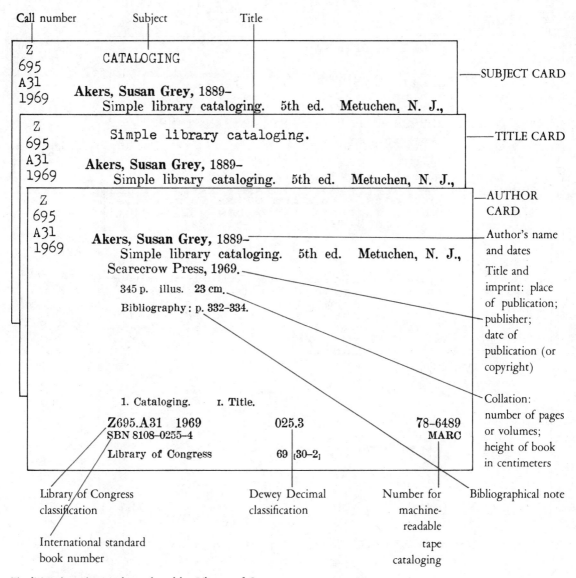

Call number   Subject   Title

Z
695
A31
1969   CATALOGING   —SUBJECT CARD

Akers, Susan Grey, 1889–
Simple library cataloging.   5th ed.   Metuchen, N. J.,

Z
695
A31
1969   Simple library cataloging.   —TITLE CARD

Akers, Susan Grey, 1889–
Simple library cataloging.   5th ed.   Metuchen, N. J.,

Z
695
A31
1969   —AUTHOR CARD

Akers, Susan Grey, 1889–   —Author's name and dates
Simple library cataloging.   5th ed.   Metuchen, N. J.,
Scarecrow Press, 1969.   Title and imprint: place of publication; publisher; date of publication (or copyright)

345 p. illus. **23 cm.**

Bibliography: p. 332–334.

                                        —Collation: number of pages or volumes; height of book in centimeters

1. Cataloging.   ɪ. Title.

Z695.**A31** 1969   025.3   78–6489
SBN 8108–0255–4   **MARC**

Library of Congress   69 ₍30–2₎

Library of Congress classification   Dewey Decimal classification   Number for machine-readable tape cataloging   Bibliographical note

International standard book number

Traditional catalog card, produced by Library of Congress

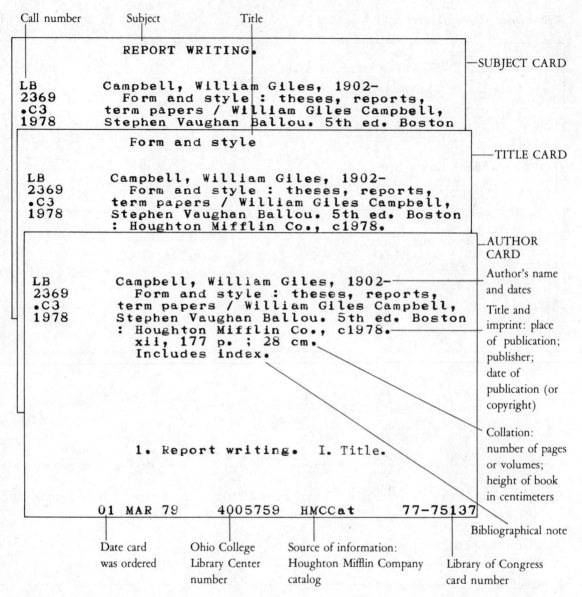

Catalog card produced by an automated cataloging system

The main divisions of the Library of Congress classification are as follows:

A	General Works	L	Education
B	Philosophy, Psychology, Religion	M	Music
		N	Fine Arts
C-D	History and Topography (except America)	P	Language and Literature
		Q	Science
E-F	America	R	Medicine
G	Geography, Anthropology, Sports and Games	S	Agriculture, Forestry
		T	Engineering and Technology
H	Social Sciences	U	Military Science
J	Political Science	V	Naval Science
K	Law	Z	Bibliography and Library Science

The main divisions of the Dewey Decimal classification are these:

000–009	General works	600–699	Technology (applied sciences)
100–199	Philosophy and related disciplines	700–799	The arts. Fine and decorative arts
200–299	Religion	800–899	Literature (belles-lettres)
300–399	Social sciences	900–999	General geography and history and their auxiliaries
400–499	Language		
500–599	Pure sciences		

FILING RULES

Librarians use rules and conventions for filing cards alphabetically, and an acquaintance with them is helpful in using the card catalog.

1. Personal surnames are filed before other "entries" or headings that begin with the same word.

London, Jack, 1876–1916.   (author entry)
LONDON, ENGLAND, DESCRIPTION AND TRAVEL   (subject entry)
London: places and pleasures.   (title entry)

2. Names beginning with *Mc* are filed as though they were spelled *Mac.*

3. Cards for books *by* an author are filed before cards for books *about* that author.

4. Titles are filed according to the first significant word, ignoring *a, an,* and *the.*

5.   Abbreviations and numbers are filed as though they were spelled out: *Dr. Strangelove* will be found under "doctor"; *U.S. News and World Report* under "United States"; *365 Days* under "three hundred sixty-five."

6.   Subject entries may be subdivided in alphabetical, geographical, or chronological order.

Alphabetical   DOGS—BREEDS
                   DOGS—PSYCHOLOGY
                   DOGS—STORIES

Geographical   BANKS AND BANKING—U.S.
                   BANKS AND BANKING—MASSACHUSETTS
                   BANKS AND BANKING—BOSTON

Chronological   FRANCE—HISTORY—BOURBONS, 1589–1789
                   FRANCE—HISTORY—REVOLUTION, 1789–1799
                   FRANCE—HISTORY—CONSULATE AND EMPIRE, 1799–1815

7.   Basic filing order is word-by-word rather than letter-by-letter.

North, Sterling, 1906–
NORTH ATLANTIC TREATY ORGANIZATION
North with the spring.
The Northeast coast.
NORTHMEN

THE REFERENCE COLLECTION

A student who needs information for a research paper will be wise to go first to the reference department of the library. The reference collection contains not only works filled with information, but also guides to other possible sources throughout the library.

BOOK CATALOGS

Catalogs in book form show what materials are available in other libraries and what books an author may have written in addition to those noted in your card catalog. The largest and best-known book catalogs are those of the British Museum* and the Library of Congress. The latter is currently called the *National Union Catalog* and lists books, music, records, motion pictures, and film strips.

* The library of the British Museum is now a part of the British Library.

LISTS OF BOOKS

The main lists of current publications in the United States are these:

Books in Print. An annual listing of books in print in the United States, indexed alphabetically by authors (2 vols.) and titles (2 vols.). There is also an annual *Subject Guide to Books in Print.*

Cumulative Book Index. A monthly list of books published in the English language, excepting government documents. Periodically several issues are combined (cumulated) into one volume.

Forthcoming Books. A bimonthly listing of books about to be published or recently published.

Publishers' Trade List Annual. A collection of publishers' book lists reprinted and bound together in alphabetical order.

LISTS OF PERIODICALS
AND NEWSPAPERS

The main lists of magazines, journals, and other publications issued in parts are these:

Ayer Directory of Publications. A standard source of information about newspapers and magazines of the United States, Puerto Rico, Virgin Islands, Canada, Bahamas, Bermuda, Panama, and the Philippines.

Standard Periodical Directory. A listing by subject of 62,000 serial publications in the United States and Canada.

Ulrich's International Periodicals Directory. A comprehensive list of periodicals of the world, arranged by subject, with an alphabetical index.

Union List of Serials in Libraries of the United States and Canada. A series that lists periodicals in the collections of major American libraries, continued in *New Serial Titles, 1950–1970* and supplements.

INDEXES TO
PERIODICAL LITERATURE

Much student writing is based on periodical articles, but these are not included in the card catalog. It is therefore necessary to use *periodical indexes* to find listings of articles on your subject.

For periodicals covering a generality of subjects, the main source is the *Readers' Guide to Periodical Literature,* which cites the articles in a number of nontechnical periodicals. It is published twice a month and cumulated in annual volumes. At the front of each issue is a list of the periodicals indexed with the abbreviations used for their titles, and a key to other abbreviations used in the citations. Articles are indexed mostly by subject and by author, but titles of creative works are also given as entries. Here is a sample from *Readers' Guide:*

CUPBOARDS
   See also
Armoires
Kitchen cabinets

Subject entry having no article listed under it, referring to other related headings that might have one.

CUPIVAC; drama. *See* Boiko, C.

Title entry, referring to the author entry for complete information.

CURARE
   Curare cure; treating pancreatitis. il
   Newsweek 89:74 My 2 '77

Subject entry for an illustrated article in *Newsweek,* Volume 89, page 74, the issue of May 2, 1977.

CURATORS. *See* Museum directors

Subject not used, referring to the one used.

CURCIO, Renato
   Terrorism on trial in Italy. il por Time
   110:58 Jl 4 '77

Author entry for an illustrated article with a portrait in *Time,* Volume 110, page 58, for July 4, 1977.

CURRENT events
   Events and people. See issues of Christian century

Subject entry referring to a section appearing in each issue of *Christian Century,* page numbers not given.

There are many periodical indexes covering specialized and technical subjects, such as

Applied Science and Technology Index
Art Index
Bibliographic Index
Biography Index
Biological and Agricultural Index
Book Review Index
Business Periodicals Index
Education Index
Engineering Index

General Science Index
Humanities Index
Index of Economic Articles in Journals
   and Collective Volumes
Index to Legal Periodicals
Music Index
Public Affairs Information Service
   Bulletin
Social Sciences Index

Similar indexes cover materials in anthologies and other collections published in book form. Among these are the *Essay and General Literature Index, Granger's Index to Poetry,* and the *Index of Plays.*

Many periodical indexes are available in databanks and may be used only through a computer terminal. In addition to *Readers' Guide* and the printed indexes to periodicals such as those listed above, articles and other references may be located by using the *Magazine Index,* a databank that indexes more than 370 periodicals. There are many other technical and special subjects covered by more than 200 other databanks.

The standard newspaper index for the United States is *The New York Times Index,* which goes back to 1851. This index will help in finding the exact date of an event and will cite the page of the *Times* on which the story appeared.

For quick reference and brief accounts of important news, the weekly world news digest *Facts on File* is very useful. Published since 1940, it records events day by day and has bimonthly, annual, and five-year indexes.

GOVERNMENT DOCUMENTS

Two lists of documents are published by the United States Government: the *Monthly Catalog of United States Government Publications* and the *Monthly Checklist of State Publications.*

UNABRIDGED DICTIONARIES

One of the meanings of *unabridged* is "being the most complete of its class." Unabridged dictionaries are large dictionaries that, because of their size, provide much more linguistic information than is available in even the best of the desk dictionaries. The best-known unabridged dictionaries are

Funk & Wagnalls New Standard Dictionary of the English Language
The Oxford English Dictionary
The Random House Dictionary of the English Language
Webster's Third New International Dictionary of the English Language

Each of these dictionaries is unabridged in another sense: it is the source or parent volume from which an abridged desk dictionary is made, though not all desk dictionaries are abridgments of larger works.

GENERAL ENCYCLOPEDIAS

The two chief general encyclopedias for academic use are the *Encyclopedia Americana* and the *Encyclopaedia Britannica.* The *Americana* is the second-oldest general encyclopedia in English and is continuously revised. The oldest is the *Britannica,* which originated in England in 1768 but is now published in the United States. It was completely revised for the fifteenth edition, published in 1974 and usually called "Britannica 3," in thirty volumes. The *Propaedia* volume is an overview of all fields of knowledge; the ten-volume *Micropaedia* is an index with brief information; the nineteen-volume *Macropaedia* treats many, though not all, of the same subjects in more detail. It is best to consult the *Micropaedia* first and then, if necessary, the *Macropaedia.* Older editions of this encyclopedia are still valuable and may even be preferable on some subjects. For example, the eleventh edition (1911) is still highly regarded for its treatment of topics in English literature.

YEARBOOKS AND ALMANACS

Yearbooks are devoted to the chief occurrences and developments of the preceding year and are published as soon as possible after its close. Most of the major encyclopedias publish an annual supplement in the form of a yearbook. Other "yearbooks" may be published less often than once a year, and still others, such as the *Yearbook of Agriculture,* cover one topic thoroughly each year.

Almanacs are compilations of miscellaneous statistics, records, events, and other bits of information. Any one of the following would make a useful and interesting addition to a student's personal library:

Hammond Almanac of a Million Facts, Records, Forecasts
Information Please Almanac, Atlas and Yearbook
Reader's Digest Almanac and Yearbook
World Almanac and Book of Facts

A number of almanacs on more specialized topics are also in print—for example, the *Almanac of American Politics,* which gives biographies and voting records of members of Congress.

SPECIALIZED REFERENCE WORKS

The following list of specialized works of reference can give only a preliminary overview of the wealth of source books available. It is divided into broad fields of knowledge and is highly selective. Other works in each area will be found in the reference collection of your library. Descriptive details of the works in this list are given in the standard source, Eugene P. Sheehy's *Guide to Reference Books* (9th edition; Chicago: American Library Association, 1976).

THE ARTS

American Architecture Since 1780: A Guide to the Styles. Arranged chronologically by the zenith points of styles.

American Art Directory. A source of information on museums, art schools, and art associations of the United States and Canada.

Art Dictionary. A classic work translated from the French and first published in 1891.

Dance Encyclopedia. All forms of dance are discussed in articles by specialists.

Dictionary of Architecture and Building: Biographical, Historical, and Descriptive. Although old, the standard dictionary in this field in English.

Encyclopedia of Painting: Painters and Painting of the World from Prehistoric Times to the Present Day. One volume arranged alphabetically and well illustrated.

Encyclopedia of World Art. A fifteen-volume set with authoritative signed articles on all countries, periods, and genres with bibliographies and many plates.

Focal Encyclopedia of Film and Television Techniques. A large volume on ways to make films and television programs.

Grove's *Dictionary of Music and Musicians.* By Sir George Grove, a standard reference work, with a supplement published in 1961.

A History of Architecture on the Comparative Method, for Students, Craftsmen, and Amateurs. A standard work by Sir Banister Fletcher, re-edited in 1961.

History of Sculpture. The standard handbook in the field.

Music Since 1900. One volume with a descriptive chronology to 1969, letters and documents, a dictionary of terms, and index.

New Oxford History of Music. An encyclopedic multivolume work, replacing an older work and covering all phases of music.

New York Times Film Reviews. Reproduces reviews of films since 1913 and gives an index of titles, persons, and awards; biennial supplements.

The Reader's Encyclopedia of World Drama. A handbook with historical accounts of theater development in addition to titles of plays and biographies of playwrights.

BIOGRAPHY

Chambers's Biographical Dictionary. An English publication giving commentaries on famous people of the world with a subject index.

Dictionary of American Biography. The classic multivolume set of scholarly biographies of noted Americans no longer living.

Dictionary of National Biography. The British equivalent and predecessor of the above.

A Dictionary of Universal Biography of All Ages and of All Peoples. An older work re-edited in 1951, giving very brief entries for many persons, with references to fuller biographies to be found elsewhere. Includes pronunciations.

McGraw-Hill Encyclopedia of World Biography. An illustrated one-volume work, published in 1973, containing signed articles.

National Cyclopaedia of American Biography. Fifty-one volumes and index containing a broad coverage of American people of accomplishment in past years.

New Century Cyclopedia of Names. Includes literary characters, names from myths and legends, and names of places and events, with pronunciations of prenames as well as surnames.

Notable American Women 1607–1950. In three volumes, with a supplement in preparation.

Webster's Biographical Dictionary. One of the most used sources of brief biographical data from all nations and times.

Who's Who. An annual listing of prominent living British persons with brief biographical data provided by the subjects themselves. *Who Was Who* is a companion set containing entries for deceased persons, with date of death.

Who's Who in America. A biennial equivalent to the British work, with a companion set of *Who Was Who in America.*

Who's Who in _____. Besides those of other nations and areas *(Who's Who in Italy; Who's Who in the West)* there are many specialized publications using this general title *(Who's Who Among American Women; Who's Who in Engineering).* Similar to *Who's Who in _____* are such works as *American Men and Women of Science* and *Directory of American Scholars.*

EDUCATION

American Universities and Colleges; American Junior Colleges. Published quadrennially by the American Council on Education, these volumes give detailed basic information on each institution.

Dictionary of Education. Definitions of educational and related terms.

Digest of Education Statistics. Published annually by the National Center for Education Statistics.

Education Directory. An annual publication of the U.S. Office of Education that lists institutions, educational officers, government officials connected with education, and educational associations, at all levels, from municipal to federal.

Educator's Complete ERIC Handbook. Gives abstracts of reports on research on the education of disadvantaged and culturally deprived children.

Encyclopedia of Education. A work in ten volumes, published in 1971.

Encyclopedia of Educational Research. Articles by leaders in the field cover recent developments in education.

The Gifted: Educational Resources. A list of public and private elementary and secondary schools having special programs for the gifted.

Guide to Educational Media. A work listing films, filmstrips, phonodiscs and tapes, slides, transparencies, videotapes, kinescopes and programed instruction materials.

A Guide to Study Abroad: University, Summer School, Tour, and Work-and-Study Programs. Describes living conditions, costs, and requirements for a large number of foreign educational programs for American students.

International Guide to Educational Documentation. An annotated list published by UNESCO of books, periodicals, pamphlets, films, and sound recordings on education, arranged by countries.

World of Learning. An annual list of educational, scientific, and cultural organizations of the world.

World Survey of Education. A four-volume publication of UNESCO dealing with education in general, primary education, secondary education, and higher education, arranged by countries.

HISTORY

American Heritage New Pictorial Encyclopedic Guide to the United States. In two volumes, arranged by states, a combination of text and pictures.

Cambridge Histories: Ancient, Mediaeval, Modern. Multivolume histories of the Western world published by Cambridge University. All three are being revised.

Chronology of the Modern World, 1763 to the Present Time. With its companion volume, *Chronology of the Expanding World, 1492–1762,* covers events in all areas since Columbus.

Dictionary of American History. In six volumes plus index, a compilation of short articles edited by James Truslow Adams. A companion volume is the *Atlas of American History.*

Documents of American History. Edited by Henry Steele Commager, this work includes documents of historic importance in the Western world from Columbus to the present.

An Encyclopedia of World History; Ancient, Medieval, and Modern. Edited by William L. Langer, a chronological treatment of world events in one volume.

Guide to Historical Literature. An annotated bibliography of selected works in history to 1957.

Guide to the Study of the United States of America: Representative Books Reflecting the Development of American Life and Thought. Published by the Library of Congress, an annotated list of works on American civilization.

Harper Encyclopedia of the Modern World. A concise one-volume reference to historical events from 1760 to 1970, arranged by eras, by areas, and by subjects.

Harvard Guide to American History, revised edition. A two-volume guide to research with essays on methods and resources and with reading lists arranged by periods.

Shepherd's *Historical Atlas.* The standard work of its kind, first published in 1911 and kept up to date, this book of maps covers world history with emphasis on Europe.

LITERATURE

American Authors 1600–1900; British Authors Before 1800; British Authors of the 19th Century; Twentieth Century Authors. Titles in a series of biographical dictionaries edited by Stanley Kunitz and Howard Haycraft.

Annual Bibliography of English Language and Literature. A source for studies on these topics, arranged by centuries of literature and types of language study.

Bartlett's Familiar Quotations. The best known of several books of quotations from poetry, prose, and drama, identifying authors and works.

Bibliography of American Literature. A historical guide in six volumes to date.

Book Review Digest. Digests of book reviews; published monthly and cumulated annually.

Cambridge Bibliography of English Literature. A major work in four volumes and supplement, not entirely replaced by the *New Cambridge Bibliography of English Literature* because of changes and omissions in the new edition.

Cambridge Histories of American and English Literature. Standard sets covering literature into the thirties.

Cassell's Encyclopaedia of World Literature. Signed articles with bibliographies by and about authors.

Columbia Dictionary of Modern European Literature. Begins just before the turn of the century and gives critical comment on works cited.

Contemporary Authors: A Bio-bibliographical Guide to Current Authors and Their Works. In eighty volumes to date, with cumulative index.

Contemporary Poets of the English Language. Edited by Rosalie Murphy and published in 1971.

A Critical History of English Literature. By David Daiches; two volumes of text written by a noted British scholar.

English Literature: An Illustrated Record. An older work valuable for its illustrations.

A History of English Drama 1660–1900. By Allardyce Nicoll, a work of six volumes with detailed articles and also lists of theaters and plays.

History of the English Novel. A ten-volume work covering the English novel from its beginnings to the early twentieth century.

A Library of Literary Criticism: Modern American Literature. Excerpts from critical writings about American authors of the twentieth century.

Literary History of England. A four-volume work edited by Albert C. Baugh, also available in one volume.

Literary History of the United States. An evaluative two-volume work often identified by the name of editor Robert E. Spiller. The second volume is a bibliography and two bibliographical supplements have been published.

Masterplots. A multivolume cyclopedia of plots of world literary works arranged alphabetically by title. Annual volumes have been published since 1954, and two volumes indexing literary characters were published in 1963.

Oxford Companions to: American Literature; Canadian History and Literature; English Literature; French Literature; the Theatre. Useful volumes for quick reference.

Oxford History of English Literature. A compilation begun in 1945 with fourteen volumes projected.

The Reader's Encyclopedia. A volume of brief references to world literature from antiquity to the present.

MYTHOLOGY AND CLASSICS

Dictionary of Greek and Roman Antiquities. By Sir William Smith, a great nineteenth-century editor, and still a standard source.

Dictionary of Mythology, Mainly Classical. By Bergen Evans, a source for mythological characters, emphasizing Greek and Roman mythology.

Everyman's Dictionary of Non-Classical Mythology. A source for non-Western myths.

Funk and Wagnalls Standard Dictionary of Folklore, Mythology and Legend. A two-volume encyclopedic dictionary covering all world cultures.

Gayley's *Classic Myths in English Literature and Art.* A famous old multivolume work, known by its editor's name; also in a one-volume edition.

The Golden Bough. By Sir James Frazer, a great exhaustive study of mythology in twelve volumes, with a supplement called *Aftermath* and a one-volume *New Golden Bough* brought up to date by Theodor H. Gaster.

A Handbook of Classical Drama. Plays by Greek and Roman dramatists are critically discussed.

Harper's Dictionary of Classical Literature and Antiquities. An older work of broad coverage, good for quick reference.

Larousse Encyclopedia of Mythology. Profusely illustrated world coverage.

Mythology. By Edith Hamilton, noted classical scholar; one volume of classical and Norse mythology comparing original with later versions of myths.

Mythology of All Races. The standard multivolume set in the field.

New Century Classical Handbook. A compilation embodying recent archaeological research, with many photographs.

Oxford Classical Dictionary and *Oxford Companion to Classical Literature.* Valuable for factual information.

Religions, Mythologies, Folklore: An Annotated Bibliography. Includes periodicals, and is arranged by subject areas as well as by type of publication.

Standard Dictionary of Folklore, Mythology and Legend. A two-volume compilation of wide coverage.

Universal Pronouncing Dictionary of Biography and Mythology. Known as "Lippincott's Biographical Dictionary," an older work covering all mythologies in brief articles.

Who's Who in the Ancient World. One of several "Who's Whos" of early eras.

PHILOSOPHY AND PSYCHOLOGY

The Cambridge History of Later Greek and Early Medieval Philosophy. A 1967 work by scholars, arranged by periods, with bibliography.

Catalogue of Renaissance Philosophers (1300–1650). A source book arranged by philosophical schools with bibliographies of the writings of the philosophers.

The Concise Encyclopedia of Western Philosophy and Philosophers. Articles by scholars on the main concepts.

Coordinate Index Reference Guide to Community Mental Health. A bibliographical publication coded by content of the work cited.

Dictionary of Philosophy and Psychology. . . . By James M. Baldwin; an old work not yet replaced.

Dictionary of Psychology. One volume that includes foreign terms.

Encyclopedia of Philosophy. An eight-volume work embracing both Eastern and Western philosophy.

Harvard List of Books in Psychology. A selected bibliography that has been added to by supplements.

History of Psychiatry: An Evaluation of Psychiatric Thought and Practice from Prehistoric Times to the Present. A comprehensive and useful work.

History of Psychology in Autobiography. A four-volume compilation of "intellectual histories" written by great psychologists about themselves.

History of Western Philosophy. By Bertrand Russell; one of several works on the history of philosophy.

How to Find Out in Philosophy and Psychology. A guide to research for undergraduates.

Professional Problems in Psychology. A valuable source for the literature of the field and for information on the profession.

Rehabilitation Literature, 1950–1955; A Bibliographic Review of the Medical Care,

Education, Employment, Welfare, and Psychology of Handicapped Children and Adults. An annotated bibliography arranged by subject.

RELIGION

Atlas of the Early Christian World. A translation from the Dutch, scholarly and thorough, with descriptions and comments.

Book of Saints. . . . A dictionary of canonized saints with brief biographies and a calendar.

Cambridge History of the Bible. A three-volume set containing long articles on the various versions of the Bible with photographs of pages from famous Bibles.

Concise Encyclopedia of Living Faiths. Long, detailed articles on religions of the world.

A Dictionary of Angels, Including the Fallen Angels. Names and attributes of angels and terms of angelology.

Dictionary of the Bible. Edited by James Hastings; a classic work.

Dictionary of Christian Ethics. Scholarly articles on modern ethical concepts and problems.

A Dictionary of Hymnology Setting Forth the Origin and History of Christian Hymns of All Ages and Nations. An old work still very useful.

Encyclopedia of Modern Christian Missions: The Agencies. History and statistics of existing Protestant missions.

Encyclopedia of Religion and Ethics. A multivolume standard work edited by James Hastings.

Exhaustive Concordance of the Bible. An index of the principal words of the Bible with their contexts, as used in the Hebrew and Greek originals and the King James, Authorized, and Revised versions.

History of Religions. In two volumes, gives detailed accounts of the religions of the civilized peoples of Asia, the Near East, and Europe.

Interpreter's Bible. . . . Twelve volumes containing the King James and Revised Standard texts in large print, accompanied by an Exegesis and an Exposition.

New Catholic Encyclopedia. . . . In fifteen volumes, the most recent encyclopedia of the Roman Catholic faith.

New Schaff-Herzog Encyclopedia of Religious Knowledge. . . . A standard work in thirteen volumes and two supplements.

Oxford Dictionary of the Christian Church. Articles by scholars, definitions of terms, and customs.

Sacred Books of the East. Translations of the works of seven non-Christian religions that have influenced the civilization of Asia.

A Source Book for Ancient Church History, From the Apostolic Age to the Close of the Conciliar Period. A standard source for early Christianity.

Treasure House of the Living Religions: Selections from Their Sacred Scriptures. An anthology of quotations with a good bibliography.

Universal Jewish Encyclopedia. . . . In ten volumes, one of several comprehensive works on Judaism.

SCIENCE AND TECHNOLOGY

The Atlas of the Universe. An encyclopedia with ninety-four plates.

Britannica Yearbook of Science and the Future. An annual illustrated work giving the latest scientific information for the general reader.

Chemical Technology: An Encyclopedic Treatment. A projected eight volumes on the economic applications of technological developments.

The Dictionary of the Biological Sciences and *Encyclopedia of the Biological Sciences.* Both edited by Peter Gray.

A Dictionary of Genetics. An aid for the student giving a chronology, a bibliography, and lists of periodicals and laboratories in the field.

Encyclopaedic Dictionary of Physics. An English publication designed to replace the older *Dictionary of Applied Physics,* and consisting of signed articles by experts.

Famous First Facts. A record of first happenings, discoveries, and inventions in the United States, with dates and descriptions of patented devices.

Geography of Commodity Production. Treats commodities of the world by their derivations: agriculture, forests, the sea, mining, and manufacturing.

Gray's *Anatomy of the Human Body.* A classic that is still re-edited.

Guide to Geologic Literature. Essays on methods of research, library facilities, and types of literature.

Guide to the Literature of Mathematics and Physics, Including Related Works on Engineering Science. A handbook with chapters on how to study, how to search the literature, and how to use the library. It also has a large annotated bibliography.

Handbook of Chemistry and Physics. The Chemical Rubber Company's standard work of reference for formulas, tables, and definitions.

Harper Encyclopedia of Science. A work of broad scope issued in four volumes in 1963, with a one-volume edition in 1967.

History of Magic and Experimental Science. An eight-volume work by Lynn Thorndike.

Horus: A Guide to the History of Science. One of several works by George Sarton on the early development of science, with an extensive bibliography.

McGraw-Hill Encyclopedia of Science and Technology: An International Reference Work. A fifteen-volume set supplemented by the *McGraw-Hill Yearbook of Science and Technology.*

Mathematical Dictionary. A handy one-volume guide giving symbols, tables, formulas, and vocabularies in other languages.

Stedman's Medical Dictionary. Gives pronunciations and derivations of medical terms.

Van Nostrand's Scientific Encyclopedia. A one-volume compendium on science.

Wildlife in Danger. A source of information about endangered species.

SOCIAL SCIENCES

American Indian Almanac. Descriptive text and illustrations by areas of the United States.

American Labor Unions: What They Are and How They Work. Gives history, structure, and activities of unions.

Biographical Dictionary of the American Congress, 1774–1961. Gives information not easily found elsewhere.

Black's Law Dictionary: Definitions of the Terms and Phrases of American and English Jurisprudence, Ancient and Modern. The standard reference.

Cambridge Economic History of Europe. In six volumes, covering the time from the Middle Ages to the present.

Ebony Handbook. Published in 1974, a useful one-volume reference work on black Americans.

Encyclopaedia of the Social Sciences. In fifteen volumes, the main comprehensive reference work in the field.

Encyclopedia of Social Work. Gives history of social welfare, biographies, and a directory of agencies.

Foreign Affairs Bibliography: A Selected and Annotated List of Books on International Relations, 1919/32–1952/62. Four volumes of critical bibliographies from the journal *Foreign Affairs,* re-edited for publication in this form.

International Bibliographies of Economics; of Political Science; of Social and Cultural Anthropology; of Sociology. Annual bibliographies published by UNESCO.

International Encyclopedia of the Social Sciences. A seventeen-volume set designed to complement the *Encyclopaedia of the Social Sciences* by describing the state of the social sciences in the 1960s.

International Library of Negro Life and History. In four volumes, an illustrated reference work, giving documents and articles arranged by historic era.

The Negro in America: A Bibliography. Arranged by topic, the second edition covers music, literature, and the arts, and has a guide to further research.

Official Congressional Directory for the Use of the U.S. Congress. Complete information about Congress published by Congress itself.

Palgrave's Dictionary of Political Economy. Three volumes of reprints of classic writings on economics; an older work reprinted in 1963.

Political Handbook and Atlas of the World: Parliaments, Parties and Press. . . . An annual publication of the Council on Foreign Relations.

Reference Encyclopedia of the American Indian. A guide to sources of information, including a bibliography and a Who's Who.

Sources of Information in the Social Sciences: A Guide to the Literature. Published in a second edition in 1973; very useful for the student.

A Statistical History of the American Presidential Elections. Many tables arranged by states and candidates of all parties.

United States Government Organization Manual. . . . An annual publication listing federal government departments, agencies, and officials.

Worldmark Encyclopedia of the Nations: A Practical Guide to the Geographic, Historical, Political, Social, and Economic Status of All Nations, Their International Relationships, and the United Nations System. Five volumes of condensed factual information, with bibliographies.

13

THE
RESEARCH
PAPER

The research paper goes under various names, but whether it is called a "research paper," a "library paper," or an "investigative paper," it is based on a student's reading on a selected subject. The student chooses the topic, reads about it in books and periodicals, takes notes, and writes a paper on his or her findings. The function of the assignment is twofold: first, to give students, through independent study, the experience of finding, organizing, and developing material on a subject of their own choice; second, to make them generally familiar with the conventions of bibliography and documentation. Since the writing of such a paper is often a requirement in courses other than English, the assignment is sometimes regarded as basic training for college work.

THE INVESTIGATIVE PROCEDURE

The paper you finally hand in will consist of the following parts: (1) a complete topic or sentence outline, (2) the text of the paper, (3) the endnotes* that identify the sources of statements made in the text, (4) the final bibliography of the works you used.

This chapter will discuss in detail the whole process of writing a research paper, from choosing a subject to presenting the final copy. But because it would be helpful to see what the finished product looks like, we suggest that you first turn to page 355 and examine the sample paper that begins there. Later you will study that paper and will probably consult it while you are writing your own to see how particular details are handled, but an introductory look at the model may give you a perspective on the variety of details with which this chapter must be concerned.†

CHOOSING A SUBJECT

The nature of the research paper rules out the following kinds of subjects:

1. one that could be developed solely from personal experience and therefore does not require research—for example, an autobiographical topic.

2. one that is so subjective that it cannot be significantly influenced by research. For example, no matter how much reading you do, you will not find any reliable answer to the question "Which is the greater poet—Yeats or Eliot?"

3. one that could be adequately developed from a single source, such as an explanation of a process.

If you avoid these subjects, any other topic that you could explore and come to a decision about may be suitable, *provided that the decision can be fully explained or supported within the time and space available for the assignment*. Ideally, your subject should arise out of your need or desire to find an answer to some question. If, as a result of previous experience, you want an answer to such questions as "Why is English spelling so illogical?" and "Is Henry James's *The Turn of the Screw* a ghost

---

* Endnotes are like footnotes in form and function. The only difference is placement, at the end of the paper instead of at the foot of the page. End placement is more convenient in typewritten material and is now generally recommended for research papers.

† The forms for bibliographical entries and endnotes given in this chapter follow those recommended by the *MLA Handbook*, which is the standard work on documentation in the fields of English and other modern languages.

story or a study of hysteria?" you have a specific subject that poses the problem for investigation. If your reading provides you with an answer to the question, you then have a thesis for your paper. Even if you are not satisfied that any one answer is sufficient, you will have a specific problem that can be discussed and explained.

Make your subject as specific as possible. A general subject can be restricted when your reading suggests that it is too broad, and this kind of restriction is normal. But the longer it takes you to restrict a general subject, the less purposeful your reading will be. If you begin with "The Novels of Henry James" and then restrict that subject, first to *The Turn of the Screw,* and then to the question of how that novel should be interpreted, much of your early reading will have no bearing on the question you finally deal with.

READING

For most research studies the reading may be divided into two stages—introductory and intensive. The introductory reading gives the background needed in order to begin the investigation intelligently. The intensive reading provides the information from which the paper will be written. Once the function of the introductory reading is understood, it becomes clear that note-taking at this stage is not profitable. The information obtained from this reading is probably not going to appear in your paper. This reading should therefore be done quickly. Indeed, the early accumulation of miscellaneous notes may actually be confusing, since a student who has notes on every aspect of the chosen subject is likely to have a harder time deciding which phase of it to concentrate on.

Usually the best sources for introductory reading are general works—articles in encyclopedias, chapters in textbooks, histories, biographical references, and specialized dictionaries. For example, if you set out to answer the question "How did English spelling become so illogical?" you might begin by checking the table of contents of several histories of the English language. If one of these was G. L. Brook's *A History of the English Language,* you would find a fifteen-page chapter on spelling that would be an excellent introduction to your investigation. Or if you think you would like to do something with mythology, you might begin by checking the list on page 322 of this textbook and then skim through one of the one-volume works cited there, perhaps Bergen Evans's or Edith Hamilton's. But do not get bogged down in this introductory reading. At this stage you are not gathering information for a paper but are reconnoitering a general subject to find an area of specialization.

PREPARING A BIBLIOGRAPHY

Your introductory reading will suggest certain books and articles that look promising for your study. Once you feel confident about the particular phase of the general subject that most interests you, you will begin to prepare a bibliography. In the sense in which you will use the term in your college work, a *bibliography* is a list of books, articles, and other publications. In this chapter it will be useful to distinguish between a working bibliography and a final one. A *working bibliography* is a set of cards identifying works you consult during your study. It is a tentative bibliography, from which you weed out cards for titles that prove on examination to have no value for your purpose, and to which you add cards for other titles that come to your attention as you read intensively in your subject. A *final bibliography* is a typewritten list placed at the end of your finished paper. It is a record, not of all the items you consulted, but of those you used in preparing your paper. It will naturally contain fewer titles than your working bibliography.

The working bibliography   Before you begin preparing a working bibliography, a few minutes' careful consideration of the problem ahead of you may save much time. Different subjects require different approaches to the preparation of a bibliography. If you are dealing with a subject recently developed, the card catalog will be of little use to you. It records only books, and the very latest material in a book just published is usually at least a year old. For a current topic you must get most of your information from newspapers and recent magazine articles. On the other hand, many subjects—the development of the alphabet, for example—have been thoroughly treated in books, and little of significance will be found about them in current periodicals. The best general sources of information are the card catalog and the *Readers' Guide to Periodical Literature.* For some subjects the best approach will be through an index to technical publications; for others, *The New York Times Index* may yield the required information most readily. Before beginning the bibliography, you should check the appropriate lists of reference works in Chapter 12.

Once you have started to prepare your bibliography, the following advice may be helpful:

1.   Try to make your bibliography selective as you prepare it. Develop the habit of guessing intelligently whether a book will be useful to you. In some subjects—space exploration, for example—an older book is likely to be out of date. Usually the best way to guess at a book's usefulness is to look at it quickly. Read the

preface, or part of it; check the table of contents; see how much space the book gives to your subject. With a little practice you will usually be able to tell within a few minutes whether the book will be of use to you.

2. Watch for critical bibliographies, which evaluate the works they list and thus tell you what sources are best and for what topics. Many studies contain such bibliographies, at the ends of chapters or the end of the whole work, and so give you valuable leads to other sources.

3. Study the indexes of books on subjects related to yours. A book on psychotherapy may contain a pertinent discussion of hypnotism. But do not begin to read it through merely in the hope that it *may* contain such information. Instead, turn to the index, see how many references are given under "hypnotism" or related headings, and sample the most likely of these references.

The working bibliography is made on 3-by-5-inch cards, with each title on a separate card. Each card should contain three essential pieces of information: (1) the name of the author, (2) the title of the work, (3) the facts of publication. In addition, a card may contain for your own convenience the library call number and a note concerning the contents of the work. The accompanying card is typical for a book.

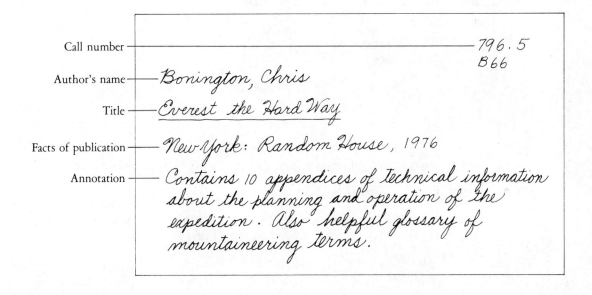

Call number —————————————————————— 796.5
                                                        B66
Author's name —— *Bonington, Chris*

Title —— *Everest the Hard Way*

Facts of publication —— *New York: Random House, 1976*

Annotation —— *Contains 10 appendices of technical information about the planning and operation of the expedition. Also helpful glossary of mountaineering terms.*

Sample bibliographical entries   The form of the entry varies with the kind of publication being cited. The major variations are illustrated in the sample bibliographical entries given below.

1.   A Book by a Single Author or Agency

> Murray, K. M. Elisabeth. Caught in the Web of Words:
>   James A. H. Murray and the Oxford English
>   Dictionary. New Haven: Yale Univ. Press, 1977.

a. The author's surname comes before the given name or initials for ease in alphabetizing. Use the name exactly as it appears on the title page.

b. If the book is the work of an agency, committee, organization, or department, instead of an individual, the name of the agency takes the place of the author's name.

c. If no author or agency is given, the citation begins with the title.

d. The title of the book is underlined.

e. The facts of publication are the place of publication, the publisher, and the date of publication, in that order.

f. If more than one place of publication is given on the title page, use only the first.

g. If no date of publication is given, use the latest copyright date, usually found on the reverse of the title page.

h. The punctuation and spacing in the sample show the preferred form.

2.   A Book by Two or More Authors

> Ashby, Eric, and Mary Anderson. The Rise of the Student
>   Estate in Britain. Cambridge, Mass.: Harvard Univ.
>   Press, 1970.

a. The names of authors after the first are not inverted (Thomas, Joseph M., Frederick A. Manchester, and Franklin W. Scott). Otherwise the form of the entry is the same as that of example 1.

b. The order of the authors' names is the same as that on the title page; hence Ashby comes first, even though Anderson would be alphabetically earlier.

3.   An Edition Other than the First

> Bailey, Sydney D. British Parliamentary Democracy. 3rd
>   ed. Boston: Houghton Mifflin, 1971.

a. If the work is a revised or later edition, the appropriate abbreviated designation (Rev. ed., 7th ed.) is placed immediately after the title and separated from it by a period.

b. Only the date of the edition being cited is given.

c. The edition number is not included in the title but follows it after a period and two spaces.

4. A Work of More than One Volume

> Johnson, Edgar. Charles Dickens: His Tragedy and
>   Triumph. 2 vols. New York: Simon and Schuster, 1952.

The number of volumes follows the title, is separated from it by a period, and is always abbreviated as shown.

5. An Edition of Another Author's Work

> Smith, Grover, ed. Letters of Aldous Huxley. New York:
>   Harper and Row, 1969.

6. An Edited Collection or Anthology

> Rothenberg, Jerome, ed. Shaking the Pumpkin:
>   Traditional Poetry of the Indian North Americas.
>   Garden City, N.Y.: Doubleday, 1972.

7. A Translation

> Hesse, Hermann. Beneath the Wheel. Trans. Michael
>   Roloff. New York: Farrar, Straus and Giroux, 1968.

8. A Pamphlet

Because there is considerable variation in the bibliographical information given in pamphlets, they are sometimes difficult to cite. Whenever possible, treat them like books, with or without an author. If the bibliographical information is so incomplete that you cannot confidently describe the pamphlet, get your instructor's advice. Following are four variant forms:

> Lichtman, Gail. Alcohol: Facts for Decisions. Syracuse,
>   N.Y.: New Readers Press, 1974.
> Florida Dept. of Highway Safety and Motor Vehicles.
>   Florida Driver's Handbook. Tallahassee, Fla., 1976.
> U.S. Dept. of Interior, Teton Dam Failure Review Group.
>   Failure of Teton Dam: A Report of Findings.
>   Washington, D.C.: GPO, 1977. [GPO is a standard
>   abbreviation for the U.S. Government Printing
>   Office.]
> Your Library: A Guide for Undergraduate Students.
>   University of Illinois, n.d.

a. The last example shows a difficult pamphlet, since the only bibliographical information given is the title and publisher.

b. The symbol *n.d.,* meaning "no date," is used to show that no date of publication or copyright is given and that the omission is not your oversight.

9.   An Essay in an Edited Collection

> Carr, Mary Jane. "Traps of Quick Sand." In This Land
>   Around Us: A Treasury of Pacific Northwest Writing.
>   Ed. Ellis Lucia. Garden City, N.Y.: Doubleday,
>   1969.

a. This entry requires two titles and both an author and an editor.

b. The title of the essay (or story or poem) is in quotation marks.

c. The title of the book is underlined and is preceded by *In.*

10.   An Article in an Encyclopedia

> Green, Benny. "Jazz." Encyclopaedia Britannica:
>   Macropaedia. 1974 ed.
> "National Parks and Monuments." Columbia Encyclopedia.
>   1963 ed.

a. Some encyclopedia articles are initialed, and the authors are identified in a special list. The article on jazz is signed "B. Gr." If the author is not identified, the entry begins with the title of the article, as in the *Columbia* example.

b. The British spelling *Encyclopaedia* is often bothersome to American students. Copy the title exactly as it is given on the title page.

c. The only fact of publication necessary is the edition or the year of publication. Pages may be omitted, since the topics are arranged alphabetically.

11.   An Article in a Journal

Journals are periodical publications dealing with a particular area of study. Examples are *The Journal of Library History, The Book Collector,* and *PMLA* (Publications of the Modern Language Association). The following samples show respectively the forms for periodicals published annually, quarterly, and monthly.

> Stewart, George R. "A Classification of Place Names."
>   Names, 2 (1954), 1-13.
> Hoffman, Frank A. "Place Names in Brown County."
>   Midwest Folklore, 11 (Spring 1961), 57-62.
> Stitzel, Judith. "Reading Doris Lessing." College
>   English, 40 (Jan. 1979), 498-503.

a. For all three of these entries the information following the title is volume, date, and page numbers in that order, with the volume in Arabic numerals and the date in parentheses.

b. For a journal published only once a year, the year alone is a sufficient date. For one published quarterly, the season (Spring, Summer, Fall, Winter) is added to the year, and for monthly periodicals the date consists of month and year.

c. When using quarterly or monthly issues bound in an annual volume by the library, check to see whether the page numbers are continuous through the volume or whether they start again from page 1 for each issue. Some journals use continuous pagination through a volume; others do not. As long as the date of each issue is given, the page numbers are not likely to be confused.

12. A Magazine Article

```
George, Phyllis.  "Sports: A Joy to the Spirit."
     Saturday Evening Post,  Oct. 1978, pp. 34-36.
Kramer, Hilton.  "The New American Photography."  New
     York Times Magazine,  23 July 1978, pp. 8-13.
```

a. The first entry shows the standard form for an article in a monthly magazine. No place of publication or publisher is given, but the month, year, and page numbers are shown. Notice the abbreviations: *p.* for "page," *pp.* for "pages."

b. The second entry shows the form for magazines published oftener than once a month and magazines issued as newspaper supplements. The day as well as the month is given.

13. A Newspaper Article

```
Whited, Charles.  "The Priceless Treasure of the
     Marquesas." Miami Herald, 15 July 1973, p. 1.
"Fall Brings Road Hazards."  The [Champaign, Ill.]
     News-Gazette, 25 Sept. 1976, p. 8, col. 4.
"Culture Shock: Williamsburg and Disney World, Back to
     Back."  New York Times, 28 Sept. 1975, Sec. 10,
     p. 1.
```

a. The first example shows the standard form for a signed article. The definite article before the name of the city is not used because it does not appear in the title of the newspaper.

b. The second example illustrates the form when the name of the city does not appear in the title, but the definite article does. In this example the column number is given because the story is not conspicuous on the page, and the column number makes identification easier.

c. When the pagination of a newspaper is not continuous throughout the paper but starts afresh in each section, the section number must be given, as shown in the third example. If sections are identified by letters rather than numbers, the section letter is used—"Sec. C, p. 2."

EXERCISE   In order to get practice as quickly as possible with the various forms illustrated in this discussion, convert the following information into conventional bibliographic form. You can check your answers against the appropriate preceding illustrations, since the number of each exercise corresponds to the number of the example in the text.

1.   A book by Hugh Fordin called Getting to Know Him: A Biography of Oscar Hammerstein II published by Random House in New York and copyrighted in 1977.

2.   A book by Seon Manley and Susan Belcher called O, Those Extraordinary Women! or the Joys of Literary Lib, published in Philadelphia by the Chilton Book Company in 1972.

3.   The second edition of a book entitled A Browning Handbook, written by William Clyde DeVane and published by Appleton-Century-Crofts of New York in 1955.

4.   A two-volume work called Examination of Sir William Hamilton's Philosophy, written by John Stuart Mill and published by Holt in New York in 1877.

5.   Thomas A. Gullason's edition of The Complete Novels of Stephen Crane, published in 1967 by Doubleday at Garden City, New York.

6.   An anthology titled From Freedom to Freedom: African Roots in American Soil, Selected Readings, edited by Mildred Bain and Ervin Lewis and published in New York in 1977 by Random House.

7.   A translation of The Complete Major Prose Plays of Henrik Ibsen by Rolf Fjelde, published by the New American Library in New York in 1978.

8.   A pamphlet entitled Animal Books for Children, prepared by the American Humane Association and printed in Denver, Colorado, in 1969.

9.   R. P. Blackmur's essay called The Craft of Herman Melville, published in the collection entitled American Literary Essays, edited by Lewis Leary and published by Thomas Y. Crowell Company of New York in 1960.

10.   An article on Mardi Gras in the 1977 edition of the Encyclopedia Americana.

11.   An article called Learning to Read: Friedrich Gedike's Primer, by David Paisey, on pages 112–121 of the Autumn 1978 issue in volume four of The British Library Journal.

12. An article entitled Nature and Cities on pages 14–16 of a magazine called Sierra for April 1978, written by Michael McCloskey.

13. An unsigned editorial entitled Rhodesia's Cycle of Futility on page 6 of Part 2 of Los Angeles Times for September 15, 1978.

The final bibliography   The final bibliography will be typed from the cards of the working bibliography and will follow the forms already discussed. It should contain a citation for each work mentioned in the endnotes.

In typing the final bibliography, which begins on a separate page, follow these directions:

1. List all entries in alphabetical order according to the surname of the author.

2. Double-space between successive lines of an entry and between entries. Also leave one extra space—that is, two spaces in all—between author and title, and title and facts of publication.

3. After the first line of an entry, indent successive lines five spaces.

4. If you are listing more than one book by the same author, do not repeat the author's name; instead of the name, type ten hyphens followed by a period, thus:

```
Richards, I. A.  Principles of Literary Criticism.  4th
     ed.  New York: Harcourt, Brace, 1930.
----------.  The Philosophy of Rhetoric.  New York:
     Oxford Univ. Press, 1936.
----------.  How to Read a Page.  New York: Norton, 1942.
```

In this example initials are used instead of given names because that is the form Richards uses on the title pages. The books are listed in order of their publication dates, but they could also be listed in alphabetical order.

NOTE-TAKING

When you begin intensive reading, you should begin taking notes. The results of your preliminary reading may be carried in your head, but you are now beginning to collect the actual evidence from which your paper will be written, and it is important to the success of all the rest of your work that both the form and the content of your notes be satisfactory.

The form of notes   All notes should be written on cards, not in notebooks. The practice of using note cards instead of notebooks has grown out of the experience of thousands of research workers. To be really useful, your notes must be so flexible that you can shuffle them to suit whatever order you finally decide on and can discard useless notes easily. Notes written solid in a notebook cannot conveniently be arranged or edited. They are fixed in the order they had in the source from which they were taken, whereas the order that suits your final purpose may be entirely different. Recording information in a notebook is therefore inefficient, no matter how easy it may seem at first glance.

Only one note should be placed on a card. Two notes on one card are inseparably bound together. Since you must be free to shuffle your notes, discard useless ones, and add supplementary ones, the only satisfactory method is to use a separate card for each.

Leave enough space at the top of each card (see page 341) so that you may write in a subject heading when you group your cards to develop your outline. Because these subject headings may be changed as your organization develops, it is wise to enter them in pencil.

Each note card should contain two kinds of information: (1) a clear reference to the exact source from which the note was made and (2) the quotation, fact, or opinion being noted. Since your bibliographical cards already contain author, title, and facts of publication, the note card usually needs no more than the surname of the author and the page number. Thus "Bonington, p. 166" would provide a clear reference. The only exception to this short form occurs when your bibliography contains two authors with the same surname or two books by the same author. To avoid confusion of authors or titles, a short form of the title would have to follow the author's name. Thus "Richards, Principles, p. 27" or "Richards, Philosophy, p. 27" would be necessary to distinguish Richards's *Principles of Literary Criticism* from his *Philosophy of Rhetoric*.

The content of notes   Your notes may contain statements of fact or of opinion, in your own words or in the words of the author from whose work they came. The two accompanying cards contrast a direct quotation and an indirect quotation from the same source. Each card bears a tentative subject label in the upper right corner.

If the wording as well as the content is taken from a source, be extremely careful to use quotation marks, both on your note card and, later, in your paper. Failure to use quotation marks on the note card may later lead you to think that the information is expressed in your own words and thus may trap you into unintentional plagiarism.

> *zero*
>
> Danzig, p. 35
> "In the history of culture the
> discovery of zero will always
> stand as one of the greatest single
> achievements of the human race."

> *Learned Superstitions*
>
> Danzig, p. 40
> Pythagoreans identified numbers
> with human qualities. Odd numbers
> male, even numbers female.
> 1 = reason   2 = opinion
> 3 = justice   4 = marriage

Whenever possible, your notes should be summaries of the source material, not direct quotations. Summarizing encourages you to *select* and *extract* the information most relevant to your purpose and to *state* the essential information *in your own words*. It thus lessens the temptation to quote excessively when you write your paper. The use of too many quotations in a research paper gives the impression that the student has merely strung together statements made by others without digesting these statements or doing any thinking about them. But in summarizing material, do take care to be sure that the summary accurately represents the content of the original source. Check your summary against the original before you consider the note card final. If you are then satisfied that you have not distorted the information in summarizing it, the economy of the summary will be constructively carried over to your paper. A summary thus helps to make both the note-taking and the writing more efficient. The accompanying note, for example, is an accurate summary of a five-paragraph passage containing about five hundred words. Notice that cards containing summaries are labeled as to the source of the information just as carefully as if they contained direct quotations. The material is taken from the work of another and must be acknowledged in endnotes.

There are two exceptions to this advice to summarize content whenever possible. The first exception is a passage that you are going to criticize. You should quote such a passage directly, and you should be careful not to distort the meaning of even a direct quotation by presenting it out of context. If the context is so long that it cannot conveniently be given in full, you are under a special obligation to be sure that the quotation faithfully represents the author's meaning. The second exception is statements that are so apt, dramatic, or forceful that they would lose some of their effect in a restatement or a summary.

Number sense

Danzig, pp. 1–3

Says number sense not to be confused with counting. Counting confined to humans, but some animals, birds, insects — crows and "solitary wasps," for example — have remarkable sense of number.

What has been said about note-taking may be summarized as follows:

1.   Put notes on cards, not in notebooks, with one note to a card.

2.   On each card identify the exact source of the note, including the page number. Abbreviations may be used when there is no danger of ambiguity.

3.   Enclose in quotation marks the actual words of an author.

4.   Summarize extensive quotations if possible, but still identify the source.

5.   Use direct quotation whenever the exact wording may be significant, especially if you are going to criticize a statement in the source.

6.   Be careful that your notes—whether direct quotations or summaries—do not distort the meaning when taken out of their original context.

THE COMPOSING PROCEDURE

OUTLINING THE PAPER

Since the research paper is usually the longest and most complex paper written in the composition course, it nearly always requires a complete outline. Indeed, many instructors make the writing of the outline a critical stage of the assignment and ask students not to begin the actual writing until the outline is approved.

Your final outline may be either a topic outline, in which all entries are subject headings, or a sentence outline, in which all entries are complete sentences. Which type you use will be determined by the kind of paper you intend to write. In general, a problem-solving paper has a topic outline, a paper developing an argument requires a sentence outline, and a classification paper may have either a topic or a sentence outline. The next few pages will explain and illustrate this statement.

Papers attempting to solve a problem usually do not have one main idea stated as a thesis; instead they present the problem, analyze it, and come to some conclusion about it. The following introduction to a problem-solving paper illustrates this procedure:

> While most critics agree that Henry James's novel *The Turn of the Screw* is one of the greatest horror stories ever written, they have disagreed vigorously for nearly fifty years about how it should be interpreted. The root of the quarrel is the character of the governess, from whose point of view and in whose words the story is told. Is she a courageous young woman fighting

a losing battle to save two innocent children from evil spirits who are trying to corrupt them? Or is she a hysterical girl who destroys the children placed in her care by her efforts to save them from ghosts which are products of her neurotic imagination?

This paper will review the controversy and evaluate it. Specifically, the paper considers three questions: What are the key issues in the controversy? What was the author's intent? Is the controversy a result of the ambiguity of the work itself? Since those who believe that the ghosts are "real" and constitute a mortal threat to the children are in the majority, their judgment will be called the *majority interpretation.* The conviction that the governess imagines the ghosts will be called the *minority interpretation.* The problem is to decide, if possible, which interpretation is better supported by the evidence of the text and of James's own comments on the story.

The topic outline suggested by this introductory statement would consist of five main headings.

    I. Introduction: the statement of the problem
   II. The key issues in the controversy
  III. The author's intent
  IV. The ambiguity of the text
   V. Conclusion

Except for the introduction and conclusion, all headings would be subdivided as fully as necessary. For example, II might be subdivided as follows:

  II. The key issues in the controversy
     A. The governess's relations with her employer
     B. The situations in which she sees the ghosts
     C. Her description of the ghosts
     D. Her relations with the children
     E. The final scene

If necessary, these subheadings could be divided into still smaller units.

Since there is no one main idea running through this outline, the paper will have no thesis. Even though the writer will finally present his or her conclusion, that is not a thesis. Not only does it not come at or near the beginning of the paper, but *the conclusion does not control the outline:* no matter what conclusion the writer reaches in V, all the headings above the conclusion would be the same. The function of the outline is simply to show the topics that have to be discussed, and nothing would be gained by trying to convert these headings into sentences.

But a paper developing an argument follows the premise-conclusion style of outline shown on page 221. The outline begins with the conclusion that is the thesis of the paper, the Roman-numeral entries state the main premises used to prove that conclusion, and the capital-letter entries provide the support for the main premise. All entries are thus clearly related to the thesis. The following abridgement of the outline on page 221 shows this relationship by arrows connecting subdivisions to main divisions and main divisions to the thesis:

Thesis: Teen-age marriages are not advisable.
I. The divorce rate for teen-age marriages is high.
   A. Dr. Laura Singer . . . says that two out of three teen-age marriages end in divorce.
   B. Dr. Harold Christensen . . . says that the younger the age of marriage, the higher the percentage of divorce.
II. Teen-age marriage is especially difficult for students.
III. Teen-age marriages restrict individual development.

These arrows show the Roman-numeral statements pointing back to the thesis and the capital-letter statements pointing back to the Roman-numeral statement that they support.

In such an outline sentences are more efficient than topic headings in showing the relation between premises and conclusions. A topic outline of the form

I. High divorce rate
   A. Dr. Laura Singer
   B. Dr. Harold Christensen
II. Student difficulties
III. Restricted development

does not clearly show that teen-age marriages are not advisable, because a reader may not see how I, II, and III lead to that conclusion, or how A and B support I. The sentence outline constructs the whole argument so that a reader can see how each sentence contributes toward the acceptance of the thesis.

In a classification paper the outline shows the classes and subclasses into which the subject can be divided. The thesis does not express a conclusion in the same sense that "Teen-age marriages are not advisable" is a conclusion. Rather, it states the number of classes that are going to be described. The outline identifies each of these classes and its subclasses. This setting-up of a classification system can be done almost as well by topic headings as by sentences. For example, the outline of the model research paper on page 355 could have been a topic outline. In fact, it began as one and was later converted to a sentence outline. In developing that paper, the author began to feel that a sentence outline would provide a tighter organization; but the structure of the paper would not have been significantly different had a topic outline been used.

Whichever form you choose, it will grow out of repeated study of your notes. You will start by grouping note cards dealing with the same topic. Then you will combine these small groups into larger ones to find the main divisions of your material. At this stage you will begin to try out topic outlines. Thus gradually you will shape an outline that satisfies you. The whole process was illustrated when we dealt with the results of the questionnaire on freshman objectives on pages 49–51.

The procedure will be greatly simplified and speeded up when you know exactly what you want to do. Therefore, the sooner you discover your real subject or your thesis, the easier your job will be. This is one of the reasons for beginning with a restricted subject, especially one that can be framed as a question. If you find your question has a single answer, that answer is your thesis. If you find that no one answer offers a sufficient explanation but that two or more answers do, you will have a classification outline, and your thesis will be something like this: "There are two (three? four?) reasons why this happened."

Once your outline is established, mark each note card with the symbol of that part of the outline to which it belongs: IA, IB, IC, IIA, and so on. Then arrange your cards in the order in which they are to be used. You are now ready to write the first draft of your paper.

WRITING THE PAPER

All that has been said about composition earlier in this book applies to the research paper. But in addition the research assignment has its special problem—the relationship between borrowed material and the use that is made of it. The research paper is necessarily written from information derived from various sources. But that information has to be reorganized and woven into an essay that is essentially the student's own work. If you have worked purposefully, you will not have much difficulty reconciling these two conditions, for you will have selected your material with a view to using it in support of a purpose you have been forming as you read. In a sense you are like a person who is building a house with bricks obtained from others. The bricks are not of the builder's making, but the design and construction of the house are. *Writing a research paper, then, is not just stringing together statements from books and magazines. It is completely reorganizing and reworking the source material into an original composition.*

Failure to recognize this sometimes results in a paper that is merely a transcription of the information in the note cards. The following excerpt from a student research paper reveals this weakness:

Article 123 of the Mexican Constitution has the sole purpose of solving the labor problem. It is looked upon as the declaration of the rights of the workmen.[10]

The workers' hours have a maximum limit of eight hours for
a day's work. At least one day's rest for every six days' work
is to be enjoyed by everyone.[11]

Children over twelve and under sixteen years of age can
work only six hours a day, and children under twelve are not
permitted to be made the subject of a contract.[12]

The minimum wage that can be received by a workman should
be considered sufficient according to the conditions of life
prevailing in the workman's particular region of the country.
This same compensation is to be paid without regard to the sex
of the worker.[13]

Wages are required to be paid in legal currency rather than
by any other representative token with which it is sought to
substitute money.[14]

_____

Notes

[10] Tannenbaum, p. 529.

[11] Tannenbaum, p. 529.

[12] Tannenbaum, p. 529.

[13] Tannenbaum, p. 529.

[14] Tannenbaum, p. 530.

What this student is doing is simply copying his notes into his paper. If that is all
he is going to do, he might as well hand in his note cards. The composition
problem is to take the raw material of the notes and process it into a unified
paragraph, perhaps one like the following:

Article 123 of the Mexican Constitution attempts to
standardize labor conditions by setting up basic principles
governing hours and salaries. It provides a maximum workweek of
six eight-hour days, prohibits the contractual hiring of
children under twelve years of age, and limits the employment of

children between twelve and sixteen to six hours a day. It
requires that all wages be paid in legal currency, thus
eliminating company scrip and other cash substitutes. It
provides for a minimum-wage scale which takes into account
differences in the standard and cost of living in various parts
of the country. It abolishes discrimination against women by
making the wage rate the same for both sexes. In general,
therefore, it seeks to establish a uniform code which will
provide the general pattern of labor-management relations
throughout the country.[10]

Notes

[10] Tannenbaum, pp. 529-30.

The first of these two versions is a series of raw notes; the second is a unified and
coherent paragraph created by the student. Both contain exactly the same facts,
but the revised version rearranges and rewords the facts to make them develop the
idea stated in the opening sentence. It also avoids the overdocumentation of the
first version by acknowledging the two pages of Tannenbaum's book as the source
for all the information in the paragraph. An instructor comparing the second
version with the notes from which it was written would clearly see that the writer
had mastered the information he was using and had shaped it to suit his own
purpose.

Because of the scope of the research paper, the composition should usually be
done in three stages: writing the rough draft, preparing the final revision, and
proofreading the finished paper. No two of these stages should be completed at a
single sitting; indeed, it is best to allow at least a day between the completion of
one and the beginning of the next.

How you should compose the rough draft will depend partly on your work
habits and partly on the nature of your material. For the average student the best
advice is to break the total job into the main units of the outline and to tackle
these units in order. The first draft of a paper so developed is likely to be a bit stiff
and to proceed rather mechanically from one step to the next, but this is not a
serious weakness if careful revision is to follow.

DOCUMENTING THE EVIDENCE

All information taken from a specific source must be documented by a citation in the endnotes that gives the exact source from which it was taken. The purpose of this convention is twofold: (1) to avoid the appearance of representing somebody else's work as your own, and (2) to let interested readers consult your sources and so check the accuracy of your investigation or carry on their own. This convention is so important in research writing that inaccurate documentation—or none at all—is regarded as a serious offense.

When to document   In general you should cite the source of any statement for which you are indebted to the work of another. For most student research this general principle can be broken down into five conditions. You should provide an endnote whenever

1.   you use a direct quotation.
2.   you copy a table, chart, or other diagram.
3.   you construct a table from data provided by others.
4.   you summarize a passage in your own words. (In this case the words are yours, but the ideas are borrowed from the passage. A good example of this practice is the revised paragraph about the Mexican Constitution on page 347.)
5.   you present specific examples, figures, or factual information taken from a specific source and used to explain or support your judgments.

To some extent, a sense of when documentation is necessary comes from experience, and part of the function of the research assignment is to provide that experience. A careful study of the sample paper on pages 356–371 should be helpful. If at any point in your work you are still uncertain whether a source should be cited, follow the general advice: "When in doubt, document it." It is easier to take out unnecessary endnotes in revision than to add them.

How to document   Documentation consists of two parts: a numbered marker that identifies the statement to be documented, and an endnote that cites the exact source of that statement. The marker is placed in the text (preferably in the first draft) at the end of and just above the statement to be documented. The endnote provides all the information necessary to cite the source. These citations begin on the first full page after the text of the paper and are numbered to correspond to their markers.

In typing your endnotes, follow these directions, all of which are illustrated in the sample paper at the end of this chapter:

1. *Spacing.* Begin your endnotes on a separate page following the text of your paper. Begin each note with the number you used in the text: 1 for the first note, 2 for the second, and so on. Each number is indented five spaces and is placed slightly above and one space before the author's name. If the note takes more than one line, all lines after the first start flush with the left margin. Double-space between lines and between notes.

2. *Author's name.* Reverse the order you used in the bibliography: begin with the given name–"John Smith," not "Smith, John." If the work has more than two authors, use "and others" after the first one–"Leon Edel and others," instead of "Leon Edel, Thomas H. Johnson, Sherman Paul, and Claude Simpson." This shorter form is used only in endnotes, not in the bibliography. When a book has an editor instead of an author (as in an anthology or a book of readings), the editor's name goes in place of the author's and is followed by "ed." After the first reference to a work, the author's or editor's name is shortened to surname only–"Smith," not "John Smith." If there is no author's or editor's name, the note begins with the title.

3. *Title.* All titles follow the form used in the bibliography, but in the second and subsequent references, the author's surname and the page number are enough–for example, "Bonington, p. 11"–provided that only one author by that name is being cited, and only one book or article by that author. Unless both these conditions are met, it will be necessary to add a short title–"Richards, Principles, p. 24."

After the first reference to an *unsigned* newspaper article, the title of the newspaper is used without the title of the article. Obviously this short form can be used only if no ambiguity results; if other endnotes are going to refer to different issues of that newspaper, a fuller reference will be needed. The short form can be used only when the endnote refers to a newspaper article already cited. When it refers to another article in the same newspaper, it requires a full citation.

4. *Facts of publication.* The place of publication, the name of the publisher, and the date of publication are enclosed in parentheses in the first citation of a work, but are omitted in subsequent references. When used, the facts of publication follow the form used in a bibliography.

5. *Volume and page numbers.* In reference to a one-volume work, the abbreviation *p.* is used for "page" and *pp.* for "pages." When the reference is to a work of more than one volume, both the volume and the page number must be given. When

both are given, the abbreviations *Vol.* and *p.* are dropped; instead the volume is indicated by a Roman numeral and the page by an Arabic numeral—"II, 28," not "Vol. II, p. 28." The page number must refer to the exact page of the source being cited; if the material comes from more than one page in the source, all necessary pages must be shown—"p. 5," or "pp. 5–6," or "pp. 5–8."

But when the reference is to a periodical rather than to a book, both the volume and the page numbers are in Arabic numerals, with the volume number first and the page number last and the date coming between these two numbers—"22 (1976), 45–46." Usually, however, no volume number is given for magazines published monthly, semimonthly, or weekly. Then the citation is by date and page numbers—"Oct. 1978, p. 140," or "10 Sept. 1976, pp. 21–23." Many newspapers are numbered in sections, with the page numbers starting over again in each new section—"Sec. A, p. 12," or "Sec. B, p. 4," or "Sec. 2, pp. 4–6." For such newspapers the order is title, date, section, page, and sometimes column number.

6. *Punctuation.* Endnotes are punctuated like sentences, with a period at the end of the note and after abbreviations, and commas between the parts except where colons are needed.

Sample endnotes   The following sample endnotes illustrate and supplement the preceding discussion. They may be used as models against which to check your own endnotes.

1.   First Reference to a Book

> ¹ Wolf Mankowitz, <u>The Extraordinary Mr. Poe</u> (New York: Summit Books, 1978), p. 43.

Subsequent reference

> Mankowitz, p. 88.

2.   Reference to a Multivolume Work

> ² Martin Blumensen, <u>The Patton Papers</u> (Boston: Houghton Mifflin, 1972, 1974), I, 134–35.

(Note: The two dates are necessary here because the first volume was published in 1972, and the second in 1974.)

Subsequent reference

> Blumensen, II, 27.

3. Reference to a Second or Later Edition

     ³ John Hope Franklin, From Slavery to Freedom: A
History of Negro Americans, 3rd ed. (New York: Knopf,
1967), p. 506.

Subsequent reference

     Franklin, p. 302.

4. Reference to an Essay in an Edited Collection

     ⁴ Henry Beston, "The Golden Age of the Canoe," in The
Great Lakes Reader, ed. Walter Havighurst (New York:
Macmillan, 1966), pp. 31-32.

Subsequent reference

     Beston, p. 35.

5. Reference to a Magazine Article

     ⁵ William H. Isbell, "The Prehistoric Ground Drawings
of Peru," Scientific American, Oct. 1978, p. 140.

Subsequent reference

     Isbell, p. 142.

     ⁶ Mario Pei, "Prospects for a Global Language,"
Saturday Review, 2 May 1970, p. 23.

Subsequent reference

     Pei, p. 25.

6. Reference to a Newspaper Article

     ⁷ Roger Kenneth Field, "Automated Medicine," New York
Times, 31 Jan. 1971, Sec. 3, p. 8, col. 2.

Subsequent reference

     Field, p. 8

     ⁸ "Senate Unit Moves to Set Aside Alaska Lands,"
Washington Post, 30 Sept. 1978, p. A6, cols. 3-5.

Subsequent reference

> `Washington Post.`

7. Reference to an Article in an Encyclopedia, Signed or Unsigned

> [9] `Thomas Babington Macaulay, "Johnson, Samuel,"`
> `Encyclopaedia Britannica, 11th ed., XV, 463.`

Note that "1910 ed." could be used in place of "11th ed."

Subsequent reference

> `Macaulay, p. 465.`

> [10] `"Entelechy," Encyclopaedia Britannica:`
> `Macropaedia, 1974 ed., XXIII, 908.`

Subsequent reference

> `Britannica, 1974, XXIII, 908.`

8. Biblical Reference by Book, Chapter, and Verse (or Verses)

> [11] `Genesis 25:29-34.`

(The title of the book is not underlined.)

9. Reference to a Play by Act, Scene, and Line

> [12] `Hamlet III, i, 56.`

FINAL CHECK AND SPECIMEN PAPER

When the endnotes have been completed and the final bibliography added, the whole paper, including endnotes and bibliography, should be carefully proofread. Before it is handed in, the paper must be identified by the author's name, course number, and date. This information can be placed on the upper right corner of the first page, though some students prefer to put it on a separate cover page which also contains the title. If your instructor has a preference in this matter, he or she will tell you. Instructors often require that the note cards from which the paper was written be handed in along with the paper. If your notes are required, be sure that they are arranged in order of use and are securely bound together or placed in an envelope.

EXERCISE   Following is a specimen research paper, complete with outline, text, endnotes, and bibliography. For your convenience in studying the structure of the paper, the appropriate outline symbols have been inserted in the margin, though they would not normally appear in your paper. First, read the text to become generally familiar with the content of the paper. Second, study the outline to see if it is a logical development of the thesis. Third, check the text against the outline symbols to see if the structure of the paper reflects the structure of the outline. Finally, check the forms of the endnotes and the bibliography.

Comment on outline   Since the specimen paper being presented in this section is a classification paper, the outline may be in either topic or sentence form. The writer has chosen a sentence outline because, by including subtopics in parallel structure within the capital-letter statements, he can get a more compact plan. For example, in a topic outline, references to Indian, Biblical, classical, and European names would have to be labeled IA1, IA2, IA3, and IA4 respectively. This kind of subdivision, if carried through the whole outline, would require about three pages instead of one. Such a topic outline would be more complex than an outline for this paper needs to be, and it would actually be harder for both the writer and reader to follow.

The outline on the opposite page is relatively easy to construct and read. The thesis announces the number of classes; each class is identified in one of the main divisions and is explained and illustrated through the subdivisions. The structure is similar to that of the classification papers you studied in Chapter 4 and to that of the enumerative paragraph in Chapter 5.

Notice that no part of this outline is labeled "Introduction" or "Conclusion." Such headings would be appropriate in a topic outline, as they were in the topic outline on page 221. But the function of this sentence outline is to develop the thesis, first through the main classes, marked by Roman numerals, and then through the subclasses, marked by capital letters. The three-part structure of the outline is therefore determined by the necessity of explaining the "three ways" in which place names have been derived. Adding "Introduction" before the first Roman numeral and "Conclusion" after the third one would confuse the forms of topic and sentence outlines. The introductory material in the first two paragraphs of the paper and the final concluding paragraph are important and should not be omitted, but they should not be shown in the outline.

Notice also that the capital-letter statements in the outline refer to subclasses, not to paragraphs. The writer of the paper may take as many paragraphs as he wishes to discuss one subclass, or he may write a transitional paragraph in going from one main division to another. He is under no requirement to give the same amount of space to each subclass.

How American Places Get Their Names

Thesis: Although American place names resist scientific classification, they tend to be derived in three ways.

I.   They are borrowed directly from an existing name.
  A. Some of them are Indian place names or the names of Biblical, classical, or European places.
  B. Some are the names of historical figures: political leaders, military commanders, religious personages.
  C. Some are the names of little-known people: early settlers and relations or friends of the person doing the naming.
II. They are corruptions of an existing name.
  A. The corruption may have come from the incompetence of translators.
  B. The corruption may have occurred through misreading of the name.
III. They are inventions that commemorate particular situations.
  A. Some are manufactured by combining parts of words or by spelling them backward.
  B. Some describe the physical characteristics of an area.
  C. Some refer to disputes or deaths.
  D. Some are the result of frustration.

How American Places Get Their Names

The problem of classifying the processes through
which place names in the United States have been derived
is a complex one. Scholars have been only partially

Introduction   successful in developing a satisfactory system. The
leading authority on the subject, George R. Stewart,
speaks of the reason for this complexity.

> The period of active naming extended over four
> centuries, during which time customs and
> fashions had a chance to change. The work was
> shared among all classes from border ruffian
> to Boston Brahmin. It drew upon the influence
> of a strong patriotism which by hero-names and
> other devices produced, often consciously, a
> national and regional flavor.[1]

Stewart has explained that the "mechanism of naming" can
be divided into nine classes, with the help of many
subclasses, though he admits that "border-line cases may
occur."[2]

Stewart's admission that even his nine-class scheme
runs into "border-line" difficulties is something of an

2

understatement. His border lines not only merge; they
sometimes overlap conspicuously, so that some words fit
as well in one category as in another. But if
occasional overlapping is accepted as a necessary evil,
it is possible for even a beginning student of place
names to show that, though they resist scientific
classification, they do tend to be derived in one of
three major ways: through direct borrowing, through the
corruption of existing names, and through the invention
of new names to meet particular situations.

Thesis

In this study a borrowed name is one that has been
adopted from an existing name. Many of the borrowed
place names in the United States are Indian names. A
list would include about half the states (Missouri,
Kentucky, Kansas, Alabama), eighteen large cities
(Chattanooga, Omaha), most of the larger lakes (Erie,
Chautauqua) and long rivers (Rappahannock,
Tallahatchie), several mountains (Mount Kahtadin, the
Appalachian chain), thousands of other geographical
features, and numerous small towns.[3] This kind of
borrowing goes back to the earliest explorers and
settlers. For example, the priests who were traveling
with the French explorers recorded a river called the

IA

3

Mississippi, from the Algonquin miss ("big") and sipi ("river"). Captain John Smith recorded the names of rivers called Patowomek and Susquesahanock.[4] Sometimes Indian place names were translated into English. Maiden Rock, Wisconsin, is named for a place famous in Indian legend because a young Indian woman leaped from a rock to her death to avoid marrying into a tribe other than her own.[5] And a rural community in Indiana, Bean Blossom, took its name from a village with the Indian equivalent of that name.[6]

Biblical, classical, and European places have often been the sources for place names. Among those from the Bible are Shiloh, Bethesda, Mount Carmel, Bethlehem, Sharon, and Lebanon. A person approaching Lebanon, Tennessee, may drive on a road lined with cedar trees and read at the city limits a sign that says "The Cedars of Lebanon," an allusion to Solomon's insistence that "they hew me cedar trees out of Lebanon" for the temple he would build.[7] Classical civilization has provided names for at least 2,200 places in the U.S.: Troy, Utica, Syracuse, Ithaca, Rome, Athens. So many classical names were assigned in central New York in the late 1700s that they were the source of scoffing--so

4

much that the man who for fifty years had served as the
state's surveyor general felt compelled to deny
responsibility for the naming.[8] Settlers from Western
Europe often brought the names of their old places of
residence with them. In Pennsylvania the English
settled in Bristol, Birmingham, and Lancaster; the Welsh
in Bryn Mawr, Caernarvon, and Brednock; the Scotch-Irish
in Drumore, Colerain, and Donegal; the Germans in
Manheim, Lititz, and Strasburg.[9] A number of U.S. towns
and cities have the names of French cities: Paris (in
forty-five states), Marseilles, Versailles, Orleans,
Lyons, Montpelier. Louisiana, named for a king of
France, is the state with the largest number of towns
and cities—122—borrowed from French place names.[10]

Borrowed place names often honor prominent people
in America's history, particularly political and
military leaders. Some of these were Indian chiefs
(Tecumseh, Powhatan, Pontiac). It is estimated that
places in about twenty states have been named for the
Seminole chief Osceola.[11] But most of the leaders whose
names have been borrowed have been whites, among whom
George Washington leads the list. Two hundred years
after his birth the places named for him "were more than

IB

5

could be surely counted--a state, thirty-three counties,
121 cities and towns and villages, 257 townships, ten
lakes, eight streams, and seven mountains." No other
person in history has been so honored with place names.
Twenty-four counties were named for Jefferson and
twenty-three for Lincoln. Both Nathanael Greene, of
Revolutionary War fame, and Ulysses Grant gave their
names to fourteen counties.[12]

Pennsylvania was named for a man who was both its
political and religious leader. The Quaker William Penn
received a land grant from Charles II in payment of a
debt. Because Quakers did not honor persons, Penn could
not propose that the colony be named for anyone,
including the king. Instead, he proposed Sylvania,
Latin for "forest land." Charles, perhaps with wry
humor, declared that the area would be called
Pennsylvania. Disappointed, Penn insisted that the name
be construed to mean "high or head woodlands," reasoning
that the Welsh word meaning "head" is pen. Though the
word was not the purest of borrowed words, it was much
too close for Penn's comfort.[13]

The Spanish and French explorers often named new
places for the saints on whose days they were

6

discovered. Lake Saint Clair in Michigan; Saint Elias,
a mountain in Alaska; and the Saint Lawrence River in
New York are three of many.[14] Ironically, the gentle
Saint Augustine, whose name was given to the oldest city
in the nation, was honored by the same Spanish explorer
who once captured about four hundred French, removed
only those who were Catholic or musicians, and ordered
the heads of all the others cut off.[15]

IC

The most common type of name-borrowing was the
naming of a town for a person little known, if at all,
beyond where he or she lived. This person was likely to
be one of the early settlers, prominent in the local
community. A record of such places would be so
extensive that dictionaries of place names normally do
not list them.

The naming of places for little-known people has a
long history, going back to the time the country was
being explored. Lewis and Clark named places for their
loved ones, who are otherwise unknown in history. Clark
named Fanny's Island for his sister, Judith's Creek for
his fiancée, and Martha's River for "the Selebrated
[sic] M. F." Lewis named Maria's River for his
sweetheart, explaining that "the waters of this

7

turbulent and troubled stream but illy comport with the
pure celestial virtue and amiable qualifications of this
lovely fair one."[16] Years later this tendency to name
places for little-known people was accelerated by the
many requests for acceptable names for post offices.
One official in the Post Office Department said that he
had named towns for all of his relatives and for "all
the kids on the block."[17]

IIA

Many U.S. place names exist in their present form
because of the process of corruption--that is, the form
of the word has been changed significantly. The
corruption often occurred because the translator was
ignorant of the original language, especially if it was
an Indian language. American Indian languages are so
different from English, French, and Spanish that many of
the Indian sounds do not even have equivalent sounds in
the languages the translators spoke. Furthermore, the
white men who reported the names usually had no training
in languages and no efficient system of recording.
Often these men recorded place names long after they had
partially forgotten what they had heard only
imperfectly.[18] The river that the white men eventually
called the Tombigbee comes from an Indian phrase similar

8

to <u>itombi-ikibi</u>;[19] Allegheny (river and mountains) is
probably a corruption of something like <u>eleuwi-geneu</u>.[20]
A great deal of confusion developed about Indian names
of the Eastern seaboard, for by the time linguists knew
enough to study the languages competently, few people
spoke them--in some cases, none. The name of a small
New Hampshire lake is an example of the confusion: a
national board for studying place names considered 132
forms of the name before settling on Winnipesaukee.[21]

    Corruption of place names has also occurred because
speakers of English were ignorant of a particular
European language. For example, the Spanish name for
Bone Island was Cayo Hueso. But people who did not know
Spanish accepted what they thought they heard, and the
name became Key West. The French called a particular
stream L'Ours Crique, or Bear Creek. Speakers of
English heard Loose Creek, and that became the name.[22]
A similar corruption caused what the French called Sumac
Couvert ("thicket of sumac bushes") to become known as
Smackover, Arkansas.[23]

    Corruption has sometimes occurred simply through a
mistake in the reading of a name. One of the most
thoroughly authenticated cases is that of Nome, Alaska.

IIB

9

Because a member of the survey crew working from a ship
did not know the name of a certain cape, he wrote a
question mark and the word Name at the appropriate place
on the map. Another member of the expedition read Nome
for Name and so recorded Cape Nome, the name that was
later printed from his record. The city took its name
from the Cape.[24]

Usually the Post Office Department, which must
officially accept a name before regular mail service can
be established, was involved in such mistakes. Often
the people in the communities accepted the erroneous
names docilely, for they cared more about getting a post
office than about how it was spelled. A new postmaster
in Alabama was asked to submit three names for his
community. He must have hoped that two of his
suggestions, Ink and Bird, would be rejected, for his
third recommendation was Arad, his son's name. But d
was mistaken for b, and the town was named Arab. In
another community, on the Chesapeake Bay, the postmaster
suggested the name Noon, since that was when the mail
boat arrived each day. But his handwriting was fancy,
and so he became instead the postmaster of Moon,
Virginia.[25]

10

Americans have invented many place names by
manufacturing names, by describing local phenomena, and
by commemorating local events. A manufactured name is
produced quite mechanically--by combining words or by
spelling backward. The names of a postmistress's
deceased husbands, Mr. Lea and Mr. Day, produced Leaday,
Texas;[26] Seroco, North Dakota, commemorates the first
item to reach there by mail, a Sears, Roebuck Company
catalog; Itmann, West Virginia, is named for I. T.
Mann.[27] Some names of border towns are manufactured:
Texarkana from Texas, Arkansas, and Louisiana; Calneva,
Calor, and Calzona from California and neighboring
states. Wabasso, Florida, is a backward spelling of the
Indian name Ossabaw; Tesnus, Texas, celebrates the
sunset; Ti, Oklahoma, reverses the initials of Indian
Territory.[28] Such manufactured names are numerous and
according to Stewart have flourished only in America.[29]

Invented names that describe geographic features
usually focus on the atypical. For example, Blowing
Rock, North Carolina, takes its name from a rock so
unusual that it was once featured in a Ripley
"Believe-it-or-Not" cartoon as "the only place in the
world where snow falls upside down." This phenomenon is

IIIA

IIIB

created by wind currents which blow from a gorge below
and up over Blowing Rock.[30] Such descriptive names are
numerous: Stinking Spring, Lookout, Marblehead, Picture
Rocks, Wind Gap, Rushingwater Creek.

Some of the descriptive names assigned by Indians
and early trappers to describe geographic features were
considered objectionable once a frontier area was
settled. Accordingly, when the Park Service and Forest
Service printed maps, they were careful not to use names
referring to private parts of human anatomy. Laird
reports an exception: ". . . <u>Trois</u> <u>Tetons</u>, a name given
by early trappers to three prominent peaks in what is
now Teton National park, was too well established to be
tampered with, and the words being French, the mammary
implications are lost on many speakers of English."[31]

A particular part of the plant life of an area has
sometimes been the source of a place name. Chicago is
an example. Seventeenth-century Frenchmen called the
place Chicagou, using the Indian name, which means
"onion." Similar words in the Algonquian language,
Stewart explains, "apply also to the skunk, and certain
kinds of bad-smelling filth." Some detractors have
suggested that the name should be "skunktown, or

12

something worse." But wild onions did grow in the area,
and three different Frenchmen reported that
interpretation in writing shortly after they heard
Chicagou. So the plant life seems to have determined
the name.[32] Less well-known place names stemming from
plant life abound: Rosharon, Texas; Verbena, Alabama;
Pea Ridge, Arkansas; Pecan Gap, Texas; and Pine Apple,
Alabama, named not for pineapple fields, but for pine
trees and apple orchards.[33]

Local disputes have been the sources for some of   IIIC
the invented names that commemorate events. One of the
most famous place names in America, Wounded Knee, South
Dakota, derived from violence.

        Two braves were in love with the same
        Indian maiden and while practicing with their
        bows and arrows near the headwaters of a
        creek, one of the Indians saw what he believed
        was an opportunity to disqualify his companion
        in the eyes of the maiden. Therefore he
        "accidentally" shot an arrow through the knee
        of his companion. This made him a cripple,
        and thus a poor hunter, and poor prospect for
        a husband. The area became known as Wounded
        Knee.[34]

13

Burnt Cabins, Pennsylvania, is another place that got
its name from a dispute. In 1730, after the Indians
complained that the white people had encroached on their
lands, the colonial government ordered that white
squatters be driven out of their cabins and that the
cabins be burned.[35] The name of Cut and Shoot, Texas,
is said to have resulted from an argument "over, of all
things, the pattern for a new church steeple!"[36] Some
disputes had happy endings. For example, Fighting
Corners, in New York, was a place where hill people and
valley people often fought; but after they quit
fighting, they named the place Friendship.[37]

Other place names commemorate deaths. Las Animas,
Colorado, took its name from el rio de las animas
perditas, which means "the river of lost souls." A
regiment of Spanish soldiers is said to have drowned
there.[38] And Strange Creek, in West Virginia, got its
name from an incident that Stewart reports: "Lost in the
forest, [William Strange] carved on a beech tree,
'Strange is my name, / and I'm on strange ground, / and
strange it is / that I cannot be found.' His skeleton
and inscription were later discovered."[39]

IIID

Frustration has been responsible for some place
names. The country had been settled so rapidly during

14

the nineteenth century that by the last quarter of the
century the Post Office Department had difficulty
keeping some sort of order in the record of names. The
Department rejected many, often to avoid multiple use of
a name in the same area, and much frustration developed
among people who wanted post offices. One California
community had so many names rejected that someone
suggested that they were not likely ever to get an
appropriate one. Another person recommended that they
try Likely, and that was accepted.[40] The Department
rejected a list of several hundred names for another
place. That community became Nameless, Georgia.[41]

But some of the frustration of establishing names
developed from citizens' inability to agree. A New York
community received its name only after a resident,
frustrated by the people's failure to agree on a
recommendation, proposed Discord to the Post Office
Department. Accord was approved.[42] The residents of
Juggville, New York, which was named for the drinking
jugs of lumbermen, were meeting to change their town's
name. Each time a name was suggested, people would
shout "No! O no!" Finally they agreed on Onoville.[43]
Wynot, Nebraska, got its name when one German settler
became so disgusted with hearing people in a meeting ask

15

"Why not this name?" and "Why not that name?" that he
yelled, "Vi not! Vi not! Name it Vi Not!"[44]

There was some frustration—and some irony, too—
at a meeting when the people of an Indiana community
chose a new name for their town.

> At a meeting in the log store, a heated
> argument ensued between an Englishman who
> wanted to call it Liverpool, a German who
> thought Brunswick would be a fine name, and a
> determined Irishman who insisted on Maloney.
> Peace was restored when a Mrs. Jackson
> suggested the name Chrubusco, to honor a
> recent victory by American troops over the
> Mexicans in the Mexican War. The Irishman
> said he couldn't pronounce it, but if it was
> for patriotic reasons he would accept it,
> "cause he was damn if he was going to have a
> foreign name for his town!" The motion was
> carried and the new post office got the
> distinctive name of Chrubusco. Years later it
> was discovered that Chrubusco was the War God
> of the ancient Indians of Mexico.[45]

16

I would like to end this paper on a personal note.
I have no illusions that my classification is leakproof.
Every student of place names will encounter overlapping
categories when trying to decide, for example, whether
Kentucky, which the Indians called something like
hentake,[46] is a borrowed name or a corrupted one. Such
decisions are typical "hard cases" in any system of
classification. What I have been concerned with is
finding a convenient way of organizing the data I have
discovered in my reading without getting bogged down in
conflicting details that would require more space than I
have available. As my thesis requires, I have dealt
only with the processes by which class names are
derived. Yet I am conscious that one cannot review the
scholarship on "more than a million"[47] place names
without acquiring insights into the history of our
country. The Indians, the Spanish, the French, and
immigrants from many countries have left the imprint of
their cultures in American place names. As one writer
puts it, "An examination of all these names, which are
now used by a mostly English-speaking population, could
not fail to yield some information about the
colonization of the United States, even if the history
were not known."[48]

These comments are numbered to correspond to the number of the endnote to which they refer. The comment is intended to call your attention to details in the form of the note and thus supplement the discussion on pages 350–353.

1.   First reference to a book. Except for the order of the author's names and the punctuation, the only differences between this note and the citation in the final bibliography are that here the facts of publication are enclosed in parentheses and the page number is given.

2.   This note consists of two parts: a citation of the source and an added comment explaining Stewart's nine classes referred to in the text. The citation is a first reference to an article in a journal. No publisher or place of publication is given, but volume, date, and page number are shown, in that order. For this particular journal, called *Names,* only the year is given for the date. Since this journal is published annually, the year alone is sufficient.

3.   Subsequent reference to a work already cited in note 1. Short form of the title is necessary to distinguish this book from others by the same author.

4.   To avoid unnecessary duplication of author and title, two different pages of the same work are cited in one note. Page 87 comes before page 33 because the reference to Mississippi in the paper comes before the reference to John Smith. It would be all right to cite Mississippi and Smith in two separate notes, but the *MLA Handbook* encourages such combination as is shown here.

6.   First reference to a journal published quarterly. Here *Spring* is necessary to avoid confusion with summer, fall, and winter issues.

7.   Citation of a Biblical source. The number preceding *Kings* distinguishes the first book of Kings from the second book; the numbers following *Kings* identify first the chapter and then the verse from which the quotation is taken. Notice that the Bible is not cited in the final bibliography. It never is.

8.   Since Mencken's work was published in an original volume followed by separate supplements, the supplement number is necessary.

17

Notes

¹ George R. Stewart, <u>Names on the Land: A</u>
<u>Historical Account of Place-Naming in the United States</u>,
revised and enlarged edition (Boston: Houghton Mifflin,
1958), p. 382.

² George R. Stewart, "A Classification of Place
Names," <u>Names</u>, 2 (1954), 2. Stewart sets up these nine
classes: "1) Descriptive names, 2) Possessive names, 3)
Incident names, 4) Commemorative names, 5) Euphemistic
names, 6) Manufactured names, 7) Shift names, 8) Folk
etymologies, 9) Mistake names."

³ Stewart, <u>Names on the Land</u>, p. 10.

⁴ Stewart, <u>Names on the Land</u>, pp. 87, 33.

⁵ Henry Gannett, <u>American Names: A Guide to the</u>
<u>Origin of Place Names in the United States</u> (Washington,
D.C.: Public Affairs Press, 1947), p. 196.

⁶ Frank A. Hoffman, "Place Names in Brown County,"
<u>Midwest Folklore</u>, 11 (Spring 1961), 60.

⁷ 1 Kings 5:6.

⁸ H. L. Mencken, <u>The American Language: An Inquiry</u>
<u>into the Development of English in the United States</u>,
supplement II (New York: Knopf, 1948), p. 532.

9.   The source of this information is both these pages.

10.   First reference to a work by two authors, in this case father and daughter. The small Roman numerals show that the information came from the Introduction, which is so numbered in the book.

12.   Another example of two widely separated pages being combined in a single note. The examples of Washington, Jefferson, Lincoln, Greene, and Grant are all used in the text to make a single point—that more places are named for Washington than for anybody else. For this purpose a single note can combine the information from the two pages cited.

14.   Subsequent reference to Gannett's work. Since Gannett, unlike Stewart, has only one book in the final bibliography, his name alone is a precise reference and no short title is needed.

18.   After the Laird citation the writer adds a comment about Mencken. He does not choose to put Mencken's remark in the text because it is not supported by other evidence and seems to be an example invented by Mencken; so he reports it as an aside in this note.

18

⁹ A. Howry Espenshade, Pennsylvania Place Names (State College, Pa.: The Pennsylvania State College, 1925), pp. 17–18.

¹⁰ René Coulet du Gard and Dominique Coulet du Gard, The Handbook of French Place Names in the U.S.A. (Chicago: Adams Press, 1974), pp. ix, xxi–xxvii.

¹¹ George R. Stewart, American Place-Names: A Concise and Selective Dictionary for the Continental United States of America (New York: Oxford Univ. Press, 1970), p. 349.

¹² Stewart, Names on the Land, pp. 164, 358.

¹³ Stewart, Names on the Land, pp. 102–04.

¹⁴ Gannett, pp. 270–71.

¹⁵ Stewart, Names on the Land, p. 19.

¹⁶ Stewart, Names on the Land, pp. 216–17.

¹⁷ Charlton Laird, Language in America (New York: World, 1970), p. 237.

¹⁸ Laird, p. 235. Mencken (p. 530) thinks that the white man's lack of knowledge of Indian languages made him vulnerable to malicious or jesting Indians. A white man, Mencken says, might ask an Indian the name for some place and be answered with the Indian equivalent of "Go to hell."

Comments on endnotes,
cont.

21.   This reference to four pages indicates that the writer is summarizing information contained in these pages of Mencken's work.

22.   First reference to an article in a magazine that is published oftener than once
a month. For such a magazine both the day and the month are necessary, and the
month is abbreviated.

25.   Same explanation as in notes 4 and 12: the Arab example comes from page
26, the Moon example from page 219.

33.   This note is necessary to document the explanation of *Pine Apple.* The origin
of the other names is self-evident.

19

[19] Stewart, <u>American Place-Names</u>, p. 488.

[20] Espenshade, p. 120.

[21] Mencken, pp. 526-29.

[22] Mario Pei, "Faraway Places with Strange-Sounding Names," <u>Saturday Review</u>, 10 Feb. 1958, p. 64.

[23] Myron J. Quimby, <u>Scratch Ankle, U.S.A.: American Place Names and Their Derivation</u> (New York: A. S. Barnes, 1969), p. 310.

[24] Stewart, <u>American Place-Names</u>, p. 331.

[25] Quimby, pp. 26, 219.

[26] Stewart, <u>American Place-Names</u>, p. 252.

[27] Mencken, p. 541.

[28] Stewart, <u>Names on the Land</u>, pp. 362-64.

[29] Stewart, <u>American Place-Names</u>, p. xxxi.

[30] Quimby, p. 52.

[31] Laird, pp. 236-37.

[32] Stewart, <u>Names on the Land</u>, pp. 86-87.

[33] Quimby, p. 258.

[34] Quimby, p. 381.

[35] Espenshade, p. 301.

[36] Quimby, p. 102.

[37] Harold W. Thompson, <u>Body, Boots & Britches</u> (Philadelphia: Lippincott, 1940), p. 451.

Comments on endnotes, cont.

48.   First reference to an article in an encyclopedia. The volume and page numbers are given because the reference is to only one page of a multipage article, and these numbers allow a reader to locate the information without reading the whole article. Notice that they are not given in the citation of this article in the final bibliography, because there only the article is being cited, not particular statements in that work.

20

[38] Gannett, p. 182.

[39] Stewart, American Place-Names, p. 462.

[40] Stewart, American Place-Names, p. 257.

[41] Gannett, p. 219.

[42] Quimby, p. 16.

[43] Thompson, p. 451.

[44] Quimby, p. 384.

[45] Quimby, pp. 85-86.

[46] Stewart, American Place-Names, p. 237.

[47] Mencken, p. 574.

[48] Ladislav Zgusta, "Names," Encyclopaedia
Britannica: Macropaedia, 1974 ed., XII, 819.

21

Bibliography

Coulet du Gard, René, and Dominique Coulet du Gard. The
    Handbook of French Place Names in the U.S.A.
    Chicago: Adams Press, 1974.

Espenshade, A. Howry. Pennsylvania Place Names. State
    College, Pa.: The Pennsylvania State College, 1925.

Gannett, Henry. American Names: A Guide to the Origin
    of Place Names in the United States. Washington,
    D.C.: Public Affairs Press, 1947.

Hoffman, Frank A. "Place Names in Brown County."
    Midwest Folklore, 11 (Spring 1961), 57-62.

Laird, Charlton. Language in America. New York: World,
    1970.

Mencken, H. L. The American Language: An Inquiry into
    the Development of English in the United States.
    Supplement II. New York: Knopf, 1948.

Pei, Mario. "Faraway Places with Strange-Sounding
    Names." Saturday Review, 10 Feb. 1958, pp. 64-65.

Quimby, Myron J. Scratch Ankle, U.S.A.: American Place
    Names and Their Derivation. New York: A. S.
    Barnes, 1969.

22

Stewart, George R. American Place-Names: A Concise and
Selective Dictionary for the Continental United
States of America. New York: Oxford Univ. Press,
1970.

----------. "A Classification of Place Names." Names,
2 (1954), 1-13.

----------. Names on the Land: A Historical Account of
Place-Naming in the United States. Revised and
enlarged edition. Boston: Houghton Mifflin, 1958.

Thompson, Harold W. Body, Boots & Britches.
Philadelphia: Lippincott, 1940.

Zgusta, Ladislav. "Names." Encyclopaedia
Britannica: Macropaedia. 1974 ed.

14

THE
BUSINESS
LETTER

The writing of a business letter as a college assignment serves a double purpose: to acquaint students with the conventional forms of business correspondence and to provide a practical application of the principles of effective composition. Of these two, the latter is the more important. The conventions of business correspondence should be understood and followed, but these conventions are easily learned. The effectiveness of any letter you write will depend, as it does in any composition, on what you have to say and how you say it.

THE FORM
OF A BUSINESS LETTER

The form of the business letter is relatively standardized. The letters in this chapter illustrate a common *block* style of arrangement, so called because no lines in any of the parts of the letter are indented. In some versions of the block arrangement, all parts start flush with the left margin, but the style shown here is usual for letters with a typewritten return address.

A business letter typically consists of seven parts, as the model on the next page shows. For your convenience as you study the letter and the discussion that follows, the various parts have been numbered.

1. *The Return Address.* This part is omitted, of course, if stationery with a printed letterhead is used, since the letterhead itself is the return address. The form used in the example is a *block heading* with *open punctuation.* In a block heading the lines are not indented; each line begins flush with the one preceding. In open punctuation no marks are used at the ends of lines, but elements within the lines are separated in accordance with the usual conventions. The two-letter abbreviation of the state is the form approved by the U.S. Postal Service as shown on page 386.

2. *The Date Line.* The date line is placed directly below the return address heading. The order in the date may be day-month-year without punctuation, as shown in the model, or month-day-year ("April 25, 1979") with a comma between day and year.

3. *The Inside Address.* This heading of three or more lines is placed flush with the left margin and follows the form established in the first heading. Abbreviations such as *Co.* and *Inc.* are used only if these terms are abbreviated in the letterheads of the companies being addressed.

4. *The Salutation.* When an individual is being addressed, the salutation usually takes one of the following forms: "Dear Mr. (or *Mrs., Ms.,* or *Miss)* Blank," or "Dear Sir (or *Madam),"* followed by a colon. The form "Dear Sirs" is seldom used in modern business letters, and such informal salutations as "Dear Bob" are acceptable only in writing to a friend. When the letter is addressed to a company or a department rather than to a named individual, the current trend is to make the salutation agree with the first line of the inside address, as shown in the sample letter on page 388. Until recently, the usual salutation in such cases was "Gentlemen," but this form has fallen into disfavor because it implies that business affairs are exclusively in the hands of males.

5. *The Body.* The body of the letter usually consists of one or more paragraphs of single-spaced text, with double spacing between paragraphs. All paragraphs start at the left margin, with no indentation to mark the opening of the paragraph.

117 Jefferson Street   *1*
Tallahassee, FL 32306
25 April 1979   *2*

    3

Mr. T. A. Swanson
Subscription Department
<u>Newstime</u>
250 N. Michigan Avenue
Chicago, IL 60601

Dear Mr. Swanson: *4*

Recently I received from you an offer of a six-months'
subscription to <u>Newstime</u> at half the newsstand price,
provided I subscribed before June 1.

I would like to take advantage of that offer, but since
I have a summer job that will require me to travel
through the Midwest, I will have no fixed address until
I return to school in the fall and therefore cannot
receive the summer issues.   *5*

Would it be possible to subscribe now and have my
subscription begin September 1? If not, can you give me
a similar rate for a nine-months' subscription from
September through May?

Sincerely yours,   *6*

Peter Wint

Peter Wint   *7*

6. *The Complimentary Close.* The most common endings are "Yours truly," "Yours sincerely," and "Sincerely yours." Such closes as "Cordially" or "Cordially yours" are used only when the writer is on familiar terms with the addressee. "Respectfully" is a formal close used chiefly in submitting a report. The complimentary close is punctuated with a comma.

7. *The Signature.* The signature consists of two parts: the written signature and the writer's typed name. Both parts are necessary. The written signature is the legal identification of the writer; the typed name below it is a safeguard against misreading. If a woman wants to be addressed as *Mrs.* or *Miss,* she may indicate the preferred form in parentheses before her typed name; otherwise she will probably be addressed as *Ms.* in a reply to her letter. The complimentary close and typed signature are in alignment and start in approximate alignment with the return address and date.

When a letter is typed by someone other than the author, the typist puts first the author's initials, then his or her own (with a colon between them) flush with the left margin and below the author's signature.

State Abbreviations

The following list shows the two-letter abbreviations of state names used by the U.S. Postal Service. Zip Code numbers may be obtained from your library or local post office.

AL	Alabama	LA	Louisiana	OH	Ohio
AK	Alaska	ME	Maine	OK	Oklahoma
AZ	Arizona	MD	Maryland	OR	Oregon
AR	Arkansas	MA	Massachusetts	PA	Pennsylvania
CA	California	MI	Michigan	RI	Rhode Island
CO	Colorado	MN	Minnesota	SC	South Carolina
CT	Connecticut	MS	Mississippi	SD	South Dakota
DE	Delaware	MO	Missouri	TN	Tennessee
FL	Florida	MT	Montana	TX	Texas
GA	Georgia	NE	Nebraska	UT	Utah
HI	Hawaii	NV	Nevada	VT	Vermont
ID	Idaho	NH	New Hampshire	VA	Virginia
IL	Illinois	NJ	New Jersey	WA	Washington
IN	Indiana	NM	New Mexico	WV	West Virginia
IA	Iowa	NY	New York	WI	Wisconsin
KS	Kansas	NC	North Carolina	WY	Wyoming
KY	Kentucky	ND	North Dakota		

THE CONTENT
OF THE LETTER

In writing the letter, be as brief and as clear as you can. There is seldom any
need to make the letter longer than one page. If it has to be longer, try to avoid
having the second page contain only a sentence or two. If you type your first draft,
as you should, you will be able to see whether a slight adjustment of the margins
will allow the final copy to go on one page, or whether you can space the letter so
that it will be at least 1½ pages long.

Brevity does not mean incomplete communication. Give your addressee all the
information he or she needs to respond to your letter. The kind of information
required will depend on the kind of letter you are writing. In this chapter we will
discuss three common kinds: a letter of inquiry, a letter asking for an adjustment,
and a letter of application for a job.

LETTER OF INQUIRY

The letter on page 385 is a typical letter of inquiry. It asks the specific information and explains why the information is needed. Sometimes, however, your
question will require not only a fuller answer than this sample letter calls for but
also considerable effort on the part of the addressee. As much as possible, reduce
that effort by making sure that your inquiry is addressed to the proper person or
department and by taking care that it is clearly worded. If you are asking a series of
questions, it is helpful to set them off from the rest of the paragraph and number
them.

LETTER ASKING
AN ADJUSTMENT

The letter asking for an adjustment, sometimes called a complaint letter, usually
reports that a product or service was not satisfactory and requests some kind of
corrective action. The letter on page 388 is an example.

The important things to remember in writing to request an adjustment are
these:

1.   Check the facts to be sure that your complaint is justified. It would be
embarrassing to discover later that the mistake was yours, not the addressee's.

221 N. Clark
Lakewood, CA 90714
June 3, 1979

Catalogue Department
Acme Products
P. O. Box 117
Van Nuys, CA 91408

Catalogue Department:

On May 10 I ordered from page 74 of your Summer
Catalogue a variable-speed reversing drill (Model
7190) at $28.49 and enclosed my check for that
amount. I am enclosing a Xerox copy of my order.

Yesterday I received a variable-speed drill which is
not reversible. This drill is similar to Model 7114
in your catalogue, where it is priced at $23.99.
This drill will not meet my needs.

Will you please send me the drill I ordered or, if
Model 7190 is no longer available at the catalogue
price, refund the purchase price? I will return the
non-reversing drill when I hear from you.

Yours truly,

Henry Dent

Henry Dent

2.   Avoid an angry or indignant tone. Do not assume that the error or failure you are reporting was intentional. Just state the facts clearly and courteously.

3.   Provide all the information your addressee will need to see that an adjustment should be made, but do not take more space than is necessary.

LETTER OF APPLICATION

In this section we assume that you are applying for a job that requires a letter of application. Many jobs do not. If you are seeking part-time work selling in a department store, pumping gas in a service station, or doing clerical work for one of the college departments, the best procedure is to apply in person to whoever does the hiring for that job. A letter of application is necessary only when the importance of the position requires that the applicants be screened before they are interviewed, or when the applicant is living at some distance and wants to arrange an interview. For example, a summer job as a typist or receptionist in your home town might be obtained by an application in person if you were at home. But if you are at college and return home only on vacations, you might want to arrange an interview for the next time you go home. In such a situation you might write a letter such as the one shown on page 390. Notice that this letter is supplemented by a data sheet. The information on the data sheet could have been incorporated in the letter, but the great advantage of a data sheet is that it enables the reader to take in all details at a glance.

LETTER WITH DATA SHEET

The letter consists typically of three parts: (1) the lead, (2) the highlights, and (3) the request for an interview.

Lead   The lead is an introductory paragraph in which you explain what job you are applying for and how you learned of it. The source of the lead is usually an advertisement or, as in our example, the recommendation of a friend or an employee in the company.

Highlights   Although your data sheet provides details, a brief paragraph highlighting your special qualifications will direct the reader's attention to your strongest points as an applicant for the job. Refer the reader to your data sheet for detailed information.

115 Sellman Hall
Mansfield College
Belton, KY 42314
May 14, 1979

Mrs. Margaret Wilson
Office Manager
Ingrahms Stationery Products
284 Main Street
Selkirk, TN 37864

Dear Mrs. Wilson:

I wonder if you will need someone to serve as a
temporary typist, receptionist, or clerk while regular
employees are on vacation during the summer. My friend
Sue Baker, who is secretary to Mr. Enders, tells me that
you often have need of such help. If that is the case
this year, I would like to apply.

At present I am a first-year student at Mansfield
College and would like to work during the three months
from June 15 to September 15 before I return to college
in the fall. Last year, in a summer job at Taylor's
Department Store, I gained experience in general office
work through the miscellaneous duties of a clerical
assistant. The attached data sheet will give you this
and other information about me.

I would be happy to come for an interview. I will be at
home in Selkirk between May 29 and June 5, but I can
probably arrange an earlier meeting if that is more
convenient for you. I can be reached by letter or
telephone at my college address. May I look forward to
hearing from you?

Sincerely yours,

Mary Helen Carter

Mary Helen Carter

MARY HELEN CARTER

Present address: 115 Sellman Hall   Phone: (606) 577-2808
                      Mansfield College
                      Belton, KY 42314

Permanent address: 28 Crescent Avenue   Phone: 565-2116
                   Selkirk, TN 37865

Education

1978-1979 Mansfield College, first year. Major not yet
          decided but probably either English or Psychology.
          Point average to date, 3.4 on a scale of 4.

1974-1978 Central High School, Selkirk. Graduated in top
          quarter of class of 96 students.
          College-preparatory program supplemented by
          electives in Advanced Typing, Art, and Speech.

Experience

1978, summer
          Taylor's Department Store, Selkirk. Clerical
          assistant in the office; duties included Xeroxing,
          typing, and relieving regular operator on
          switchboard.

1976 and 1977, Christmas seasons
          Taylor's. Sales clerk.

Personal Details

Age: 19

Health: Excellent

Hobbies: Amateur theatricals, photography

Activities:
          (Mansfield College) Drama Club
          (Central High School) Class representative on the
             Student Council, 1976, 1977, 1978; assistant editor
             of Centerpiece, the senior yearbook; parts in two
             Gilbert and Sullivan operettas.

References

The following people, all from Selkirk, have kindly told me that
they will be glad to provide references whenever I need them:

Ms. Dorothy Stanley   Mr. William White
Assistant Office Manager   Director of Music and Drama
Taylor's Department Store   Central High School
Bus. phone 222-8482   Bus. phone 222-5069

Dr. Alan Kincaid   Rev. Alexander Lee
Counselor   Minister
Central High School   First Presbyterian Church
Bus. phone 222-5069   Bus. phone 565-3107

Request for an interview   For the kind of job for which a letter of application is necessary, the employer will want to see and talk with several applicants. If the job is a desirable one, there will be many applicants. Not all of these will be chosen for interviews, but those who are will be chosen on the evidence of their letters. The immediate purpose of your letter, then, is to obtain an interview. For this reason, take pains with your letter and always ask for an interview.

DATA SHEET

Put your name at the top of the sheet. Immediately under it give the address and telephone number at which you can be reached.

Group your data under the following headings, which are arranged roughly in order of importance: Education, Experience, Personal Details (optional), and References. (An applicant with considerable work experience would probably put that heading first.) A prospective employer is guided chiefly by the information under the first two headings, but personal details and references can also contribute pertinent information.

Education   As a college freshman you have a rather limited educational background. Probably most other applicants for the job will also have at least a high school diploma. When you are ready to graduate from college, you will have a more impressive educational record, but meanwhile you make the most of what you have. If your scholastic rank or grade-point average is high, you will want to include that information, as Mary Helen Carter does in her data sheet. Perhaps you have taken some courses that are definitely or possibly job-related, such as Ms. Carter's electives in advanced typing (clerk-typist) and speech (receptionist). Arrange your list of items in reverse chronological order—that is, from present to past.

Experience   Some undergraduates who have returned to college after a period in business, industry, or military service may have much to report under this heading, but most freshmen have had very limited work experience. If this is true in your case, make the most of whatever part-time or occasional job experience you can offer, and let the prospective employer decide whether it is enough to qualify you for further consideration. Even if the jobs you have held bear no relation to the kind of job for which you are now applying, any work experience counts in your favor, especially if you can back it up with a reference from a former employer who found you capable and dependable. Again, use reverse chronology in your listing.

Personal details   Under the optional heading "Personal Details" you may include factual information about yourself not given elsewhere in your letter or data sheet. By law, there are many personal data that an employer may not require an applicant to provide. You may volunteer whatever information you wish, but it is advisable to select those details that bear most directly on your potential to do the job for which you are applying. For example, your membership in student organizations or honor societies, your election to club or class office, or even your hobbies might suggest to an employer some job-related qualities that reinforce your other data.

References   As references, choose three or four people who have indicated that they think well of you and who are in a position to vouch for your education, experience, and character. Always ask their permission to use their names as references. Give their full names, job titles, and mailing addresses. It is considerate to provide also the business telephone numbers of any who live in the same town or telephone area as the prospective employer.

LETTER WITHOUT A DATA SHEET

If you do not have much detailed information to supply in a data sheet, you may prefer to omit the data sheet and incorporate in a letter the elements discussed above. A letter without a data sheet usually consists of five or six brief paragraphs starting with the lead. Successive paragraphs cover education, experience, personal information (optional), and references (an offer to supply them or a listing on a separate sheet). The letter closes with a request for an interview and information on how you can be reached by mail and telephone.

THE STYLE OF THE LETTER

Here are the most important things to keep in mind in preparing the final draft of a letter of application:

1.   Follow the conventional business forms shown in earlier pages.

2.   Compose the letter so that it makes an attractive appearance on the page, or on two pages if a second is necessary.

3.   Be sure that the letter is completely free of errors of grammar, punctuation, and spelling, and of strikeovers and interlinear corrections. Such errors are likely to disqualify an applicant from further consideration. You cannot talk about your

character in your letter of application, but you can display competence through neatness and accuracy.

4.   Avoid slang, colloquialisms, and jargon. Especially avoid outdated business jargon such as "Re your advertisement," "Pursuant to the request for an inter-view," "With reference to my educational background, I would say . . . ," or anything else that is not natural in your writing but sounds like the way you think business people write.

5.   Do not try to be impressive by using big or flowery words or unusual constructions. A letter of application is a formal communication, but the employer is looking for clearly presented information, not a sample of a literary style.

6.   Do not make judgments about yourself or your qualifications. It is all right to say, "I feel that the experience in the speech course and the theater has helped me to overcome a certain shyness in situations where I have to speak in public." But it is not all right to say, "This experience makes me well qualified to perform the duties that will be expected of me." Let the facts of the data sheet and the testimony of your references help the employer to judge whether or not you are likely to perform well on the job.

7.   Do not try to flatter the employer. Statements such as "Your company is so widely known as a leader in its field that I would be honored to be a small cog in so great a machine" sound insincere and are more likely to harm than help an applicant's chances.

EXERCISES   A.   In the following letter all parts except the salutation and the body have been omitted to save space. Study the letter and then discuss it in class.

> Dear Sir:
>
> This is an application for a position.
>
> For months I have been investigating different firms interested in hiring college graduates that have majored in foreign economics and export trade. In the course of my investigation I have found there is a place in your organization for a man of my talents and education.
>
> Your firm is interested in people who have majored in economics, with particular stress on foreign trade. I have studied every phase of economics and am well prepared.
>
> I have not yet had any job---I'm still young---but I am confident I can meet your requirements.

> The college officials will recommend me, if you will
> write them.
>
> I shall be glad to have an interview with you. Any time
> will do.

B. Using Mary Helen Carter's application as a model, write a letter with accompanying data sheet for any position for which you feel qualified. Do not invent details of education or experience. Simply do the best you can with what you have to offer.

HANDBOOK

OF

GRAMMAR

AND

USAGE

THE EVOLUTION OF ENGLISH

The language that Americans speak and write is descended from the language spoken by the English, Scottish, and Irish immigrants who founded the British colonies in America. Their language, in turn, was descended from the languages of Germanic tribes who, during the fifth and sixth centuries, invaded Britain and settled there. One of these tribes, the Angles, later became known as the Englisc (English) and gave their name to a country and a language, both of which they shared with other peoples—the Saxons, the Jutes, and, later, the Danes and the Normans.

The language that has come down to us from that Anglo-Saxon beginning has undergone great changes. Modern college students find Chaucer's fourteenth-century English something of a puzzle. And before Chaucer—well, judge for yourself. Here is the opening of the Lord's Prayer as it was written in the ninth, fourteenth, and seventeenth centuries, respectively:

Old English	Middle English	Modern English
Fæder ūre þū þe eart on heofonum, sī þīn nama gehālgod. Tōbecume þīn rīce, Gewurþe ðīn willa on eorðan swā swā on heofonum.	Oure fadir that art in heuenes, halwid be thi name; thi kyngdom cumme to; be thi wille don as in heuen and in erthe.	Our Father which art in heaven, Hallowed be thy name. Thy kingdom come. Thy will be done on earth as it is in heaven.

A contrast of these three versions offers a brief but revealing impression of the changes that occurred in the language during eight hundred years, and these differences would seem even greater if we could reproduce also the changes in sound that took place. For example, Old English *ū* and *ī* were pronounced like the *oo* in *boot* and the *e* in *me* respectively, so that *ūre* was pronounced "oo'ruh" and *sī,* "see."

In grammar the major change has been the simplification of grammatical forms. Old English (700–1100) was a highly *inflected* language, one that made grammatical distinctions by changes in the form of a word. For example, nouns were declined in five cases (nominative, genitive, dative, accusative, and instrumental) as well as in singular and plural numbers. Adjectives and the definite article were declined to agree with the nouns they modified. Here is the declension, in the singular only, of "the good man" with the approximate pronunciation enclosed in quotation marks at the right:

Case	Declension	Pronunciation
N. (*man* as subject)	sē gōda mann	"say goada man"
G. ("of the good man" or "the good man's")	ðaes gōdan mannes	"thas goadan mannes"
D. ("to the good man")	ðǣm gōdan menn	"tham goadan men"
A. (*man* as object)	ðone gōdan mann	"thonna goadan man"
I. ("by the good man")	ðȳ gōdan menn	"thee goadan men"

In Modern English the article and the adjective are not declined at all. The noun retains the genitive case and has singular and plural forms. We distinguish between subject and object by word order, and we have replaced the dative and instrumental endings by the prepositions *to* and *by.* As a result, the whole declensional system has been greatly simplified. Verbs still show considerable inflection, though much less than in Old English.

Along with this simplification of grammatical forms went a great increase in vocabulary as new words were introduced through association with foreign cultures. During the eighth and ninth centuries Scandinavian raiders settled along the coast and brought into the language some fourteen hundred place names and about one thousand common words. In 1066 the Normans conquered England, and for three hundred years their French language dominated the court and the affairs in which the nobility was most involved—government, army, law, church, art, architecture, fashions, and recreation. Between 1100 and 1500 over ten thousand French words were absorbed into the language. During the fourteenth, fifteenth, and sixteenth centuries English writers borrowed heavily from Latin. It is estimated that more than half of the present English vocabulary came from Latin, either directly or through one of the Romance languages, especially French. And as the English-speaking countries grew in political, economic, and cultural importance, their language borrowed from all over the world the words it needed to name the things and ideas that Anglo-Americans were acquiring. Today the vocabulary of the English language is international in origin, as the following list illustrates:

algebra (Arabic)	dollar (German)	polo (Tibetan)
amen (Hebrew)	flannel (Welsh)	silk (Chinese)
bantam (Javanese)	garage (French)	shampoo (Hindi)
boor (Dutch)	garbage (Italian)	ski (Norwegian)
caravan (Persian)	inertia (Latin)	tag (Swedish)
cashew (Portuguese)	kimono (Japanese)	toboggan (American Indian)
chorus (Greek)	leprechaun (Old Irish)	vodka (Russian)
coffee (Turkish)	polka (Polish)	whiskey (Gaelic)

STANDARDS OF USAGE

A description of a language is a description of the speaking and writing habits of the people who use it. Since there are some 300,000,000 users of English, widely separated geographically, culturally, and socially, many differences distinguish the English of one group from that of the others. These variations within a common language are called *dialects*. For example, in some ways the English spoken in Britain differs from that spoken in the United States. The British say "lift" when we would say "elevator," "torch" when we would use "flashlight," "bonnet" when we would speak of "the hood of a car"; they pronounce *garage* with the accent on the first syllable and *controversy* with the accent on the second; and they pronounce *schedule* as though it were written "shedule." Yet, despite many such differences, American and British English are mutually understandable dialects of a common language. A visitor to either country may be often amused but seldom confused by national differences.

Within the United States there are noticeable differences between the speech of natives of Atlanta and that of people raised in Boston, the Bronx, or Chicago. Even in a single city there will be language variations that can be attributed to differences in education and cultural background. But seldom do these differences interfere with communication. A Harvard professor and a Detroit factory worker would be able to carry on a conversation about the World Series, enjoy Archie Bunker or Johnny Carson on television, and read the news in the *Detroit Free Press*. Their individual dialects would be less important than the language they have in common.

The dialect that American schools have historically taught is called *Standard English*. This is a social rather than a regional dialect. *Webster's Third New International Dictionary* defines it as

> the English that with respect to spelling, grammar, pronunciation, and vocabulary is substantially uniform though not devoid of regional differences, that is well-established by usage in the formal and informal speech and writing of the educated, and that is widely recognized as acceptable wherever English is spoken and understood.

We can simplify this definition by saying that Standard English is the usage of educated speakers and writers of English. Schools generally stress this dialect, and it is the standard by which expository writing in schools and colleges is judged.

Even within Standard English, though, decisions about what is acceptable usage are sometimes troublesome for three reasons. First, in an evolving language, usage will change. The change will be greatest in the vocabulary, as new words are introduced, old words are given new meanings, and some words cease to be used. Spellings, pronunciations, styles of punctuation, and grammatical constructions that were not recognized by one generation may be accepted by another, and there is likely to be a "usage gap" between what people think standard usage is and what it has, in fact, become.

Second, educated speakers and writers vary their usage with the situation, so that there are differences between the way they speak with their friends and the way they write on serious matters for strangers. These differences are not between educated and uneducated usage but between different styles within the standard dialect. Whether formal or informal usage is preferable depends not on which is more "correct" but on which is more appropriate to the writing or speaking situation.

Finally, many people have strong opinions about usage and approve or condemn certain uses no matter what the facts are.

These three conditions sometimes make it difficult for people to agree on whether particular constructions are or are not standard usage. For example, even on such an apparently simple question as whether "alright" is an accepted spelling, reputable dictionaries disagree. *Webster's Third New International* says it is, *The American Heritage Dictionary* calls it "a common misspelling," and *Webster's New World Dictionary* labels it "a disputed spelling."

When judgments about particular usages are so divided, the division suggests that the usage is changing and that the two forms are in competition. This is a common situation in a living, hence changing, language. In the past *honour, labour,* and *valour* have lost out to *honor, labor,* and *valor* in American usage; *shirt* and *skirt,* which were originally English and Norse variants of the name for a garment worn by either men or women, have become different words with different meanings; foreign pronunciations have been naturalized (French *coupé* has lost its accent and changed its pronunciation from "coo-pay" to "coop"); foreign plurals have been forced into English patterns *(gymnasia* became *gymnasiums; data are* has retained the plural verb in formal and scientific writing, but become *data is* in informal writing). No doubt each of these changes was first condemned as a mistake, then called a disputed usage, and finally accepted as standard. The history of the language shows that when mistakes become common enough they cease to be mistakes.

Despite specific disagreements, there is still general agreement about the main conventions of Standard English. These conventions are generalizations about how the language is used, and as long as the generalizations actually report educated usage, they provide norms against which we can check our own practices. If we want to call these generalizations "rules," we can do so, as in "rules of spelling," "rules of punctuation," "rules of grammar"; but it would be misleading to include them all under the heading "rules of grammar," since spelling and punctuation are not parts of grammar. The blanket term to cover them all would be "rules of usage."

The handbook that follows is a reference section in which you can check your usage against the norms of standard English. The material is organized under eight main headings, the first five of which are marked by an identifying letter: *sentence structure* (**S**), *diction* (**D**), *word order* (**WO**), *grammatical forms* (**GF**), *punctuation* (**P**), *mechanics* (spelling, capitalization, italics, and so on), a *glossary* of grammatical and literary terms, and a *checklist* that identifies particular words and constructions that frequently give student writers trouble. Under each lettered heading, the numbered sections deal with specific parts of the subject. Thus sections S2–S4 deal with the distinction between sentences and nonsentences; S6–S9 deal with inconsistencies in sentence patterns. It is assumed that your instructor will decide from your writing which conventions you need to study and will refer you to the section or sections dealing with them.

S

SENTENCE
STRUCTURE

S1 REVIEW OF SENTENCE ELEMENTS

Know how to recognize the basic elements in any sentence.

The basic elements of a sentence are subject, verb, object, complement, modifier, and connective. These elements can be represented by the symbols S, V, O, C, M, and +; they are identified in the following examples:

	S	V
1.	Nobody	came.

(Simple subject followed by *intransitive* verb—a verb that does not require an object.)

```
    S    V    O
```
2. We have time.   (Subject followed by *transitive* verb
                                      and its necessary object.)

```
    M    S    V    C
```
3. Her father is a lawyer.   (Subject preceded by its modifier, then
                                      followed by *linking* verb and its noun
                                      complement.)

```
    S    V    +    V    O
```
4. They washed and polished the car.   (Compound verb connected by *and.*)

Each of these four sentences says something about its *subject.* What it says about that subject is called the *predicate.* The predicate may be just an intransitive verb (example 1), a transitive verb and its object (example 2), or a linking verb and its complement (example 3). The subject and one of these basic forms of the predicate make a basic, or kernel, sentence.

The most common **subjects** are nouns and pronouns, but a group of words (a *phrase*) may also serve as a subject, as in the following examples:

Most of the books were damaged.

The end of the story puzzled me.

When a group of words has a subject and verb of its own, it is called a *clause.* A clause, too, may serve as the subject of a sentence. In

What everyone wants is more time

the italicized words make up a clause that serves as the subject.

Verbs may be single words or phrases, but never clauses. When they require an object to complete the predicate, they are called *transitive* verbs, as in "He caught the ball," in which the transitive verb *caught* is completed by the direct object *ball.* When a verb does not require an object to make a complete predicate, it is called *intransitive,* as in "I refused"; "They arrived"; "The child cried." Many verbs may be transitive or intransitive according to the structure of a sentence: "She *sings* (transitive) the National Anthem at every game," or "She *sings* (intransitive) beautifully." A verb is called a *linking* verb when it completes the predicate by linking the subject to a following noun or adjective. For example, compare these two sentences:

She telephoned a doctor.

She became a doctor.

In both sentences *doctor* is necessary for a complete predicate. In the first sentence *doctor* is the **object** of the transitive verb *telephoned,* because the doctor received the action performed by the subject. But in the second sentence no action is performed on the doctor. The verb *became* merely links the subject to the doctor. In such sentences we say that *doctor* is not the object but the **complement** of the verb. In the following sentences the italicized adjectives are complements of linking verbs:

Mary looks *tired.*

That offer seems *reasonable.*

Dad remained *unconvinced.*

The most common linking verb is some form of the verb *to be (is, are, was, were, have been,* and so on), but *become, get, feel, look, seem, smell, taste,* and some other verbs may serve as links between the subject and the complement.

EXERCISE   Identify each of the underlined elements as a subject, verb, object, or complement by writing the appropriate letter above it.

1.   They tried it and it worked.

2.   Nobody likes her; she is too sarcastic.

3.   That dog looks vicious.

4.   Those who trust you will not need an explanation.

5.   I doubt that he will go, but I'll ask him.

6.   Did you get the tickets?

7.   Part of the sentence is illegible.

8.   They paid you a compliment.

9.   The trouble with Bill is that he is too sensitive.

10.   We discovered that it was our fault.

In general, a **modifier** describes a subject, object, complement, or another modifier or tells where, when, why, how, or under what conditions the action of the verb takes place. The italicized modifiers in the following sentences illustrate these uses:

Old soldiers never die.	(Modifies the subject.)
We had a *second* chance.	(Modifies the object.)
Honesty is the *best* policy.	(Modifies the complement.)
They came *early.*	(Modifies the verb—tells when.)
What do you have *in your hand?*	(Modifies the verb—tells where.)

I will go, *if you pay my way.*   (Modifies the verb—tells under what
                                     conditions.)

She had a *disturbingly* hostile look.   (Modifies the modifier *hostile.*)

Connectives (or *conjunctions*) are sentence elements that join other elements in a sentence. They usually come between the elements they join. The two most common types are coordinating and subordinating connectives. A **coordinating connective** *(and, or, nor, but, either . . . or, neither . . . nor, yet)* joins two grammatically similar elements:

He fought cleverly *and* courageously.   (Connects two adverbs.)

I'll do it, *but* I won't like it.   (Connects two main clauses.)

A **subordinating connective** does two things: it joins two clauses and subordinates one to the other. Thus if we change "He is cross. He is tired" to "He is cross because he is tired," we have connected two main clauses and reduced the second one to a subordinate clause by the use of the subordinating connective *because.* In the following examples the subordinate clauses are in parentheses and the connectives are in italics:

I don't know (*why* he did it).

He did not say (*when* he would return).

You may go (*whenever* you please).

In these examples the subordinating connective comes between the clauses it joins. But a subordinate clause may precede the main clause, and then the connective will come at the beginning of the sentence:

(*If* you seriously object), I won't do it.

(*Because* I flatter him), he likes me.

(*Since* you are in a hurry), I won't bother you about it now.

Using subordinating connectives as clues, enclose in parentheses all subordinate   **EXERCISE**
clauses in the following sentences, and state whether they act as subjects, objects, complements, or modifiers.

1. I will do whatever you say.

2. What he told me is none of your business.

3. The book that I bought cost eight dollars.

4. The man who is wearing the plaid shirt is his uncle.

5. If that is how you feel, why don't you leave?

6. The people who lived in that house moved to Minnesota.

7. He said that he was terribly embarrassed.

8. This is the book that I want.

9. I would like to know why they did it.

10. When you are ready, call me.

VERBS AND VERBALS

Much of the trouble with verbs comes from a failure to distinguish verbs from verbals. **A verbal** is derived from a verb but does not act as one in a sentence. In the sentences

Wrestling is a body-building sport.

To wait is sometimes not easy.

He spoke in *threatening* terms.

the italicized words may look like verbs, but they do not act as verbs. *Wrestling* and *to wait* are the subjects of their sentences; *threatening* modifies *terms*.

Verbals are of three types: infinitives, participles, and gerunds. **Infinitives** are verbals of the type *to do, to choose, to be seeking, to have said.* Usually, but not always, they begin with the infinitive marker *to.* They often serve as subjects, objects, or complements and may occasionally act as modifiers.

To do that takes nerve.	(Infinitive phrase is the subject.)
He asked *to be excused.*	(Infinitive phrase is object of *asked.*)
He seems *to be worried.*	(Infinitive phrase is complement of *seems.*)
I bought it *to read,* if I have time *to spare.*	(Infinitives are modifiers.)

A **participle** is a word or phrase that is derived from a verb but acts as a modifier. The present participle ends in *-ing (crying, smiling, sulking).* Most past participles end in *-ed (disgusted, abused, inspired),* but many are irregular *(chosen, grown, kept, slung).* The following sentences illustrate forms and uses of participles:

His *fighting* days are over.	(Present participle modifies subject.)
He is a *fighting* fool.	(Present participle modifies complement.)
Discouraged by the lack of public support the mayor resigned.	(Past participle modifies *mayor.*)
Goldsmith wrote a poem about a *deserted* village.	(Past participle modifies *village,* the object of *about.*)

Having been deserted by her husband, she supported the family. (Passive form of past participle modifies subject *she.*)

A **gerund,** or verbal noun, has the same form as the present participle but is used as a subject, object, or complement in a sentence.

Thinking is hard work. (Gerund is subject of *is.*)

That will take some *doing.* (Gerund is object of *will take.*)

What bothers them is his *swearing.* (Gerund is complement of *is.*)

Identify infinitives, participles, and gerunds in the following sentences and tell   **EXERCISE** whether they act as subjects, objects, complements, or modifiers.

1.   Nobody wants to tell him.

2.   This is a thrilling story.

3.   The course requires too much reading.

4.   To play as well as she does takes more time than I can afford.

5.   A drunken man is usually a bore.

6.   Disappointed by the results, he gave up the experiment.

7.   With screeching brakes, the car came to a jarring stop.

8.   That will take some thinking.

9.   Not to have invited her would have caused trouble.

10.   Feeling sorry for yourself will not solve the problem.

S2   PERIOD FAULT AND SENTENCE FRAGMENT

Use complete sentences, not sentence fragments, in expository writing. Especially avoid separating a subordinate clause or phrase from its main clause by a period.

Sentence fragment	Explanation	Full Sentence
We decided to stay home for the holidays. *Because the gasoline shortage made driving too uncertain.*	*The italicized element is a subordinate clause and therefore only part of a sentence. It must be included in the full sentence, as shown at the right.*	We decided to stay home for the holidays because the gasoline shortage made driving too uncertain.

Sentence fragment	Explanation	Full Sentence
Professor Carlson gave us a choice. Either *to write a 1000-word essay out of class or to take a midterm exam in class.*	*The infinitives* to write *and* to take *are verbals, not verbs; therefore, the words after the first period are not a sentence.*	Professor Carlson gave us a choice, either to write a 1000-word essay out of class or to take a midterm exam in class.
Several of my friends earn a major part of their college expenses. *Attending* classes during the day, *working* in the early evening, and then *studying* later at night.	*The italicized words are verbals, not verbs. They are changed to verbs at the right.*	Several of my friends earn a major part of their college expenses. They attend classes during the day, work in the early evening, and then study later at night.

In the examples to the left above, a period comes between a main clause and a subordinate clause or phrase. The words following that period are a **sentence fragment**—a part of a sentence punctuated as if it were a complete sentence. The incorrect use of the period represented here is a **period fault.** As the revisions indicate, period faults may be corrected either by changing the period to a comma, thus incorporating the separated phrase or clause into the sentence to which it belongs, or by expanding the fragment into a main clause so it can stand as an independent sentence.

EXERCISE   In the following sentences correct the period faults:

1. He has only one ambition. To play professional football.

2. Having come this far. We must see the matter through.

3. In a persuasive speech you should try to appeal to the whole audience. Not just to those who believe as you do.

4. We made our way up the mountain trail with much difficulty. Slipping on rocks and snagging our clothes in the underbrush.

5. Anticipating that our team would be named to the top twenty. We forgot that our defense was only mediocre.

6. Whatever challenge the office presents. I believe our new member of Congress will meet it successfully.

7. When our mayor announced, "I will not compromise on any issue on which I have taken a stand." That's when I began to question his judgment.

S 3   FUSED SENTENCES

Do not fuse two sentences by omitting necessary terminal punctuation between them.

Fused sentences

There are several words similar in meaning to the word *happiness* three of them are *bliss, contentment,* and *felicity.*

Be sure to set your alarm by dawn we must be well on our way.

Fused sentences can be quite confusing to a reader when we know how to revise them we can easily avoid the confusion.

Why do you ask how does it concern you?

Separated sentences

There are several words similar in meaning to the word *happiness.* Three of them are *bliss, contentment,* and *felicity.*

Be sure to set your alarm. By dawn we must be well on our way.

Fused sentences can be quite confusing to a reader. When we know how to revise them, we can easily avoid the confusion.

Why do you ask? How does it concern you?

Revise the fused sentences in these examples:

EXERCISE

1.   At the half it seemed that the Jets would be in the playoffs when the game was over they were out of the running.

2.   Let's make up our minds about this matter there is certain to be much disagreement, whatever we decide.

3.   The food service in the student union must be investigated unless better food is served business will drop drastically.

4.   We must know what we mean when we punctuate we use punctuation marks to make our meaning clear.

5.   Every lesson we have learned so far in the campaign has proved to be helpful in the last half of the campaign, though, there will certainly be much more to learn.

6.   I find it difficult to believe he would act in such a way that is not at all like him.

7.   Why do you want to make such an offer if you know they will refuse it what do you hope to gain?

S 4   R U N - O N   S E N T E N C E S

Do not string together a number of main clauses with *but, and, for, so,* or *and so.*

Sentences so formed are called **run-on sentences.** They can be improved if part of the material is made subordinate to the rest, as shown in the following revisions:

Run-on sentence	Revision
The committee was trying to coordinate the events for Homecoming weekend, but various campus organizations were secretly engaged in plans to outshine each other, for competition among these organizations goes far back into the school's history, and so persuading them to cooperate was no easy task.	While the committee was trying to coordinate the events for Homecoming weekend, various campus organizations were secretly engaged in plans to outshine each other. Because competition among these organizations goes far back into the school's history, persuading them to cooperate was no easy task.

EXERCISE   Remove the run-on effect in the following examples:

1.   I was not sure which flight Jim would arrive on, so I met all the planes coming in from Atlanta, but he was on none of them and so I decided that I was wrong about which day he was coming.

2.   You object to having been misled, and so do I, and so we should be able to find a common ground for agreement.

3.   I examined all reasonable transportation possibilities and I concluded that indeed I was stranded, so I called the professor whose exam I was to take next day and told her that I would probably be absent, and then I started to hitchhike back to school.

4.   I was interested in learning about Thomas Wolfe's method of writing auto-biographical fiction, and so I read his first novel and then I read the section of the Nowell biography dealing with his early life, and the comparison was fascinating.

5.   John Malcolm Brinnin wrote a book called *Dylan Thomas in America,* but Mrs. Thomas disapproved of it, so she insisted that a statement from her appear at the beginning of the book, for she wanted to record her disapproval.

6.   Our freshman writing instructor told us about various theories for teaching writing, and then we asked him what scholarly research had to say about the matter, and so he explained the difficulty of conducting research on the subject, and then he said, "There's not much that is conclusive."

S5   COMMA SPLICE

Do not join main clauses by only a comma unless they are in series.

The use of a comma instead of a period or a semicolon between main clauses not linked by a coordinating conjunction is a **comma splice.** A comma by itself is a purely internal mark of punctuation, and a reader may read through it and be confused:

Registration for the new term begins Monday, on Wednesday classes begin.

In the following example, the italicized element could attach to either clause:

The United Fund drive was a great success, *thanks to several citizens' groups,* the campaign was better organized than ever before.

Which clause is the writer qualifying? Readers are free to guess, but they will get no help from the sentence. It could mean either

The United Fund drive was a great success, thanks to several citizens' groups. The campaign was better organized than ever before.

or

The United Fund drive was a great success. Thanks to several citizens' groups, the campaign was better organized than ever before.

Comma splices can be corrected in any one of three ways.

1.   The simplest way is to change the faulty comma to a period or a semicolon, whichever gives the more desirable degree of separation.

Comma splice	Revision
No conclusive evidence has been uncovered, the committee will meet again tomorrow.	No conclusive evidence has been uncovered. The committee will meet again tomorrow.
The team lost six games, at least three of these losses were due to fumbles.	The team lost six games; at least three of these losses were due to fumbles.

2.   A second way is to provide a coordinating conjunction between the two main clauses, thus making the comma acceptable.

Comma splice	Revision
Much has been said, we believe that much more needs to be said.	Much has been said, but we believe that much more needs to be said.

3.   The third way is to subordinate one main clause to the other.

Comma splice	Revision
Members of the Drama Guild have rehearsed carefully for tonight's show, the director feels certain it will be a success.	Members of the Drama Guild have rehearsed so carefully for tonight's show that the director feels certain it will be a success.

When two main clauses are joined by a transitional connective—*consequently, however, moreover, nevertheless, therefore*—the usual punctuation between them is a semicolon, though a period is not uncommon.

It's too late to get a plane reservation; however, you could go by bus.

When two short independent clauses are closely related, informal usage permits a comma by itself.

The war is over, the fighting is not.

EXERCISE   Using whatever method seems best, correct the comma splices in the following sentences:

1.   Practice ran very late tonight, Coach said that we would not work out tomorrow morning.

2.   The comma splice can confuse the reader, it is usually less troublesome, though, than the fused sentence.

3.   You don't have to pay for it today, all you need is a five-dollar deposit.

4.   Professor Thompson refused to miss our final class to attend a professional meeting, moreover, he definitely expected us to be in class to hear his summarizing lecture.

5.   I made the best decision I could at the time, looking back, I see what I should have done differently.

6.   Pay attention, before you go you must be familiar with the entire plan.

7.   We never once questioned Luke's integrity, strange as it now seems, we would have trusted him with anything.

8.   On the first day of our tour our guide took us to the Senate because it was so close, the House of Representatives was our next stop.

9.   We were able to notify all the committee members of the emergency meeting, although there were others who should have attended, enough were present to make a quorum.

10.   Although the election was over, the excitement among the campaign workers wasn't, enjoying their memories of ten months together, they stayed around campaign headquarters until daylight.

S6   FAULTY PARALLELISM

Sentence elements that are parallel in function should be parallel in grammatical form.

For a detailed discussion of parallel and balanced sentences, see pages 129–134.

Faulty parallelism	Explanation	Revision
The two matters that most concern the leading candidates for class president are *winning* the election and then *to persuade* opposing factions in student government to work together harmoniously.	*The first part of the compound complement of* are *is a gerund phrase starting with* winning; *the second part is an infinitive phrase starting with* to persuade. *The two should be in parallel form. In the revision the infinitive has been changed to a gerund.*	The two matters that most concern the leading candidates for class president are winning the election and then persuading opposing factions in student government to work together harmoniously.
The report is chiefly about *inflationary trends* in the last decade and *that the consumer has lost confidence* in the quality of many products.	*The compound object of* about *consists of a phrase and a subordinate clause. Each part of the object should be a phrase.*	The report is chiefly about inflationary trends in the last decade and the consumer's loss of confidence in the quality of many products.

Sentence elements in a series should have the same form: a phrase should be followed by a phrase, a clause by a clause, a noun by a noun, and a verb by a verb. The following sentence contains a series that lists the powers of a commission:

The commission has the power *to investigate, to conciliate, to hold* hearings, *to subpoena* witnesses, *to issue* cease-and-desist commands, *to order* reinstatement of a discharged employee, and *to direct* the hiring of a qualified applicant.

Most of this sentence consists of a series of infinitive phrases, each identifying one of the powers of the commission and modifying the noun *power*. Since all elements in the series have the same function, they all have the same form. They could have been put in a form other than the infinitive: "The commission has the power *of investigating, of conciliating, of holding* hearings," and so on. But the forms should not shift, as they do in the following sentence—from noun, to infinitive, to gerund, to verb-verb-verb, and back to infinitive again:

The commission has the power *of investigation, to conciliate, holding* hearings, *subpoena* witnesses, *issue* cease-and-desist commands, *order* reinstatement of a discharged employee, and *to direct* the hiring of a qualified applicant.

EXERCISE   Rewrite the following sentences to correct faulty parallelism:

1.   In high school we were asked to write legibly and that we should be concerned with accuracy.

2.   The evangelist ended the service with a hymn and calling on sinners to repent.

3.   Sentence elements performing parallel functions but that are not written in parallel grammatical form should be revised.

4.   The article cites three main causes for the energy crisis: the greatly increased demand for oil in industrialized countries; the fact that the big oil companies had not built new refineries to meet this demand; and that the supply of oil depends to some extent on the political situation, which has become more unstable.

5.   The narrator in *Invisible Man* was idealistic, intelligent, and tried to advance the cause of black people.

6.   By examining newspaper files, magazine articles, and obtaining interviews with knowledgeable people, I was able to gather the information I needed.

7.   The executives of a corporation must be concerned with keeping the price of their product competitive and that the stockholders make a reasonable profit.

8.   In President Carter's first two years in office, his main challenges were to persuade Israel and the Arab nations to reach a peace agreement and finding a way to control inflation in the United States.

9.   Manipulative commercials encourage people to want things they do not need and in buying things that they cannot afford.

10.   Because he has always been wealthy and with indulgent parents, he has never been forced to accept responsibility.

S7   DANGLING MODIFIERS

Avoid dangling modifiers

Any modifier that does not clearly relate to some word in the sentence can be said to dangle. The most troublesome dangling modifiers are verbal phrases at the beginning of a sentence. As the revisions below show, a writer can remove an opening dangling modifier by either (1) revising the main clause so that its subject can be modified by the introductory phrase, or (2) rewriting the opening phrase as a subordinate clause.

Dangling modifier	Explanation	Revised version
Expecting an important call, the telephone was always at my elbow.	*There is nothing in the sentence for* expecting *to modify. Making* I *the subject of the main clause (method 1 above) removes the dangling modifier.*	Expecting an important call, I stayed close to the telephone.
Discouraged by the score, the stadium began to empty.	*Without something in the main clause to modify,* discouraged *dangles. Making* fans *the subject of the main clause (method 1) corrects the error.*	Discouraged by the score, the fans began to leave the stadium.
Waiting for my date in the lobby, two men in tuxedos got into a violent argument.	*The introductory phrase does not modify anything in the main clause. Changing the phrase into a subordinate clause (method 2) corrects the error.*	While I was waiting for my date in the lobby, two men in tuxedos got into a violent argument.

Sometimes a dangling modifier is an elliptical clause—that is, a subordinate clause some elements of which are not expressed. The simplest way to revise a dangling elliptical clause is to supply the missing elements to complete the clause.

Dangling modifier	Revised version
When only five, my father began to teach me how to swing a golf club.	When I was only five, my father began to teach me how to swing a golf club.
While in training, Mother did not have to insist on my getting plenty of sleep.	While I was in training, Mother did not have to insist on my getting plenty of sleep.

A dangling modifier at the end of the sentence is more likely to be awkward or unemphatic than ambiguous:

Dangling modifier	Revised version
Every member of our research team worked conscientiously, thus producing one of the best projects Professor Ames has ever received.	Because every member of our research team worked conscientiously, we produced one of the best projects Professor Ames has ever received.

The cause-to-effect order is presented more emphatically if the sentence begins with a subordinate clause and ends with a main clause, as in the revised version.

EXERCISE   Correct the dangling modifiers in the following sentences:

1.   Although working steadily each day, time ran out before I could complete the job.

2.   To qualify for the award, the committee requires that candidates have perfect attendance.

3.   When a senior in high school, my English teacher had so many students that he was not able to give close attention to individual students' writing problems.

4.   Having heard the weather report, our trip was postponed.

5.   By telling the story in the first person, the reader is more likely to grant the narrator's credibility.

6.   In order to study the effects on their hearts, pigs are jogging up to five miles.

7.   By quoting two authoritative sources, my reader should realize that my information is trustworthy.

8.   Studying about life during the Middle Ages, Chaucer's work became more meaningful to us.

9.   Secure in the knowledge that we had finally arrived safely, a good night's sleep was welcome.

10.   Upon hearing a sharp click the suds subsided and the dial on the top of the washing machine read "drain."

S 8   SHIFTS IN SUBJECTS AND VERBS

1.   Avoid any unnecessary shifts in the person and number of a pronoun subject.

Shifted pronouns	Explanation	Revised version
One hopes that an effective speaker is a good person, but *you* cannot prevent a bad person from learning and using all the means of persuasion.	*The subject shifts from the impersonal pronoun* one *to the second person pronoun* you. *The revisions remove this shift. (A shift from* one *to* he *or* she *would also be acceptable as a revision.)*	One hopes that . . . , but one cannot. . . . *or:* You hope that . . . , but you cannot. . . .

Shifted pronouns	Explanation	Revised version
I cannot understand how a *person* can have so many different feelings about something *they* plan to do.	Person *is singular and should have a singular pronoun, as shown at the right.*	I cannot understand how a person can have so many different feelings about something he or she plans to do.

Remove the shifts in person or number in these sentences: E X E R C I S E

1. When one gets through a three-hour examination, you are exhausted.

2. I tried to understand quadratic equations, but there is a limit to how much math a person can learn.

3. In a situation like that, so many things can happen that one cannot foresee them all. All we can do is decide on a plan and then make whatever changes you have to.

4. Loyalty means having complete confidence in someone, even if they are under suspicion.

5. The book says that the battle took place in 1847, but they are wrong.

2. Avoid unnecessary shifts in the subject within successive sentences of a paragraph.

Although it is not necessary for all sentences in a paragraph to have the same subject, keeping the same subject running through a paragraph whenever possible is one means of preserving unity.

Shifting subjects	Explanation	Revision
When *we* began our composition course, there was little *knowledge* about the importance of strategy in the writing of a paper. *Correctness* in spelling, punctuation, and grammatical usage was what had been drilled into us; but the *effects* of interrelationships among speaker, audience, and occasion were foreign to us.	*Both these sentences have the same logical subject, the students' unawareness of the role of rhetorical strategy in their writing; but the two sentences contain four grammatical subjects. This unnecessary shifting of subject weakens the unity of the passage. The revision reduces the subject to one form—we.*	When we began our composition course, we knew little about the importance of strategy in the writing of a paper. We knew the necessity for correctness in spelling, punctuation, and grammatical usage; but we were unaware of the effects of interrelationships among speaker, audience, and occasion.

EXERCISE   Rewrite the following passages to improve unity by keeping a common subject in all sentences of each passage:

1.   The worries about entrance examinations leave the minds of the students before they depart for the campus. The last days are spent shopping for clothes during the day and partying with friends at night. Their families receive little attention, and entrance examinations are no longer thought of.

2.   I often have difficulty writing the first draft of a paper. The chief problem is finding a main idea to write about. A blank page seems to produce a blank mind. When possible topics do occur, they don't work out. After a few sentences or a paragraph, there is nothing more to say and the wastepaper basket begins to fill up with discarded sheets. All this shows lack of concentration, which seems to be the main weakness in my writing.

3.   Avoid unnecessary shifts in the forms of verbs. Keep voice and tense consistent.

Shifted verb forms	Explanation	Revised version
Members from the House and Senate *met* in conference committee for five consecutive days, but no agreement *was reached*.	*The shifting from active voice in the first clause to passive in the second clause is awkward. The revision keeps both verbs in the active voice.*	Members from the House and Senate met in conference committee for five consecutive days but reached no agreement.
The older girls *had* a party to get us acquainted, and it *was* deeply *appreciated* by me.	*The shift from active voice in the first clause to passive in the second is unnecessary and awkward. The revision subordinates one clause and keeps both verbs in the active voice.*	I appreciated the party that the older girls gave to get us acquainted.
As centuries *passed*, the dress patterns *become* more and more complicated.	*The tense changes from past to present. Since both actions happened in the past, both verbs should be in the past tense.*	As centuries passed, the dress patterns became more and more complicated.
He *said* he *will* call for me at eight.	*The writer is confusing the tenses for direct and indirect discourse. Either form at the right will do.*	He said he would call for me at eight. He said, "I will call for you at eight."

Revise the following sentences to get rid of awkward shifts in voice and   EXERCISE
tense:

1.   The more we learned about the proposal, the clearer the issues become.

2.   We spent the whole class hour discussing that question, but no agreement was
arrived at.

3.   I wrote inviting her to the party, but no answer was received.

4.   When the problem was discussed in class, it becomes quite simple.

5.   As Douglas talked, I reminded myself that we will have to reserve judgment
about him but that he will have to prove himself.

6.   One behavioral scientist has said that he believed permissiveness in the schools
leads to student contempt for the schools.

7.   Professor Wallingford said that she will return our papers at the next class
session.

8.   The rescue party worked for hours to extricate the child from the wreckage,
and finally the efforts were successful.

9.   He said we would be late for class anyway, so let's finish our Cokes and not
worry.

10.   In choosing a mate for the rest of your life, certain qualities should be looked
for.

S9   INCOMPLETE CONSTRUCTIONS

Do not omit words necessary to the structure of a sentence.

Leaving out a word or phrase that is necessary to the structure or meaning of a
sentence may result in an awkward or ambiguous statement. The following
sentences illustrate this error, which should be caught in proofreading:

Incomplete	Explanation	Complete
The playwright tried for months, but no play.	*Incomplete contrast. The conjunction* but *requires a verb to balance the sentence.* Could not finish *is necessary to complete the contrast.*	The playwright tried for months but could not finish the play.

Incomplete	Explanation	Complete
I don't approve of the assumption which he began.	*Omitted preposition. With a choice of two forms for the subordinate clause—"with which he began" or "which he began with"—the writer has failed to supply* with *in either position.*	I don't approve of the assumption with which he began. or: I don't approve of the assumption which he began with.
Investigation showed that the foreman took the defect in the engine more seriously than his employers.	*Omitted verb causing a possible ambiguity. The comparison is not of en-gine and employers, but of foreman and employers. The clause with employers as subject needs a verb.*	Investigation showed that the foreman took the defect in the engine more seriously than his employers did.
The problem was his cousin was too honest to cooperate in the scheme.	*Omission of the subordinating conjunction that allows the subject of the subordinate clause, cousin, to be misread for a moment as the complement of was.*	The problem was that his cousin was too honest to cooperate in the scheme.
This decision is as hard, if not harder, than any we have had to make.	*This construction mixes two expressions: "as hard as" and "harder than." Than will not serve as connective for both expressions. The sentence could be revised to read: "This decision is as hard as, if not harder than, any we have had to make"; but this construction is so awkward that many people prefer to avoid it and use instead one of the revisions at the right.*	This decision is one of the hardest we have had to make. or: This decision is at least as hard as any we have had to make. or: This decision may be the hardest we have had to make.

Revise the following sentences to complete the incomplete constructions: **EXERCISE**

1. We studied the subject as carefully as our opposition.

2. I question the premise which the argument depends.

3. I scribbled and outlined until I had exhausted my imagination, but no satisfactory result.

4. Jason Compson, in *The Sound and the Fury,* is as despicable, if not more despicable, than any character in all of Faulkner's fiction.

5. Senator Benson has spoken more convincingly against the denial of civil rights than his opponent.

6. We have insisted, and continue throughout the campaign, on equal opportunity for every ethnic group.

7. I sometimes think our professor has a better understanding of *Macbeth* than Shakespeare.

8. The recommendation that is as valuable, or perhaps more valuable, than any the steering committee received came from a housewife whom the committee chairman inadvertently failed to mention.

9. Our expectation is the proposal will be rejected at the polls.

10. In the last quarter State launched a furious passing attack and its fifth straight victory.

D

DICTION

D1 USING A DICTIONARY

Become familiar with at least one good college-level desk dictionary.

Since a good dictionary may well contain more useful information on more subjects than any other one book you are likely to use, it is a good idea to own one. Useful dictionaries are of two sizes: the so-called unabridged, and the collegiate, or desk, size. Unabridged dictionaries are listed on page 315. The following desk dictionaries are those most commonly recommended for student use:

The American Heritage Dictionary of the English Language
Funk & Wagnalls Standard College Dictionary

The Random House Dictionary of the English Language, College Edition
Webster's New Collegiate Dictionary
Webster's New World Dictionary of the American Language, College Edition

All these dictionaries are equipped with useful study aids that are supplied by their publishers on request.

When you look up a word in a dictionary, try to find out as much as you can about it. A good desk dictionary records many kinds of information about a word, as the entry on page 426 shows.

Although dictionaries vary in detail, they all give the following kinds of information. Check your dictionary against this list and make notes on any variations.

1. *Spelling and syllabication.* The entry word is spelled and is divided into syllables, usually by dots: *con•tract.* When a given word has more than one acceptable spelling, all accepted spellings are listed: *ax, axe.* (For your own and your readers' peace of mind, it is a good idea to choose one of these accepted spellings and to stand by that spelling in all the writing you do.)

2. *Pronunciation.* Immediately after the entry word is the pronunciation, usually in parentheses. Each dictionary has its own pronunciation key, usually printed at the foot of the page. Words of more than one syllable also include one or more accent marks (′ ′) placed before or after syllables to indicate secondary or primary stress. Note that *contract* has alternative pronunciations depending on whether it is used as a noun or a verb.

3. *Part of speech.* The abbreviation is given for the part of speech in which the word is used (*n., v., adj.,* and so on). If a word is used in several parts of speech, all meanings for each part of speech are grouped together: all noun meanings are grouped, all verb meanings, and so on.

4. *Abbreviations.* Most dictionaries list common abbreviations, though not always near the beginning of the entry.

5. *Grammatical features.* Irregular plurals are given for nouns (*mice, oxen*), principal parts for verbs, and comparative forms for adjectives and adverbs that do not take *more* and *most.*

6. *Meanings.* Within part-of-speech groupings, meanings are given in historical order, in order of frequency of use, or from primary or basic to secondary or extended. Check the front matter of your dictionary to see which order it uses.

7. *Etymology.* When it is known, the origin of the word is given. Thus *contract* is one of a large class of words that came into English from Latin via Old French. It is made up of the prefix *con-* (from Latin *com-,* "together") and the root *tract* (from Latin *trahere,* "to draw").

Spelling and   Pronunciations   Grammatical features:
syllabication   Parts of speech   principal parts

                                    Abbreviations   Meaning within
                                                           part-of-speech groupings

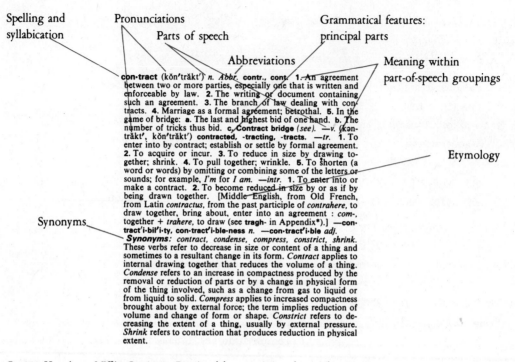

con·tract (kŏn'trăkt') *n. Abbr.* contr., cont. **1.** An agreement
between two or more parties, especially one that is written and
enforceable by law. **2.** The writing or document containing
such an agreement. **3.** The branch of law dealing with contracts. **4.** Marriage as a formal agreement; betrothal. **5.** In the
game of bridge: **a.** The last and highest bid of one hand. **b.** The
number of tricks thus bid. **c.** Contract bridge *(see).* —*v.* (kon-
trăkt', kŏn'trăkt') **contracted,** **-tracting,** **-tracts.** —*tr.* **1.** To
enter into by contract; establish or settle by formal agreement.
2. To acquire or incur. **3.** To reduce in size by drawing together; shrink. **4.** To pull together; wrinkle. **5.** To shorten (a
word or words) by omitting or combining some of the letters or
sounds; for example, *I'm* for *I am.* —*intr.* **1.** To enter into or
make a contract. **2.** To become reduced in size by or as if by
being drawn together. [Middle English, from Old French,
from Latin *contractus,* from the past participle of *contrahere,* to
draw together, bring about, enter into an agreement : *com-,*
together + *trahere,* to draw (see **tragh-** in Appendix*).] —contract'i·bil'i·ty, con·tract'i·ble·ness *n.* —con·tract'i·ble *adj.*
 Synonyms: *contract, condense, compress, constrict, shrink.*
These verbs refer to decrease in size or content of a thing and
sometimes to a resultant change in its form. *Contract* applies to
internal drawing together that reduces the volume of a thing.
Condense refers to an increase in compactness produced by the
removal or reduction of parts or by a change in physical form
of the thing involved, such as a change from gas to liquid or
from liquid to solid. *Compress* applies to increased compactness
brought about by external force; the term implies reduction of
volume and change of form or shape. *Constrict* refers to decreasing the extent of a thing, usually by external pressure.
Shrink refers to contraction that produces reduction in physical
extent.

Etymology

Synonyms

8.   *Labels.* Labels are used to indicate usage (*Nonstandard, Slang, Informal*), dialect
(*Dial.*), region (*Brit., Southern*), and specialization (*Law, Med.*). A word not
labeled (*contract,* for example) is in standard general use.

9.   *Synonyms and antonyms.* Dictionaries vary in the positioning of these elements
and in the space given to them. Check the front matter of your dictionary if in
doubt.

EXERCISE   The following quiz will test your knowledge of your own dictionary. Check your
answers by the introductory pages and by reference to particular entries.

1.   Does your dictionary record variant spellings of the same word in one entry or
in different entries? Is one spelling necessarily "more correct" than an alternate
spelling?

2.   How is pronunciation indicated in your dictionary? Is there a key to the symbols at the bottom of the page, or only in the introductory matter?

3.   Where are the etymologies shown: after the inflectional forms, or at the end of the entry? In many dictionaries, *L* is the symbol for Latin. Other common origins are *Gr* (Greek), *F* (French), *N* (Norse), *O* (Old, as in *Old English, Old French*). If you are not sure how to interpret these symbols, where in your dictionary can you find out?

4.   In what order are the definitions given? If you are not sure, where can you find out?

5.   How are foreign words identified—that is, words that are still considered foreign rather than English, and so have to be underlined in manuscript or italicized in print? If you are not sure, how can you find out? (Hint: Check *gestalt, bon voyage, in absentia.*)

6.   For which of the following entries are synonyms or antonyms given: *ambition, deface, fiendish, luster, restive, voracious?*

7.   How are the following words pronounced: *acclimate, alias, banal, data, ennui, impious, impotent, joust, schism, Wagnerian?*

The things you most need to know about a new word are its pronunciation, etymology, and meanings. Knowing the pronunciation not only helps you pronounce a word correctly in reading aloud or in speaking, but also helps you fix the word in your memory. Since the way a word looks is often no safe clue to how it sounds, we have all had the embarrassing experience of making a very obvious mispronunciation when called upon to read an unfamiliar word aloud. Even such fairly common words as *abyss, blatant, caprice, decade, echelon, façade, gauge,* and *ribald* can be troublesome for a person who has met them in reading and has never heard them spoken.

The etymology of a word gives you its family history and thus makes your knowledge of it more complete. When you learn that *crucial* comes from the Latin word for *cross,* you can see that in a crucial decision, we figuratively stand at a crossroads and decide which way we will go; and you may discover an unsuspected relationship among *crucial, crucify, crusade,* and *crux.*

As for the meaning of a word, it should be clear that unless you know what a word means, you cannot use that word effectively in speech or in writing. Failure to use the right word or to use the word right is an error in diction.

The errors in diction identified in sections **D2** through **D6** have all been discussed earlier in the text, chiefly in Chapter 7. For help with avoiding any of these errors in your writing, consult the pages referred to.

D 2   WRONG MEANING

The italicized word does not mean what the writer intended it to mean:

The state's attorney said that the man would be *persecuted.*

The word wanted here is *prosecuted.* The error may be a misspelling, or it may reveal a confusion of two words of similar appearance but different meanings, like *casual–causal, concave–convex, detracted–distracted, official–officious,* and *prescribe–proscribe.* For a fuller list of such pairs, see the Checklist of Troublesome Usages at the end of this book.

D 3   INCONSISTENT DICTION

Words may be inconsistent for two reasons: (1) because they are too formal or too colloquial for the context in which they are being used, or (2) because they are not appropriate to the writer's purpose.

1. Avoid diction that is too formal or too colloquial for the style of your paper.

See pages 156–158.

2. Avoid connotations that work against your purpose.

Example: *Notorious* and *famous* both have the general meaning of being well known, but the first has unfavorable connotations, the second favorable: "a notorious criminal," but "a famous writer."

D 4   VAGUE DICTION

See "Eliminating Vagueness," pages 169–172.

D 5   TRITE DICTION

See "Eliminating Triteness," pages 175–177.

D 6   INAPPROPRIATE IMAGE

A figure of speech will be inappropriate if:

1.   it attempts to combine one or more images in one *metaphor* (see page 179).

2.   it presents a *personification* that is so exaggerated that a reader will not accept it (see page 167).

3.   it makes an *allusion* to some person or event that a reader is not likely to understand (see page 167).

WO

WORD
ORDER

WO1 NORMAL ORDER
AND ACCEPTED INVERSIONS

NORMAL ORDER

The normal order of words in English sentences may be summarized as follows:

1. Except in questions and expletive-type sentences ("Why do you despair?" "There is a ray of hope"), the standard order of the main sentence elements is subject–verb–object or complement. An indirect object precedes the direct object: "He sent me flowers."

2. Single adjectives or series of adjectives precede, and adjective phrases follow, their headword–the word they modify: "a *trusted* man *of the people*."

3. Adverbs usually follow the verbs they modify, but may come elsewhere. Adverbs modifying adjectives or other adverbs precede the headword: "He is *very* old"; "They dance *remarkably* well."

4. Main clauses usually precede subordinate clauses, but the following exceptions are common:

a. Adjective clauses immediately follow their headwords: "The man *who did it* should be punished."

b. Adverbial clauses, especially conditional clauses, often precede the main clause: "*If you do that,* you'll be sorry."

c. Noun clauses acting as subjects or objects occupy the subject or object position: "*That he will accept* is taken for granted." "He says *that you are afraid.*"

5. Closely related elements are kept as close together as possible. Thus a preposition precedes the object and its modifiers ("the top *of the highest mountain*"); modifiers remain close to their headwords; and subject-verb, verb-object, and pronoun-antecedent combinations are not separated more than the special needs of the sentence require. In short, the order of elements in a sentence should reveal relationships, not obscure them.

ACCEPTED INVERSIONS

Any inversion of normal word order tends to attract attention and to emphasize the inverted expression. If this emphasis is desirable and if the departure from normal order is not outlandish or unidiomatic, a writer may gain interesting variety in sentence structure by moderate use of inversion.

If it does not create misinterpretation or awkwardness, an element may be transposed from its normal order for emphasis.

Normal order	Emphatic inversion
They laid him down *slowly and sadly.*	*Slowly and sadly* they laid him down.
The Cowboys don't stand a chance *without Roger Staubach.*	*Without Roger Staubach,* the Cowboys don't stand a chance.
The doctor arrived *at last.*	*At last* the doctor arrived.
Will you help me *if I agree?*	*If I agree,* will you help me?
Don't take his word for it *under any circumstances.*	Don't *under any circumstances* take his word for it.
Oliver asked, "Please, sir, may I have some more?"	"Please, sir," Oliver asked, "may I have some more?"

In this last example the inversion is made not so much for emphasis as to provide variation in the order of the "he asked," "she said," "they answered" tags that accompany direct discourse. These tags may come at the beginning, the middle, or the end of the quotation.

W O 2   A M B I G U O U S   O R D E R

Be sure that the relationship between modifying words, phrases, or clauses and the elements they modify is clear.

If a modifier is so placed that it could modify either of two elements, its reference will be ambiguous and the intended meaning will be unclear. Even if the reader is able to make the correct interpretation, the writer's carelessness will be apparent.

Ambiguous order	Explanation	Revised order
I thought of writing *often* but never did.	*The adverb* often *can modify either* thought *or* writing. *If it is intended to modify* thought, *put it immediately before or after that verb.*	I often thought of writing but never did.
The Chinese vase was a wedding gift *that was stolen.*	Since adjective clauses follow the nouns they modify, a reader may interpret *gift* as the antecedent of *that.* The revision removes this possibility.	The Chinese vase that was stolen was a wedding gift.

EXERCISE   Remove possible ambiguities in the following sentences by changing the position of misleading modifiers:

1. My mother planted the rosebush in her garden that I gave her on Mother's Day.

2. The children watched while the magician drew out a rabbit with shining eyes.

3. No boy would treat his father like that unless he was spiteful.

4. The list of expenses tells the story of the man who wrote it quickly and clearly.

5. There is a panel discussion tonight about drug addiction in the student lounge.

6. Bill promised on his way home to pick me up.

7. I was so surprised that I forgot what I intended to say to her when I met her.

8. At one time his neighbors said he had been in jail.

9. Richard Burton played the part of the man who was corrupted by power superbly.

10. There was a noisy disturbance when the speaker said that at the back of the hall.

11. The car is in the garage that he wrecked.

12. They talked about going on a second honeymoon frequently but never did.

WO3   AWKWARD SEPARATION OF ELEMENTS

Avoid unnecessary separation of a subject and its verb, a verb and its object or complement, a modifier and its headword, or a preposition and its object.

Unnecessary separation of closely related elements can distort the sentence pattern and interfere with ease of reading.

Awkward separation	Explanation	Revised order
My *father,* after considering what the trip would cost and how long it would take, *refused* to go.	*Awkward separation of subject and verb. The unnecessary interruption of the main clause by a phrase and two subordinate clauses distorts the structure of the main clause.*	After considering what the trip would cost and how long it would take, my father refused to go.
Who *will believe,* considering his reputation and the lack of any confirming evidence, *what he says?*	*Awkward separation of italicized verb and object.*	Considering his reputation and the lack of any confirming evidence, who will believe what he says?
Her parents are neither in favor *of* nor opposed to the *marriage.*	*Awkward separation of preposition* of *and its object. The revision at the right is the best way of expressing the idea.*	Her parents neither favor nor oppose the marriage.

W O 4   U N E M P H A T I C   O R D E R

Any word order that reduces a desired emphasis in a sentence should be avoided or revised. This principle was discussed in "Emphatic Word Order" and "Climactic Order" on pages 138–140. What follows is a supplement to that earlier treatment, not a substitute for it.

1. Do not place relatively unimportant material at the end of a sentence.

The end of a sentence is a point of major stress. Putting unimportant information there will give that information more emphasis than it deserves and produce an anticlimax. For example, in the sentence

Last night our car was stolen while we were in the theater.

the most important information—that the car was stolen—is in a position of less emphasis than the less important information that the owners were in the theater at the time. A more appropriate emphasis can be obtained by putting the theft at the end:

Last night, while we were in the theater, our car was stolen.

This kind of faulty emphasis is most conspicuous when an unimportant qualification ends the sentence. Compare:

Unemphatic ending	More emphatic ending
He has never been married, *as far as I know.*	*As far as I know,* he has never been married.
She is innocent, *in my opinion.*	*In my opinion,* she is innocent.

2. Do not weaken an important concluding statement by reducing it to a participial phrase.

Many a good sentence ends with a participial phrase, but to use such a phrase for an idea that is important enough to deserve a main clause often makes a lame ending. For example, in

He fell from the roof, *thus breaking his neck.*

the italicized phrase is at least as important as the main clause, yet it is grammatically subordinate and trails off weakly. The idea in the phrase is important enough to come at the end, but it deserves a stronger grammatical form:

He fell from the roof and broke his neck.

3. **Do not put a conjunctive adverb at the end of a sentence.**

Conjunctive adverbs, also called transitional connectives, are words like *accordingly, consequently, furthermore, however, nevertheless, therefore* that connect and make a transition between two sentences or two main clauses of a compound sentence:

> He thinks she deceived him deliberately; *consequently,* he is in no mood for a reconciliation.

> We have repeatedly tried to make friends with them and have been consistently repulsed. *Nevertheless,* we'll try again.

> I am willing to advise you. I will not, *however,* accept responsibility for what you do.

Since a connective should come between the things it connects, the normal positions for a conjunctive adverb are at the beginning of the second sentence or clause, as in the first and second examples above, or *near* the beginning of the second clause, as in the third example. For maximum emphasis on the conjunctive adverb, place it at the very beginning of the second sentence.

Revise the following sentences to improve awkward or unemphatic order: **EXERCISE**

1. The cause of death was heart failure rather than drowning in the coroner's judgment.

2. Her parents, even, do not know where she is.

3. The challenger knocked down the champion six times in two rounds, thus shocking the crowd.

4. The plane made a successful takeoff although its tires had been riddled by the FBI marksmen, who were there to prevent the hijacking.

5. The Supreme Court refused to consider the appeal, according to the late news last night.

6. I think Wayne's personality will irritate other members of the council. I'll have to vote for him, however.

7. The chairman said the minutes would be accepted, there being no objection.

8. The best argument for democracy is to consider its alternatives, I firmly believe.

9. The instructor promised that she would give the class some sample questions to study for the exam after much pleading from the students.

10. The evidence shows, if you examine it carefully and impartially, that the best baseball is played in the National League.

11. I am neither in support of nor opposed to the bill.

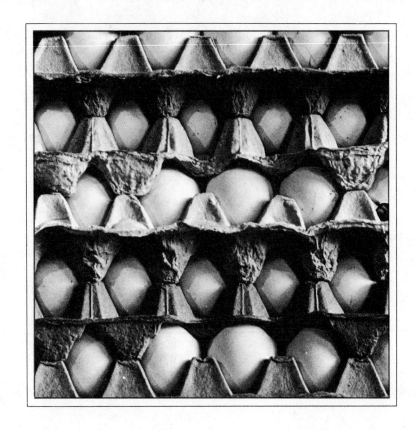

GF1 PRINCIPAL PARTS OF VERBS

1. Use the accepted principal parts of verbs.

The great majority of English verbs form the present participle by adding *-ing* to the present-tense form *(walk, walking)*; they form the past tense and the past participle by adding *-ed* to the first principal part *(walked, walked)*. All exceptions are specifically listed in a good dictionary. The following list contains the principal parts of the irregular verbs that cause most trouble:

Present tense	Present participle	Past tense	Past participle
am, is, are	being	was, were	been
bear	bearing	bore	borne
beat	beating	beat	beaten
begin	beginning	began	begun
bite	biting	bit	bitten
blow	blowing	blew	blown
break	breaking	broke	broken
bring	bringing	brought	brought
burst	bursting	burst	burst
cast	casting	cast	cast
choose	choosing	chose	chosen
come	coming	came	come
deal	dealing	dealt	dealt
do	doing	did	done
draw	drawing	drew	drawn
drink	drinking	drank	drunk
eat	eating	ate	eaten
fall	falling	fell	fallen
fly	flying	flew	flown
forbid	forbidding	forbade	forbidden
forsake	forsaking	forsook	forsaken
freeze	freezing	froze	frozen
give	giving	gave	given
go	going	went	gone
grow	growing	grew	grown
hang*	hanging	hung	hung
have	having	had	had
know	knowing	knew	known
lay	laying	laid	laid
lie	lying	lay	lain
ride	riding	rode	ridden
ring	ringing	rang	rung
rise	rising	rose	risen
run	running	ran	run
see	seeing	saw	seen
shake	shaking	shook	shaken

* The verb *to hang*, used in the sense of "to execute," is regular: *hang, hanged, hanged.*

Present tense	Present participle	Past tense	Past participle
shoe	shoeing	shod	shod
shrink	shrinking	shrank (shrunk)	shrunk
sing	singing	sang (sung)	sung
sink	sinking	sank (sunk)	sunk
sit	sitting	sat	sat
slay	slaying	slew	slain
slink	slinking	slunk	slunk
speak	speaking	spoke	spoken
spin	spinning	spun	spun
spring	springing	sprang (sprung)	sprung
steal	stealing	stole	stolen
strive	striving	strove	striven
swear	swearing	swore	sworn
swim	swimming	swam	swum
take	taking	took	taken
teach	teaching	taught	taught
tear	tearing	tore	torn
throw	throwing	threw	thrown
wear	wearing	wore	worn
weave	weaving	wove	woven
win	winning	won	won
write	writing	wrote	written

2. Distinguish between the forms for the past tense and the past participle.

In verb phrases the past participle, not the past-tense form, should follow an auxiliary verb ("has *been*"). Except when a verb is acting as an auxiliary ("*had* gone," "*was* crying"), its past-tense form is not used in combination with another verb.

Nonstandard form	Standard form
It is *broke.*	It is *broken.*
These tires are *wore* out.	These tires are *worn* out.
He has *began* all over again.	He has *begun* all over again.
I *seen* him do it.	I *saw* him do it.
The river is *froze* solid.	The river is *frozen* solid.
Everybody has *went* home.	Everybody has *gone* home.

Nonstandard form	Standard form
Have you *wrote* to him?	Have you *written* to him?
They *come* back yesterday.	They *came* back yesterday.

3. **Distinguish between the uses and forms of *lie* and *lay*, *rise* and *raise*, *sit* and *set*.**

The principal parts of these verbs are as follows:

Present	Present participle	Past	Past participle
lie	lying	lay	lain
lay	laying	laid	laid
rise	rising	rose	risen
raise	raising	raised	raised
sit	sitting	sat	sat
set	setting	set	set

Each pair has principal parts that are similar, though not the same, in form and general meaning. The chief difference in each pair is that the first verb is *intransitive,* the second *transitive.* That is, the first does not need an object to complete the action of the verb; the second does need an object. Determining the accepted form, therefore, depends on the answers to two questions: (1) Does the sentence require a transitive or an intransitive verb? (2) What are the principal parts of the required verb?

In the examples that follow, the unacceptable forms at the left are revised at the right.

Unacceptable	Explanation	Acceptable
We *laid* breathless with suspense.	*The sentence contains no object; therefore, the intransitive verb is wanted. The past form of* lie *is* lay.	We lay breathless with suspense.
It was *setting* on the table.	*No object; therefore, the intransitive form* sitting *is required.*	It was sitting on the table.
They have *lain* the carpet.	*Carpet is the object; therefore, the transitive* laid *is required.*	They have laid the carpet.

Unacceptable	Explanation	Acceptable
He *raised* up and went to the bench.	*No object; intransitive* rose *is required.*	He rose and went to the bench.
It has been *laying* there all night.	*No object; intransitive* lying *is required.*	It has been lying there all night.

EXERCISE   Write the acceptable form in the following sentences:

1. We (lay, laid) on the pier and dozed.
2. I would like you to (rise, raise) my wages.
3. Go out and (rise, raise) the flag.
4. (Set, Sit) down and rest for a while.
5. Finally, the curtain (raised, rose).
6. They were (laying, lying) in wait for us.
7. We (laid, lay) down for a rest.
8. They were (setting, sitting) the chairs in a circle.
9. He (raised, rose) himself on his elbow.
10. Clothes were (laying, lying) all over the room.

GF2   TENSE FORMS

(For identification of the basic tenses, see page 527.)

1.   Avoid illogical sequence of tenses.

a.   Keep the tenses of main clauses consistent. Do not shift needlessly from one tense to another.

Inconsistent	Explanation	Consistent
She laughed, and I asked her what she knew about him. She *laughs* again, this time much louder.	*In the first sentence all verbs are in the past tense; in the second,* laughs *is in the present tense. There is no reason for the shift to occur here.*	She laughed, and I asked her what she knew about him. She *laughed* again, this time much louder.

Inconsistent	Explanation	Consistent
For five rounds the young challenger danced and ducked and jabbed and piled up points. Then the champion found an opening—and Bam! The fight *is* over.	*All the verbs except the last one are in the past tense. The last shifts to historical present. Either that tense or the simple past should be used throughout.*	For five rounds the young challenger danced and ducked and jabbed and piled up points. Then the champion found an opening—and Bam! The fight *was* over.

b.   **Keep the tense of a subordinate clause in logical sequence with that of the main clause.**

Illogical	Explanation	Logical
They *have made* so much money last year that they *bought* a second store.	*The present perfect (have made) suggests action more recent than the simple past (bought); it is illogical to use the present perfect for the earlier action.*	They *made* so much money last year that they *have bought* a second store.
Before I was introduced to her, I *heard* rumors about her reputation.	*Since the rumors came before the introduction, the past perfect tense should be used in the main clause.*	Before I was introduced to her, I *had heard* rumors about her reputation.

2.   **In converting direct discourse to indirect discourse, observe the normal change in tense.**

Direct discourse repeats the actual words of the speaker, and verbs should be in the tense the speaker used. When direct discourse is converted to indirect, the tenses of the original are, when possible, pushed one stage farther into the past. Thus present becomes past, and past becomes past perfect. Since there is no tense more past than past perfect, a verb in that tense does not change.

Direct discourse	Explanation	Indirect discourse
He said, "I *want* to read that novel."	*Change simple present to simple past.*	He said that he *wanted* to read that novel.
He said, "I *wanted* to read that novel yesterday."	*Change simple past to past perfect.*	He said that he *had wanted* to read that novel yesterday.

Direct discourse	Explanation	Indirect discourse
He said, "I *had wanted* to read that novel until I *saw* the movie."	*Leave the verbs as they are. There is no way to make* had wanted *more past than it is, and to change* saw *to* had seen *would destroy the sequence of tenses.*	He said that he *had wanted* to read that novel until he *saw* the movie.

The following examples contrast faulty and correct conversion from direct to indirect discourse:

Direct discourse	Faulty conversion	Correct conversion
I said, "She *is* a good risk."	I said she is a good risk.	I said she *was* a good risk.
I asked, "*Have you talked* to your doctor?"	I asked if he talked to his doctor.	I asked if he *had talked* to his doctor.

3.　Observe the relationships of tense between verbs and verbals.

The tense of a verbal is not determined by the tense of the verb in the main clause. Regardless of the tense of the verb, a present participle expresses an action occurring at the same time as that of the verb. A perfect participle expresses time before that of the verb. A present infinitive indicates either the same time as that of the verb or a later time. A perfect infinitive suggests time before that of the verb.

Rounding the last turn, he *was* ahead by two yards.	*The present participle* (rounding) *and the past-tense verb refer to actions occurring at the same time.*
Having unblocked the drain, she *washed* her hair.	*The perfect participle* (having unblocked) *refers to an action before that of the verb* (washed).
I *tried to telephone* you.	*The verb* (tried) *and the present infinitive* (to telephone) *refer to actions occurring at the same time.*
I *expect to hear* from him tomorrow.	*The expectation is now; the hearing has yet to occur. Therefore, the present infinitive refers to a time later than that of the verb.*
They *are reported to have reached* an agreement.	*The perfect infinitive* (to have reached) *points to a time before the reporting.*

Faulty sequence	Explanation	Correct sequence
Asking the blessing, we began to eat.	*Since the blessing was asked before the eating began, the perfect participle is required.*	*Having asked* the blessing, we began to eat.
Having faced the spectators, the referee signaled a holding penalty.	*Since both actions took place at the same time, the present participle is required.*	*Facing* the spectators, the referee signaled a holding penalty.
We meant to *have told* you earlier.	*The perfect infinitive suggests that the telling occurred before the intention. The present infinitive is the required form.*	We meant *to tell* you earlier.
I am sorry *to overlook* that fact.	*Since the overlooking occurred before the regret, the perfect infinitive should be used.*	I am sorry *to have overlooked* that fact.

Revise the following sentences where necessary to correct illogical or faulty sequence of tenses: **EXERCISE**

1. Because the social committee has planned so carefully, everything went just fine.

2. Billy insisted that his antique Cadillac runs as smoothly as last year's model.

3. Practicing all week against a zone defense, our team was puzzled when Riply played man to man.

4. It was clear that just before I arrived they had a serious quarrel.

5. We were told to have packed our bags before breakfast.

6. The treasurer is lucky to find the error before the meeting on the budget.

7. Even before the jury pronounced her guilty, the accused woman sensed that they were not sympathetic toward her.

8. Finishing the prewriting stage of my paper, I was ready to begin my rough draft.

9. We arranged to have submitted our papers before leaving campus.

10. I had planned to write the letter before I had gone to the party, but Karen asked me to come earlier than I intended.

GF3   CASE

Case is a system of inflection that shows the relation of nouns and pronouns to other words in the sentence. English has three cases: **subjective** (or *nominative*), **possessive** (or *genitive*), and **objective** (or *accusative*). In general, a noun or pronoun is in the subjective case when it acts as a subject, in the objective case when it acts as an object, and in the possessive case when it modifies a noun as in "*his* bicycle," "the *boy's* dog," "the *girl's* future."

English nouns, pronouns, and adjectives were once fully inflected to show case, but in modern English, word order and idiomatic constructions have largely replaced case endings. Adjectives are no longer inflected for case; nouns are inflected only in the possessive case: "the *fireman's* hat." Only pronouns (and chiefly the personal pronouns) still make any considerable use of case forms. The study of case in modern English, therefore, is pretty much restricted to pronouns.

1.   The case of a pronoun is determined by its function in its own clause.

If a pronoun is the subject of its clause, it takes the subjective case; if it is an object within its clause, it takes the objective case; if it is a modifier, it takes the possessive case. But notice that: (1) a pronoun subject of an infinitive takes the objective case ("I want *him to see* it"); and (2) the complement of the verb *to be* takes the subjective case in formal usage ("It was not *I* who said that").

Pronouns take the *subjective* case when

1.   they are subjects of verbs: "*I* think that *he* missed."
2.   they are in apposition with subjects: "Three men—Fred, Roy, and *I*—were elected delegates."
3.   they are complements of the verb *to be:* "I am sure it was *he*."

Pronouns take the *objective* case when

1.   they are objects of verbs: "Mother likes *her*."
2.   they are objects of prepositions: "They pointed at *me*."
3.   they are in apposition with objects: "They gave *us*—Dave and *me*—the money."
4.   they are subjects or objects of infinitives: "I want *her* to go"; "We didn't expect to see *him*."

Pronouns take the *possessive* case when

1.   they modify a noun or a pronoun: "Those are *my* six children, this is *his* one."

2. they precede and modify a gerund: "What's wrong with *her* swimming?" "*His* winning was a surprise."

TROUBLESOME CONSTRUCTIONS

In general, errors in case occur for two reasons: (1) because the function of a pronoun is obscured; and (2) because a case form inappropriate in writing is so often used in speech that the colloquial form seems more natural than the more formal one. Often these two reasons merge. That is, a particular construction requires more deliberate analysis than speakers have time to give it and so encourages a colloquial usage that competes with the formal one.

The following pages point out the constructions that create most of the irregularities in the use of case forms.

2. Most errors in case occur in a few constructions. Learn to recognize and deal effectively with the following:

a. Interrupting constructions with *who* or *whom*.

Any construction that interrupts the normal pattern of a clause is likely to obscure the function of a pronoun in the clause. In the following sentence it is quite clear that *who* is the subject of *won* and takes the subjective case:

That is the man who won the prize.

But if we introduce an interrupting clause—"they say"—into the sentence, the function of *who* becomes less clear:

That is the man who they say won the prize.

There is now a tendency to assume that *who* is the object of *say* and to put it in the objective case. But its function has not changed. "They say" has no grammatical relationship to any element in the sentence. The faulty analysis suggested by the interrupting construction often leads to the use of the wrong case.

Wrong case	Explanation	Correct case
The man *whom* they think did it has been arrested.	*Pronoun is subject of* did, *not object of* think.	The man *who* they think did it has been arrested.
She introduced me to a man *whom* she said was her boss.	*Pronoun is subject of* was, *not object of* said.	She introduced me to a man *who* she said was her boss.

Wrong case	Explanation	Correct case
The police identified the woman *who* they had arrested.	*Pronoun is object of* had arrested, *not a subject.*	The police identified the woman *whom* they had arrested.

b. *Whoever* and *whomever.*

These two relative pronouns follow the rule that the case of a pronoun is determined by its function in its own clause. But because they often follow a transitive verb or the preposition *to,* they are often mistaken as objects when actually they are not objects.

Faulty	Explanation	Correct
Invite *whomever* will come.	*Pronoun is subject of* will come; *object of* invite *is the clause* whoever will come.	Invite *whoever* will come.
Send it to *whomever* you think would like it.	*Relative pronoun is subject of* would like. *The preposition* to *and the qualifying clause* you think *do not affect its case.*	Send it to *whoever* you think would like it.

c. Complement of the verb *to be.*

In written usage a pronoun complement of the verb *to be* takes the subjective case: "It was *he.*" See page 534 in the Checklist of Troublesome Usages.

d. Comparative with *than* or *as.*

The case of a pronoun following *than* or *as* in a comparison often causes difficulty. In such comparisons as the following, *than* and *as* are connectives between a full clause and an elliptical (incompletely expressed) one:

He is at least as old as *she.*	(If the elliptical clause were completely expressed, the sentence would read: "He is at least as old as *she is.*")
I am about twenty pounds lighter than *he.*	("I am about twenty pounds lighter than *he is.*")
The judge liked us better than *them.*	("The judge liked us better than *he liked them.*")

In the expanded form it is clear that *than* and *as* are connectives joining two clauses. Pronouns in shortened comparisons take the same case they would take if the comparisons were fully expanded. That is, a pronoun takes the subjective case if it is the subject of an unexpressed verb and the objective case if it is the object of such a verb.

e. Possessive with a gerund.

A pronoun preceding and modifying a gerund takes the possessive case: "I am opposed to *his going*." In formal writing, a noun modifying a gerund also takes the possessive case: "Imagine *John's saying* that!" Both colloquial usage and informal usage usually ignore this latter convention and put the noun modifier in the objective case: "Imagine *John saying* that!"

The following sentences further illustrate the use of the possessive case when a noun or a pronoun modifies a gerund:

There is really no excuse for *his failing* the course.

We are embarrassed by *their* continual *begging*.

They object to *my having signed* the petition.

Mary's interrupting annoys him.

Their believing that doesn't surprise me.

We could not sleep because of the *baby's crying*.

In the following sentences some of the italicized case forms are acceptable and some are not. Where a wrong form has been used, write the acceptable form.

EXERCISE

1. Reverend Clark is the person to *whom* we'll go for advice.
2. Barbara and she are the ones *who* I believe should receive the award.
3. *Us* union members are happy about the *company's* being so generous.
4. You, not *me,* must make the decision.
5. You suspect Jennifer's friends, but she is more likely to be guilty than *they.*
6. Our school officials did not like *us* heckling the visiting speaker.
7. I will be pleased to work with *whomever* you appoint to the job.
8. I will be pleased to work with *whoever* accepts the job.
9. Nielson is the candidate *who* the party leaders prefer.
10. The comments were directed at *we* two, you and I.
11. I'll support *whomever* has the best chance of defeating the incumbent.
12. In the dim light I thought *her* to be Mary.

GF4   SUBJECT-VERB AGREEMENT

In grammar the term **agreement** is used to describe the relationship between the inflectional forms of different elements within a sentence. When two related elements (subject and verb, pronoun and antecedent) show the same kind of inflection, they are said to agree. Thus a verb agrees with its subject if its form shows the same number and person as the subject. A pronoun agrees with its antecedent if both show the same gender, number, and person. The fundamental convention of agreement is that *the inflectional endings of two related elements should agree as far as possible.*

1. **Verbs agree with their subjects in number and person.**

A singular subject requires a singular verb, a plural subject a plural verb. If the subject is a personal pronoun, inflected for person, the verb agrees in person. If the subject is a noun, it is always considered to be in the third person and takes the third-person form of the verb.

I am late.	(subject first person singular; verb first person singular)
He is sorry.	(subject third person singular; verb third person singular)
The *man works* slowly.	*(works* third person singular to agree with *man)*

TROUBLESOME CONSTRUCTIONS

The following constructions cause most troubles in subject-verb agreement:

a.   **When two or more singular subjects are connected by *and,* a plural form of the verb is required.**

He and his brother *are* identical twins.
Tom, Sarah, Griff, and I *make* a good foursome.
A fool and his money *are* soon parted.

There are three exceptions to this rule: First, when each of the singular subjects is considered individually, the verb is singular. This usage is most frequent after *each* or *every.*

Here, every man and woman *works* for the good of the organization.
Each boy and girl *makes* a separate report.

Second, when the two singular subjects refer to the same person or thing, the singular verb is used.

His pride and joy *is* his new car.

Grape juice and ginger ale *is* a good drink.

Third, mathematical computations may take either a singular or a plural verb.

Five and five *is* ten.
or:
Five and five *are* ten.

Two times three *is* six.
or:
Two times three *are* six.

b.   When two or more singular subjects are connected by *or, nor,* **or** *but,* **a singular form of the verb is required.**

Quigley or Stein *is* to be elected.

Neither Saundra nor Hugh *has* a chance.

Not Sue but Betty *was* invited.

Not only his wife but even his mother *finds* him selfish.

c.   When one of two subjects connected by *or, nor,* **or** *but* **is singular and the other is plural, the verb agrees in number with the nearer one.**

Neither Lewis nor his lawyers *were* there.

Not only the boys but also their father *encourages* it.

d.   When two subjects connected by *or* **or** *nor* **differ in person, the verb agrees with the nearer.**

Neither you nor Ted *works* this evening.

Jean or you *are* to go.

Either Red or I *have* won.

When following this rule creates an awkward sentence, restate the idea in a form that is both correct and natural. For example, rather than write

Neither Ben nor I am to blame.

You or he is the leading contender.

restate these sentences as follows:

> Ben is not to blame, and neither am I.
> You and he are the leading contenders.

e. A singular subject followed immediately by *as well as, in addition to, including, no less than, with, together with,* or a similar prepositional construction, requires a singular verb.

> The husband as well as the wife *needs* advice.
> The senator together with his assistants *was* praised.
> The president no less than the secretary *is* responsible.
> The store in addition to the farm *was* sold.

Because this rule sometimes creates some strained sentences, it is sometimes best to avoid the construction altogether and to write:

> Both the husband and the wife *need* advice.
> The senator and his assistants *were* praised.
> The president *is* just as responsible as the secretary.
> The store and the farm *were* sold.

f. A singular subject followed by a phrase containing a plural noun requires a singular verb.

> The *attitude* of these men *is* definitely hostile.
> The *leader* of the rebel forces *has* been captured.
> *One* of the women in the back row *looks* sick.
> A *list* of the names of all survivors *is* on file.

In conversation, a plural modifier immediately before a verb often leads to a plural verb. This is most likely to happen in sentences like the last example, in which the subject is followed by a long modifier containing two plural nouns. This colloquial usage has less justification in writing, since the more deliberate nature of writing and revision makes it easier to identify *list* as a singular subject requiring a singular verb.

g. Indefinite pronouns such as *anybody, anyone, each, either, everybody, neither, nobody, no one,* and *somebody* generally require a singular verb.

> *Anybody* who does that *is* just reckless.
>
> *Anyone* who wants to *has* the right to split this with me.
>
> *Each* of them *makes* fifty dollars a week.
>
> *Somebody has been using* my bicycle.
>
> *Nobody* in town *admits* having seen him.
>
> *Everybody has* the same chance.

h. The pronouns *any* and *none* take either singular or plural verbs.

> *Are any* of you *going* to the show?
>
> *Any* of these times *is* satisfactory.
>
> *None works* so faithfully as he.
>
> *None are expected* from the district.

i. When the subject is a relative pronoun, the verb agrees with the antecedent of that pronoun.

> He is one of the *men who act* as advisers.
>
> This is one of those *problems that have* two solutions.

j. When the expletive *there* or the adverb *here* comes at or near the beginning of a sentence, the verb agrees with the subject that follows the verb.

> Here *is* your *money.*
>
> Here *are* the *receipts.*
>
> There *are* no second *chances.*
>
> There *are* a *man* and a *boy* in that boat.
>
> *Is* there a *chance* of his winning?
>
> *Were* there many *people* present?

This usage is not strictly observed in speech, because we often begin a sentence with an expletive followed by a single subject and then add more subjects before we finish the sentence. For example:

Did I see anyone you know at the party? Well, there was Juana Salazar, and Rae Carroll, and Dan Snyder.

In speech, we cannot conveniently revise the verb to take care of these additional subjects. But we do have such an opportunity in writing, and hence a plural verb is expected in such sentences.

k. When a sentence begins with the expletive *it*, the verb is always singular, regardless of the number of the subject.

It *is* the *Johnsons.*

It *is* *we* whom they want.

l. The complement of the verb *to be* does not affect the number of the verb.

Books are her chief source of enjoyment.

Her chief *source* of enjoyment *is* books.

One *thing* you must be ready for *is* their attempts to break up the meeting.

Their *attempts* to break up the meeting *are* one thing you must be ready for.

If this rule produces an awkward sentence, the wisest thing to do is to revise the sentence.

Awkward	Revised
The amusing *thing* about campaign speeches *is* the attempts that both sides make to represent themselves as the only friends of the people.	In campaign speeches, it is amusing to see how both sides attempt to represent themselves as the only friends of the people.

m. A collective noun takes a singular verb when the class it names is thought of as a unit, a plural verb when the members of the class are thought of as individuals.

Singular	Plural
The jury *is* finally complete.	The jury *were* divided in their opinions.
The family *holds* an annual reunion.	My family *have* never been able to agree.
The clergy *is* wretchedly underpaid.	The clergy *are* supporting this proposal from their pulpits.

This rule also applies to such nouns as *number, part,* and *rest.*

Singular	Plural
A large number *is* expected.	A number of errors *have* been found.
Only part of the order *was* delivered.	A great part of the people *have* no opinion on the question.
The rest of the page *is* illegible.	The rest of the votes *are* about equally divided among the three candidates.

n. Titles of books, magazines, movies, newspapers, plays, and the like take a singular verb.

The Sound and the Fury is a fine novel.

The Outcasts was not a success at the box office.

The *New York Times* is his bible.

o. Plural numbers take a singular verb when they are used in a phrase to indicate a sum or a unit.

A million dollars *is* a great deal of money.

Ten years *is* too long to wait.

Nine percent *is* good interest.

Forty hours *is* the regular work week.

p. Certain nouns that are plural in form generally take a singular verb. Some of these are *civics, economics, electronics, linguistics, mathematics, measles, mumps, news, physics, semantics.*

Economics *has* been called the dismal science.

No news *is* good news.

Semantics *is* the study of meanings.

Which of the forms in parentheses is the right one?   **EXERCISE**

1. Neither he nor his sons (was, were) present at the reading of the will.

2. Neither my sister nor my mother (plans, plan) to attend the physical fitness sessions for women.

3. The instructor as well as the students (was, were) at fault.

4. Each of the candidates for the position (has, have) exceptionally high qualifications.

5.   He is one of the students who (plans, plan) to attend the extra class session tomorrow.

6.   There (is, are) both food and firewood in the snowbound cabin.

7.   The jury (is, are) expected to reach its decision very quickly.

8.   Fifty hours (is, are) the amount of work time I contracted for.

9.   It (is, are) the Joneses who are particularly concerned about the new zoning regulations.

10.   The jury (is, are) to be isolated in individual hotel rooms each night during the trial.

GF5   PRONOUN-ANTECEDENT AGREEMENT

1.   Pronouns agree with their antecedents in gender, number, and person.

The **antecedent** of a pronoun is the noun or pronoun to which it refers. In "The children missed their parents," the antecedent of *their* is *children,* and in "She packed her suitcase," the antecedent of *her* is *She.* The rule requires that if the antecedent is plural, the pronoun must be plural (*their*); if the antecedent is feminine, the pronoun must take the feminine form (*she, her*); if the antecedent is declined for person, the pronoun should be in the same person. But a pronoun need not agree with its antecedent in case, since it takes its case from its function in its own clause.

Example	Explanation
The *men* got *their* wages.	Their *is third person plural to agree with* men. *The plural form of the pronoun is the same for all genders.*
The *girl* found *her* watch.	Her *is third person feminine singular to agree with* girl.
The *boy* misses *his* dog.	His *is third person masculine singular to agree with* boy.
The *plane* changed *its* course.	Its *is third person neuter singular to agree with* plane.
Mario and *Carlos* are looking for *their* parents.	*Two or more antecedents connected by* and *take a plural pronoun.*

TROUBLESOME CONSTRUCTIONS

Most troubles with agreement of pronouns occur in only a few constructions, and arise because of conflict between formal and colloquial usage. Generally, in formal usage the *form* of the antecedent, not its *meaning,* determines the number of the pronoun; whereas in colloquial usage number tends to be governed by *meaning.* For example, *everybody* is singular in form but plural in meaning, since it refers to more than one person. Formally, *everybody* requires the singular *his* or *her;* colloquially, *everybody* is often followed by the plural *their.*

a. *Each, either,* or *neither,* followed by a phrase containing a plural noun, takes a singular pronoun.

Each of the girls is sure *she* is going to win.

Neither of the men would admit *his* mistake.

Either of these women may lose *her* position.

b. *Everybody, each, either, everyone, neither, nobody,* or *a person* takes a singular pronoun.

Each has *his or her* own group of supporters.

Everybody had *his or her* work in good shape.

Nobody had *his or her* speech ready today.

Everyone was keeping *his or her* fingers crossed.

A *person* who begins to cut classes may find *himself or herself* in trouble.

As these examples show, English does not have a singular personal pronoun that refers to both male and female in such sentences as "Each student should do _____ own work." Traditionally, the masculine form of the pronoun has been used when the sex of the antecedent is unknown or when the antecedent refers to both sexes. But many people now urge that the linguistic discrimination implied in this traditional use should be avoided whenever possible. If the use of both masculine and feminine forms results in an awkward construction (as in some of the examples above), a sentence may be recast in the plural or reworded to eliminate the gender form. For example: "Students should do their own work"; "Nobody had a speech ready today"; "Cutting classes may lead to trouble."

c. **The impersonal *one* takes the third person pronoun unless the style is very formal.**

> *One* must watch *his or her* step with that group.
>
> *One* can't really blame *himself or herself* for that.
>
> If *one* had a second chance, how much wiser *he or she* might be.

In a very formal style the impersonal pronoun is sometimes used throughout.

> Under such conditions *one* laments *one's* utter incapacity to be of any genuine service.
>
> *One* finds *oneself* wishing that the evidence were more convincing.

d. **A collective noun takes either a singular or a plural pronoun, depending on whether the group is considered as a unit or as a number of individuals.**

Singular	Plural
The *family* keeps pretty much to *itself.*	The *family* may have *their* private quarrels, but *they* always agree in public.
The judge reprimanded the *jury* for *its* disregard of the evidence.	At the request of the defense attorney, the *jury* were polled and *their* individual verdicts recorded.
The *team* had *its* back to the wall.	The *team* are electing *their* captain.

e. **The relative pronoun *who* is used when the antecedent is a person; *which* is used when the antecedent is a thing; *that* is used to refer to persons, animals, or things.**

> This is the *man who* drove the car.
>
> The *girl who* found it is here.
>
> The *woman that* I mean had brown hair.
>
> Here is the *parcel which* (or *that)* she left.
>
> This is the *cow that* jumped over the moon.

The possessive form *whose* is theoretically limited to persons, but it is often used when the more formal *of which* seems awkward.

> The *nation whose* conscience is clear on that score is exceptional.
>
> The *newspaper whose* reporters are most alert gets the most scoops.

Indicate which of the forms in parentheses is the preferred form.

1.   Each boy must take (his, their) turn.

2.   Nobody will commit (himself or herself, themselves) to a definite plan.

3.   One shouldn't be too confident until (one has, you have) tried it.

4.   The team lost (its, their) opening game at home and won the first game (it, they) played away from home.

5.   The horse (who, that) won the Kentucky Derby went on to win the Preakness and the Belmont.

6.   My high school graduating class will hold (its, their) first reunion this Christmas.

7.   Neither of the bicycles (is, are) worth (its, their) price.

8.   Everybody has (his or her, their) own opinion about what we should do.

9.   The janitor (who, which) found the money was given a reward.

10.   The faculty are quite divided about whom (it, they) (wants, want) to be the next president.

GF6   VAGUE PRONOUN REFERENCE

A pronoun should refer clearly to a specific antecedent. If it refers to a whole clause, or to one of two possible antecedents, or to an unidentified antecedent, the reference may be vague.

Vague reference	**Explanation**	**Revision**
I lost a front tooth, *which* embarrassed me.	Which *refers to the whole main clause. In the revision the sentence is recast in order to avoid the vague reference.*	Losing a front tooth embarrassed me.
Because Kyle is more interested in literature than in biology, he sometimes slights *it*.	*The pronoun* it *has no clear antecedent and might refer to either literature or biology. The revision avoids the ambiguity.*	Kyle's interest in literature sometimes makes him slight biology.

Vague reference	Explanation	Revision
The crash is being investigated. At present *they* think the planes must have collided.	*The antecedent of* they *is not identified. The statements would be improved by substituting the noun* investigators *for the nonspecific pronoun.*	The crash is being investigated. At present the investigators think the planes must have collided.

EXERCISE   Revise the following sentences to make all pronoun references clear:

1.   The defendant was visibly upset. At that very moment they were in the next room deciding his fate.

2.   We have already overspent our budget for the play, but we need money for props and for set construction, which is a major problem.

3.   In revival meetings it is customary for them to offer testimonies.

4.   Hunters should be careful about how they carry guns when they are loaded.

5.   Mark Twain did not like his early work on *Huckleberry Finn,* which caused him to consider destroying the partially completed manuscript.

6.   The figure skaters anxiously awaited the decision as they tabulated their score cards.

7.   Fred and Sue agreed to have a church wedding, which pleases their parents.

8.   My job in New York was only three blocks from my apartment and the working hours were during the daytime, which pleased my mother.

9.   Kemper would draw sketches of birds and trees which showed where his interests lay.

10.   Students living in an apartment must do their own cooking and cleaning, which will take some of their time.

GF7   FAULTY COMPLEMENT

1. Avoid using an illogical or awkward construction as a complement of the verb *to be.*

The verb *to be* is usually either an auxiliary verb ("I *am* learning") or a linking verb ("Honesty *is* the best policy"). As a linking verb, it joins its complement to its subject and thus acts as a kind of equal sign: honesty = best policy. Readers expect two things of this linking verb: (1) that it will be followed by a complement, and (2) that the complement can be logically equated with the subject. They will be bothered if either of these expectations is not met.

Thus if they read the sentence, "Honesty is in the little details of everyday life," they will miss the promised linking relationship and will want to make the sentence read, "Honesty is best expressed in the little details of everyday life," thus changing *is* from a linking to an auxiliary verb (*"is* expressed").

Similarly, readers who meet the sentence, "Honesty is what you do in such a situation," will feel that the complement throws the equation out of balance, since it equates the abstract noun *honesty* with a statement of action. They will want to revise the sentence to read, "The honest thing to do in such a situation is to tell the truth," so that each side of the equation refers to an action (*to do* and *to tell*).

To avoid such annoying constructions, make sure that the complement of *to be* can be logically equated with the subject. If it cannot, or if the equation results in a wordy or awkward sentence, either revise the form of the complement or rewrite the sentence to get rid of the linking verb.

Illogical or awkward complement	Explanation	Revised sentence
Before I built the house, all I had learned about carpentry was from watching my father.	*The equation requires some statement of* what *I knew, not* how *my knowledge was obtained. Of the various possible revisions, perhaps the best is to substitute a more active verb that does not promise an equation.*	Before I built the house, all that I knew about carpentry *I had learned from* watching my father.
The chief disadvantage of weeping willows is the branches are brittle and break easily.	*The omission of* that *between* is *and the* branches *invites the misreading that* branches *is the complement. When that is inserted, however, the complement is seen to be the entire clause, of which* branches *is the subject.*	The chief disadvantage of weeping willows is *that* the branches are brittle and break easily.

2.   Avoid the use of *is when, is where,* and *is if* when the complement of *to be* is intended to describe or define the subject.

This advice is a special application of the more general statement given in rule 1. The use of an adverbial clause instead of a noun phrase or clause is one kind of illogical complement that occurs frequently in student definitions. This error and its revision are illustrated by the following examples:

Faulty complement	Explanation	Revision
Plagiarism is *when you represent another person's writing as your own.*	*The reader expects to find out* what *plagiarism is, not* when *it is. The construction calls for a noun phrase similar to the italicized phrase at the right.*	Plagiarism is *the representation of another's writing as one's own.*
Manslaughter is *where a person is killed deliberately but without premeditation.*	*Again, the construction requires a statement of* what *manslaughter is, not* where *it is.*	Manslaughter is *the deliberate but unpremeditated killing of a person.*
A comma splice is *if a comma is used to separate two independent sentences that are not connected by a coordinating conjunction.*	*The complement should tell* what *a comma splice* is, *not* how *a comma splice is made. Use a noun such as* use *at the right.*	A comma splice is *the use of a comma to separate two independent sentences that are not connected by a coordinating conjunction.*

3.   Use the adjective form as the complement of a sensory verb.

A **sensory verb** is one that identifies some action of the senses—seeing, hearing, feeling, tasting, smelling. Since the complement of a sensory verb usually describes the subject rather than the action of the verb, it should be an adjective, not an adverb. Turning the construction around and expressing the complement as an adjective, as in the parenthetical phrases below, helps illustrate the adjectival function of the complement:

The table feels smooth.   (smooth-feeling table)

The barrel looks clean.   (clean-looking barrel)

That note sounded flat.   (flat-sounding note)

The syrup tasted sweet.   (sweet-tasting syrup)

To use an adverb after these verbs would suggest that the writer was describing the manner in which the feeling, looking, sounding, and tasting were performed. Unless the modifier completing a sensory verb is clearly intended to describe the action suggested by the verb, an adjective is the correct form. The adverb is appropriate in the following sentences:

The blind man touched the paper lightly.

The doctor tasted the liquid cautiously.

Revise the following sentences to correct faulty complements: EXERCISE

1.   My only preparation for college chemistry was from a junior high school course in general science.

2.   I feel badly about having caused you so much trouble.

3.   Forgery is when one signs another person's name to a document.

4.   I heard on last night's news where flooding has reached disaster proportions in some areas of the country.

5.   Goal tending is if a defensive basketball player touches the ball after it has begun its downward path toward the goal.

6.   The result of our conference was in reaching complete accord.

7.   The most unusual food I have ever had was when I ate a serving of boiled snails.

8.   In tennis a double fault is where the server fails twice successively to hit the ball into the appropriate part of the opponent's court.

9.   The boxer's chief disadvantage is his opponents have learned that he has a "glass chin."

10.   The judge explained that perjury is if a witness lies under oath.

GF8   CONFUSION OF ADJECTIVE AND ADVERB

Modifiers that are faulty because of word order are discussed in **WO2**. This section is limited to errors in the forms of modifiers.

1. **Do not use an adjective to modify a verb.**

Adjective for adverb	Correct
The old car still runs *good*.	The old car still runs *well*.
Do it as *careful* as you can.	Do it as *carefully* as you can.
Listen *close* to what I tell you.	Listen *closely* to what I tell you.

2. **Do not use an adjective to modify an adverb or another adjective.**

Adjective for adverb	Correct
He is *considerable* better today.	He is *considerably* better today.
It is *sure* difficult to decide.	It is *surely* difficult to decide.

3. **Do not use an adverb as the complement of a sensory verb unless you clearly intend to modify the verb, not the subject.**

See **GF7**.

4. **When a modifier could modify either a noun or a verb, indicate by the form which one you intend.**

Adverb	Adjective
Tie the knot *tightly* and *securely*.	Tie the boat *tight* to the dock.
Her husband held her *firmly*.	He kept his resolutions *firm*.
John spoke out *forthrightly*.	His answers seemed *forthright*.

EXERCISE   Rewrite the following sentences to revise or delete faulty modifiers:

1. Speak gentle though you feel angry.
2. We are sure pleased that you could work with us today.
3. The polluted pond smelled horribly.
4. Fasten the hatches secure, for we expect strong wind and high waves tonight.
5. React as calm as you possibly can.
6. We have just come from a real exciting movie.
7. When Laura saw the grade on her algebra exam, she looked happily.
8. Keep him safely until the danger is past.
9. Now listen careful while I tell you once again.
10. I am considerable poorer for having bought a used car.

P

PUNCTUATION

The common marks of punctuation are the following:

period	.	quotation marks	" "
comma	,		or ' '
semicolon	;	apostrophe	'
colon	:	dash	—
question mark	?	parentheses	( )
exclamation mark	!	square brackets	[ ]

Most of these marks have highly specialized functions, and once these functions are understood, it is easy enough to use the specialized punctuation marks correctly. The chief exception, perhaps, is the comma, which is at once the most common mark of punctuation and the one with the most complex uses.

P 1   USES OF THE COMMA

The comma is used to make the internal structure of a sentence clear. It does so in three general ways: (1) by separating elements that might otherwise be confused, (2) by setting off interrupting constructions, and (3) by marking words out of normal order.

1. Use commas to separate elements that might otherwise seem to run together. Use them as separators in the following ways:

a. To prevent a confused, ambiguous, or awkward reading.

The most important use of the comma is to prevent a confused, ambiguous, or awkward reading. All other uses are subordinate to this one. Notice how the confused sentences at the left are made clear at the right by the use of commas.

Ambiguous	Explanation	Clear
Mr. Smith our milkman has been hurt.	*Is this a statement to or about Mr. Smith?*	Mr. Smith, our milkman has been hurt. *or* Mr. Smith, our milkman, has been hurt.
I do not care for money isn't everything.	*In order that* money *will not seem to complete* care for, *a comma should be inserted after* care.	I do not care, for money isn't everything.
A hundred yards below the bridge was flooded.	*Comma necessary to avoid misreading of* bridge *as the object of* below.	A hundred yards below, the bridge was flooded.

b. To separate two main clauses joined by a coordinating conjunction (*and, or, nor, but, for*).

The comma prevents possible misinterpretation on first reading; specifically, it keeps the subject of the second main clause from being misread as a second object in the first clause.

He sold his tractor and his fields went unplowed.

The club owner traded the catcher and the shortstop, his roommate, was angry.

In both these sentences the noun following the conjunction appears at first glance to be part of a compound object of the first verb. A comma before the conjunction shows clearly that the two nouns are in different clauses:

He sold his tractor, and his fields went unplowed.

The club owner traded the catcher, and the shortstop, his roommate, was angry.

When there is no danger of a confused reading, the comma becomes less necessary and may be omitted.

c.   **To separate elements in a series.**

Churchill promised the English only *blood, sweat, toil,* and *tears.*

Reading, swimming, and *dancing* are my favorite recreations.

It was said of Washington that he was *first in war, first in peace,* and *first in the hearts of his countrymen.*

North passed, East bid two spades, South bid three hearts, and *West doubled.*

We were tired, hungry and *disconsolate.*

As these illustrations show, a series may consist of clauses, phrases, or single words, and all items in a series should have the same grammatical form. The comma before the conjunction joining the last two items in a series is optional and may be omitted, as it is in the last example.

Commas are not used to separate adjectives in series under the following conditions:

1.   When the adjectives do not individually modify the same headword. For example, in "a new silk dress," *silk* modifies *dress,* but *new* modifies *silk dress.* This kind of sequence is different from the kind of sequence in "a dark, drizzly, cold day," in which each adjective individually modifies *day.*

2.   When the series is so commonly used that there is no need to separate the adjectives: "a nice little old lady" or "a red white and blue flag."

d.   **To separate contrasted elements in a "this, not that" construction.**

He is sick, not drunk.

We are disgusted, not angry.

This is a problem that must be handled with sympathy, not harshness.

e.   To separate directly quoted material from such speech tags as "he said," "she answered," and "we replied."

She said, "You are only half right."

"This," I declared, "is the last straw."

"Nobody asked you, sir," she said.

"But," he asked, "what if they do decide to come?"

Since the quotation marks themselves set off the quoted material, no confusion would result if the comma were omitted; but convention requires the comma. Whether the punctuation should come *inside* or *outside* the quotation marks is discussed in **P9**.

f.   To separate elements in dates, addresses, and place names.

January 1, 1976; Dec. 25, 1979	(comma between day and year)
She dated the check January 23, 1979, before remembering that the year was now 1980.	(comma between day and year and after year)
875 Main Street, Galesburg, Illinois	(comma between street and city and between city and state)
Chicago, Illinois, is the third-largest city in this country.	(comma before and after the state)
He was born in London, England.	(comma between city and country)

g.   In the following miscellaneous constructions: in figures—

22,745; 1,000,000; 150,743,290

in names followed by titles—

R. W. Leeds, M.D.

at the end of the salutation in informal letters—

Dear Joe,

after an introductory *yes* or *no*—

Yes, I'll do it.

In the following sentences insert commas if they are needed for ease of reading or are conventionally required:

1.   The largest city in the world is Jacksonville Florida if you judge by area not population.

2.   I'll have orange juice waffles with maple syrup and black coffee.

3.   When we finished sanding and staining the desk looked beautiful.

4.   "But the name is Manson not Mason" said Aunt Lois.

5.   After all it was not such a difficult shot for a professional.

6.   The yard was strewn with empty cartons newspapers scraps of lumber and discarded tires.

7.   Throughout his speech was a masterful exhibition of how to talk around a question without answering it.

8.   Father went to the airport to meet his sister and Mother came with me to the reception.

9.   Lyndon Baines Johnson, thirty-sixth President of the United States, was born near Stonewall Texas on August 27 1908 and died on January 22 1973.

10.   No I cannot wait any longer for the train leaves in ten minutes.

2.   Use commas to set off an interrupting construction.

Any element that comes between a subject and its verb, a verb and its object or complement, or any two elements not normally separated may be called an *interrupting construction.* If the interruption is awkward, it should be avoided; but many interrupters are necessary. These should be set off by commas, so that a reader can recognize the basic pattern of the sentence.

But we must distinguish between constructions that actually interrupt and those that come between related elements without interrupting them. For example, in

The girl, *you say,* has gone.

the italicized clause comes between subject *(girl)* and verb *(has gone).* The interrupter need not occupy this position. The sentence could have been written

You say that the girl has gone.

The girl has gone, you say.

But in the sentence

The girl *you want* has gone.

the italicized clause identifies the particular girl and cannot be moved without weakening the sentence. The clause modifies the subject so closely that we may consider "The girl you want" as the "whole subject" of *has gone.* A modifying phrase or clause which is so closely related to another element that it is felt to be a part of that element should not be set off with commas, since the commas would distort the relationship, not clarify it. The italicized modifiers in the following sentences are so necessary that they are not considered interrupting constructions:

The man *with him* is his brother.

The woman *at the piano* is his wife.

The leader *of the revolt* has been captured.

As you study the following uses of commas to set off interrupting constructions, notice this about them: *an interrupting construction between subject and verb, or verb and object, or verb and complement requires two commas to enclose it.* These commas act like mild parentheses and *are always used in pairs.*

a. To set off an appositive.

An **appositive** is a noun or pronoun, a noun phrase, or a noun clause that is considered grammatically equivalent to the noun or pronoun it refers to:

His father, *the president of the company,* will be responsible.

They want us, *you and me,* to go.

I felt that her main point, *that everybody must be on time,* was directed chiefly at me.

I want to see Dr. Roberts, *the guidance counselor.*

The first three examples show that the appositive is often a particular kind of interrupter. The fourth appositive does not interrupt the main clause, but is conventionally separated from the rest of the sentence by a comma.

But when an appositive is necessary to identify the subject, it is not considered an interrupting construction and is not set off with commas:

Your son *John* called.

John is necessary to identify the son who called.

b.   To set off nouns of address.

A **noun of address** is a common or proper noun used to name a listener to whom we are speaking directly: "I wish, *Dad,* that you would reconsider your decision." "I understand, *Mrs. Ellison,* that you are now a grandmother." Such nouns may come at the beginning, middle, or end of a sentence, so that strictly speaking they are not always interrupters. But they are always set off from the rest of the sentence by commas.

I would like to ask you, *Mr. Jones,* for your opinion.

Sir, I'd like to ask a question.

Listen, *chum,* I've had enough of you!

I wish I were going with you, *Brenda.*

c.   To set off conjunctive adverbs and other transitional markers.

Conjunctive adverbs (*however, moreover, therefore,* and the like), sometimes called **transitional connectives,** are adverbs that serve to connect main clauses or sentences. Usually they provide a transition between two such statements, and they come *near,* or *at,* the beginning of the second one.

We planned our demonstration for noon sharp. We thought, moreover, that we could bring it off.

Most students seemed excited enough. Some, however, were already expressing doubts.

Commas around *therefore* are sometimes omitted.

I am therefore canceling the order.

d. To set off a nonrestrictive modifier.

A modifier of a noun is said to be **restrictive** when it specifies a particular member or members of a group. In "The President *who said that* was Lincoln," the italicized modifier restricts the whole class of Presidents to a particular one. When a modifier does not limit a class to a particular group or individual but modifies the whole class, it is said to be **nonrestrictive.** Thus in "The President, *who is both the chief of state and the leader of his party,* holds one of the most powerful offices in the world," the italicized modifier refers to all Presidents of the United States and does not restrict the statement to any particular one. It is nonrestrictive.

A modifier of a verb or predicate is restrictive when it limits the action of the verb. Thus in "I'll go *if I must*," the italicized conditional clause states under what conditions the going will occur. Similarly, in "I did it *because I was forced to*," the italicized clause states why the speaker had to do a particular thing. In both examples the information provided by the modifier is so closely related to the action indicated by the verb that the meaning of the whole sentence would be considerably changed if the modifier were omitted.

The following sentences illustrate the punctuation of restrictive and nonrestrictive modifiers:

Restrictive	**Nonrestrictive**
All students *who were absent* will be required to do an additional assignment.	College graduates, *who represent a superior intellectual group,* must accept the responsibility of leadership.
Soldiers *who have flat feet* are not assigned to the infantry.	Soldiers, *who are selected by physical fitness tests,* should show a sickness rate lower than that of the total population.
He comes and goes *as he pleases.*	Just one more picture, *if you please.*
Speak *when you are spoken to.*	He asked me, *when she had gone,* who she was.

The best practical test of whether a modifier is restrictive in its context is to see if leaving it out would seriously distort the meaning of the sentence. Restrictive modifiers are so closely related to their headwords that they cannot be left out without distortion of the original meaning. Nonrestrictive modifiers, by contrast, can be omitted without significant change in the meaning. Compare the following omissions with the original versions above:

All students . . . will be required to do an additional assignment.	(This is not what the original statement meant.)
College graduates . . . must accept the responsibility of leadership.	(This is substantially what the original statement meant.)
Soldiers . . . are not assigned to the infantry.	(Not the original meaning.)
Soldiers . . . should show a sickness rate lower than that of the total population.	(The original meaning has not been substantially changed.)

He comes and goes.	(This was not the idea of the original sentence.)
Just one more picture.	(The omission does not change the meaning.)
Speak.	(The omission distorts the original meaning.)
He asked me . . . who she was.	(No significant change of meaning.)

In the following sentences, provide commas to set off appositives, nouns of address, conjunctive adverbs, and nonrestrictive modifiers. Some sentences may require no additional punctuation. **EXERCISE**

1. Dad did you know that Dr. Jones our chemistry professor once played professional hockey?

2. Mary asked, "Joe why don't you talk to the man in charge the managing editor?"

3. Yes her mother is a doctor—not however of medicine but of philosophy.

4. The man who said that must have been joking.

5. The man whoever he is must be found.

6. Don't shoot till you see the whites of their eyes.

7. Fred asked me when he called last night if we were still going to have the picnic.

8. The children looking very disappointed thanked us anyway.

9. The instructor said in addition that some of the test answers were illegible.

10. I left a call with the switchboard operator to be sure of getting up in time to catch my plane.

11. Dad you said we could go if we had finished our work. You promised moreover that we could use the car even though the direction signal is not working.

12. A radio report which may or may not be true states that John Whalen our line coach has an offer from a professional team that he will probably accept.

13. The challenger who was clearly the underdog before the match made his defeat of the champion look so easy that the sportswriters began to hail him as one of the truly great champions.

14. However the wig that she bought in the bargain basement was the best of the three.

15.   The bus driver Mr. Peterson who is usually an easygoing person was in a bad mood today scolding the children at the slightest provocation.

3.   Use commas to mark an inversion.

a.   To emphasize an inverted element.

Any word, phrase, or clause written out of its normal position is said to be *inverted*. To emphasize an inverted element, a writer sets it off with commas.

Myself, I will vote in favor of it.

Except for physics, my courses are not difficult.

But if the inversion is so common as to seem normal, the comma is usually omitted. No commas would be used in the following inversions:

Yesterday I had a bad time of it.

In 1913 the concept of total war was unknown.

In the following sentences the verbs are underlined.

b.   To set off a long introductory phrase or an adverbial clause preceding the main clause.

When a sentence opens with a long phrase or adverbial clause, use a comma between this element and the main clause:

1.   *Pulling over to the curb at the first opportunity,* I waited for the fire engines to pass.

2.   *If there is going to be any difficulty about this request,* I would rather withdraw it.

3.   *Being ignorant of the facts of the situation,* I could say nothing.

4.   *When you say that,* smile.

This usage is often considered optional, but the comma is generally used under the following conditions:

1.   when the opening phrase contains a verbal, as in examples 1 and 3
2.   when it is a subordinate clause, as in example 2
3.   when it is an obvious inversion, as in example 4

The comma should always be used if it makes the meaning clearer and the reading easier.

In the following sentences insert commas to set off inversions and introductory   E X E R C I S E
constructions where desirable.

1. Whatever he says take it with a grain of salt.

2. Whatever he says will be worth listening to.

3. If he is going to fly off the handle like that at the slightest provocation I think
you should stop dating him.

4. As far as I know they plan to stay here this summer.

5. Whatever the merits of the proposal it comes too late to be considered.

6. Whether you like it or not this is the final decision.

7. After the show we walked home together.

8. Since he has not answered any of our letters even those we sent by registered
mail we must assume that he is not interested.

9. Knowing that his only chance to win might depend on stealing second base
the manager sent in a runner for Milney.

10. Confused and hurt by her parents' attitude the girl ran sobbing to her room.

P 2   MISUSE OF THE COMMA

Too many commas can be more annoying than too few. Observe the following
"don't's":

1. Do not use a comma instead of a period between sentences.

Using a comma instead of a period between sentences may cause serious misinterpretation. (See "Comma Splice," **S5**.)

Comma splice	Clear
He spoke very quietly, as I listened, I had the impression that he was speaking to himself.	He spoke very quietly. As I listened, I had the impression that he was speaking to himself.
There was nothing more to be said, when they took that attitude, further negotiation became impossible.	There was nothing more to be said. When they took that attitude, further negotiation became impossible.

2. Do not use a comma between closely related elements except to mark an interrupting construction.

The comma should reveal the structure of a sentence, not disguise it. Closely related elements (subject and verb, verb and object, verb or noun and modifier) should not normally be separated. If these elements must be interrupted, using a pair of commas to enclose the interrupting construction helps to bridge the interruption.

Faulty comma	Correct
My car, is at the service station.	My car, which is at the service station, needs a thorough overhauling right away.
He said, that he would try.	He said, when I asked him, that he would try.
The student who lost his money, may need it badly.	The student, who had lost money on other occasions, was reprimanded for his carelessness.

The last pair of illustrations contrasts a restrictive and a nonrestrictive clause (see page 469). There should be no comma in the sentence at the left because the subordinate *who*–clause is a restrictive modifier.

3.   Do not use commas excessively.

It is not necessary to use commas in a particular construction simply because convention recommends them. Convention describes general practice and should usually be followed, but there are times when slavishly following the rules will chop a sentence to pieces. In such cases omit any punctuation that is not necessary to control the reading of the sentence. Exception: You may not omit commas that set off nonrestrictive modifiers or appositives.

The following examples illustrate excessive and adequate punctuation:

Excessive	Adequate
However, it is not, in my opinion, desirable.	However, it is not in my opinion desirable.
Yesterday, a little, old lady, in a dilapidated, old Ford, picked me up and brought me home.	Yesterday a little old lady in a dilapidated old Ford picked me up and brought me home.
Sometimes, she would appear in an elaborate beach outfit, sometimes, she wore a simple, white suit, and, occasionally, she put on a red, white, and blue bathing suit, with a detachable skirt.	Sometimes she would appear in an elaborate beach outfit, sometimes she wore a simple white suit, and occasionally she put on a red white and blue bathing suit with a detachable skirt.

P 3   USES OF THE SEMICOLON

1.   Use a semicolon to separate closely related independent clauses not connected by a conjunction.

> Try this one; it looks like your color.
>
> His mother won't let him; she is afraid he might get hurt.
>
> Your car is new; mine is eight years old.

In each of these sentences a period could be used instead of the semicolon. But the clauses, even though grammatically independent, are felt to be so closely related that a period makes too sharp a separation.

The semicolon provides a more emphatic separation than the comma; it affords a closer tie than the period. It is therefore the most suitable mark to balance two contrasted ideas parallel in form:

> Take care of the children; the adults can take care of themselves.
>
> It was not the hours or the pay that discouraged me; it was the constant monotony of the work.

2.   Use a semicolon between independent clauses joined by a transitional connective (conjunctive adverb).

Transitional connectives are words like *also, besides, consequently, furthermore, hence, however, in addition, likewise, moreover, nevertheless, still, then, therefore.* Since these connectives are not subordinating conjunctions, they require a stronger mark of punctuation than a comma.

> His argument has some merit; *however,* he goes too far.
>
> His eyes went bad; *consequently,* he had to resign his job as a proofreader.
>
> She argued brilliantly; *still,* her opponent had the stronger case.

3.   Use a semicolon to separate elements in a series that themselves contain commas.

> Among those present were Dr. Holmes, pastor of the First Methodist Church; A. C. Levitt, superintendent of schools; B. L. Rainey, manager of the Benson Hotel; and M. T. Cord, vice president of Miller and Sons.

Commas between the elements in this series would be confused with the commas that set off the appositives.

P 4   MISUSE OF THE SEMICOLON

1.   Do not use a semicolon as the equivalent of a colon.

Although the names suggest a close relationship, the semicolon and the colon have quite different uses and are not interchangeable. The colon (see **P7**) is used chiefly to indicate that something is to follow, usually a series of items; the semicolon separates parallel elements and is never used to introduce a series. In the following examples the faulty semicolon is followed by the correct colon in parentheses:

> My records show that the following students have not handed in the assignment; (:) Mr. Andrews, Mr. Richardson, Mr. Smith, and Ms. Wallace.
>
> Dear Sir; (:) May I call your attention to an error. . . .

2.   Do not use a semicolon as the equivalent of a comma.

A semicolon cannot be substituted for a comma between a main clause and a subordinate construction. In the following examples the faulty semicolon is followed by the correct comma in parentheses:

> Although I seldom have trouble with grammar or spelling; (,) I never seem to use the right punctuation.
>
> We stayed up until two o'clock in the morning; (,) hoping that they would arrive.

P 5   THE PERIOD

1.   A period is used to mark the end of a declarative sentence.

Unless a sentence is intended as a question, a command, or an exclamation, it is declarative and is closed by a period.

> Today is Tuesday.
>
> We have three days to go.

2.   A period is used to mark an accepted abbreviation such as the abbreviation of a title—

Col., Dr., Hon., Mrs., Rev.

degree—

B.A., B.S., M.D., Ph.D.

name—

John A. Jones, Chas. W. Brown

month—

Jan., Feb., Aug., Nov.

state—

Ala., Ga., Me., Ill., Wash. (*but also:* AL, GA, ME, IL, WA—no period is used in the capital-style, two-letter state abbreviations)

miscellaneous—

Ave., St., vol., p., U.S.A., B.C., A.D.

Notice, however, that periods are not used in such shortened forms as *exam, gym, prom, per cent, 1st, 2nd, 3rd.* Periods are usually omitted also in abbreviations of government agencies—*USNR, TVA, AEC, FBI, CIA.*

3. **A period is used before a decimal and between dollars and cents.**

The error is less than .01 inch.

The correct answer is 57.39.

The price tag read $11.98.

P6 QUESTION AND EXCLAMATION MARKS

1. **The main use of the question mark is to indicate that a sentence is to be understood as a question.**

Whose is this?

You mean he's ill?

But if the question is a courteous way of stating a request, the end punctuation is a period, not a question mark:

Will you please hand in your papers now.

The question mark is sometimes used in parentheses to query the accuracy of the preceding word:

These amateurs (?) make a comfortable living out of sports.

As a device for irony, however, it is generally weak. Avoid:

Those funny (?) remarks are uncalled for.

Notice that a question reported in indirect discourse does not take a question mark:

They asked where we were going.

2.   The exclamation mark is used to show that a statement is imperative or that it is spoken with strong emotion.

Be quiet!
Don't just stand there! Do something!
Oh, what a mess!

P 7   THE COLON

Use a colon:

1.   To indicate that something is to follow, especially a formal statement or series.

Here are the facts: The money was there five minutes before he entered the room; it was missing immediately after he left; the next day he bought a new record player, though he had already spent all this month's allowance.

2.   In place of a comma before long direct quotations.

In his most famous speech Bryan said: "You shall not press down upon the brow of labor a crown of thorns; you shall not crucify mankind upon a cross of gold."

This is her statement as reported in the papers: "I have never advocated such ideas; I do not advocate them now; I do not approve of them; I have no reason to believe that I ever will approve of them."

3. Before a clause that restates in different words the idea of the preceding clause.

> *Romeo and Juliet* is one of the great experiences in film. It is not, to be sure, the greatest: the creation of new dramatic poetry is more important than the re-creation of old.
>
> Except for differences of subject matter, the rules of grammar are in essence like the laws of physics and chemistry: they are scientific generalizations about the facts.

In such uses the clause after the colon says, in another way, what the clause before the colon has already said. But the restatement is not needless repetition: it illustrates or amplifies the content of the preceding clause.

4. Between clauses when the second clause provides an example of something stated in the first.

> Very few baseball players can be called superstars: Reggie Jackson is one of those few.

5. In certain specialized uses: after the salutation in formal letters—

> Dear Sir:

between hours and minutes—

> The train is due at 8:36.

between chapter and verse in Biblical citations—

> Isaiah 12:2–4

between volume and page in a magazine citation—

> *College English* 29:253–285

between place and publisher in a bibliography—

> Boston: Houghton Mifflin

P8 QUOTATION MARKS

This section is limited to the use of quotation marks. The position of other punctuation in relation to quotation marks is treated separately in the next section. Quotation marks may be double (" ") or single (' ').

DOUBLE QUOTATION MARKS

1. Double quotation marks have the following uses:

a. To enclose the actual words of a speaker (direct discourse).

> I said, "That's your worry."
> "Bob," he said, "you can't do that!"
> "What is the matter?" she asked.

Since all the words of a speaker are enclosed in quotation marks, an interrupting "he said," "she replied," or the like requires two sets of quotation marks in the sentence. Notice also that when direct discourse is reported as indirect discourse, quotation marks are not used.

> She asked what was the matter.

b. To identify words that are being discussed as words.

> The word "garage" comes from French; the word "piano" comes from Italian.
> "Buxom" originally came from the Old English verb meaning "to bend."

This use of quotation marks to call attention to a word is sometimes extended to include technical terms *(A "field" in mathematics is not what it is in agriculture)* and slang terms *(Her brother "socked" her in the eye and "beaned" her with a ruler).* Though occasionally acceptable, this usage is often overdone. Quotation marks do not make a term appropriate. If a word is appropriate in context, it can usually stand without quotation marks; if it is not appropriate, it should not be used.

Another method, preferred by some writers, is to underline or italicize the word being cited (see page 508).

> *To be* is the trickiest verb in the language.

c. To enclose the titles of essays, short stories, articles, poems, paintings, songs, television programs, and the like (but not books).

(For an alternative form for paintings and musical compositions, see page 507.)

I think Hemingway's best short story is "The Snows of Kilimanjaro."

It was Cole Porter who wrote "Begin the Beguine."

Two of my otherwise highbrow mother's favorite television programs were "The Waltons" and "All in the Family."

He says that Da Vinci's "Mona Lisa" is a portrait of an Italian noblewoman.

d. In bibliographies, to distinguish the title of a selection from that of the book from which it is taken.

Faulkner, William. "Two Soldiers." In *Collected Stories of William Faulkner.*
   New York: Random House, 1950.

For additional examples of this use, see pages 336–337. Notice that titles of books are either underlined or set in italics, not enclosed in quotation marks.

SINGLE QUOTATION MARKS

2. Single quotation marks are used to mark quotations within quotations.

When it is necessary to include one set of quotation marks within another, the internal quotation is placed within single marks, the longer quotation within double marks:

When the director said, "Let's try that passage again, beginning with 'Once more into the breach,' and remember that this is a battle, not a declamation contest," there was an audible Bronx cheer from one of the veterans.

P9 PUNCTUATION WITH QUOTATION MARKS

The question often comes up whether punctuation should be placed *inside* or *outside* quotation marks. The procedure recommended by the *MLA Handbook* is to place commas and periods *inside* the quotation marks, and all other marks *outside* them. But if a question mark or exclamation mark is part of the quotation, it is placed *inside* the quotation marks. This recommendation may be detailed as follows:

1. **When the quoted words are followed by a comma, put the comma inside the quotation marks.**

"If you insist," I said, "I'll do it."

The word "bread," for example, has both standard and slang meanings.

A comma after "he said," "she replied," and similar tags should be placed immediately after these phrases, as in the first example above.

2. **A period, like a comma, always goes inside the quotation marks.**

That is not the way to spell "eclectic."

He said, "You can always count on Tom to muddy the issue."

3. **If a quotation ends with both single and double quotation marks, the final period comes inside both sets of marks.**

Here is an excerpt from my brother's letter: "Today in class Mr. Blair quoted Wordsworth's line 'A six years' darling of a pigmy size,' and said it appeared in one edition as 'A six years' darling of a pig my size.'"

4. **If the quotation is a question, the question mark goes inside the quotation marks; if the whole sentence in which a quotation appears is a question but the quotation is not, the question mark goes outside.**

Somebody yelled, "Why don't you go home?" (What was yelled was a question.)

Did he actually say, "Let Williams do it"? (The quotation is not a question, but the whole sentence is. The question mark goes outside the quotation marks, and no other end punctuation is used.)

Well, how *do* you spell "eclectic"? (The whole sentence is a question, not just the word "eclectic.")

5. **The exclamation mark, like the question mark, goes inside if the quotation itself is an exclamation; otherwise it goes outside.**

"Get out of my sight!" he yelled. (The quoted portion is an exclamation.)

But I *did* say "Friday"!   (The whole sentence is an exclama-
                                 tion; "Friday" is not.)

His only answer was "Nonsense!" (Only the quoted word is an exclama-
                                 tion.)

6. If a semicolon is used to separate a quotation from the rest of the sentence, it always goes outside the quotation marks.

He said, "You can be confident that I'll do it"; but I was not the least bit confident.

7. When a dash is used to indicate that a remark was left unfinished, it is included within the quotation marks.

Occasionally speakers are interrupted or for some reason fail to finish what they have begun to say. Whenever this happens, a dash is used to show that the quotation is not finished.

"But Mary said—" she began, then stopped suddenly.

Nicholson said loudly, "In my opinion, our instructor is—" Just then the instructor walked into the room.

Notice that a concluding period is not used after the dash.

P10   THE APOSTROPHE

The apostrophe (') has three general uses:
1. To indicate the possessive case of nouns and some pronouns.

To indicate the possessive, an apostrophe followed by *s* is added to the regular form of the following types of nouns and pronouns:

1.   both singular and plural nouns that do not end in *s:*

boy's, girl's, ox's, mouse's, tooth's, antenna's
men's, women's, oxen's, mice's, teeth's, antennae's

2.   singular nouns ending in *s:*

James's, Charles's, Keats's, Burns's, Dickens's

Usage for this group varies. Some writers omit the final *s*: *James', Charles'*. When a noun already contains two or more *s* sounds, these writers are especially reluctant to add the final *s*. They would strongly prefer, for example, *Massachusetts', mistress', Jesus'*. But since most written communications are not read aloud, the repetition of *s* sounds is not so objectionable as it might seem to be. With singular nouns ending in *s*, then, follow your own preference.

3. indefinite pronouns:

anybody's, anyone's, everybody's, one's, nobody's, someone's

An apostrophe without an *s* is added to form the possessive of plural nouns that end in *s*. Most plural nouns, of course, fit into this category.

babies' clothing, lions' manes, birds' nests, teachers' personalities

2.   To indicate the omission of letters or figures.

I've, can't, hasn't, isn't, '48 (1948), the class of '39

3.   To indicate the plural of letters or figures.

Let's begin with the *A*'s.
Mr. Cardoza's application was misfiled among the *K*'s.
Her *S*'s look like *8*'s.

P 1 1   ELLIPSIS

1.   The basic use of an ellipsis (. . .) is to mark the omission of one or more words from a quotation.

If the omitted words were preceded in the original quotation by a comma or other punctuation mark necessary to the meaning of the shortened quotation, the punctuation mark is given and then the three dots of the ellipsis (, . . .). If the ellipsis comes at the end of a sentence, it is followed by a fourth dot to mark the concluding period (. . . .). The following ellipses (note the plural form) illustrate the conventions:

Original quotation

In a famous speech after the British defeat at Dunkirk, Churchill said: "Even though large tracts of Europe and many old and famous States have fallen or may fall into the grip of the Gestapo and all the odious apparatus of Nazi rule, we shall not flag or fail. We shall go on to the end. We shall fight in France, we shall fight on the seas and oceans, we shall fight with growing confidence and growing strength in the air, we shall defend our island, whatever the cost may be. We shall fight on the beaches, we shall fight on the landing grounds, we shall fight in the fields and in the streets, we shall fight in the hills; we shall never surrender, and even if, which I do not for a moment believe, this island or a large part of it were subjugated and starving, then our Empire beyond the seas, armed and guarded by the British Fleet, would carry on the struggle, until, in God's good time, the new world, with all its power and might, steps forth to the rescue and the liberation of the old."

Elliptical quotation

In a famous speech after the British defeat at Dunkirk, Churchill said: ". . . we shall not flag or fail. We shall go on to the end. . . . We shall fight on the beaches, . . . we shall fight in the fields and in the streets . . . ; we shall never surrender. . . ."

2. A second use of ellipsis is to indicate that a progression of numbers continues beyond the last figure given.

1, 4, 7, 10, 13, . . .

P 12 DASH

The dash should not be used as a general utility mark in place of a comma, period, semicolon, or colon. It is a specialized punctuation mark that serves the following purposes:

Use the dash:

1. To stress a word or phrase at the end of a sentence.

In the whole world there is only one person he really admires–himself.

And now it is my pleasure to present a man whom we all know and admire and to whom we are all deeply indebted–the Reverend Dr. Mason.

Absence makes the heart grow fonder–of somebody else.

2. To set off a summary of, or conclusion to, an involved sentence.

To live as free people in a free country; to enjoy, even to abuse, the right to think and speak as we like; to feel that the state is the servant of its people; to be, even in a literal sense, a trustee and a partner in the conduct of a nation–all this is what democracy means to us.

3. To mark an interrupted or unfinished construction.

"I'd like to," he said, "but I'm–"
"You're what?" I asked.
"Well, I'm–I–you see, I've never done anything like that before, and I won't–I mean, I see no reason to start now."

4. In pairs, to set off a pronounced interruption.

There will never again be–you may be sure of this–so glorious an opportunity.

This answer–if we can call it an answer–is completely meaningless.

P 13 PARENTHESES AND BRACKETS

PARENTHESES

1. The three most common uses of parentheses are:

a. To enclose an explanation, qualification, or example.

His wife (he married about a year ago) is a member of a fine New England family.

Nice (in the old sense of "discriminating") has almost fallen out of use.

Foreign words (*data,* for example) slowly become naturalized and lose their foreign characteristics.

b. To enclose cross-references.

(See Appendix A.)

(See page 271.)

(Consult *Webster's Biographical Dictionary.*)

George Bellows described the world of sports in vivid oil paintings like *Dempsey and Firpo* (see Plate VI).

c. In formal business transactions, to repeat a sum previously stated in words.

I enclose three hundred dollars ($300.00) to cover my share of the costs.

BRACKETS

Square brackets are used chiefly to enclose an editorial or a clarifying explanation or comment within a passage being edited, reported, or quoted. The words within the brackets are supplied by the editor or reporter. The Latin word *sic,* meaning "thus," is included in brackets after an error to indicate that the error is in the original statement.

The entry reads, "The father died of numonia [sic]."

Smith is unjustified in claiming, "What he [Faulkner] meant to write is 'back door,' not 'black door.' "

A. Where necessary, rewrite the following sentences, inserting appropriate punctuation. If sentences are correct as they stand, simply mark them OK.

REVIEW EXERCISES

1. Mr. Reynolds the insurance agent had not arrived by nine o'clock.

2. I wonder whats keeping him Dad grumbled. Are you sure that he said he would call at eight o'clock.

3. Yes quite sure I replied. He said to me Tell your father I will call at eight o'clock.

4. I have not seen Mrs. Manlin for some time since her husband was killed she spends a lot of time at her mother's place.

5. Gutenberg the inventor of movable type was motivated by a desire to make the Bible more widely available.

6. I hear that the man who was responsible for the accident has been arrested.

7. The speaker who was obviously embarrassed said that he did not answer questions of such a personal nature.

8. No wonder her hair looks different she's wearing a wig.

9. Some of the shutters had fallen to the ground others were hanging from one corner and a few were firmly locked in place across the windows.

10. Seated at the speakers' table were Fred Hanley, superintendent of schools, Dr Mason, dean of the College of Education, Mrs Helen Loftus, president of the Parent Teachers Association, and the chairman, Professor Robbins.

11. The girl who received first prize a silver cup was our neighbors' daughter.

12. A dog that's frightened by the sound of gunshots is no good for hunting.

13. However important these facts may have been eight years ago they have no significance today.

14. Trevino despite the pressure he was under continued to joke with the gallery.

15. He said when I asked him that he expected to take a brief vacation.

16. She said When I asked his opinion he answered if you want legal advice I'll be glad to talk with you in my office.

17. Donald said if I remember correctly that he would be out of town for the next three or four days.

18. Where the old ice house used to be there is now a little stone cottage with a white picket fence around it.

19. Giggling almost hysterically the children either could not or would not explain what had happened.

20. Mules though less speedy than horses in open country are both faster and surer on those narrow mountain tracks.

B. The following selection is now punctuated only at the ends of the sentences. Add whatever internal punctuation you think necessary and be able to explain why.

The plight of a normal person who finds himself committed to a mental institution and unable to convince anyone he is not insane is a standard plot for horror fiction. But in a remarkable study last week Dr David L Rosenhan professor of psychology and law at Stanford University and seven associates reported just such a nightmare in real life. To find out how well psychiatric professionals can distinguish the normal from the sick they had themselves committed to mental institutions. Their experiment reported in the journal *Science* clearly showed that once inside the hospital walls everyone is judged insane.

The pseudopatients five men and three women included three psychologists a pediatrician a psychiatrist a painter and a housewife all of whom were certifiably sane. In the course of the three-year study the volunteers spent an average of nineteen days in a dozen institutions private and public in New York California Pennsylvania Oregon and Delaware. Each pseudopatient told admitting doctors that he kept hearing voices that said words like empty hollow and void suggesting that the patient found his life meaningless and futile. But beyond falsifying their names and occupations all the volunteers described their life histories as they actually were. In so doing they gave the doctors every chance to discern the truth. I couldn't believe we wouldnt be found out Rosenhan told *Newsweek*'s Gerald Lubenow. But they werent. At eleven hospitals the pseudopatients were promptly diagnosed as schizophrenic and at the twelfth as manic-depressive.

As soon as they had gained admission the volunteers studiously resumed normal behavior. They denied hearing voices and worked hard to convince the staff members that they ought to be released. But such efforts were to no avail doctors and nurses interpreted everything the pseudopatients did in terms of the original diagnosis. When some of the volunteers went about taking notes the hospital staff made such entries in their records as patient engages in writing behavior. The only people who realized that the experimenters were normal were some of the patients. Youre not crazy said one patient. Youre a journalist or a professor. Youre checking up on the hospital. (Copyright Newsweek, Inc. 1973, reprinted by permission.)

S p   SPELLING

If you have trouble with spelling, the first step toward improvement is to take an inventory of your errors. In a notebook keep a written record of the words *that you actually misspell in your writing.* This is your basic list. Review it periodically and keep it up to date by crossing out the words you have mastered and by adding new words that you have recently misspelled.

When you study your list, concentrate on the *part* of the word that you have misspelled. Generally we misspell not words, but syllables. For example, most students who misspell *secretary* interchange the second and third vowels; most misspellings of *tragedy* come from placing an extra *d* before the *g;* and misspellings of such words as *receive, belief,* and *friend* come from reversing the *i* and *e.* Identifying your specific errors allows you to concentrate on the syllable in which the error occurs.

For words that prove unusually troublesome it often helps to learn or invent some memorizing device: a rule, a slogan, a jingle—anything, no matter how absurd, that will remind you of the correct spelling of a particular syllable. The rule of "*i* before *e* except after *c,*" which is stated as a jingle on page 494, and the rules for prefixes and suffixes are generally useful memorizing devices. It may help, too, to remember statements like "A good secretary keeps a secret," "Remember the gum in argument," and "Every cemetery has a meter in the middle." Or you may capitalize the danger spots in practice—*tRAGedy, mainTENance, desPERate.* If these devices help you, use them; if not, invent your own.

Finally, so far as possible, don't worry about spelling while writing the first drafts of your papers. Wait until revision. If you break off writing a paragraph to use the dictionary, you may lose a thought you cannot recapture. Put a check in the margin and go on. Then, when the first draft is finished, you can look up the spellings of all the words you have checked. Indeed, a student with severe spelling troubles should proofread every draft of each paper at least once for spelling alone.

In short, then: (1) keep a spelling record, (2) study it at regular intervals, (3) identify the trouble spot in each word, (4) figure out a way to remember the correct spelling, and (5) check your spelling when you proofread.

THE MOST COMMON TRAPS IN SPELLING

Although any word that is not spelled the way it sounds may give trouble, six types of words are especially likely to cause errors. Let us look briefly at these error-causing word types.

Words containing a "colorless" vowel A vowel in an unstressed position (*ago, agent, awkward, maintenance, incredible, bachelor*) is likely to be pronounced as a very weak "uh." This sound is called the *colorless,* or *neutral, vowel.* Because its sound gives no clue to its spelling, the colorless vowel is responsible for many spelling errors. There is nothing to guide you in spelling this sound. The only solution is to memorize the vowel in any word that repeatedly causes trouble. The best help is a memorizing device, such as magnifying the syllable in question—*balANCE, independENT, eliGIble, sponSOR, forEIGN, chaufFEUR.*

Words with *ie* or *ei*   Words like *niece, receive,* and *friend* are frequently mis-spelled through the interchanging of the *e* and the *i.* Most of these errors may be easily removed by following rule 4 on page 494 and memorizing the eleven exceptions.

Words with similar sounds but different meanings   Such words as *altar, alter; peace, piece; weak, week; weather, whether* are easily confused, as are the con-trasted pairs given on page 495.

Words with irregular plural forms   Most English nouns are made plural by the addition of *-s* to the singular form. All plurals formed in any other way may be considered irregular. The most troublesome plurals to spell are those of nouns ending in *o* or *y.* Such nouns have regular *s* plurals when the *o* or *y* immediately follows a vowel *(cameo, cameos; key, keys; studio, studios),* but are generally irregular when the *o* or *y* follows a consonant *(cargo, cargoes; veto, vetoes; lady, ladies; torpedo, torpedos).* See rules 6 and 7 on page 494.

Words in which the final consonant is doubled before a suffix beginning with a vowel   Some words double a final consonant before adding a suffix beginning with a vowel *(refer, referred),* while others do not *(benefit, benefited).* This inconsistency causes many spelling errors, and the "rule" is so cumbersome and has so many exceptions that students often prefer to study the individual words that cause them trouble. The more useful part of the rule concerning doubled conso-nants is given as rule 9 on page 495.

Common exceptions to general rules   Any exceptional spelling is likely to be difficult because of the tendency to make it conform to the regular pattern. For example, a student who is not sure how to spell *seize* is likely to interchange the *e* and *i* because of the *i*-before-*e* rule. Similarly, the rule that a silent *e* at the end of a word is retained in adding a suffix beginning with a consonant leads many students to misspell *argument.* Words like these are exceptions to general rules and cause many spelling errors. The only safe procedure is to *memorize the exceptions along with the rule.* Whenever a rule is given in the following pages, the common exceptions are noted as well. Study these as carefully as you study the rule itself.

RULES OF SPELLING

Only the most useful rules are given here.

1. **The prefixes *un-, dis-, mis-* do not affect the spelling of the root.**

   Thus, *unafraid* but *unnecessary; disappoint* but *dissatisfy; misrepresent* but *misspell.* And

   > unable, unknown, unopened; *but* unnatural, unnerved, unnoticed
   >
   > disable, disorder, disregard; *but* disservice, dissimilar, dissolve
   >
   > misbehave, misconduct, misguided; *but* misshapen, misspent, misstatement

2. **When a suffix beginning with a consonant is added to a word ending in silent *e*, the *e* is retained.**

   > absolutely, achievement, extremely, indefinitely, sincerely

   Exceptions to this rule include *argument, awful, duly, ninth, probably, truly, wholly.*
   Three common words have alternative spellings: *abridgment, abridgement; acknowledgment, acknowledgement; judgment, judgement.*

3. **When a suffix beginning with a vowel is added to a word ending in silent *e*, the *e* is dropped unless it is required to indicate pronunciation or to avoid confusion with a similar word.**

   > accumulating, achieving, boring, coming, grievance, icy

   Following are examples of the kinds of exceptions mentioned in the rule:

   a. *e* retained to keep *c* or *g* soft

   > advantageous, changeable, courageous, manageable, noticeable, outrageous, peaceable, serviceable, singeing, tingeing, vengeance

   b. *e* kept to prevent mispronunciation

   > canoeist, eyeing, hoeing, mileage, shoeing

   c. *e* kept to prevent confusion with other words

   > dyeing, singeing

4.   The order of the vowels in the *ie* combination *(ceiling, niece)* is explained in the jingle:

> Write *i* before *e*
> Except after *c*
> Or when sounded like *ay*
> As in *neighbor* and *weigh.*

Exceptions to the rule include *counterfeit, either, foreign, forfeit, height, leisure, neither, seize, seizure, sovereign, weird.*

5.   Words ending with the sound "seed" are usually spelled *-cede.*

accede, concede, intercede, precede, recede, secede

There are only four exceptions to this rule. Three of them end in *ceed (exceed, proceed, succeed);* the fourth is the only English word that ends in *sede (supersede).*

6.   Singular nouns ending in a consonant plus *y* form their plurals by changing the *y* to *i* before adding *-es.*

This rule also applies to the third person singular of verbs.

ally, allies; baby, babies; city, cities; cry, cries; try, tries

The plurals of proper names often add *-s* immediately after the *y* and are an exception: *the Kellys, the Marys, the Sallys.*

Notice that singular nouns ending in a vowel plus *y* are regular and simply take on an *-s* on becoming plural: *attorneys, donkeys, valleys.*

7.   Singular nouns ending in a consonant plus *o* generally form their plurals by adding *-es.*

buffaloes, cargoes, echoes, heroes, potatoes, torpedoes, vetoes

There are many exceptions. The chief exceptions are musical terms: *altos, bassos, pianos, solos, sopranos.* Others are *autos, cantos, dynamos, Eskimos, quartos.*

Notice that singular nouns ending in a vowel plus *o* are regular and simply add *-s* to form the plural: *cameos, folios, radios, studios.*

8.   Most singular nouns ending in *s, ss, sh, ch, x,* or *z* form their plurals by adding *-es.*

Jameses, Joneses, ashes, bushes, matches, pitches, foxes, taxes, buzzes

Exceptions include *fish* and *Swiss* (both of which are plural as well as singular forms) and borrowed Greek nouns ending in *is (ellipsis, ellipses; thesis, theses)*.

9. Words of one syllable double the final consonant before adding a suffix beginning with a vowel if (1) they end in a single consonant, and (2) they contain a single vowel.

begging, fitting, spinning

This rule holds only if *both* conditions are satisfied. Thus a word of one syllable ending in *two* consonants does not double the final consonant before a suffix beginning with a vowel (ac*t*ing, as*k*ed, par*t*ing, sif*t*ed). And a one-syllable word containing *two* vowels does not double the final consonant (bea*r*ing, cree*p*ing, dea*l*ing, ree*l*ing, soa*r*ing).

A. Errors in the following words may be classified as errors in spelling or errors in diction, since both meaning and spelling are involved in their correct use. Check those words that you are unsure of and look them up in the Checklist of Troublesome Usages, which begins on page 529.

REVIEW EXERCISES

access–excess
adapt–adopt
advice–advise
affective–effective
all together–altogether
allusion–illusion
capital–capitol
censor–censure
cite–sight–site
complement–compliment
continual–continuous
council–counsel
decent–descent
desert–dessert
economic–economical
elicit–illicit
emigrant–immigrant
eminent–imminent

formally–formerly
ingenious–ingenuous
irrelevant–irreverent
judicial–judicious
loath–loathe
loose–lose
luxuriant–luxurious
moral–morale
personal–personnel
principal–principle
prophecy–prophesy
respectfully–respectively
right–rite
sensual–sensuous
stationary–stationery
suit–suite
troop–troupe

B.   Following is a list of words frequently misspelled by college students. Under-line those words that you know you have trouble with and review them from time to time. The list may also serve as a handy reference when you proofread your papers.

abbreviate	annual	bearing
absence	antecedent	becoming
absurd	anxiety	beggar
accelerate	apartment	beginning
accidentally	apparatus	believe
accommodate	apparent	beneficial
accomplish	appearance	benefited
according	appropriate	biscuit
accumulate	arctic	boundaries
accustom	argument	breathe
achievement	arising	brilliant
acoustics	arithmetic	Britain
acquaintance	arouse	Britannica
acquitted	arranging	bulletin
across	article	buoyant
address	artillery	bureau
aggravate	ascend	buried
aggression	association	burying
airplane	athlete	business
alleviate	athletics	busy
alley	attempt	cafeteria
allotted	attractive	calendar
allowed	audible	candidate
ally	audience	carburetor
although	authorities	carrying
always	automobile	casualties
amateur	auxiliary	causal
ambiguous	awkward	ceiling
ammunition	bachelor	celebrity
among	balance	cemetery
amount	balloon	certain
analogous	barbarous	changeable
analysis	barring	changing
analyze	battalion	characteristic

chauffeur

chief

choosing

chosen

clause

climbed

clothes

colloquial

colonel

column

coming

commission

commitment

committed

committee

companies

comparatively

compel

compelled

competent

competition

complaint

completely

compulsory

concede

conceivable

conceive

condemn

condescend

connoisseur

conqueror

conscience

conscientious

considered

consistent

contemptible

control

controlled

convenient

copies

corner

coroner

corps

corpse

costume

countries

courteous

courtesy

cries

criticism

criticize

cruelty

cruise

curiosity

curriculum

custom

cylinder

dealt

debater

deceitful

deceive

decide

decision

defendant

deferred

deficient

definite

definition

democracy

dependent

descendant

description

desirable

despair

desperate

destruction

developed

development

diaphragm

diary

dictionary

dietitian

difference

digging

diphtheria

disappearance

disappoint

disastrous

discipline

discussion

disease

dissatisfied

dissipate

distribute

doesn't

dominant

don't

dormitories

dropped

drunkenness

echoes

ecstasy

efficiency

eighth

eligible

eliminate

embarrass

emphasize

employee

encouraging

encyclopedia

enthusiastic

environment

equipment

equipped

equivalent

erroneous

especially	glorious	indispensable
eventually	government	inevitable
exaggerate	grammar	influential
exceed	grandeur	innocent
excel	grievous	inoculate
excellent	guarantee	intellectual
exceptional	guardian	intelligence
excitement	guidance	intentionally
exercise	handicapped	intercede
exhaust	handkerchief	interested
exhilaration	harass	interpret
existence	hearse	interrupt
experience	height	irreligious
explanation	heinous	irresistible
extensive	heroes	irresponsible
extracurricular	hesitancy	itself
extremely	hindrance	judicial
exuberance	hoarse	khaki
fallacious	hoping	knowledge
fallacy	horde	laboratory
familiar	humorous	legitimate
fascinate	hurries	leisure
February	hygiene	library
fiery	hypocrisy	lightning
financial	hysterical	literature
financier	illiterate	loneliness
forehead	illogical	losing
foreign	imaginary	magazine
foremost	imagination	magnificent
forfeit	imitative	maintain
forty	immediately	maintenance
frantically	implement	maneuver
fraternities	impromptu	manual
friend	inadequate	manufacture
fulfill, fulfil	incidentally	mathematics
gaiety	incredible	mattress
generally	indefinitely	meant
genius	independent	medicine
genuine	indicted	medieval

messenger
millionaire
miniature
minute
mischievous
misspelled
modifies
modifying
momentous
mosquitoes
mottoes
mountainous
murmur
muscle
mysterious
necessary
necessity
neither
nervous
nevertheless
nickel
niece
ninety
ninth
noticeable
notorious
nowadays
obedience
obliged
obstacle
occasionally
occur
occurred
occurrence
official
omission
omit
omitted
opinion

opportunity
optimistic
organization
original
orthodox
outrageous
overrun
pamphlet
parallel
parliament
participle
particularly
pastime
peaceable
perceive
perform
permissible
perseverance
persuade
phrase
physical
physician
picnicked
piece
playwright
pleasant
possess
possessive
possible
potatoes
practice
prairie
preceding
predominant
preference
preferred
prejudice
preparation
prevalent

primitive
privilege
probably
professor
prominent
pronounce
pronunciation
propeller
protein
psychology
pursue
pursuing
putting
quantity
quarantine
questionnaire
quizzes
realize
recede
receipt
receive
receiving
recognize
recommend
reference
referred
relevant
religion
religious
remembrance
reminiscence
rendezvous
repetition
replies
representative
reservoir
resistance
restaurant
rhetoric

rheumatism	stomach	typical
rhythmical	stopped	tyranny
ridiculous	strength	unanimous
sacrifice	strenuously	undoubtedly
sacrilegious	stretched	unnecessary
safety	struggle	until
salary	studying	usage
sanctuary	subordinate	useful
sandwich	subtle	using
scarcely	succeed	usually
scene	success	vacancy
scenic	successful	vacuum
schedule	suffrage	valuable
secretarial	superintendent	vengeance
secretary	supersede	victorious
seized	suppress	view
sensible	surprise	vigilant
sentence	swimming	vigorous
sentinel	syllable	village
separate	synonym	villain
sergeant	synonymous	warrant
severely	tangible	warring
shining	tariff	weird
shriek	tasting	welfare
siege	technical	whole
sieve	technique	wholly
similar	temperament	wiry
sincerely	tenant	woman
sincerity	tendency	women
skeptical	thorough	won't
slight	thought	worried
soliloquy	tournament	worrying
sophomore	traffic	writing
source	tragedy	written
specifically	transferred	yacht
specimen	tremendous	your
spontaneous	tries	you're (you are)
statement	truly	zoology
statue	twelfth	

Abr   ABBREVIATIONS

In general, abbreviations should satisfy two conditions: they must be standard forms recognized by dictionaries, and they must be appropriate to the context. The first condition rules out such slang abbreviations as *b.f.* (boyfriend) and *n.g.* (no good). The second implies that many standard abbreviations *(advt., Ave., Feb., Xmas)* are inappropriate in most student essays and that abbreviations of certain titles *(Col., Dr., Mrs., Ms., Rev.)* are used only when followed by the name of the person to whom the title applies.

The following is a summary of the most common standard abbreviations. For the correct form of abbreviations not included in this list, you should consult your dictionary.

Abbreviations may be used for: bibliographical terms—

cf., vol., pp.

names of days (in dates only)—

Sun., Mon., Tues., Wed., Thurs., Fri., Sat.

names of months (in dates only)—

Jan., Feb., Aug., Sept., Oct., Nov., Dec.

names of organizations—

AFL, U.S. Steel, IBM, YMCA, UNESCO

names of government agencies (abbreviations of government agencies generally do not require periods)—

CIA, FBI, HUD, SEC, TVA

names of states (in addresses only), and signs.

See the complete list of abbreviations for state names on page 386.

When the context permits, the following signs are used as abbreviations: & (ampersand; see Glossary), $ (dollar), £ (British pound sterling), % (per cent), and " " (ditto marks, used in tabulations to repeat the item immediately above the marks).

Caps   USE OF CAPITAL LETTERS

1.   **Capitalize the first word of every sentence and of every line of regular poetry.**

> Ask for Mr. Lane. He is in charge of services.
>
> Too bad! Better luck next time.
>
> Earth has not anything to show more fair;
> Dull would he be of soul who could pass by
> A sight so touching in its majesty. . . .
>   —Wordsworth, "Composed upon Westminster Bridge"

2.   **Capitalize the first word of a direct quotation.**

> Who said, "We have met the enemy, and they are ours"?
> She looked puzzled and asked, "For example?"

3.   **Capitalize proper nouns.**

> She works for the National Broadcasting Company.
> I find French easier than German.
> The Amazon is longer than the Mississippi.

Note: Words that were originally proper nouns but have taken on more general meanings are regarded as common nouns and are not capitalized: *boycott, calico, china* (dishes), *port* (wine), *tweed.*

4.   **Capitalize adjectives formed from proper nouns.**

> They seem to be ignorant of the *American* point of view.
> There is a *Miltonic* quality in this verse.
> The inductive method has been called the *Baconian* method.

Note: Words originally derived from proper nouns cease to be capitalized when they are used as allusions rather than as direct references to the original noun. For example, *colossus, draconian, herculean, meandering,* and *panic* do not take capitals. *Philippic* is capitalized when it refers directly to the orations made by Demosthenes but not when it is used to describe some other denunciatory speech.

5.   Capitalize nouns or pronouns referring to the deity. Also capitalize *Bible* and *Biblical* when they refer to Scripture.

> God, Lord, our Father, Savior, Messiah, Trinity, Holy Ghost, He, His, Him
>
> Although she does not seem to be a particularly religious person, she reads a passage from the Bible every day.

Note: When *bible* and *biblical* do not refer to Scripture, they are not capitalized: "*Das Kapital* is the bible of the Communist party." Some dictionaries also accept *biblical* as an alternative spelling of *Biblical*.

6.   Capitalize names of offices only when they are used as titles.

Capitalized	Not capitalized
District Attorney Johnson	Tell it to the district attorney.
Prime Minister Thatcher	Heath is a former prime minister.
The death of Chairman Mao resulted in major changes in official Chinese policies.	Stella Iantosca was made chairperson of the committee.
Professor Swanson	She is a college professor.

Note: *President, Presidential, Presidency,* and *Executive* are capitalized when they refer to the office of President of the United States: "One of these men will be our next President"; "the Presidency is at stake"; "Executive privilege." The same style is followed for *Vice President* and its derivatives.

7.   Capitalize *north, south, east,* and *west* and their derivatives only when they refer to geographical areas.

Capitalized	Not capitalized
We found the South charming.	Next year we are going south.
Her parents live in the East.	New York is east of Chicago.
They live on the West Side.	The west side of the field is wet.
The Southern armies fought gallantly.	The house has a fine southern exposure.

8.   Capitalize titles of books, names of magazines, titles of plays, and the headings of chapters or sections of a work.

The general practice is to capitalize all significant words in a title, including the first word.

A Child's History of the United States
The Return of the Native
Mourning Becomes Electra

Some publishers, however, capitalize every word in the title.

A Child's History Of The United States

Either form is acceptable, but be consistent.

9. Capitalize the names of days of the week, months, and holidays.

New Year's Day will fall on Tuesday.
The favorite vacation months are July and August.

10. Avoid unnecessary capitalization.

In general, do not use capitals unless they are required by one of the conventions stated above. The modern tendency is to use capitals sparingly. Especially avoid unnecessary capitalization of the names of the seasons, of family relationships *(father, mother, sister, uncle),* and of such words as *army, college, freshman, navy, sophomore, university,* unless they are being considered as proper nouns.

Capitalized	Not capitalized
He is a captain in the Army of the United States.	In foreign affairs an army is a political instrument.
Whom do you pick in the Army-Navy game, General?	The general said we must have an army and a navy second to none.
Uncle Bill and Aunt Martha are here.	All the uncles and aunts were present.
Where is Sanford Community College?	He wants a college education.
Boston University will have a strong team next year.	He is a university professor.
Are you going to the Freshman Mixer?	Are you a freshman or a sophomore?
The Summer Festival starts next week.	I like summer best and winter least.
Oh, Mother, I can't do that!	Is your mother at home?

Hyph HYPHENATION

Hyphens are used for two purposes: to divide a word at the end of a line, and to join two or more words of a compound that is not written solid.

1.   Use a hyphen to break a word at the end of a line.

This use of the hyphen is less frequently necessary in typed or handwritten copy than it is in print. In student writing, words should be broken at the ends of lines only when failure to hyphenate would result in obviously long or short lines. If hyphenation seems necessary, the following conditions should be observed:

a.   Do not break words of one syllable.

If there is not room at the end of a line for a word such as *burst, change, drink, through,* carry the whole word over to the next line.

b.   Break words only between syllables.

When in doubt about syllabication, consult your dictionary.

c.   Do not separate a suffix of fewer than three letters from the rest of the word or break on a one-letter prefix.

An *-ing* may be carried over to the next line, but single letters or *-al, -le, -ly,* and *-ed* endings should not be. Words like *about, against,* and *open* should not be broken.

d.   Break compound words between the elements of the compound.

Compound word	End-of-line hyphenation
armchair	arm- chair
blackbird	black- bird
sailboat	sail- boat
self-denial	self- denial (not: self-de- nial)

e.   Subject to the limitations stated in rules b and c, hyphenate between prefix and root or between root and suffix.

Between prefix and root	Between root and suffix
ante- cedent	adapt- able
be- loved	back- ward
com- mit	depend- able
con- tagious	ego- ism
dis- appear	kitchen- ette
inter- rupt	lemon- ade
intro- duce	mile- age
per- suade	racket- eer
trans- late	trouble- some

2.   Use a hyphen between elements of a compound when usage calls for it.

Hyphenation of compounds varies so much that (1) for any particular word, the only safe authority is a reliable, up-to-date dictionary, and (2) whenever usage is uncertain, a writer is allowed a choice between competing usages.

Some compounds *(applesauce, blackboard, steamship)* are written solid; others *(dirt cheap, place kick, wedding ring)* are nearly always written as separate words; still others *(father-in-law, ready-made, up-to-date)* are hyphenated.

A hyphen is required in the following types of compounds:

a.   Hyphenate a compound modifier preceding a noun.

a self-made man, a well-dressed woman, a pay-as-you-go tax, a round-by-round report, an off-the-cuff judgment, a tear-jerking film, a Sunday-morning golf game, a heart-to-heart talk

Compound numerical modifiers follow this rule: "twenty-seven dollars," "one hundred and twenty-five pounds," "a two-thirds majority." When a compound numeral is used as a noun, it is hyphenated: "All the men in Ward Room II should be commended, for all twenty-five of them volunteered for special duty." But whole numbers below twenty-one are single words and are not hyphenated· "their nineteenth anniversary," "the sixteenth of May."

Notice that a compound modifier *following* a noun is usually not hyphenated: "The woman was well dressed"; "The machine is worn out."

b.   Hyphenate a compound consisting of a prefix and a proper noun.

pro-Russian, un-American, anti-Castro

c. Hyphenate compounds of *ex* ("former") and a noun.

ex-wife, ex-sweetheart, ex-President

d. Hyphenate to avoid confusion with another word.

re-cover (to prevent confusion with *recover)*
re-creation (to prevent confusion with *recreation)*

e. Hyphenate most compounds beginning with *self.*

self-satisfied, self-government, self-conceit

But *selfless* and *selfsame* are written solid.

Ital USE OF ITALICS AND UNDERLINING

Words in print are made to stand out by using a special kind of slanting type called *italic;* they are similarly set off in manuscript or typewritten material by underlining.

1. Italics or underlining is used for the following purposes:

a. To indicate that a word is still considered a foreign element in the language.

In printed material	In manuscript
were *en rapport*	were en rapport
voted *in absentia*	voted in absentia

b. To mark titles of books, magazines, newspapers, movie and stage productions, musical compositions, and paintings, and the names of airplanes, ships, and trains.

In printed material	In manuscript
Mencken's *The American Language*	Mencken's <u>The American Language</u>
last month's *Esquire*	last month's <u>Esquire</u>
Beethoven's *Eroica*	Beethoven's <u>Eroica</u>
Da Vinci's *Last Supper*	Da Vinci's <u>Last Supper</u>
Lindbergh's *Spirit of Saint Louis*	Lindbergh's <u>Spirit of Saint Louis</u>
the French liner, the *France*	the French liner, the <u>France</u>

But notice that (1) Bible is not italicized and (2) titles of musical compositions, paintings, and other works of art may be either italicized or enclosed in quotation marks (see page 480).

c. To call attention to a word being named.

In printed material	In manuscript
The word *judgment* has two spellings	The word <u>judgment</u> has two spellings.
What does *discriminate* mean?	What does <u>discriminate</u> mean?

Quotation marks are also used for this purpose (see page 480), but when in a printed work it is necessary to place quotation marks around a great many single words, an editor will sometimes attempt to improve the appearance of the page by substituting italics for quotation marks. The need for this substitution almost never exists in student writing.

d. To emphasize a word, letter, or number.

In printed material	In manuscript
Not *moral,* but *morale.*	Not <u>moral,</u> but <u>morale.</u>
Is this letter an *a* or an *o*?	Is this letter an <u>a</u> or an <u>o</u>?

No FORMS OF NUMBERS

Whether numbers should be written in words *(twenty-five)* or figures *(25)* depends partly on the nature of the writing. In scientific, statistical, and technical writing, figures are used whenever possible. In essays and literary publications, numbers are more frequently written in words, and the more formal the style is, the less often are figures used.

1. **Figures are used in writing days, hours, and street numbers.**

    January 22, 1967   5:00 A.M.   17 Main Street
    January 1   6:15 P.M.   417 Fifth Avenue

Notice that figures are used for street numbers but that street names, even when they are numbers, are usually written out and capitalized to avoid confusion with other numbers.

2. **Figures are used in recording sums of money other than round sums.**

    $2.75; 98 cents (*but:* a hundred dollars; thirty cents)

If the style is informal, even round sums may be expressed as figures.

    $40 million; 100 dollars; 30 cents; 40,000 spectators

3. **Use figures for large numbers that would be awkward to write out.**

    365 days; 1,760 yards; 14,320 students

4. **Use figures in citing volume, chapter, and page references.**

    This whole question is discussed in Volume 2 of Brand's work.
    Soil erosion is discussed in Chapter 5, beginning on page 84.

5. **Do not use figures at the beginning of a sentence.**

    Sixty percent is a passing grade.   (*not:* 60% is a passing grade.)

6. **Generally avoid figures when a number can be conveniently expressed in one word.**

    one, five, third, quarter, twelve

But in an informal style and in scientific writing, numbers over ten are frequently expressed in figures.

7. **Do not use figures in a formal invitation or reply.**

on Saturday the twenty-third of June

at seven o'clock in the evening

This most formal usage is an exception to the practice recommended in rule 1 above.

8. **Roman numerals are used chiefly as volume and chapter numbers in some books and as page numbers in the front matter of books.**

Because Roman numerals are so little used, many people have trouble reading them. If you are one of these people, you will find that most of the difficulty is eliminated once you recognize the key numerals and understand the principle by which they are combined.

The key numerals are i (1), v (5), x (10), l (50), c (100), d (500), m (1,000). Occasionally these are written in capitals: I, V, X, L, C, D, M. The basic principle is that a higher number is created either by adding a numeral to a lower number—xi, for example, is x (10) plus i (1), or 11—or by subtracting a numeral from a higher number—xc is c (100) minus x (10), or 90.

Units	Tens	Hundreds
i(1)	x(10)	c(100)
ii(2)	xx(20)	cc(200)
iii(3)	xxx(30)	ccc(300)
iv(4)	xl(40)	cd(400)
v(5)	l(50)	d(500)
vi(6)	lx(60)	dc(600)
vii(7)	lxx(70)	dcc(700)
viii(8)	lxxx(80)	dccc(800)
ix(9)	xc(90)	cm(900)

REVIEW EXERCISE In the following sentences make any corrections that you think would be necessary in a college composition:

1. Doctor Lindon is a chemistry prof at the U of Toronto.

2. Columbus discovered America in anno Domini fourteen hundred and ninety-two.

3. 4 days after medication the sore was completely healed.

4. Her father is a Lt. Col. in the army of the U.S.

5. That is a Senior course. Freshmen and Sophomores are not eligible for it, but Juniors may take it with the Instructor's permission.

6. My father's birthday falls on father's day this year.

7. When he got out of the Navy he studied for the ministry.

8. It has rained heavily on each of the last 5 days.

9. Faulkner incorporated altered versions of several of his short stories, including Spotted Horses, in his novel The Hamlet.

10. What day of the week was new year's day in 1973?

11. Rev. David Smith lives at seventy-one Grand Ave.

12. Bill says that his Mother-in-law is one of the finest women he knows.

13. The birth certificate shows that he was born on January thirty-one at five minutes after eleven, post meridiem.

14. The bill came to $6.15. That was fifteen cents more than I had.

15. The King James bible is called the Authorized Version. It was translated by a committee of biblical scholars.

16. 78 was the median score on this test; the highest score was 98, and the lowest, 39.

17. I suppose pas de deux and tour jeté are French terms, but what do they mean?

18. The word is concave, not convex.

19. As a star in many american and european movies of the twenties and thirties, including Emperor Jones, Othello, King Solomon's Mines, and The Proud Valley, Paul Robeson is one of the great figures in black film history.

20. The careers of Harry S. Truman and Lyndon B. Johnson, although different in many respects, show interesting similarities. Both were democratic senators who were elected vice presidents and succeeded to the presidency on the death of a president. After serving the unexpired term they were elected chief executive, served four years, and refused to run again. They died within a month of each other, and for the first time in our history the American flag flew at half-mast to honor simultaneously the memory of two presidents.

This glossary is a reference section that explains grammatical and literary terms. Page references following an explanation refer you to a fuller treatment in the text. Words not listed in this glossary may be checked in the index at the end of the book.

absolute An element that has no specific grammatical relationship to any other term in a sentence, yet clearly belongs in the sentence.

> *Nonsense,* it is all a hoax.
>
> *Good heavens,* is it that late?
>
> *No,* I won't do it.
>
> He said—*believe it or not*—that he had played in the Rose Bowl.

accent marks When French words are written in English, their accent marks *(café, mère, fête)* are treated as part of their spelling, but when such words are no longer considered foreign, the accent mark generally is dropped. When in doubt whether the accent mark is needed, consult your dictionary.

In English, accent marks are used chiefly to indicate primary and secondary stress: *ak′ sent′.*

accusative case In modern English, the objective case, as in *him, her, me, us, them.*

acronym An abbreviation pronounced as a word and made up of the first letters of the title being abbreviated: *CORE* (Congress of Racial Equality), *NASA* (National Aeronautics and Space Administration).

active voice One of two "voices" of a verb, the other being *passive.* See **voice.**

A.D. Abbreviation for Latin *anno Domini,* "in the year of the Lord." Opposite of B.C., "before Christ." Used to distinguish dates before and after the beginning of the Christian era: "He lived from 31 B.C. to A.D. 12"; "From 100 B.C. to 100 A.D. is two hundred years." Note that B.C. always follows the figure; A.D. may follow or precede the figure.

adjectives and adverbs Adjectives and adverbs can often but not always be distinguished by their forms. Most adverbs end in *-ly,* but so do a few adjectives: *silly, lively, manly.* A few adverbs (among them *clean, fast, straight*) do not have *-ly* endings, and some have two forms: *late, lately; loud, loudly; slow, slowly.* Adjectives and adverbs are best recognized by their function in a sentence: adjectives modify nouns or pronouns; adverbs modify verbs, adjectives, or other adverbs. See also **comparison.**

agreement The convention that verbs agree in number with their subjects and that pronouns agree in gender, number, and person with their antecedents.

alliteration Repetition of the same consonant, especially an initial consonant, in several nearby words in prose or poetry: "*T*ippecanoe and *T*yler *t*oo"; "The *m*oan of doves in i*mm*e*m*orial el*m*s, / And *m*ur*m*uring of innu*m*erable bees." Alliteration is a common device in poetry, but it should be used with restraint in ordinary prose since its overuse or inappropriate use may seem affected.

A.M., P.M., a.m, p.m.   Abbreviations for the Latin phrases *ante meridiem* ("before noon"), *post meridiem* ("after noon"). The abbreviation A.M. is used to indicate the period from midnight to noon; P.M. from noon to midnight: "He works from 8 P.M. to 4 A.M." These abbreviations can be used only after a figure. Either capital or small letters may be used in manuscript, and in printed books small capitals frequently are used.

ampersand   The sign "&," an abbreviation for *and,* is used in some company names ("G. & C. Merriam Co.") and in various types of notation. Except in statistical tabulation it is not acceptable in college writing.

analogy in argument   See pages 233–236.

analogy in language   The process by which words change their forms to fit a dominant pattern. Because the dominant way of forming the past tense in English is to add -*ed* or -*d* to the present tense, small children are likely to say "buyed" for *bought* and "catched" for *caught* by analogy with *cried, sighed, tried,* and the like. Similarly, the regular pattern of forming English plurals is to add -*s* to the singular form, so foreign words imported into English tend to adjust to this pattern. Thus the Latin plural *gymnasia* becomes *gymnasiums* and the Hebrew plural *cherubim* becomes *cherubs.*

antagonist   See **protagonist.**

antecedent   The noun or pronoun to which a following pronoun refers.

anticlimax   The putting of a minor fact or detail at the end of a sentence or passage where a reader expects a climactic point: "I recommend Miss Smith for her high intelligence, moral integrity, and attractive smile." Putting the least important information at the end can destroy the effectiveness of a sentence. However, skillful writers deliberately employ anticlimax for humorous effect. In *Pudd'nhead Wilson* Mark Twain says, "Adam and Eve had many advantages, but the principal one was that they escaped teething."

antonym   A word opposite in meaning to a given word. Thus, *love* is the antonym for *hate.*

apposition   In grammar, two constructions are in apposition when the second follows and identifies the first, as in "Mr. Botts, *the chemistry teacher,* has resigned."

Arabic numerals   The numbers 1, 2, 3, etc., as contrasted with Roman numerals I, II, III, etc.

assonance   The similarity of vowel sounds in words that do not rhyme (w*e,* w*ee*p; f*i*ne, wh*i*te).

asterisk   The sign "*." A single asterisk is sometimes used as a footnote marker. A row of asterisks is sometimes used to indicate that the action of the story has been broken off or to suggest that time has passed.

auxiliary verb   A "helping" verb that combines with another verb to form a verb phrase: "I *am* going"; "He *has been* talking." The most common auxiliaries are *be, can, do, have, may, must, ought, shall, will.*

basic sentence   A sentence in its simplest form, usually just a subject and predicate without any modifiers: "The rain came." "She laughed." See page 122.

B.C. See **A.D.**

big words   The stylistic fault of using longer and more learned words than the context requires.

blank verse   Unrhymed verse with the dominant metrical pattern of five feet to a line, each foot containing one unstressed and one stressed syllable. The following line from Marc Antony's funeral oration illustrates the pattern:

If you have tears, prepare to shed them now.

caret   The symbol "$_\wedge$," used to identify the place in a printed, typed, or written line at which something is to be inserted.

case   A system of inflection that shows the relation of nouns and pronouns to other words in the sentence. See pages 444–447.

circumlocution   Literally, "roundabout speech." An attempt to avoid a direct statement by a circuitous reference, as in "She is expecting an addition to the family" for "She is pregnant."

clause   A group of words containing its own subject and predicate. When a clause can stand alone as a sentence, it is a *main clause;* when it acts as the subject, object, complement, or modifier within a sentence, it is a *subordinate clause.*

cliché   A synonym for "trite expression." See page 175.

clipped words   Any word formed by clipping off part of a longer word, as *cab* or *taxi* from *taxicab,* or *phone* from *telephone.* Clipped words are not considered abbreviations and are not followed by periods. They are generally acceptable in all but the most formal of styles. Common examples are *ad, auto, bike, bus* (from *omnibus*), *exam, flu* (from *influenza*), *gas* (from *gasoline*), *gym, lab, mike* (from *microphone*), *photo, tarp* (from *tarpaulin*), *vet* (from *veteran* or *veterinarian*), *wig* (from *periwig*), *zoo* (from *zoological garden*).

coherence   The quality of being logically integrated. In composition, chiefly used to refer to the integration of sentences within a paragraph. See pages 104–112.

collective noun   A noun that refers to a group or class of individuals: *army, audience, committee, team.* For the agreement of a collective noun and its verb, see page 452.

colorless vowels   When vowels are in an unstressed position, they are sometimes pronounced as a weak "uh," as in *ag*o, sof*a*, bal*a*nce, *a*gent, el*e*ph*a*nt, incred*i*ble, bachel*o*r, cor*o*ner, nerv*ou*s. Such colorless vowels frequently cause spelling errors. See page 491.

comma splice   The use of a comma instead of a period or semicolon between two independent clauses that are not connected by a conjunction. See page 413.

comparison   A change in the form of an adjective or adverb to show degree of comparison. There are three degrees: positive, comparative, superlative. There are three methods of indicating comparison in English: (1) adding *-er* for the comparative and *-est* for the superlative; (2) prefixing *more* for comparative and *most* for superlative; (3) using different words for each degree. Methods 1 and 2 are regular; 3 is irregular.

	Positive	Comparative	Superlative
Method 1:	strong	stronger	strongest
Method 2:	beautiful	more beautiful	most beautiful
Method 3:	good, well	better	best
	bad, ill	worse	worst
	far	farther, further	farthest, furthest
	little	less, lesser	least
	much, many	more	most

complement   Literally, a completing construction. Used in grammar chiefly to refer to the construction that completes a linking verb. See pages 404–406.

compound verbs   Two or more finite verbs in the same clause: "He *called* and *apologized* for his error."

compound words   Combinations of two or more words, the parts of which may be written solid *(blindfold),* hyphenated *(father-in-law),* or separately *(blood bank).* When in doubt about the spelling, consult your dictionary.

conjugation   The inflection of a verb to show its different forms, chiefly those indicating number, person, and tense.

conjunction   Also called *connective.* See below.

connective   Also called *conjunction.* See page 404.

connotation   See page 152.

context   The situation or environment in which a word or statement occurs. It may be verbal, physical, or psychological. A *verbal context* is the surrounding words in a sentence or paragraph. Thus in "That strike *looked like a ball to me,*" the italicized words form a verbal context that tells a listener which of several meanings of *strike* to choose. A *physical context* is the physical environment in which an utterance is made, as when miserable weather conditions provide an ironic meaning for "Nice day, isn't it?" A *psychological context* is the state of mind in which a statement is made, as when a frustrated child screams at its mother, "I hate you!" These contexts must be considered in interpreting the statement. Any interpretation that ignores the context may seriously distort what was meant.

coordination   The combining of grammatical structures into pairs or series having the same grammatical function and form. See page 126.

copula   See **linking verb.**

couplet   Two successive lines of poetry that rhyme, as in Coleridge's

The one red leaf, the last of its clan,
That dances as often as dance it can, . . .

dangling modifier   Any modifier that has nothing to modify in a sentence. See page 416.

dative case   In Old English and in some other languages, generally the case of the indirect object; in Modern English expressed by word order ("He gave *me* the book") or by a prepositional phrase ("Send it to *her*").

deadwood   The use of unnecessary words that should be pruned from a sentence. See pages 143–145.

declension   The inflection of a noun to show its different forms for number and case.

definite article   *The* as contrasted with the indefinite article *a* or *an.*

demonstrative   *This, that, these, those* are called demonstratives when they are used as pointing words: "This is the man"; "That coat is mine."

denotation   See page 152.

dialects   Variant forms of a common language which show differences in pronunciation, vocabulary, and grammar characteristic of a particular regional or social group. See "Standards of Usage," pages 400–401.

dieresis   A diacritical (distinguishing) mark consisting of two dots placed over the second of two like vowels to show that they are to be pronounced separately: *reëntry, coöperation, coördination.* In Modern English the dieresis is so little used that it is not included among the characters on a standard typewriter keyboard. Such vowels are often separated by a hyphen without a dieresis: *re-entry. Cooperation* and *coordination* are now commonly written without either a dieresis or a hyphen.

diphthong   A combination of two vowel sounds run together to sound like a single vowel. Examples are the "ah-oo" sounds combining into a single sound in *shroud* and *cloud* and the "aw-ee" sounds combining in *boy* and *toy.*

direct discourse   A quotation of the exact words of a speaker or writer as contrasted with *indirect discourse,* in which the content of the message is reported but not quoted. Contrasted in

> He said, "Send me a copy of the letter."   (direct discourse)
>
> He told me to send him a copy of the letter.   (indirect discourse)

direct object   See **object.**

distance   A term used in a discussion of style to indicate a writer's attitude toward the reader. See page 186.

documentation   The citing of the source of information either in a footnote or an endnote. See page 349.

e.g.   An abbreviation for the Latin phrase *exempli gratia* ("for the sake of example"; "for example"). Used to introduce an example in publications, such as dictionaries, in which space must be conserved. Seldom used in freshman writing.

ellipsis   A punctuation mark consisting of three dots (. . .) used to indicate the omission of words within a statement. See page 484.

elliptical construction A construction which is literally incomplete but in which the missing terms are understood.

> I am taller than he (is tall).
>
> Who told him? (It was) Not I (who told him).

endnotes Notes placed at the end of a paper or article to identify the sources from which the information was obtained. For the form of such notes, see pages 349–353.

epigram A short, pithy statement, usually witty or cynical, in either prose or verse.

> Yes, the meek shall inherit the earth—six feet of it.
>
> Here lies our sovereign lord, the King,
> Whose word no man relies on,
> Who never said a foolish thing,
> And never did a wise one.

etymology The study of the derivation of words.

euphemism A word or phrase used as a substitute for a term with unfavorable connotations. A common example is the use of "lady dog" or "girl dog" for *bitch.* When used to refer to a female dog, *bitch* is no more objectionable a word than *doe* or *mare;* but as a slang word it has acquired such unfavorable connotations that some people avoid it altogether and use the euphemisms given above.

expletive In such sentences as "There are two answers to the question" and "It seems to me that you are mistaken," the words *There* and *It* are called *expletives.* In these sentences the order is expletive-verb-subject, the expletive occupying the normal position of the subject.

fallacy An error in reasoning. For common fallacies, see pages 236–242.

figure of speech A literary device that involves an imaginary comparison between two things that are normally quite unlike. The most common figures of speech are discussed on pages 163–167.

fine writing Often used as an uncomplimentary term for writing that, because of its attempts to be "literary," is artificial or pretentious.

finite verb A verb form that can be conjugated to show number, person, and tense and can serve as a predicate in a sentence, as contrasted with infinitives, participles, and auxiliary verbs, which cannot be so conjugated or used.

footnotes Notes used at the foot of a page to identify a source of information. See also **endnotes.**

free verse Poetry that does not conform to conventional meter and rhyme patterns but has cadence, lines of irregular length, and imagery—for example, these lines from Amy Lowell's "A Decade":

When you came, you were like red wine and honey,
And the taste of you burnt my mouth with its sweetness.
Now you are like morning bread,
Smooth and pleasant.
I hardly taste you at all for I know your savour,
But I am completely nourished.

function words   Words used chiefly to show grammatical relationships between sentence elements: "worked *at* the store," "students *in* class," "ran *and* played," "laughed *because* he won."

gender   A grammatical division of words into masculine, feminine, and neuter categories. Grammatical gender is important in highly inflected languages such as Latin and German. It is only partly related to differences in sex. For example, *nauta* ("sailor") in Latin is a feminine noun, *das Kind* ("child") in German is neuter. Except for personal pronouns *(he, she, it)* and a few feminine forms of nouns *(actress, niece)*, English makes little use of grammatical gender.

genitive case   The possessive case.

gerund   The *-ing* form of a verb when used as a noun: "*Sewing* bored her."

headword   The chief word in a phrase: a noun modified by one or more adjectives ("an old tall *tale*"), or a verb modified by one or more adverbs ("they *danced* mechanically"), or a noun in a prepositional phrase ("at the *beginning*").

historical present   Also called *dramatic present.* The use of the present tense in narrative style to record action in the past: "His friends *try* to persuade him to escape, but Socrates *reasons* with them and *shows* them he must die."

homonyms   Words that are pronounced alike: *air, heir; blew, blue.*

hyperbole   An obvious exaggeration as in "When she said she would tell my father, I was scared to death."

idiom   A usage characteristic of the language or dialect in which it is used. We say "How do you do?"; the French say "How do you carry yourself?" Neither of these expressions is more logical than the other. One is an English idiom, the other a French idiom.

Because idioms are traditional rather than logical, they can be learned only by experience, not by rule. There is, for example, no rule that will tell us in advance what preposition to use with what verb. We say "aim *at*," "abide *by*," "account *for*," "meet *with*," and "move *on*." A foreigner who knows what *get* means will find that that knowledge is of little use in interpreting the meaning of "get ahead," "get along," "get away," "get by," "get on," "get over," "get through," "get with it."

i.e.   An abbreviation of the Latin phrase *id est* ("that is"), used to introduce a restatement or an explanation of a preceding word or phrase. Its use is generally confined to publications in which space must be conserved; it is rarely used in freshman writing.

imperative mood. See **mood.**

indefinite article   *A* or *an* as contrasted with the definite article *the.*

indicative mood See **mood.**

indirect object See **object.**

Indo-European The ancestral language from which most of the languages of India and Europe are assumed to have descended. The accompanying chart shows in simplified form the relationship of some European languages to Indo-European.

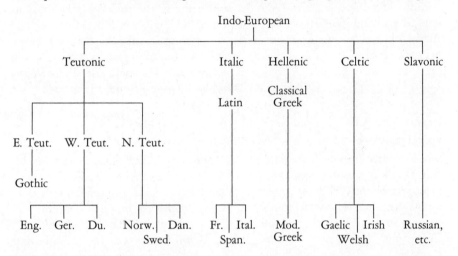

infinitive A verbal form, usually prefixed by *to* (*"to have* and *to hold"*) that can serve as a subject, object, complement, or modifier in a sentence but cannot serve as a verb. See page 408.

inflection Changes in the basic form of a word to indicate such grammatical concepts as case, number, tense, person, and degree. The system of a verb's inflection is called its *conjugation,* that of nouns and pronouns is their *declension,* and that of adjectives and adverbs is their *comparison.*

intensives Such modifiers as *much, so, too, very* are called intensives when they merely add emphasis to the words they modify: "much obliged," "so tired," "too bad," "very good." The pronouns that combine with *-self* may also be used as intensives: "You *yourself* are the best judge"; "He built the cabin *himself*"; "She *herself* is to blame"; "I will do it *myself*"; "We *ourselves* were surprised at the news"; "They *themselves* must accept responsibility."

interjection A word, phrase, or clause used as an exclamation, usually to suggest some degree of emotion. Examples are

Oh no, don't do that!

For heaven's sake, take it easy!

You better believe I'll do it.

Wow! What a blunder!

The name comes from a Latin phrase meaning "to throw in." Interjections have no grammatical relation to other parts of the sentence: they do not act as subjects, verbs, modifiers, objects, complements, or connectives, and can sometimes stand alone as sentences or sentence fragments. See **absolute.**

intransitive   See **verb.**

irony   A mode of statement in which the writer implies almost the opposite of what is explicitly stated. The writing proceeds on two levels at the same time: one stating a literal meaning and the other suggesting to the reader a quite different implied meaning. The most famous example in English is Jonathan Swift's *A Modest Proposal,* which, under the guise of proposing a workable plan for improving the economy of Ireland, makes a scathing criticism of England's exploitation of the Irish. Two examples of irony are presented in this book: the student essay "Why We Need More Westerns on Television" (page 17) and the passage from *The Adventures of Huckleberry Finn* on page 188.

jargon   See page 172.

kernel sentence   Also called a *basic* sentence. See page 122.

linking verb (copula)   A verb that is neither transitive (that is, requires an object) nor intransitive, but is completed by a noun, pronoun, or adjective acting as a complement. The most common linking verb is some form of the verb *to be,* but *become, feel, look, seem, smell, taste,* and some other verbs may link the subject to a complement: "His uncle *is* a minister"; "Tom *was* late"; "That dress *becomes* her"; "We *felt* disappointed"; "It *smells* bad"; "They *look* tired." In each of these sentences the construction following the italicized linking verb completes the verb but is not an object.

localism   Any usage that is confined to a particular region.

loose sentence   A technical term used to describe a sentence in which the main clause is completed before the end. The opposite of a periodic sentence. Loose sentences are standard sentences and should not be thought faulty.

lower case   A printer's term for small letters, in contrast with *caps* (capital letters). Printers and editors abbreviate *lower case* to *l.c.*

main clause   See **clause**

malapropism   A humorous, though unintentional, confusion of words similar in form and sound: "Henry VIII died of an *abbess* on his knee"; "An important event in early English history was the invasion of the *Dames.*" The error is named for Mrs. Malaprop, a character in Sheridan's play *The Rivals,* whose speech often illustrates this kind of confusion.

mechanics   In composition, a general term for matters of spelling, capitalization, hyphenation, abbreviation, and the like. See page 490. The term is sometimes extended to details of grammar, punctuation, and usage generally.

meter   From Latin and Greek words meaning "measure." In poetry, lines are measured by feet, and feet are measured by stressed and unstressed syllables.

Measurement of feet	Measurement of lines
ˇ ´ = iambic *(ăgó)*	monometer = 1 foot
´ ˇ = trochaic *(bóuntў)*	dimeter = 2 feet

˘ ˘ ′ = anapestic *(ŭnăwáre)*   trimeter = 3 feet

′ ˘ ˘ = dactylic *(béautĭfŭl)*   tetrameter = 4 feet

′ ′   = spondaic *(báckstáge)*   pentameter = 5 feet

˘ ˘   = pyrrhic *(mŭrmŭr)*   hexameter = 6 feet

                             heptameter = 7 feet

In the scansion of poetry these two kinds of measurement join. For example: iambic tetrameter ("Whŏse wóods/ thĕse áre/ Ĭ thínk/ Ĭ knów"); anapestic trimeter ("Thŏugh Ĭ sáng/ ĭn mў cháins/ lĭke thĕ séa"); trochaic trimeter followed by iambic trimeter ("Áy, the/ báll ĭs/ flýĭng,/ Thĕ láds/ plăy heárt/ aňd soúl").

Middle English English language and literature from 1100 to 1500.

mixed metaphor A metaphor that confuses two or more images. See page 178.

Modern English English language and literature since 1500.

mood Of the three moods of English verbs—indicative, imperative, and subjunctive—the indicative is by far the most common. A verb is in the indicative mood unless

1. it expresses a command or entreaty ("*Sit* down!" "Please *listen* to me"), in which case it is in the imperative mood.

2. it is used in one of the following ways, in which case it is in the subjunctive mood:

   a. to express a condition contrary to fact: "If I *were* you, I would go."

   b. to grant a concession: "*Be* it as you say."

   c. to state an improbability: "If this *were* the end of the matter, I'd be happy."

   d. to conduct certain parliamentary proceedings: "I move that the committee *go* on record"; "It is moved and seconded that this measure *be* adopted."

The form used for the imperative mood is always the same as the first principal part. The subjunctive, once fully inflected, is so little used in Modern English that we need consider only the forms for the simple present and past tenses of the verb *to be*. These are *be* for all persons in the singular and plural of the simple present, and *were* for all persons in the singular and plural of the simple past.

morpheme A grammatical term used to designate any segment of a word that has meaning and cannot be broken into smaller meaningful units. Thus *dog* has one morpheme, but *dogs* has two, because the plural ending *-s* has grammatical meaning. *Unfaithful* has three morphemes—*un-, faith,* and *-ful,* all of which have meaning—but *elephant* has only one morpheme, because it cannot be divided into smaller meaningful units. In this kind of analysis all prefixes and suffixes and all inflectional endings are considered morphemes.

morphology The study of the forms of words, especially their inflection.

MS., ms.   Abbreviations for *manuscript*. The plural is *MSS.* or *mss.*

Ms.   An abbreviation (pronounced "Miz") used to address a woman without indicating whether she is married *(Mrs.)* or unmarried *(Miss).*

nominative case   The case of a noun or pronoun when it is used as a subject; sometimes called the *subjective* case.

nonrestrictive modifier   See the discussion of restrictive and nonrestrictive modifiers on page 469–471.

nonstandard usage   Any usage not accepted as standard English: "they was"; "he ain't"; "them's my books."

noun   A part of speech usually inflected for number and case and used as subject, object, or complement in a sentence: *man, action, house, flower.* It may be used in the possessive case as a modifier: "the *man's* garden."

noun clause   A subordinate clause serving usually as the subject, object, or complement in a sentence—that is, used in the positions in which a noun is normally used.

object   A noun, pronoun, or noun clause that completes the action of a transitive verb: "We bought the *car*"; "I asked *her*"; "She said *that she would think about it.*" In these examples the italicized words are *direct objects.* An *indirect object* identifies the recipient of the action indicated by a verb-object combination: "We bought *Dad* a car"; "The children gave *her* a party"; "He gave the *beggar* a dollar."

Old English   English language and literature from 700 to 1100. We have no Old English literature from before 700.

onomatopoeia   The use of words that sound like the things they represent: *buzz, crack, cuckoo, hiss, meow, purr.*

parallelism   See pages 129–132.

paraphrase   The restatement of someone else's writing in one's own language.

parenthetical construction   A parenthetical element interrupts the flow of the discourse in order to give an explanation, qualification, or example. For the punctuation of parenthetical or interrupting constructions, see pages 467–469.

parts of speech   In traditional grammar the eight parts of speech are nouns, pronouns, verbs, adverbs, adjectives, prepositions, conjunctions, and interjections.

passive voice   See **voice.**

period fault   An error caused by using a period between parts of a sentence. See page 409.

periodic sentence   See pages 134–136.

persona   The personality a writer reveals in his or her writing. The term originally meant "mask" and referred to the practice in ancient Greek drama of wearing different masks for different roles. See also **voice** (in writing).

personification   See page 167.

phonetics   The science dealing with the sounds of language. The sounds are represented by phonetic symbols that ignore the appearance of a word and record only its pronunciation. When words are spelled as they are pronounced, the spelling is said to be phonetic; thus *tho* is a phonetic spelling, but *though* and *colonel* are not.

phonology The study of the sounds in speech. Phonology includes *phonemics* (the study of small units of sound) and *phonetics* (see above).

plagiarism A literary fraud in which one writer represents as his or her own the work of another. In its most blatant form the plagiarized material is copied from its source without quotation marks and without acknowledgment. In college classes the punishment for deliberate plagiarism may range from a failing grade on the paper to a failing grade in the course. To avoid unintentional plagiarism in a paper, follow the practices recommended on page 340.

P.M., p.m. See **A.M.**

précis A summary that preserves the organization and principal content of an original longer work.

predicate That part of a sentence that makes a statement about the subject. The predicate may consist of an intransitive verb, with or without modifiers; or of a transitive verb and its object, with or without modifiers; or of a linking verb and its complement, with or without modifiers.

predicate adjective An adjective that completes a linking verb: "His mother is *sick*"; "Oh, it is *beautiful!*"; "I am *afraid.*"

predicate noun Same function as *predicate adjective* above: "Her mother is a *writer*"; "Her brother became a successful *lawyer.*"

prefix A word or syllable placed before the root of another word to form a new word: *anti*bodies, *pre*writing, *mis*used, *un*able.

premise That part of an argument from which the conclusion is drawn. See pages 217–221.

preposition A connective word that links a following noun or pronoun to another word in the sentence, usually a noun or verb: "He sat *on* the desk"; "There is room *at* the top"; "We looked *into* it."

prepositional phrase A phrase consisting of a preposition, its object, and the modifiers of the object. Prepositional phrases act as adjectives ("His house *in the country* has been sold") or adverbs ("You will find her *in the kitchen*").

principal parts See **verb.**

pronoun Pronouns are usually divided into five classes: personal, relative, reflexive, demonstrative, and indefinite.

Personal pronouns refer to nouns and may serve as subjects, objects, complements, and modifiers in sentences. The following chart shows their inflection for person, gender, number, and case:

Number	Case	1st person	2nd person	3rd person mas.	3rd person fem.	neut.
Singular	Subjective	I	you	he	she	it
	Possessive	my (mine)	your(s)	his	her(s)	its
	Objective	me	you	him	her	it

Plural	Subjective	we	you	they	
	Possessive	our(s)	your(s)	their(s)	} all genders
	Objective	us	you	them	

Relative pronouns *(that, who, which, what,* and their compounds with *-ever)* are called relative because they "relate" a subordinate clause to an antecedent in a main clause. They thus act as subordinating connectives. Of these pronouns only *who* and its compounds are inflected for case: *who* (subjective), *whose,* (possessive), *whom* (objective).

When a pronoun object refers to the same antecedent as the subject in such a way that the subject performs the action of the verb on itself, the pronoun is called *reflexive.* Examples are "She hurt *herself,*" "He blamed *himself,*" "They corrected *themselves.*"

Demonstrative pronouns *(this, that)* are inflected only for number *(these, those)* and agree in number with the nouns they modify: "*this* kind," "*these* kinds."

Indefinite pronouns *(all, any, both, each, either, none, one, somebody,* and the like) often refer to antecedents that are less definite than those of other pronouns. Except for the possessive form in *one's, everybody's, nobody's, somebody's,* they are not inflected.

protagonist   The principal character in a story. He or she may be opposed by an *antagonist.* These words come from the Greek *agonistes,* meaning "competitors in games," and the prefixes *pro-* ("for") and *anti-* ("against"). In Shakespeare's *Othello,* Othello is the protagonist and Iago the antagonist.

quatrain   In poetry, a stanza of four lines, either rhymed or unrhymed.

referent   A term used in a discussion of meaning to indicate the thing to which a word refers. *Referent* is pronounced with the stress on the first syllable.

restrictive modifiers   See the discussion of restrictive and nonrestrictive modifiers on page 469–471.

Roman numerals   See page 510.

run-on sentence   See page 412.

semantics   That part of the study of language that is concerned with meaning as contrasted with phonetics (pronunciation), morphology (form), and syntax (grammatical relations within a sentence).

sentence   A unit of discourse consisting of a subject and predicate and their modifiers, if any. Sentences may be classified either rhetorically or grammatically. In Chapter 6 of this book they are classified rhetorically as standard, balanced, and periodic. Grammatically they are classified as simple, compound, complex, and compound-complex, each of which categories is illustrated below.

1.   *Simple.* One clause, a main clause: "Charlie shot a squirrel."

2.   *Compound.* Two or more main clauses: "Charlie shot a squirrel, and Beth scolded him."

3. *Complex.* One main clause and one or more subordinate clauses: "Charlie shot a squirrel while he and Beth were walking in the woods."

4. *Compound-complex.* Two or more main clauses and one or more subordinate clauses: "Charlie shot a squirrel and Beth gathered wildflowers while they were walking in the woods."

sentence fragment   See pages 409–410.

series   Parallel constructions arranged in succession: "She was *tall, tanned,* and *lean.*" The elements of a series may be single words, phrases, or subordinate or main clauses, but all elements must have the same grammatical form. See page 465.

sic   A term inserted into a quotation, usually in square brackets, to notify the reader that the word preceding *sic* was written in the form given: "The sign said firmly: 'No person will be allowed on the premises unless duely [sic] authorized.' "

silent letters   Letters that are not pronounced—the *k* in *knot,* the *b* in *climb,* the *p* in *psychology.*

slanting   Selecting material so that it suggests a judgment that could not be made if all the material available were presented. See page 211.

split infinitive   An infinitive is "split" when one or more words come between the marker *to* and the rest of the infinitive: "*to* wholly *comprehend."* When the split results in an awkward construction ("He wanted *to* at the same time *protect* his family"), it should be avoided; but if it provides a desired emphasis ("The prosecution failed *to* completely *demolish* the alibi") there can be no reasonable objection to it.

spoonerism   An unintentional shift in the sounds of a word—"She slyly shipped aboard" for "She shyly slipped aboard." The error is named for the Rev. William A. Spooner, who often made such mistakes.

strong verb   One of a class of irregular verbs that form the past tense and past participle by changing the vowel of the present tense: *break, broke, broken; ride, rode, ridden.*

stylebooks   Books that offer advice about details of usage. Three of the best stylebooks are the *MLA Handbook* (Modern Language Association), *A Manual of Style* (University of Chicago Press), and the *United States Government Printing Office Style Manual.*

subjunctive   One of three moods of English verbs, the other two being imperative and indicative. See **mood.**

subordinate clause   See **clause.**

subordination   The reduction of a main clause to a subordinate clause or phrase. See pages 124–126.

suffix   A syllable added at the end of a word to make a derived word, as in *like* + *ly* = *likely; child* + *hood* = *childhood.*

syllogism   A form of deductive argument that can be presented as a conclusion drawn from a major and minor premise.

major premise: Mammals bear their young alive.

minor premise: Whales are mammals.

conclusion: Whales bear their young alive.

symbol   (in literature)   See pages 282–283.

synonyms   Two or more words with the same meaning. Contrasted with antonyms, which have opposite meanings. *Brave* and *valiant* are synonyms; *brave* and *cowardly* are antonyms.

syntax   That part of the study of language that is concerned with the relations of words within a sentence.

tense   The system of changes in the form of verbs to indicate the time at which an action took place.

theme   Used in two ways in a composition course: (1) the dominant idea of an essay or book as in "The theme of the essay is that self-deception is the commonest of vices"; (2) a general name for a composition assignment as in "Write a 500-word theme for Monday." The first meaning is synonymous with *thesis* as it is used in this book.

tone   The attitudes of a writer toward the subject and the reader as these attitudes are revealed in the written material. See pages 182–188.

tragic flaw   In Greek tragedy, a decisive flaw or weakness in the hero's character that brings about his or her downfall. For example, it is the rashness of Oedipus at critical moments in his life that contributes to his unintentional violation of the moral laws and to the punishment he imposes upon himself. The term has been extended to English tragedy: Macbeth's tragic flaw is excessive ambition, and Othello's is irrational jealousy.

transition   From a Latin root meaning "to go across." Transitions link one part of a paper to another. The transitional devices may be individual words, phrases, clauses, sentences, or short paragraphs. See pages 109, 115–116.

transitive   See **verb.**

verb   Such words as *be, caught, do, eat, pray, run, said, thought, walked* belong to a large class of words that name actions or states of being and are inflected for number, person, tense, and mood. Each verb has four *principal parts,* from which its various forms are derived. The accompanying table shows the principal parts of regular and irregular verbs.

	Present tense	Present participle	Past tense	Past participle
Regular	walk	walking	walked	walked
	deal	dealing	dealt	dealt
	have	having	had	had

Irregular	buy	buying	bought	bought
	speak	speaking	spoke	spoken
	bet	betting	bet	bet
	am, are	being	was, were	been

As this table shows, the present participle is formed by adding *-ing* to the present-tense form. In regular verbs both the past tense and the past participle are formed by adding the suffix *-ed, -d,* or *-t* to the present-tense form. Most irregular verbs form the past tense by changing the vowel of the present tense: *buy, bought; speak, spoke.* Some, like *buy,* retain the past-tense form for the past participle; others, like *speak,* retain the vowel change but add *-en* for the past participle. Some irregular verbs, like *bet,* retain the same form in all prinicpal parts: *cast, cost, hit, hurt, let, put, set, shed, shut, split, spread, thrust.* The verb *to be* is so irregular that we will treat it separately after we have discussed the inflection of the other verbs.

Inflection for person and number. The only inflection for person and number occurs in the form for the third person singular, which is marked by the addition of *-s* to the present form. Thus: "I (we, you, they) *walk,*" but "he (she, it) *walks.*" Slight variations of this rule are *have* and *do,* which in the third person singular become *has* and *does,* respectively. Otherwise, the same form is used for all persons in both singular and plural, whether the verb is regular or irregular.

Inflection for tense. Although many tenses can be identified in English, we will deal here with only the six basic tenses.

1. *Simple present:*   They walk.   They speak.
2. *Present perfect:*   They have walked.   They have spoken.
3. *Simple past:*   They walked.   They spoke.
4. *Past perfect:*   They had walked.   They had spoken.
5. *Simple future:*   They will walk.   They will speak.
6. *Future perfect:*   They will have walked. They will have spoken.

An inspection of these tenses shows that the simple present and the simple future come from the first principal part, although the simple future also uses the auxiliary verb *will;* the simple past comes from the past-tense form; and all the perfect tenses combine the past participle with the auxiliary verb *have* or *had.*

The inflection of the verb *to be* in these six tenses is as follows:

1. *Simple present: am* in first singular, *is* in third singular, *are* in the rest
2. *Present perfect: have been* in all persons and numbers except *has been* in third singular
3. *Simple past: was* in first and third singular, *were* in all others
4. *Past perfect: had been* in all persons and numbers
5. *Simple future: will be* throughout, except that *shall* may be used for *will* in first person singular and plural
6. *Future perfect: will have been* throughout, except that *shall* may be used for *will* in first person singular and plural

Inflection for mood. See **mood.**

Verbs are also identified as *transitive* or *intransitive.* a verb is transitive when it requires an object to complete the predicate ("We *left* him alone"); when it does not require an object, it is intransitive ("All the girls *have left*").

verbal　See pages 408–409.

voice (of verb)　English verbs have two voices: *active* ("A man opened the door") and *passive* ("The door was opened by a man"). When a verb is changed from active to passive, the object of the active verb becomes the subject of the passive verb. The passive voice is formed by adding the past participle to the appropriate tense form of the verb *to be:* "The door *is opened (was opened, will be opened)."*

voice (in writing)　A term used in a discussion of style to identify the person or personality speaking in a literary work. See pages 189 and 191.

vulgate　Synonymous with *nonstandard;* any usage characteristic of uneducated speech.

This checklist identifies certain words and constructions that sometimes require attention in composition classes. Some of the entries are pairs of words that are quite different in meaning yet similar enough in spelling to be confused (see **principal–principle**); some, such as the use of *without* as a synonym for *unless,* are nonstandard usages that are not acceptable in college writing (see **without = unless**); some are informal constructions that may be appropriate in some situations but not in others (see **guess**).

The judgments recorded here about usage are based on the Usage Notes contained in *The American Heritage Dictionary,* supplemented by the following sources: *Webster's Third New International Dictionary, Webster's New World Dictionary,* Theodore M. Bernstein's *The Careful Writer,* Margaret M. Bryant's *Current American Usage,* Bergen and Cornelia Evans's *A Dictionary of Contemporary Usage,* and Robert C. Pooley's *The Teaching of English Usage.* Since these authorities do not always agree, it has sometimes been necessary for the authors of this textbook to decide which judgments to accept. In coming to decisions, we have attempted to represent a consensus, but readers should be aware that on disputed items the judgments recorded in this checklist are finally those of the authors.

Since dictionaries do not always distinguish between formal, informal, and colloquial usage, it has seemed useful in the checklist to indicate whether particular usages would be appropriate in college writing. The usefulness of this advice, however, depends on an understanding of its limitations. In any choice of usage, the decision depends less on what dictionaries or textbooks say than on what is consistent with the purpose and style of the writing. The student and instructor, who alone have the context of the paper before them, are in the best position to answer that question. All that the checklist can do is to provide a background from which particular decisions can be made. The general assumption in the checklist is that the predominant style in college writing is informal rather than formal or colloquial. This assumption implies that calling a usage informal in no way suggests that it is less desirable than a formal usage.

access–excess   *Access* means "approach" or "admission": "an access road"; "having access to the records." *Excess* means "beyond what is normal or desirable": "He worries to excess"; "a tax on excess profits."

ad   *Ad* is the clipped form of *advertisement.* The full form is preferable in a formal style, especially in letters of application. The appropriateness of *ad* in college writing depends on the style of the paper.

adapt–adopt   *Adapt* means "to adjust to meet requirements": "The human body can adapt itself to all sorts of environments"; "It will take a skillful writer to adapt this novel for the movies." *Adopt* means "to take as one's own" ("He immediately adopted the idea") or—in parliamentary procedure—"to accept as law" ("The motion was adopted").

advice–advise The first form is a noun, the second a verb: "I was advised to ignore his advice."

affect–effect Both words may be used as nouns, but *effect,* meaning "result," is usually the word wanted: "His speech had an unfortunate effect"; "The treatments had no effect on me." The noun *affect* is a technical term in psychology. Though both words may be used as verbs, *affect* is the more common. As a verb, *affect* means "impress" or "influence": "His advice affected my decision"; "Does music affect you that way?" As a verb, *effect* is rarely required in student writing but may be used to mean "carry out" or "accomplish": "The pilot effected his mission"; "The lawyer effected a settlement."

affective–effective See **affect–effect**. The common adjective is *effective* ("an effective argument"), meaning "having an effect." The use of *affective* is largely confined to technical discussions of psychology and semantics, in which it is roughly equivalent to "emotional." In this textbook *affective* is used to describe a tone that is chiefly concerned with creating attitudes in the reader. See pages 182–185.

aggravate *Aggravate* may mean either "to make worse" ("His remarks aggravated the dispute") or "to annoy or exasperate" ("Her manners aggravate me"). Both are standard English, but there is still some objection to the second usage. If you mean *annoy, exasperate,* or *provoke,* it would be safer to use whichever of these words best expresses your meaning in preference to *aggravate.*

ain't Except to record nonstandard speech, the use of *ain't* is not acceptable in college writing.

alibi The use of *alibi* as a verb ("He alibied for me") is not acceptable. Its use as a noun in the legal sense of being elsewhere when a crime was committed ("The police could not disprove the suspect's alibi") is thoroughly acceptable. Its use to mean "excuse" ("She had a good alibi for being late") is a colloquial usage to which there is some objection in college writing. *Excuse* is the preferred word.

all (not all that) The use of "not all that interested" to mean "not much interested" is generally not acceptable in college writing.

all the farther, further Colloquial in some areas but generally unacceptable in college writing. Use "as far as."

all together–altogether Distinguish between the phrase ("They were all together at last") and the adverb ("He is altogether to blame"). *All together* means "all in one place"; *altogether* means "entirely" or "wholly."

allow When used to mean "permit" ("No smoking is allowed on the premises"), *allow* is acceptable. Its use to mean "think" ("He allowed it could be done") is nonstandard and is not acceptable in college writing.

allusion–illusion An allusion is a reference: "The poem contains several allusions to Greek mythology." An illusion is an erroneous mental image: "Rouge on pallid skin gives an illusion of health."

alright A common variant spelling of *all right,* but there is still considerable objection to it. *All right* is the preferred spelling.

among, between   See **between, among.**

amount, number   *Amount* suggests bulk or weight: "We collected a considerable amount of scrap iron." *Number* is used for items that can be counted: "He has a large number of friends"; "There are a number of letters to be answered."

an   Variant of indefinite article *a*. Used instead of *a* when the word that follows begins with a vowel sound: "an apple," "an easy victory," "an honest opinion," "an hour," "an unknown person." When the word that follows begins with a consonant, or with a *y* sound or a pronounced *h,* the article should be *a:* "a yell," "a unit," "a history," "a house." Such constructions as "a apple," "a hour" are nonstandard. The use of *an* before *historical* is an older usage that is now dying out.

and/or   Many people object to *and/or* in college writing because the expression is associated with legal and commercial writing. Generally avoid it.

angle   The use of *angle* to mean "point of view" ("Let's look at it from a new angle") is acceptable. In the sense of personal interest ("What's your angle?"), it is slang.

anxious = eager   *Anxious* should not be used in college writing to mean "eager," as in "Gretel is anxious to see her gift." *Eager* is the preferred word in this context.

any = all   The use of *any* to mean "all," as in "He is the best qualified of any applicant," is not acceptable. Say "He is the best qualified of all the applicants," or simply "He is the best-qualified applicant."

any = any other   The use of *any* to mean "any other" ("The knife he bought cost more than any in the store") should be avoided in college writing. In this context, use "any other."

anyone = all   The singular *anyone* should not be used in writing to mean "all." In "She is the most talented musician of anyone I have met here," drop "of anyone."

anywheres   A nonstandard variant of *anywhere*. It is not acceptable in college writing.

apt = likely   *Apt* is always appropriate when it means "quick to learn" ("He is an apt student") or "suited to its purpose" ("an apt comment"). It is also appropriate when a predictable characteristic is being spoken of ("When he becomes excited he is apt to tremble"). In other situations the use of *apt* to mean "likely" ("She is apt to leave you"; "He is apt to resent it") may be too colloquial for college writing.

as = because   *As* is less effective than *because* in showing causal relation between main and subordinate clauses. Since *as* has other meanings, it may in certain contexts be confusing. For example, in "As I was going home, I decided to telephone," *as* may mean *while* or *because.* If there is any possibility of confusion, use either *because* or *while*–whichever is appropriate.

as = that   The use of *as* to introduce a noun clause ("I don't know as I would agree to that") is colloquial. In college writing, use *that* or *whether.*

as to, with respect to = about   Although "as to" and "with respect to" are standard usage, many writers avoid these phrases because they sound stilted: "I am not concerned as to your cousin's reaction." Here "about" would be more appropriate than either "as to" or "with respect to"; "I am not concerned about your cousin's reaction."

at   Avoid the redundant *at* in such sentences as "Where were you at?" and "Where do you live at?"

author (verb)   *Author* is not fully accepted as a verb. "To write a play" is preferable to "to author a play."

awful, awfully   The real objection to *awful* is that it is worked to death. Instead of being reserved for situations in which it means "awe inspiring," it is used excessively as a utility word. (See page 170.) Use both *awful* and *awfully* sparingly.

bad = badly   The ordinary uses of *bad* as an adjective cause no difficulty. As a predicate adjective ("An hour after dinner I began to feel bad"), it is sometimes confused with the adverb *badly*. After the verbs *look, feel,* and *seem,* the adjective is preferred. Say "It looks bad for our side," "I feel bad about the quarrel," "Our predicament seemed bad this morning." But do not use *bad* when an adverb is required, as in "He played badly," "a badly torn suit."

bank on = rely on   In college writing "rely on" is generally preferred.

being as = because   The use of *being as* for "because" or "since" in such sentences as "Being as I am an American, I believe in democracy" is nonstandard. Say "Because I am an American, I believe in democracy."

between, among   In general, use *between* in constructions involving two people or objects and *among* in constructions involving more than two: "We had less than a dollar between the two of us"; "We had only a dollar among the three of us." The general distinction, however, should be modified when insistence on it would be unidiomatic. For example, *between* is the accepted form in the following examples:

> He is in the enviable position of having to choose between three equally attractive young women.

> A settlement was arranged between the four partners.

> Just between us girls . . . (when any number of 'girls' is involved)

between you and I   Both pronouns are objects of the preposition *between* and so should be in the objective case: "between you and me."

bi-, semi-   *Bi-* means "two": "The budget for the biennium was adopted." *Semi-* means "half of": *semicircle. Bi-* is sometimes used to mean "twice in." A bimonthly paper, for example, may be published twice a month, not once every two months, but this usage is ambiguous; *semimonthly* is preferred.

but that, but what   In such a statement as "I don't doubt but that you are correct," *but* is unnecessary. Omit it. "I don't doubt but what . . ." is also unacceptable. Delete "but what" and write *that.*

can = may   The distinction that *can* is used to indicate ability and *may* to indicate permission ("If I can do the work, may I have the job?") is not generally observed in informal usage. Either form is acceptable in college writing.

cannot help but   In college writing, the form without *but* is preferred: "I cannot help being angry." (Not: "I cannot help but be angry.")

can't hardly   A confusion between *cannot* and *can hardly.* The construction is unacceptable in college writing. Use *cannot, can't,* or *can hardly.*

capital–capitol   Unless you are referring to a government building, use *capital.* The building in which the U.S. Congress meets is always capitalized ("the Capitol"). For the various meanings of *capital,* consult your dictionary.

censor–censure   Both words come from a Latin verb meaning "to set a value on" or "tax." *Censor* is used to mean "appraise" in the sense of appraising a book or a letter to see if it may be released ("All outgoing mail had to be censored") and is often used as a synonym for "delete" or "cut out" ("That part of the message was censored").

  Censure means "to evaluate adversely" or "to find fault with" or, as a noun, "rebuke": "The editorial writers censured the speech"; "Such an attitude will invoke public censure."

center around   Some people object to the contradiction between *center,* which means "focus," and *around:* "The question of his eligibility centers around the accuracy of the registrar's report." Since *around* adds nothing of value in the sentence, "centers on" is the preferred form.

cite–sight–site   *Cite* means "to refer to": "He cited chapter and verse." *Sight* means "spectacle" or "view": "The garden was a beautiful sight." *Site* means "location": "This is the site of the new plant."

commentate   *Commentate* is not generally accepted either as a transitive verb ("Howard Cosell commentated the game between the Bears and the Vikings") or as an intransitive verb ("Walter Cronkite has commentated for CBS ever since I can remember"). Use *announced* or *reported,* or rephrase the sentence to use an appropriate noun: *commentator, announcer, reporter.*

compare, contrast   *Compare* can imply either differences or similarities; *contrast* always implies differences. *Compare* can be followed by either *to* or *with.* The verb *contrast* is usually followed by *with.*

  Compared to her mother, she's a beauty.

  I hope my accomplishments can be compared with those of my predecessor.

  His grades this term contrast conspicuously with the ones he received last term.

complected   Nonstandard form of *complexioned.* Not acceptable in college writing.

complement–compliment   Both words can be used as both nouns and verbs.

Complement speaks of completion: "the complement of a verb"; "a full complement of soldiers to serve as an honor guard"; "Susan's hat complements the rest of her outfit tastefully." *Compliment* is associated with praise: "The instructor complimented us for writing good papers."

complement of *to be* The choice between "It is I" and "It's me" is a choice not between standard and nonstandard usage but between formal and colloquial styles. This choice seldom has to be made in college writing, since the expression, in whatever form it is used, is essentially a spoken rather than a written sentence. Its use in writing occurs chiefly in dialogue, and then the form chosen should be appropriate to the speaker.

The use of the objective case in the third person ("That was her") is less common and should probably be avoided in college writing except when dialogue requires it.

consensus of opinion Since *consensus* means "collective opinion," the addition of *of opinion* is redundant. In the following sentence *of opinion* should be deleted: "The leader asked for an informal show of hands so she could discover whether there was a consensus of opinion."

considerable The use of *considerable* as a noun ("I have spent considerable on this project") is not appropriate in college writing. Write "considerable money" or "a considerable amount of money." The adjective form ("I was considerable surprised") is not acceptable when the adverbial form *considerably* is needed.

continual–continuous Both words refer to a continued action, but *continual* implies repeated action ("continual interruptions," "continual disagreements"), whereas *continuous* implies that the action never ceases ("continuous pain," "a continuous buzzing in the ears").

cope The verb *cope*, meaning "to contend with," is usually followed by the preposition *with* and its object: "We found it difficult to cope with inflated prices."

could of = could have Although "could of" and "could have" often sound alike in speech, *of* is not acceptable for *have* in college writing. In writing, "could of," "should of," "would of," "might of," and "must of" are nonstandard.

council–counsel *Council* is a noun meaning "a deliberative body": "a town council," "a student council." *Counsel* can be either a noun meaning "advice" or a verb meaning "to advise": "to seek a lawyer's counsel," "to counsel a person in trouble." One who offers counsel is a *counselor*: "Because of his low grades Quint made an appointment with his academic counselor."

credible–creditable–credulous All three words come from a Latin verb meaning "to believe," but they are not synonyms. *Credible* means "believable" ("His story is credible"); *creditable* means "commendable" ("John did a creditable job on the committee") or "acceptable for credit" ("The project is creditable toward the course requirements"); *credulous* means "gullible" ("Only a most credulous person could believe such an incredible story").

cute A word used colloquially to indicate the general notion of "attractive" or "pleasing." Its overuse shows lack of discrimination. A more specific term is often preferable.

His daughter is cute.   (lovely? petite? pleasant? charming?)

That is a cute trick.   (clever? surprising?)

He has a cute accent.   (pleasant? refreshingly unusual?)

She is a little too cute for me.   (affected? juvenile? clever?)

data is   Since *data* is the Latin plural of *datum,* it logically requires a plural verb, and always does in scientific writing: "These data have been double checked." In popular usage *datum* is almost never used and *data* is treated as a singular noun and given a singular subject: "The data has been double checked." Either "data are" or "data is" may be used in popular writing, but only "data are" is acceptable in scientific writing.

debut   *Debut* is a noun meaning "first public appearance." It is not acceptable as a transitive verb ("The Little Theater will debut its new play tonight") or as an intransitive verb ("Cory Martin will debut in the new play").

decent–descent   A decent person is one who behaves well, without crudeness and perhaps with kindness and generosity. *Decent* can mean "satisfactory" ("a decent grade," "a decent living standard"). *Descent* means "a passage downward"; a descent may be either literal ("their descent into the canyon") or figurative ("hereditary descent of children from their parents," "descent of English from a hypothetical language called Indo-European").

desert–dessert   The noun *desert* means "an uncultivated and uninhabited area"; it may be dry and sandy. *Desert* can be an adjective: "a desert island." The verb *desert* means "to abandon." A *dessert* is a sweet food served as the last course at the noon or evening meal.

different than   Although both "different from" and "different than" are common American usages, the preferred idiom is "different from."

distinterested–uninterested   The distinction between these words is that *disinterested* means "unbiased" and *uninterested* means "apathetic" or "not interested." A disinterested critic is one who comes to a book with no prejudices or prior judgments of its worth; an uninterested critic is one who cannot get interested in the book. Dictionaries disagree about whether this distinction is still valid in contemporary usage and sometimes treat the words as synonyms. But in college writing the distinction is generally observed.

don't   *Don't* is a contraction of "do not," as *doesn't* is a contraction of "does not." It can be used in any college writing in which contractions are appropriate. But it cannot be used with a singular subject. "He don't" and "it don't" are nonstandard usages.

double negative   The use of two negative words within the same construction. In certain forms ("I am not unwilling to go") the double negative is educated usage for an affirmative statement; in other forms ("He hasn't got no money") the double negative is nonstandard usage. The observation that "two negatives make an affirmative" in English usage is a half-truth based on a false analogy with mathematics. "He hasn't got no money" is unacceptable in college writing, not because two negatives make an affirmative, but because it is nonstandard usage.

economic–economical   *Economic* refers to the science of economics or to business in general: "This is an economic law"; "Economic conditions are improving." *Economical* means "inexpensive" or "thrifty": "That is an economical purchase"; "He is economical to the point of miserliness."

effect–affect   See **affect–effect.**

effective–affective   See **affective–effective.**

either   Used to designate one of two things: "Both hats are becoming; I would be perfectly satisfied with either." The use of *either* when more than two things are involved ("There are three ways of working the problem; either way will give the right answer") is a disputed usage. When more than two things are involved, it is better to use *any* or *any one* instead of *either:* "There are three ways of working the problem; any one of them will give the right answer."

elicit–illicit   The first word means "to draw out" ("We could elicit no response from them"); the second means "not permitted" or "unlawful" ("an illicit sale of drugs").

emigrant–immigrant   An emigrant is a person who moves *out of* a country; an immigrant is one who moves *into* a country. Thus, refugees from Europe and elsewhere who settled in the United States were emigrants from their native countries and immigrants here. A similar distinction holds for the verbs *emigrate* and *immigrate.*

eminent–imminent   *Eminent* means "prominent, outstanding": "an eminent scientist." *Imminent* means "ready to happen" or "near in time": "War seems imminent."

enormity, enormous, enormousness   *Enormous* refers to unusual size or measure—synonyms are *huge, vast, immense:* "an enormous fish," "an enormous effort." *Enormousness* is a noun with the same connotations of size and can be applied to either good or bad effects: "The enormousness of their contribution is only beginning to be recognized"; "The enormousness of the lie almost made it believable." But *enormity* is used only for evil acts of great dimension: "The enormity of Hitler's crimes against the Jews shows what can happen when power, passion, and prejudice are all united in one human being."

enthused   *Enthused* is colloquial for *enthusiastic:* "The probability of winning has caused them to be very enthused about the campaign." In college writing use *enthusiastic.*

equally as   In such sentences as "He was equally as good as his brother," the *equally* is unnecessary. Simply write "He was as good as his brother."

etc.   An abbreviation for the Latin *et cetera,* which means "and so forth." It should be used only when the style justifies abbreviations and then only after several items in a commonly used kind of series have been identified: "The data sheet required the usual personal information: age, height, weight, marital status, etc." An announcement of a painting contest that stated, "Entries will be judged on the basis of use of color, etc.," would not tell contestants very much about the standards by which their work is to be judged. Avoid the reduntant *and* before *etc.*

excess–access   See **access–excess.**

expect = suppose or suspect   The use of *expect* for *suppose* or *suspect* is colloquial. In college writing use *suppose* or *suspect:* "I suppose you have written to him"; "I suspect that we have made a mistake."

fact   Distinguish between facts and statements of fact. A fact is something that exists or existed. It is neither true nor false; it just *is.* A statement of fact, or factual statement, may be true or false, depending on whether it does or does not report the facts accurately. But there are no true or false facts.

Avoid padding a sentence with unnecessary use of "a fact that," as in "It is a fact that all the public opinion polls predicted Truman's defeat in the 1948 election." The first five words of that sentence add no meaning. Similarly, "His guilt is admitted" says all, in fewer words, that is said by "The fact of his guilt is admitted."

famous, notorious   *Famous* is a complimentary and *notorious* an uncomplimentary adjective. Well-known people of good repute are famous; those of bad repute are notorious, or infamous.

farther–further   The distinction that *farther* indicates distance and *further* degree is not unanimously supported by usage studies. But to mean "in addition," only *further* is used: "Further assistance will be required."

feature = imagine   The use of *feature* to mean "give prominence to," as in "This issue of the magazine features an article on juvenile delinquency," is established standard usage and is appropriate in college writing. But this acceptance does not justify the slang use of *feature,* meaning "imagine," in such expressions as "Can you feature that?" "Feature me in a dress suit," "I can't feature him as a nurse."

fewer = less   *Fewer* refers to quantities that can be counted individually: "fewer male than female employees." *Less* is used for collective quantities that are not counted individually ("less corn this year than last") and for abstract characteristics ("less determination than enthusiasm").

field   *Field,* in the sense of "an area of study or endeavor," is an overused word that often creates redundance: "He is majoring in the field of physics"; "Her new job is in the field of public relations." Delete "the field of" in each of these sentences.

finalize   One of many *-ize* words that people associate with business and government jargon. Avoid *finalize* in college writing.

fine = very well   The colloquial use of *fine* to mean "very well" ("He is doing fine in his new position") is probably too informal for most college writing.

flaunt = flout   Using *flaunt* as a synonym for *flout* confuses two different words. *Flaunt* means "to show off": "She has a habit of flaunting her knowledge to intimidate her friends." *Flout* means "to scorn or show contempt for": "He is better at flouting opposing arguments than at understanding them." In the right context either word can be effective, but the two words are not synonyms and cannot be used interchangeably.

formally–formerly   *Formally* means "in a formal manner": "They dressed formally." *Formerly* means "previously": "He was formerly with A. C. Smith and Company."

fortuitous–fortunate   *Fortuitous* means "by chance," "not planned": "Our meeting was fortuitous; we had never heard of each other before." Do not confuse *fortuitous* with *fortunate,* as the writer of this sentence has done: "My introduction to Professor Kraus was fortuitous for me; today she hired me as her student assistant." *Fortunate* would be the appropriate word here.

funny   Often used in conversation as a utility word that has no precise meaning but may be clear enough in its context. It is generally too vague for college writing. Decide in what sense the subject is "funny" and use a more precise term to convey that sense. See the treatment of vagueness on pages 169–172.

get   A utility word. *The American Heritage Dictionary* lists thirty-six meanings for the individual word and more than sixty uses in idiomatic expressions. Most of these uses are acceptable in college writing. But unless the style is deliberately colloquial, avoid slang uses of *get* meaning "to cause harm to" ("She'll get me for that"), "to cause a negative reaction to" ("His bad manners really get me"), "to gain the favor of" ("He tried to get in with his boss"), and "to become up-to-date" ("Get in the swing of things").

good   The use of *good* as an adverb ("He talks good"; "She played pretty good") is not acceptable. The accepted adverbial form is *well.*

This discussion does not apply to the use of *good* as an adjective after verbs of hearing, feeling, seeing, smelling, tasting, and the like. See **bad.**

good and   Used colloquially as an intensive in such expressions as "good and late," "good and ready," "good and tired." The more formal the style, the less appropriate these intensives are. In college writing use them sparingly, if at all.

guess   The use of *guess* to mean "believe," "suppose," or "think" ("I guess I can be there on time") is accepted by all studies on which this list is based. There is still objection to its use in formal college writing, but it should be acceptable in an informal style.

had (hadn't) ought   Nonstandard for *ought* and *ought not.* Not acceptable in college writing.

hanged, hung   Alternative past participles of *hang.* For referring to an execution, *hanged* is preferred; in other senses, *hung* is preferred.

hopefully   Opinion is divided about the acceptability of attaching this adverb loosely to a sentence and using it to mean "I hope": "Hopefully, the plane will arrive on schedule." This usage is gaining acceptance, but there is still strong objection to it. In college writing the safer procedure is to avoid it.

idea   In addition to its formal meaning of "conception," *idea* has acquired so many supplementary meanings that it must be recognized as a utility word. Some of its meanings are illustrated in the following sentences:

The idea (thesis) of the book is simple.

The idea (proposal) she suggested is a radical one.

I got the idea (impression) that he is unhappy.

It is my idea (belief, opinion) that they are both wrong.

My idea (intention) is to leave early.

The overuse of *idea,* like the overuse of any utility word, makes for vagueness. Whenever possible, use a more precise synonym.

illicit–elicit   See **elicit–illicit.**

illusion–allusion   See **allusion–illusion.**

immigrant-emigrant   See **emigrant–immigrant.**

imminent–eminent   See **eminent–imminent.**

imply–infer   The traditional difference between these two words is that *imply* refers to what a statement means, usually to a meaning not specifically stated but suggested in the original statement, whereas *infer* is used for a listener's or reader's judgment or inference based on the statement. For example: "I thought that the weather report implied that the day would be quite pretty and sunny, but Marlene inferred that it meant we'd better take umbrellas." The dictionaries are not unanimous in supporting this distinction, but in your writing it will be better not to use *imply* as a synonym for *infer.*

individual   Although the use of *individual* to mean "person" ("He is an energetic individual") is accepted by the dictionaries, college instructors frequently disapprove of this use, probably because it is overdone in college writing. There is no objection to the adjective *individual,* meaning "single," "separate" ("The instructor tries to give us individual attention").

inferior than   Possibly a confusion between "inferior to" and "worse than." Say "inferior to": "Today's workmanship is inferior to that of a few years ago."

ingenious–ingenuous   *Ingenious* means "clever" in the sense of "original": "an ingenious solution." *Ingenuous* means "showing frank simplicity": "Her ingenuous confession disarmed those who had been suspicious of her motives."

in regards to   The only acceptable form in writing is "in regard to."

inside of, outside of   *Inside of* and *outside of* generally should not be used as compound prepositions. In place of the compound prepositions in "The display is inside of the auditorium" and "The pickets were waiting outside of the gate," write "inside the auditorium" and "outside the gate."

Inside of is acceptable in most college writing when it means "in less than": "I'll be there inside of an hour." The more formal term is *within.*

Both *inside of* and *outside of* are appropriate when *inside* or *outside* is a noun followed by an *of* phrase: "The inside of the house is quite attractive"; "He painted the outside of his boat dark green."

in terms of   An imprecise and greatly overused expression. Instead of "In terms of philosophy, we are opposed to his position" and "In terms of our previous experience with the company, we refuse to purchase its products," write "Philosophically, we are opposed to his position" and "Because of our previous experience with the company, we refuse to purchase its products."

invite (noun)   Sometimes used for *invitation,* as in "an invite to the picnic." In college writing *invitation* is preferred.

irregardless   A nonstandard variant of *regardless.* Do not use it.

irrelevant–irreverent   *Irrelevant* means "having no relation to" or "lacking pertinence": "That may be true, but it is quite irrelevant." *Irreverent* means "without reverence": "Such conduct in church is irreverent."

it's me   This construction is essentially a spoken one. Except in dialogue, it rarely occurs in writing. Its use in educated speech is thoroughly established. The formal expression is "It is I."

judicial–judicious   Judicial decisions are related to the administering of justice, often by judges or juries. A judicious person is one who demonstrates good judgment: "A judicious person would not have allowed the young boys to shoot the rapids alone."

kind of, sort of   Use a singular noun and a singular verb with these phrases: "That kind of person is always troublesome"; "This sort of attitude is deplorable." If the sense of the sentence calls for the plural *kinds* or *sorts,* use a plural noun and a plural verb: "These kinds of services are essential." In questions introduced by *what* or *which,* the singular *kind* or *sort* can be followed by a plural noun and verb: "What kind of shells are these?"

The use of *a* or *an* after *kind of* ("That kind of a person is always troublesome") is usually not appropriate in college writing.

kind (sort) of = somewhat   This usage ("I feel kind of tired"; "He looked sort of foolish") is colloquial. The style of the writing will determine its appropriateness in a paper.

latter   *Latter* refers to the second of two. It should not be used to refer to the last of three or more nouns. Instead of *latter* in "Michigan, Alabama, and Notre Dame have had strong football teams for years, and yet the latter has only recently begun to accept invitations to play in bowl games," write *last* or *last-named,* or simply repeat *Notre Dame.*

learn = teach   The use of *learn* to mean "teach" ("He learned us arithmetic") is nonstandard and is not acceptable in college writing.

leave = let   The use of *leave* for the imperative verb *let* ("Leave us face it") is not acceptable in college writing. Write "Let us face it." But *let* and *leave* are interchangeable when a noun or pronoun and then *alone* follow: "Let me alone"; "Leave me alone."

lend   See **loan, lend.**

less   See **fewer.**

liable = likely   Instructors sometimes object to the use of *liable* to mean "likely," as in "It is liable to rain," "He is liable to hit you." *Liable* is used more precisely to mean "subject to" or "exposed to" or "answerable for": "He is liable to arrest"; "You will be liable for damages."

like = as, as though   The use of *like* as a conjunction ("He talks like you do"; "It looks like it will be my turn next") is colloquial. It is not appropriate in a formal style, and many people object to it in an informal style. The safest procedure is to avoid using *like* as a conjunction in college writing.

loan, lend   Both forms of the verb are accepted in educated American usage. *Lend* is the preferred form.

loath–loathe   The form without *e* is an adjective meaning "reluctant," "unwilling" ("I am loath to do that"; "He is loath to risk so great an investment"), and is pronounced to rhyme with *both*. The form with *e* is a verb meaning "dislike strongly" ("I loathe teas"; "She loathes an unkempt man") and is pronounced to rhyme with *clothe*.

loose–lose   The confusion of these words causes frequent misspellings. *Loose* is most common as an adjective: "a loose button," "The dog is loose." *Lose* is always used as a verb: "You are going to lose your money."

luxuriant–luxurious   These words come from the same root but have quite different meanings. *Luxuriant* means "abundant" and is used principally to describe growing things: "luxuriant vegetation," "a luxuriant head of hair." *Luxurious* means "luxury-loving" or "characterized by luxury": "He finds it difficult to maintain so luxurious a lifestyle on so modest an income"; "The furnishings of the clubhouse were luxurious."

mad = angry or annoyed   Using *mad* to mean "angry" is colloquial: "My girl is mad at me"; "His insinuations make me mad." More precise terms—*angry, annoyed, irritated, provoked, vexed*—are generally more appropriate in college writing. *Mad* is, of course, appropriately used to mean "insane."

majority, plurality   Candidates are elected by a *majority* when they get more than half the votes cast. A *plurality* is the margin of victory that the winning candidate has over the leading opponent, whether the winner has a majority or not.

mean = unkind, disagreeable, vicious   Using *mean* to convey the sense "unkind," "disagreeable," "vicious" ("It was mean of me to do that"; "He was in a mean mood"; "That dog looks mean") is a colloquial use. It is appropriate in most college writing, but since using *mean* loosely sometimes results in vagueness, consider using one of the suggested alternatives to provide a sharper statement.

medium, media, medias   *Medium,* not *media,* is the singular form: "The daily newspaper is still an important medium of communication." *Media* is plural: "Figuratively, the electronic media have created a smaller world." *Medias* is not an acceptable form for the plural of *medium.*

might of   See **could of.**

mighty = very   *Mighty* is not appropriate in most college writing as a substitute for *very.* Avoid such constructions as "He gave a mighty good speech."

moral–morale   Roughly, *moral* refers to conduct and *morale* refers to state of mind. A moral man is one who conducts himself according to standards for goodness. People are said to have good morale when they are cheerful, cooperative, and not too much concerned with their own worries.

most = almost   The use of *most* as a synonym for *almost* ("I am most always hungry an hour before mealtime") is colloquial. In college writing *almost* would be preferred in such a sentence.

must (adjective and noun)   The use of *must* as an adjective ("This book is must reading for anyone who wants to understand Russia") and as a noun ("It is reported that the President will classify this proposal as a must") is accepted as established usage by the dictionaries.

must of   See **could of.**

myself = I, me   *Myself* should not be used for *I* or *me.* Avoid such constructions as "John and myself will go." *Myself* is acceptably used as an intensifier ("I saw it myself"; "I myself will go with you") and as a reflexive object ("I hate myself"; "I can't convince myself that he is right.")

nauseous = nauseated   *Nauseous* does not mean "experiencing nausea"; *nauseated* has that meaning: "The thought of making a speech caused her to feel nauseated." *Nauseous* means "causing nausea" or "repulsive": "nauseous odor," "nauseous television program."

nice   A utility word much overused in college writing. Avoid excessive use of *nice* and, whenever possible, choose a more precise synonym.

That's a nice dress.   (attractive? becoming? fashionable? well-made?)

She's a nice person.   (agreeable? charming? friendly? well-mannered?)

nice and   Intensives like "nice and easy" and "nice and comfortable" are colloquial. The more formal the style, the less appropriate such expressions are.

notorious   See **famous.**

nowheres   Nonstandard variant of *nowhere.* Do not use it in college writing.

off, off of = from   Neither *off* nor *off of* should be used to mean "from." Write "Jack bought the old car from a stranger," not "off a stranger" or "off of a stranger."

OK, O.K.   Its use in business to mean "endorse" is generally accepted: "The manager OK'd the request." In college writing *OK* is a utility word and is subject to the general precaution concerning all such words: do not overuse it, especially in contexts in which a more specific term would give more efficient communication. For example, contrast the vagueness of *OK* at the left with the discriminated meanings at the right.

The mechanic said the tires were OK.

The mechanic said the tread on the tires was still good.

The mechanic said the pressure in the tires was satisfactory.

one   See **you = one.**

only   The position of *only* in such sentences as "I only need three dollars" and "If only Mother would write!" is sometimes condemned on the grounds of possible ambiguity. In practice, the context usually rules out any but the intended interpretation, but a change in the word order would often result in more appropriate emphasis: "I need only three dollars"; "If mother would only write!"

on the part of The phrase "on the part of" ("There will be some objection on the part of the students"; "On the part of businesspeople, there will be some concern about taxes") often makes for a wordy style. Simply say "The students will object," "Businesspeople will be concerned about taxes."

outside of See **inside of.**

party = person The use of *party* to mean "person" is appropriate in legal documents and the responses of telephone operators, but these are special uses. Generally avoid this use in college writing.

per = a "You will be remunerated at the rate of forty dollars per diem" and "The troops advanced three miles per day through the heavy snow" show established use of *per* for *a*. But usually "forty dollars a day" and "three miles a day" would be more natural expressions in college writing.

percent, percentage *Percent* (alternative form, *per cent*) is used when a specific portion is named: "five percent of the expenses." *Percentage* is used when no number is given: "a small percentage of the expenses." When *percent* or *percentage* is part of a subject, the noun or pronoun of the *of* phrase that follows determines the number of the verb: "Forty percent of the wheat is his"; "A large percentage of her customers pay promptly."

personal–personnel *Personal* means "of a person": "a personal opinion," "a personal matter." *Personnel* refers to the people in an organization, especially employees: "Administrative personnel will not be affected."

plenty The use of *plenty* as a noun ("There is plenty of room") is always acceptable. Its use as an adverb ("It was plenty good") is not appropriate in college writing.

plurality See **majority.**

première *Première* is acceptable as a noun ("The première for the play was held in a small off-Broadway theater"), but do not use it as a verb ("The play premièred in a small off-Broadway theater"). Write "The play opened . . ."

preposition (ending sentence with) A preposition should not appear at the end of a sentence if its presence there draws undue attention to itself or creates an awkward construction: "They are the people whom we made the inquiries yesterday about." But there is nothing wrong with writing a preposition at the end of a sentence to achieve an idiomatic construction: "Isn't that the man you are looking for?"

principal–principle The basic meaning of *principal* is "chief" or "most important." It is used in this sense both as a noun and as an adjective: "the principal of a school," "the principal point." It is also used to refer to a capital sum of money, as contrasted with interest on the money: "He can live on the interest without touching the principal." *Principle* is used only as a noun and means "rule," "law," or "controlling idea": "the principle of 'one man, one vote' "; "It is against my principles."

prophecy–prophesy   *Prophecy* is always used as a noun ("The prophecy came true"); *prophesy* is always a verb ("He prophesied another war").

proved, proven   When used as past participles, both forms are standard English, but the preferred form is *proved:* "Having proved the first point, we moved to the second." *Proven* is preferred when the word is used primarily as an adjective: "He is a proven contender for the championship."

quote   The clipped form for *quotation* ("a quote from *Walden*") is not acceptable in most college writing. The verb *quote* ("to quote Thoreau") is acceptable in all styles.

rarely ever, seldom ever   The *ever* is redundant. Instead of saying "He is rarely ever late" and "She is seldom ever angry," write "He is rarely late" and "She is seldom angry."

real = really (very)   The use of *real* to mean "really" or "very" ("It is a real difficult assignment") is a colloquial usage. It is acceptable only in a paper whose style is deliberately colloquial, such as "Why We Need More Westerns on Television" (page 17). The writer of that paper uses the phrase "real low-cut dresses" for a humorous effect. In most college writing the accepted form would be *really:* "really low-cut dresses."

refer back   A confusion between *look back* and *refer.* This usage is objected to in college writing on the ground that since the *re-* of *refer* means "back," *refer back* is redundant. *Refer back* is acceptable when it means "refer again" ("The bill was referred back to the committee"); otherwise, say *refer* ("Let me refer you to page 17").

respectfully–respectively   *Respectfully* means "with respect": "respectfully submitted." *Respectively* means roughly "each in turn": "These three papers were graded respectively A, C, and B."

right (adv.)   The use of *right* as an adverb is established in such sentences as "He went right home" and "It served her right." Its use to mean *very* ("I was right glad to meet him") is colloquial and should be used in college writing only when the style is colloquial.

right–rite   A *rite* is a ceremony or ritual. This word should not be confused with the various uses of *right.*

said (adj.)   The use of *said* as an adjective ("said documents," "said offense") is restricted to legal phraseology. Do not use it in college writing.

same as = just as   The preferred idiom is "just as": "He acted just as I thought he would."

same, such   Avoid using *same* or *such* as a substitute for *it, this, that, them.* Instead of "I am returning the book because I do not care for same" and "Most people are fond of athletics of all sorts, but I have no use for such," say "I am returning the book because I do not care for it" and "Unlike most people, I am not fond of athletics."

scarcely   In such sentences as "There wasn't scarcely enough" and "We haven't scarcely time," the use of *scarcely* plus a negative creates an unacceptable double negative. Say "There was scarcely enough" and "We scarcely have time."

scarcely than   The use of "scarcely than" ("I had scarcely met her than she began to denounce her husband") is a confusion between "no sooner . . . than" and "scarcely . . . when." Say "I had no sooner met her than she began to denounce her husband" or "I had scarcely met her when she began to denounce her husband."

seasonable–seasonal   *Seasonable* and its adverb form *seasonably* mean "appropriate(ly) to the season": "She was seasonably dressed for a late-fall football game"; "A seasonable frost convinced us that the persimmons were just right for eating." *Seasonal* means "caused by a season": "increased absenteeism because of seasonal influenza," "flooding caused by seasonal thaws."

seldom ever   See **rarely ever.**

-selfs   The plural of *self* is *selves.* Such a usage as "They hurt themselfs" is nonstandard and is not acceptable in college writing.

semi-   See **bi-, semi-.**

sensual–sensuous   *Sensual* has unfavorable connotations and means "catering to the gratification of physical desires": "Always concerned with satisfying his sexual lust and his craving for drink and rich food, the old baron led a totally sensual existence." *Sensuous* has generally favorable connotations and refers to pleasures experienced through the senses: "the sensuous comfort of a warm bath," "the sensuous imagery of the poem."

shall, will   In American, as contrasted with British, usage the dominant practice is to use *will* in the second and third persons to express either futurity or determination, and to use either *will* or *shall* in the first person.

In addition, *shall* is used in statements of law ("Congress shall have the power to . . ."), in military commands ("The regiment shall proceed as directed"), and in formal directives ("All branch offices shall report weekly to the home office").

should, would   These words are used as the past forms of *shall* and *will* respectively and follow the same pattern (see **shall, will**): "I would [should] be glad to see him tomorrow"; "He would welcome your ideas on the subject"; "We would [should] never consent to such an arrangement." They are also used to convert a *shall* or *will* in direct discourse into indirect discourse.

Direct discourse	Indirect discourse
"Shall I try to arrange it?" he asked.	He asked if he should try to arrange it.
I said, "They will need money."	I said that they would need money.

should of   See **could of.**

sight–site–cite   See **cite–sight–site.**

so (conj.)   The use of *so* as a connective ("The salesperson refused to exchange the merchandise; so we went to the manager") is thoroughly respectable, but its overuse in college writing is objectionable. There are other good transitional connectives—*accordingly, for that reason, on that account, therefore*—that could be used to relieve the monotony of a series of *so*'s. Occasional use of subordination

("When the salesperson refused to exchange the merchandise, we went to the manager") would also lend variety to the style.

some The use of *some* as an adjective of indeterminate number ("Some friends of yours were here") is acceptable in all levels of writing. Its use as an intensive ("That was some meal!") or as an adverb ("She cried some after you left"; "This draft is some better than the first one") should be avoided in college writing.

somewheres Nonstandard variant of *somewhere*. Not acceptable in college writing.

sort of See **kind of.**

stationary–stationery *Stationary* means "fixed" or "unchanging": "The battle front is now stationary." *Stationery* means "writing paper": "a box of stationery." Associate the *e* in *stationery* with the *e*'s in *letter.*

suit–suite The common word is *suit:* "a suit of clothes"; "Follow suit, play a diamond"; "Suit yourself." *Suite,* pronounced "sweet," means "retinue" ("The President and his suite have arrived") or "set" or "collection" ("a suite of rooms," "a suite of furniture"). When it refers to furniture, an alternative pronunciation is "suit."

sure = certainly Using *sure* in the sense of "certainly" ("I sure am annoyed"; "Sure, I will go with you") is colloquial. Unless the style justifies colloquial usage, use *certainly* or *surely.*

swell = good, fine Using *swell* as a synonym for *good* or *fine* ("It was a swell show"; "We had a swell time") is slang. It is generally inappropriate in college writing.

take and This usage ("In a fit of anger he took and smashed the bowl") is not acceptable in college writing. Simply use *smashed:* "In a fit of anger he smashed the bowl."

terrific Used at a formal level to mean "terrifying" ("a terrific epidemic") and at a colloquial level as an intensive ("a terrific party," "a terrific pain"). Overuse of the word at the colloquial level has made it almost meaningless.

thusly Not an acceptable variant of *thus.*

tough The use of *tough* to mean "difficult" ("a tough assignment," "a tough decision") and "hard fought" ("a tough game") is accepted without qualification by reputable dictionaries. But its use to mean "unfortunate," "bad" ("The fifteen-yard penalty was a tough break for the team"; "That's tough") is colloquial and should be used only in a paper written in a colloquial style.

troop–troupe Both words come from the same root and share the original meaning, "herd." In modern usage *troop* can refer to soldiers and *troupe* to actors: "a troop of cavalry," "a troop of scouts," "a troupe of circus performers," "a troupe of entertainers."

try and "Try to" is the preferred idiom. Write "I will try to do it" in preference to "I will try and do it."

type = type of *Type* is not acceptable as a variant form of *type of.* In "That type engine isn't being manufactured anymore," add *of* after *type.*

uninterested–disinterested   See **disinterested–uninterested.**

unique   The formal meaning of *unique* is "sole" or "only" or "being the only one of its kind": "Adam was unique in being the only man who never had a mother." The use of *unique* to mean "rare" or "unusual" ("Americans watched their television sets anxiously as astronauts in the early moon landings had the unique experience of walking on the moon") has long been popular, but some people still object to this usage. The use of *unique* to mean merely "uncommon" ("a unique sweater") is generally frowned upon. *Unique* should not be modified by adverbs that express degree: *very, more, most, rather.*

up   The adverb *up* is idiomatically used in many verb-adverb combinations that act as verbs—"break up," "clean up," "fill up," "get up," "tear up." Avoid unnecessary or awkward separation of *up* from the verb with which it is combined, since such a separation makes *up* look at first like an adverb modifying the verb rather than an adverb combining with the verb in an idiomatic expression. For example, "They held the cashier up" and "She made her face up" are awkward. Say "They held up the cashier," "She made up her face."

use to   The *d* in "used to" is often not pronounced; it is elided before the *t* in *to*. The resulting pronunciation leads to the written expression "use to." But the acceptable written phrase is "used to": "I am used to the noise"; "He used to do all the grocery shopping."

used to could   Nonstandard for "used to be able to." Not acceptable in college writing.

very   A common intensive, but avoid its overuse.

wait on   *Wait on* means "serve": "A clerk will be here in a moment to wait on you." The use of *wait on* to mean "wait for" ("I'll wait on you if you won't be long") is a colloquialism to which there is some objection. Use *wait for:* "I'll wait for you if you won't be long."

want in, out, off   The use of *want* followed by *in, out,* or *off* ("The dog wants in"; "I want out of here"; "I want off now") is colloquial. In college writing supply an infinitive after the verb: "The dog wants to come in."

want to = ought to, should   Using *want to* as a synonym for *should* ("They want to be careful or they will be in trouble") is colloquial. *Ought to* or *should* is preferred in college writing.

ways   Colloquial for *way* in such sentences as "You must have come a long ways." Use *way* instead of *ways.*

where . . . at, to   The use of *at* or *to* after *where* ("Where was he at?" "Where are you going to?") is redundant. Simply write "Where was he?" and "Where are you going?"

will, shall   See **shall, will.**

-wise   Avoid adding the suffix *-wise,* meaning "concerning," to nouns to form such combinations as *budgetwise, jobwise, tastewise.* Some combined forms with *-wise* are thoroughly established *(clockwise, otherwise, sidewise, weatherwise),* but the fad of coining new compounds with this suffix is generally objected to in English classes.

without = unless   *Without* is not accepted as a conjunction meaning "unless." In "There will be no homecoming festivities without student government sponsors them," substitute *unless* for *without.*

with respect to   See **as to.**

worst way   When "in the worst way" means "very much" ("They wanted to go in the worst way"), it is too informal for college writing.

would, should   See **should, would.**

would of   See **could of.**

would have = had   *Would* is the past-tense form of *will,* but its overuse in student writing often results in awkwardness, especially, but not only, when it is used as a substitute for *had.* Contrast the following sentences:

Awkward	Revised
If they *would have done* that earlier, there *would have been* no trouble.	If they *had done* that earlier, there *would have been* no trouble.
	or:
	Had they *done* that earlier, there *would have been* no trouble.
We *would want* some assurance that they *would accept* before we *would make* such a proposal.	We *would want* some assurance of their acceptance before we *made* such a proposal.

In general, avoid the repetition of "would have . . ." in the same sentence.

Xmas   An abbreviation for *Christmas* much used in business and advertising. The full word is preferred in college writing.

you = one   The use of *you* as an indefinite pronoun instead of the formal *one* is characteristic of an informal style. If you adopt *you* in an informal paper, be sure that this impersonal use will be recognized by your readers; otherwise, they are likely to interpret a general statement as a personal remark addressed specifically to them.

Generally avoid shifting from *one* to *you* within a sentence. See page 418.

yourself   *Yourself* is appropriately used as an intensifier ("You yourself told me that") and as a reflexive object ("You are blaming yourself too much"). But usages such as the following are not acceptable: "Marian and yourself must shoulder the responsibility" and "The instructions were intended for Kate and yourself." In these two sentences, replace *yourself* with *you.*

The plural form is *yourselves,* not *yourselfs.*